RESILIENT
CITY

RESILIENT
CITY

The Economic Impact of 9/11

Howard Chernick, Editor

Russell Sage Foundation, New York

The Russell Sage Foundation

The Russell Sage Foundation, one of the oldest of America's general purpose foundations, was established in 1907 by Mrs. Margaret Olivia Sage for "the improvement of social and living conditions in the United States." The Foundation seeks to fulfill this mandate by fostering the development and dissemination of knowledge about the country's political, social, and economic problems. While the Foundation endeavors to assure the accuracy and objectivity of each book it publishes, the conclusions and interpretations in Russell Sage Foundation publications are those of the authors and not of the Foundation, its Trustees, or its staff. Publication by Russell Sage, therefore, does not imply Foundation endorsement.

Library of Congress Cataloging-in-Publication Data
Resilient city : the economic impact of 9/11 / edited by Howard Chernick.
   p. cm.
  "Reflects the joint efforts of a working group formed by the Russell Sage Foundation"—Ack.
Includes bibliographical references and index.
  ISBN 0-87154-160-2 (cloth)   ISBN 0-87154-170-X (paperback)
  1. New York (N.Y.)—Economic conditions. 2. September 11 Terrorist Attacks,
2001—Economic aspects—New York (State)—New York. 3. World Trade Center (New
York, N.Y.) I. Chernick, Howard. II. Russell Sage Foundation.
HC108.N7R47 2005
330.9747'1044—dc22   2005046592

Text design by Genna Patacsil.

RUSSELL SAGE FOUNDATION
112 East 64th Street, New York, New York 10021
10 9 8 7 6 5 4 3 2 1

CONTENTS

CONTRIBUTORS

HOWARD CHERNICK is professor of economics at Hunter College and the Graduate Center of the City University of New York.

JOSHUA CHANG is director of the Partnership for New York City.

OLIVER D. COOKE is research associate of the Fiscal Policy Institute in New York City.

FRANZ FUERST is research associate of the Center for Urban Research of the City University of New York

ANDREW F. HAUGHWOUT is research officer in the business conditions function of the Federal Reserve Bank of New York

EDWARD W. HILL is Professor and Distinguished Scholar of Economic Development at Cleveland State University's Levin College of Urban Affairs and Nonresident Senior Fellow at the Metropolitan Policy Program of the Brookings Institution.

SANDERS KORENMAN is professor in the School of Public Affairs at Baruch College of the City University of New York

IRYNA LENDEL is a doctoral candidate at Cleveland State University's Levin College of Urban Affairs and a research staff member at the college's Center for Economic Development.

JAMES A. PARROTT is deputy director and chief economist of the Fiscal Policy Institute in New York City.

CORDELIA W. REIMERS is professor emrita of economics at Hunter College and the Graduate Center of the City University of New York.

JONATHAN A. SCHWABISH is senior director of the Partnership for New York City.

FOREWORD

IN THE GRIM WEEKS after the terrorist attack on the World Trade Center on September 11, 2001, many New Yorkers asked themselves how they could contribute their talents and abilities to help their fellow citizens and assist in the effort to restore and revitalize the city. As a research organization with a long history of studying social and economic conditions in the city, the Russell Sage Foundation naturally turned toward the idea of using the analytic capacities of social science to assess the shocking blow New York had suffered and analyze the underlying dimensions of what we fervently hoped would be its full recovery. In the following months, the foundation assembled a working group of nineteen experts on New York and supported their coordinated research on the economic, social, and political implications of the terrorist attack on the city. Now, four years later, we are pleased to present the results of their efforts in three volumes.

Resilient City, edited by economist Howard Chernick, assesses the impact of September 11 on the city's economy. By and large, the book tells a remarkable story of recovery. Fears that New York's competitive position in the world economy would deteriorate as firms fled the city proved to be unfounded. The attractions that New York has always offered—high density and a large, skilled labor force—kept most businesses in the city, despite the perceived threat of another attack. Manhattan's enormous commercial real estate market managed to absorb the loss of 10 percent of its available inventory and still accommodate 80 percent of the firms forced to relocate from downtown. While demand for space in tall buildings suffered a temporary slump, occupancy rates for buildings of more than fifty stories returned to near normal levels over the three-year period following the attack. The job market fared less well, suffering a net loss of over 125,000 jobs by September 2004. By some estimates, it may take another five years for the city's job base to return to its pre-attack peak. The attack has also increased New York City taxes by about 8 percent and caused commercial insurance costs to soar. To the extent that these increased costs raise the price of doing business in New York, the city's long run competitiveness could suffer. While no one can predict the eventual consequences of the attack, the price signals in the real estate and financial markets remain positive. Housing prices and rents have risen more steeply than in the rest of the country, and the shares of firms headquartered in New York City are not selling at a discount. Remarkably, four years after the attack, confidence in the city seems fully restored.

Wounded City, edited by anthropologist Nancy Foner, is a book that digs below the aggregate outcomes revealed by economic statistics to look at especially vulnerable neighborhoods and groups of workers. Here the stories are about lasting scars and painful dislocations. The garment industry in Chinatown nearly collapsed due to security restrictions near Ground Zero that prevented the movement of merchandise, leaving thousands of immigrant workers jobless. Cabdrivers in the city, most of them Muslim, suffered from the increased hostility of their customers and the loss of business as tourism declined, leaving many of them in debt to pay the leases for their taxi medallions. The precipitous drop in air travel after September 11 eliminated thousands of New York jobs in the airline industry, stranding many workers with little prospect of regaining their jobs despite massive federal subsidies for the airlines. Communities as disparate as the Muslims in Jersey City and the white ethnic neighborhoods of Belle Harbor in the Rockaways suffered lasting trauma. Belle Harbor endured the double disaster of its many firefighters lost on September 11, followed eight weeks later by the crash of American Flight 587. The Muslim community in Jersey City experienced both an increase in hate crimes and assaults from their neighbors, and the impact of detentions, investigations, and raids by law enforcement agencies in the wake of the attack. *Wounded City* shows how New York communities and workers have struggled to cope with these problems, some more successfully than others. New York is healing, but the process remains uneven and incomplete.

Contentious City, edited by political scientist John Mollenkopf, offers valuable insights into the bewildering contest among the political actors who have grappled with decisions about how to rebuild the World Trade Center site and memorialize those who lost their lives in the attack. Stories of this ongoing political battle have filled the New York press almost daily for the past four years. As *Contentious City* is published, the outcome remains in doubt, but the political experts who contributed to the book do an excellent job of exploring the underlying logic that continues to drive the process. After the veneer of public participation in discussions about the redesign of the site wore off, the decision process revealed itself as a strikingly undemocratic contest among the governor, the mayor, the Port Authority, and the lease holder. In this game, the city and its citizens held very few cards. As a result, the narrow goal of restoring the commercial revenues from the site has generally trumped broader efforts to establish mixed residential and commercial use for the downtown area and to improve its transportation links to the rest of the city. This, despite the fact that commercial vacancies downtown are at a historic peak and demand for commercial space remains distinctly weaker in downtown than midtown. As our books go to press, it appears likely that some version of the Freedom Tower will be built. It is much less certain that tenants will be ready to occupy this space at viable prices, or that the predominantly commercial redevelopment of the site will be best for the city in the long run.

The brutal shock of September 11 caused profound human suffering for the thousands of New Yorkers who lost loved ones, and a new sense of vulnerability still experienced by everyone in the city. It is commonplace to say that nothing will ever be the same after September 11, and in many ways this is true. But the reaction to the attack also revealed much about the persistent character of the city—the enormous strength and flexibility of its economy, the vitality as well as the fragility of its communities, and the byzantine complexities of its power politics. The tools of social science, deftly wielded in these volumes, bring all these underlying constancies of New York life into sharp relief in an effort to probe the deeper dimensions of what has happened in the wake of September 11. As citizens of New York, we would like to contribute these volumes as a small part of the city's ongoing effort to understand and improve itself—and to recover from its darkest hour.

Eric Wanner
President
Russell Sage Foundation

ACKNOWLEDGMENTS

THIS BOOK reflects the joint efforts of a working group formed by the Russell Sage Foundation to study the economic impact on New York City of the September 11, 2001, terrorist attack on the World Trade Center. The book is part of a larger effort, called the New York City Recovery Project, to investigate the social, political, and economic effects of the attack. The members of the economic effects working group were Howard Chernick (chair), Franz Fuerst, Andrew Haughwout, Edward Hill, Sanders Korenman, James Parrott, and Cordelia Reimers. I would like to collectively thank our group for helping all of us to refine the questions, methods of analysis, and findings during almost three years of work toward an overall economic evaluation of this terrible event. I particularly relied on my colleague at Hunter College, Cordelia Reimers, for frequent consultations about the project, and I am grateful for her always sage advice. Thanks are also due to the additional chapter authors, including Iryna Lendel, co-author with Edward Hill; Oliver Cooke, co-author with James Parrott; and Jonathan Schwabish and Joshua Chang, co-authors of a separate chapter on the impact of 9/11 on the market for insurance in New York City. I would also like to thank participants in the conference sponsored by the Russell Sage Foundation in May 2004, particularly the paper discussants: Annette Bernhardt, Jan Brueckner, David Howell, Robert Inman, Alan Krueger, and Hugh Kelly. The conference was a great help to all of us in advancing the research studies.

Thanks are also due to two anonymous reviewers for their careful reading of the entire manuscript and their many insights and suggestions for improvement. I would also like to thank my friends and colleagues, Nancy Foner and John Mollenkopf, chairs of the social effects working group and political effects working group, respectively, and longtime students of New York City, for attending our workshops and conferences and for sound advice and friendly encouragement throughout the project.

Finally, thanks are due to the Russell Sage Foundation, particularly president Eric Wanner, for suggesting that we study the economic impacts of 9/11, for help in conceptualizing the problem, and for providing the appropriate mixture of encouragement and prodding necessary to complete our study. I would also like to thank Bindu Chindaga, for administrative assistance, and Suzanne Nichols, director of publications for Russell Sage. Both have been great to work with, and Suzanne has kept us to our deadlines with patience and firmness, both of which qualities were sorely needed.

CHAPTER 1

Introduction

Howard Chernick

WHEN TWO hijacked Boeing 767–200ER series aircraft struck the twin towers of the World Trade Center (WTC) on the morning of September 11, 2001, and caused them to collapse, New York City suffered an enormous and horrifying blow. Some 2,749 individuals perished. This represented the largest number of Americans killed in a single day in 139 years. The sense of pain and loss was intense, not only for the families of those who were killed but for all New Yorkers and much of the nation. In the weeks after the attack fear and anger were widespread, and New York City became a public space for grieving.

THE ECONOMIC IMPACT OF THE 9/11 TERRORIST ATTACK ON NEW YORK CITY

The terrorist attack was also an attack on the economy of New York City. The immediate economic losses were staggering. The New York City Comptroller's Office estimated that $13.4 billion worth of office space was destroyed and $16.6 billion worth was damaged (Comptroller, City of New York 2002). Economic activity in lower Manhattan all but ceased for several weeks. Some 13,000 jobs, mainly in the financial sector, were immediately relocated outside of the city. Economic losses quickly spread from the immediate site of the attack to key New York City industries, including travel and tourism. Between 75,000 and 100,000 jobs were lost in New York City during the fourth quarter of 2001 as an immediate result of the attack (Fiscal Policy Institute 2001; Comptroller, City of New York 2002). Gross city product (GCP), which is the single most comprehensive measure of economic activity, fell by $11.5 billion in the quarter following the attack; by July 2002 it had fallen by a total of $17.6 billion (Comptroller, City of New York 2002). Total losses to GCP through 2004 are estimated at more than $50 billion. Most estimates of total ensured losses in New York City range between $40 billion and $50 billion (Schwabish and Chang, this volume).

In a series of reports, economists at the Federal Reserve Bank of New York have also tried to assess the overall economic impact of the 9/11 attack. In an initial assessment, based on employment data available through June 2002, Jason Bram, James Orr, and Carol Rapaport (2002a) estimate that lost wages for those killed in the attack and those whose earnings were displaced ranged from $11 billion to $14 billion. Losses from destruction of buildings and public infrastructure were equal to $21.6 billion. In the first month after the attack New York City lost 51,000 private-sector jobs. Bram and his colleagues estimate that between 75 and 90 percent (38,000 to 46,000) of those jobs were lost because of the 9/11 attack. By February 2002, the drop in employment due to the attack had risen to somewhere between 49,000 and 71,000 lost jobs. However, by June 2002 the employment impact had begun to recede: direct losses were down to 28,000 to 55,000 jobs. This assessment of the timing of the effects of 9/11 on job loss in the city is supported by Edward Hill and Iryna Lendel (this volume), who find that the pre-9/11 trend in jobs was regained sometime between eight and twelve months after the attack.

Losses were concentrated in particular industries. Through June 2002 there was a loss of 27,000 jobs in the key financial services sector, though about 30 percent of this drop represented jobs that were relocated, mainly to northern New Jersey. Apart from financial services, the most direct effects of the attack were felt in the restaurant, hotel, and air transportation sectors. Hotel employment declined by 15 percent between September 2001 and March 2002, but had rebounded to about a 5 percent loss by May 2002. Air transportation employment fell by 20 percent in the immediate aftermath of the attack (compared with a 10 percent drop nationally), and it had not yet rebounded at all by June 2002 (Bram et al. 2002a).

Revised employment data from 2003 suggest that the impact of the attack, though still very substantial, was somewhat less than originally thought (Bram 2003). This reassessment reflects the fact that the decline in New York's economy in the period preceding the attack, from its cyclical peak of 3.8 million jobs in December 2000, was greater than indicated by the initial data.[1] Based on jobs data through 2003, the Office of Management and Budget (2004) has also revised downward its estimates of the initial impact. OMB finds that of 116,000 jobs lost between the third quarter of 2001 and the fourth quarter of 2002, 50,000 were the result of the attack. This agency puts the loss in gross city product in the fourth quarter of 2001 at $10 billion and the short-run loss in city tax revenues at $720 million. As a fraction of total output, as measured by GCP, these estimates range from 2 to 4 percent.

OVERALL FINDINGS

There is no question that in the short run the 9/11 attack was spectacularly successful in disrupting the social and economic fabric of a great city. The economic losses were almost fifty times as great as had been suffered in any previous terrorist attack (Schwabish and Chang, this volume). The questions asked in this volume, however, address the long-term impact of the terrorist attack: How severe have been the longer-lasting economic effects of the 9/11 attack? Has 9/11 lessened the attractiveness of NYC as a place to do business, to live, and to re-create, or have the natural economic advantages of the nation's largest city been strong enough to overcome the terrible shock suffered by the city?

To investigate these questions, the Russell Sage Foundation commissioned a three-year study of the economic effects of 9/11, along with parallel studies of the social and political effects of the attack. Reflecting our ultimate optimism about the future of our city, the study is called the New York City Recovery Project. Drawing on the intellectual capital based in New York's universities, governmental institutions, and research organizations—one of the city's great strengths—we assembled a team of leading economic researchers to investigate various aspects of the economic effect of 9/11. The resulting papers consider the effects of the attack on the overall economic competitiveness of New York City as well as the specific effects on low-wage workers, office markets, housing demand, insurance costs, the share prices of New York–based firms, and the fiscal condition of the city. Given the widespread fear and anxiety generated by the attack, we also look for evidence of behavioral changes in individuals as revealed by changes in child care arrangements. Such changes are a kind of leading indicator of changes in the city's quality of life and may affect the size and flexibility of the labor force.

The basic conclusions of the study are optimistic. Despite the magnitude of the losses, the sheer size of New York's economy kept the effects relatively small as a fraction of total economic activity, and the flexibility of markets in New York has enabled the city to recover much of its economic vibrancy. Like a very large firm with many production sites, the size of New York's office market enabled it to compensate for the disruption in one geographic area by substituting other facilities, mainly in midtown, thus keeping workers in the city. In the three years since the attack the city has made significant strides toward recovery. Despite the widespread apprehension that the terrorist attack would lead to a substantial deconcentration of firms and employment to less vulnerable locations outside of the city, particularly in the key financial services sector, the economic advantages of agglomeration—that is to say, the productivity-enhancing features of many firms being grouped together geographically and the cost savings for consumers from having many highly specialized service providers grouped together in one place—have remained dominant. Firms have been able to relocate many employees to equally dense or denser locations in midtown. As of 2004, vacancy rates for commercial office space in Manhattan are lower than for any other major metropolitan area in the country, and rents continue to be significantly higher. A vigorous residential real estate market has led to robust growth in property-related tax revenues, and this growth has helped to alleviate the severity of the fiscal pressure induced by the 9/11 attack. Labor market impacts, while severe, have been relatively short-lived. Overall, the impact on the disadvantaged was not found to be significantly different than in other large cities. Thus, the economic advantages that New York City derives from its sheer scale appear to be highly persistent. The city's economy has shown itself to be resilient to even the harshest of shocks.[2]

Nonetheless, significant problems remain. As discussed in the companion volume to this study on the social impact of 9/11, case studies reveal that there were severe impacts on specific groups who live or work in lower Manhattan and on particular industries (see, for example, Chin 2005). Although some of these effects were too small relative to the city as a whole to be detected in the available household survey data, James Parrott and Oliver Cooke (this volume) found earnings declines for low-wage households in the range of 10 percent between the last quarter of 2001 and the first quarter of 2002. In the time period of our study, the loss in New York City employment was greater than for the nation as a whole, and the recovery has been more sluggish. As of December 2004, New York was still 125,000 private-sector jobs below the level just before 9/11 (Comptroller, City of New York 2005). The number of jobs in 2003 was 6.5 percent below the December 2000 peak (Parrott and Cooke, this volume), and the average number of jobs in 2004 was still more than 4 percent below the average for the peak year of 2000 (Hill and Lendel, this volume). Though profits have rebounded, employment in the securities industry remains far below its pre-recession peak. The sluggishness in hiring after 2002 is not directly due to 9/11, but Erica Groshen, Simon Potter, and Rebecca Sela (2004) and Hill and Lendel (this volume) argue that the attack reinforced and accelerated ongoing structural changes, particularly in the financial sector. Since structural change involves the movement of routine jobs out of New York City (Hill and Lendel, this volume), this acceleration has increased the amount of temporary economic dislocation.

Terrorism-related increases in the cost of insurance for New York firms have diminished the city's comparative advantage as a location for economic activity, though the amount is difficult to quantify. To deal with the enormous fiscal deficits brought about at least in part by the attack, there has been a large increase in city indebtedness and an almost 10 percent increase in taxes as a fraction of personal income. Given the short-term stability of New York's property tax, approximately one-third of the increase in tax burdens is an automatic consequence of the decline in personal income. This means that the remaining two-thirds stems from the increase in rates for income, sales, and property taxes. It is still too early to tell whether there will be substantial adverse effects in the long run from these increases in private- and public-sector prices.

The generally optimistic results are in line with previous studies showing that man-made disasters typically do not destroy the basis for cities and that their long-run effects have tended to be relatively minor (Glaeser and Shapiro 2002; Harrigan and Martin 2002). These results also have important implications in terms of the impact of terrorism on the overall productivity of the economy. Researchers have increasingly come to recognize the crucial role of cities in promoting productivity growth. Dense economic activity is favorable to the realization of significant increasing returns to scale, with the extra output translated into higher wages, land prices, and returns to entrepreneurs who have invested in the city.[3] Moreover, increased employment density appears to lead to higher rates of growth in employment in the future. A likely source of this higher growth is the spillover of knowledge from one industry or occupation to another.

If the dangers of terrorism can serve to unravel the close relationships across firms and industries that are the hallmark of dense cities and the source of their economic strength, then not only are urban economies at risk, but so is the overall economy. The fact that New York, despite the lingering problems from the World Trade Center attack, has shown significant powers of resilience and recovery is thus reassuring in terms of overall national economic performance.

Conspicuously absent from the volume is any extensive discussion of the economic future of lower Manhattan. Given the ongoing program of rebuilding, such a discussion must perforce remain largely descriptive and speculative, hence outside the domain of the empirically based studies in this volume. This omission should not be taken to mean that the issue is not important to the economy of New York City. The rebuilding process is discussed extensively in the companion volume on the political impact of 9/11 (Mollenkopf 2005). Nonetheless, the chapters on the real estate markets do offer some intriguing hints as to the nature of the demands for space in lower Manhattan. Although demand for office space in lower Manhattan has held up better than expected, the attack served to accelerate a long-term shift in office employment, particularly in the securities industry, from lower Manhattan to midtown (Fuerst, this volume). The rent differential between the two areas has increased. These movements of employment and the associated market price signals suggest that some shift away from commercial use of land in the downtown area toward greater use for residential purposes is appropriate (Haughwout, this volume; Glaeser and Shapiro 2002).

METHODOLOGICAL ISSUES

Any study of the economic effect of 9/11 suffers from the difficult methodological problem of separating the effects of the attack from those of two other important economic events: the national recession, which began in March 2001, and the collapse of the stock market, which began in 2000. We must address a counterfactual—what would have been the condition of New York City's economy had there been no terrorist attack?—that is particularly difficult to evaluate because the effects of the attack were not limited to the New York City region. Instead, it had national repercussions, prolonging and exacerbating the economic slowdown that had begun in 2001.[4] The national repercussions in turn have had substantial effects on the New York City economy. These various lines of causality imply that a precise decomposition of effects is well nigh impossible. To illustrate, airline employment fell by 10 percent nationally in the aftermath of the attack, and by 20 percent in New York City (Bram et al. 2002a). Because the drop in airline travel nationally was so directly related to 9/11, the full 20 percent decrease in New York should be ascribed to the attack, rather than just the difference between the New York effect and the national effect. By contrast, the strong impact of the stock market on the city's economy, even after September 11, should be categorized as a national effect rather than a 9/11 effect.

While the effects in the first six to twelve months after September 11 almost certainly understate the long-run impact, the longer the time frame for analysis, the more the 9/11 effects are conflated with the ongoing national economic slowdown. In the time frame of our studies, it has not been possible to completely disentangle the 9/11 effects from the economic recession. Though our study has had the luxury of a longer-term perspective than many analyses of 9/11, still, as of this writing, only three years have elapsed since the attack. Given the lags in which data are produced, many of the analyses can report on economic developments only through 2002. Hence, what we present here should be viewed as a short- to intermediate-run assessment of economic impacts rather than a true long-run evaluation.

The overall macro estimates of the economic costs to New York City attributed to 9/11 depend on the difference between the actual performance of the New York economy post-9/11 and the pre-9/11 forecast. Straight-line estimates, essentially linear extrapolations of performance in the period just before 9/11, have tended to give the largest estimates of the impact of 9/11 (Dolfman and Wasser 2004). Forecasting methods that take national trends into account have in general attributed a greater share of post-9/11 losses to the recession than to the attack itself (Bram 2003).

To isolate the various impacts of 9/11, the studies in this project make use of several types of comparisons. While no single one is sufficient, the cumulative weight of the various comparisons increases our confidence in the overall findings. The first and most obvious approach is to compare "just before" to "just after"; most of the studies presented in this volume start with this type of evaluation. The Parrott-Cooke chapter refines the before-after comparison by comparing the impacts in three subperiods in order to better isolate the effects of 9/11 from those of the recession. They compare job losses by industry or occupational grouping for the pre-9/11 period, an immediate impact period (August 2001 to January 2002), and a post-9/11 recession period (January 2002 to August 2003).

Most of the other studies use both time and geography as the basis for comparison, with an increasingly broad range in the definition of the affected area. If the effects of the attack diffuse outward from the immediate site, then in principle the strongest effects of 9/11 should be observed in the immediate area of the attack, with successively weaker impacts on the entire city and the metropolitan area. In general, the results in this volume, combined with the findings of *Wounded City*, the social impacts volume (Foner 2005), support this proposition.

In the most pinpointed comparisons, Andrew Haughwout, Franz Fuerst, and Sanders Korenman, in their respective chapters on housing, commercial offices, and child care arrangements, compare results in the areas closest to the World Trade Center to the rest of New York City. Edward Hill and Iryna Lendel also look at changes in Manhattan and New York City employment and earnings as a share of the entire metropolitan area. The low-wage labor market chapter by Cordelia Reimers compares employment and earnings outcomes for New York City residents to five other cities; Hill and Lendel make a similar comparison for jobs. These authors chose cities with industrial structures similar to New York's because the national recession would be likely to have a similar impact on these cities. Hence, differences between New York and the other cities can be more reliably attributed to 9/11.

As discussed by Reimers, because 9/11 affected transportation and tourism all over the country and the world, the city comparison is an imperfect control. At best, it isolates the direct effects of the World Trade Center destruction in New York City as opposed to the more diffuse effects of the reaction to 9/11 on the national and world economies. Another potential weakness in comparing New York City to a set of other cities is rooted in the very reason for choosing them. If the attack promotes a perception that all large and dense cities are vulnerable to terrorist attack, then there could be a particularly strong economic impact on the comparison cities as well. For example, insurance costs might be expected to rise more, or firm values to decline more, in big cities as opposed to the nation as a whole. If true, the comparison with other large cities would be biased toward not finding any differences. For this reason, comparisons to the nation as a whole, as provided in chapters 4 (Haughwout on housing), 5 (Korenman on the stock market), and 8 (Reimers on labor), are an important complement to the comparisons with other cities.

The power of the comparisons is amplified by using both time and place together. In chapter 5 on the stock prices of New York City–based firms, Korenman relies on simple visual inspection of the trend lines for New York and non–New York firms before and after the attack. In chapter 8, Reimers uses multiple regression analysis to control for demographic characteristics in assessing before-and-after differences between New York City and the comparison cities. Other chapters make comparisons with the previous economic slowdown in New York precipitated by the 1987 crash on Wall Street. Because asset prices would be expected to adjust relatively rapidly to perceived changes in the economic competitiveness of New York, several of the chapters pay particular attention to changes in prices for commercial buildings, housing, and New York–based firms as an early indication of any long-term erosion in the value of a New York City location.

The chapters use a wide variety of data sources to evaluate the 9/11 impacts. The labor market analyses are drawn from the Current Population Survey (CPS), the Current Employment Survey, and the Unemployment Insurance Covered Wages and Employment data. The CPS, which is the household survey used to measure official unemployment rates and poverty rates, is the only monthly or annual survey that identifies workers' characteristics. The Employment Survey measures employment and payrolls by employer location and industry, but it provides no information on workers' characteristics or place of residence. The office market studies use data provided by various real estate organizations in New York City, and housing data come from a federal housing price index and the New York City Housing and Vacancy Survey (HVS). Stock market share values come from the 2001 Compustat annual file. In chapter 9 on child care arrangements, Korenman uses data from the Columbia University Social Indicators Survey.

THE INDIVIDUAL CHAPTERS

The Effects of 9/11 on Economic Competitiveness

Part I of the book addresses the effect of 9/11 on the competitiveness of New York City. In chapter 2, Edward Hill and Iryna Lendel take a broad look at the performance of New York City's economy in the past twenty to thirty years in terms of jobs, economic output, and productivity. They use the most recent data from the North American Industry Classification System (NAICS) and a technique based on the export-base model of city comparative advantage. They find that Manhattan's economic strength is concentrated in three broad industry classifications: financial services and corporate finance; cultural services and performing arts; and information, broadcast entertainment, and publishing. Other critical parts of Manhattan's economic base, such as insurance and the headquarters and office business function, are shared with the larger regional economy. Hill and Lendel's long-sweep review finds a progressive narrowing of the economic base of Manhattan combined with an unprecedented increase in output per job. This increase is reflected in the fact that even though the New York area's share of jobs has declined substantially compared to the next six largest metropolitan areas, its share of output has declined much less.

The terrorist attack did accelerate cyclical and long-term trends that were under way. This structural adjustment can be seen most clearly in finance, the sector of the economy most directly affected by the attack. To save on costs, the finance industry has been relocating its routine functions outside of New York City for many years. However, the rate of change after the attack is striking. Employment in the finance and insurance sector dropped every month after September 2001, except for June 2004. Manhattan lost 14 percent of its finance employment (56,000 jobs) while the suburban portion of the region lost 5 percent.

Hill and Lendel find no evidence that the 9/11 attack caused permanent damage to New York City as a business location. Looking forward, however, they argue that there are risks for New York. Competition for jobs and income, both within the region and with other cities, continues to increase. The city's most prominent industries must continue to innovate so as to provide a stream of new products and services that will justify the high costs of location in the central city.

In chapter 3, Franz Fuerst analyzes the effect of 9/11 on the market for commercial office space. His overall message is that in the three years since the attack, New York's office building market has held up surprisingly well. Some 31.1 million square feet of office space—approximately 10 percent of the total inventory of New York City and 60 percent of downtown's class A space—was destroyed or severely damaged by the 9/11 attack. The damaged and destroyed space equals the inventory of major office locations such as Atlanta and Miami. Widely derided as a white elephant, the World Trade Center (WTC) complex eventually proved to be a desirable location for financial services companies with a need for large floorplates. However, it was not until the Wall Street and dot-com booms of the 1990s that the WTC achieved 90 percent private occupancy.

All other things being equal, the sharp decrease in the supply of office building space would have been expected to raise rents and reduce vacancy rates in Manhattan. This did not happen, for three reasons. First, the decrease in supply was offset by a pronounced decrease in demand for office space, owing to the combined effects of 9/11 and the recession. Second, it turns out that real vacancy rates prior to 9/11 were higher than indicated by the data because firms were inventorying large amounts of unused space at various locations throughout Manhattan. Third, the higher prices for space in alternative midtown locations led firms to economize by reducing the amount of space per worker. In aggregate, companies that had occupied buildings in the affected area rented about 15 percent less space in their alternative locations. Fuerst estimates that half of the anticipated demand from tenants displaced from the attack site was accommodated through backfill into existing space, reduced staff, subleasing, and reduced space per worker. Contrary to expectations that the WTC attack would dramatically drive down the price of office buildings in New York, there was a significant increase in sales prices per square foot. Though factors such as low interest rates may have had some influence, in retrospect this price behavior seems at the least to be consistent with the trends in rents and vacancy levels.

Where did displaced tenants go? The core markets of midtown and downtown Manhattan captured about 80 percent of the stream of displaced tenants after 9/11 through reoccupation of restored buildings, backfill of previously underutilized space, and new leases. The back-office agglomerations for Wall Street located along the New Jersey waterfront dominate the residual. Notably, as of September 2003, more than half or the originally displaced tenants had returned to a downtown location. However, a number of leases in the downtown area were due to expire in 2004 and 2005, and there is some risk that, despite the substantial federal subsidies for public and private infrastructure, many tenants may choose not to renew at that time. The finding of limited spatial and temporal effects is also supported by a regression analysis. Though the downtown market, especially the World Trade Center submarket, was affected more clearly in the first two years after the attacks than the other submarkets, even in these submarkets the changes in vacancy rates have been moderate. That is a much weaker medium-term impact of the attacks than expected.

In light of the attack, tall buildings might have been expected to be particularly vulnerable to apprehensions about security. The tallest buildings (fifty stories or more) did record a sharp hike in vacancies after 9/11, even relative to buildings of forty to forty-nine stories, but in general the expected flight of tenants from tall office buildings has not occurred in the first three years following the attack. Over time the vacancy rate differential for the tallest building has decreased. Thus, the attack on the tallest buildings of all seems unlikely to permanently alter Manhattan's signature industrial characteristic, which is an enormous density of employment supported by very high ratios of capital (in the form of buildings) to land.

In chapter 4, Andrew Haughwout investigates the effect of 9/11 on the demand for New York City locations. He starts by noting that the price of vacant land reflects the attractiveness of a city, as influenced by factors such as perceived safety, taxes, and public services. However, because we do not observe the prices of vacant land, particularly in a city as built up and dense as New York, changes in land prices must be inferred from the prices (and rents) for improved properties—that is, residential dwellings and office buildings. In his analysis of housing prices, Haughwout is able to control for the characteristics of structures so that the remaining variation may plausibly be argued to reflect the price of land.

If the WTC attack led to a perception that living or working in New York City exposes people to significant safety risks in comparison to other locations, then we might expect a noticeable decline in both business and residence demands for New York locations. The premise is that if demand suddenly decreased, the change would be rapidly capitalized in real estate prices. The problem in interpreting price data as a reflection of changes in perceptions is that the city was buffeted by a recession that overlapped 9/11, and the recession might affect housing prices as well. Haughwout argues that the decline in the New York City economy from 2001 to 2003 was about average in its severity; therefore, the changes in housing prices can be interpreted as indicative of the long-run effects of 9/11. To take account of concurrent national trends in housing demand, he compares New York's prices to those in the rest of the nation.

He first looks at prices of single-family homes in the New York primary metropolitan statistical area (PMSA), as compared to the nation as a whole. Using the quarterly index of housing prices produced by the Office of Federal Housing Enterprise Oversight (OFHEO), he finds that housing prices in the New York PMSA gained ground compared to the rest of the nation, both before and in the two years after the attack. However, because the OFHEO data cover only single-family homes, they may not pick up changes in the demand for New York City locations compared with the rest of the metropolitan area. To estimate the 9/11 effect on housing prices and rent levels in New York, Haughwout uses data from the New York City Housing and Vacancy Survey (HVS), a survey of about 18,000 housing units that is done roughly every three years. The advantage of the HVS is that it identifies the specific neighborhood where a house is located and has detailed information on housing characteristics. He estimates a set of regression equations in which housing price (or rent level) depends on the year, the neighborhood, and a set of housing characteristics. The results indicate that both housing prices and rents in New York City were higher in 2002 than in 1999 and that the increase in housing prices was significantly greater than the national increase. However, rents in New York City increased at about the same rate as the nation during this period. Focusing on Manhattan, he finds the same pattern: prices rose faster than in the rest of the nation, and rents rose at about the same rate. Looking at rents in the areas closest to the WTC site itself, he finds that rent levels actually rose relative to the rest of New York City. This surprising result may be due to the temporary subsidies offered to tenants in the affected areas.

Using data from the National Real Estate Index, Haughwout also looks at trends in prices and rents for office buildings in the midtown and downtown areas, again in comparison to the rest of the country. He finds that rents in the downtown area did fall between 2001 and 2002, but the rate of decline was no greater than in the rest of the nation. The same result holds for midtown rents. By the end of 2003, however, rents seemed to have stabilized in both these areas. Evidence from prices of buildings suggests some post-9/11 weakening of demand for downtown office space, relative to the rest of the nation, and a strong increase in demand for midtown space. Thus, though there has been some shift in demand toward midtown, overall the market for office space in the immediate vicinity of the attack has held up relative to the nation. These price signals—very strong in midtown, weaker in lower Manhattan—lead Haughwout to the intriguing conclusion that the reconstruction of downtown should emphasize more residential housing as opposed to full replacement of the destroyed office space. The overall results support the conclusion that the economic impacts of 9/11 on New York City have been modest.

In chapter 5, Sanders Korenman looks at the value of New York–based companies to investigate the hypothesis that investors believe that the locational advantages of New York City have been reduced by the attack on the WTC. The share price for publicly traded companies is determined, in theory, by the present value of expected future earnings of the corporation. If investors fear that New York is no longer as desirable a place to do business after 9/11, then this perception should translate rapidly into a reduced value for the shares of New York firms. However, if investors believe that losses are only temporary, then there would be small effects on the share prices. Reduced profits could stem from higher costs or from what Korenman calls "incumbency" effects— workers in New York firms becoming less productive owing to the trauma of having lived through the 9/11 attack.

The sample consists of companies in the S&P 1500 in 2001, tracked between January 1997 and June 2002. New York companies are defined as having their corporate headquarters located in New York City or the New York City region. Korenman performs simple graphical before-after comparisons between the stock prices of firms headquartered in "New York" and stock prices for other firms. In various models, "New York" is defined alternatively as New York

City, New York State, or the tri-state area of New York, New Jersey, and Connecticut. He presents both comparisons for all New York City–based firms and industry-specific comparisons.

Overall, he finds little evidence that investors expected a major adverse impact on New York firms' profitability as a result of the terrorist attack on the World Trade Center. Stock valuations and company sales were already in decline months before the attack, but the attack did not seem to cause major breaks from this trend. Although the overall comparison suggests some decline in New York–based firms after 9/11, decomposition of the effects by industry suggests that the decline was due to a nationwide decline in those industries in which New York specializes, particularly the FIRE (finance, insurance, and real estate) sector. To the extent that there are any observed effects of the attack, they appear to be spread throughout the tri-state region rather than focused on New York City. Thus, Korenman's stock market valuation approach reinforces the conclusion of Haughwout's analysis of property values: neither study finds a negative effect on asset values of the 9/11 attack.

The 9/11 attack accentuated in a dramatic way a new type of business risk, that of a terrorist attack. New York City is at higher risk for losses than other cities because of its large concentration of symbolic targets and its density of economic activity. The city has sixty-seven buildings with fifty or more floors, almost twice as many as Chicago, and more than the next thirteen cities combined. If the attack causes the cost of insurance to rise substantially in New York relative to other cities, then its economic competitiveness could be seriously affected.

In chapter 6, Jonathan Schwabish and Joshua Chang consider the issue of insurance costs. Insurance claims of about $47 billion have been paid to New York City firms and individuals as a result of 9/11, over forty-seven times as much as has ever been paid for a terrorist attack. The first response to the severe losses to insurers from the 9/11 attack was to exclude acts of terrorism from policies, leaving many firms in high-risk areas with inadequate or highly costly coverage. As a result, the federal government created a backstop insurance program through the Terrorism Risk Insurance Act of 2002. A major problem for the efficient pooling of risk through insurance markets is the potential for adverse selection, which occurs when there is much greater demand for insurance among those who are most at risk. This is particularly the case for insurance against terrorist attacks. A risk-modeling firm has calculated that the relative risk, in terms of average annual insured losses, is over four times as great in New York as it is in Los Angeles, and three times as great as in Chicago. The recommended rates of insurance against terrorism are 66 percent higher in the densest cities than in other large cities, and thirty times as high as the rest of the United States.

At this point the evidence on the consequences of higher insurance costs in

New York is mainly anecdotal. For example, the ratings on mortgage-backed securities totaling $4.5 billion for a number of important properties in New York have been downgraded owing to the inability of the owners of the under-lying properties to obtain full terrorism insurance coverage. A survey by the New York City Comptroller found that premiums for property and casualty coverage increased dramatically following 9/11 and that the availability of cov-erage fell. The rate of increase was significantly greater in New York than in the rest of the nation. This evidence suggests that the long-term economic risk to New York City posed by terrorism may be greater than the short-term risk.

Schwabish and Chang point out that it would be inefficient to allow the densest cities, which are places with very high-factor productivity, to bear the full cost of additional terrorism insurance and that there is a strong public good argument for at least some federal role. They conclude their chapter by considering a number of policy options for the provision of terrorism insur-ance: having the federal government act as the reinsurer of last resort, as was done in Great Britain; mandating a certain minimum level of terrorism insur-ance for all large firms to minimize the adverse selection problems; and real-locating funds under the Homeland Security Act to mitigate the hazards of future attacks in the densest cities. At present, the awarding of most of the homeland security grants has not been based on any real assessment of need or risk.

The Effects of 9/11 on Labor Markets and Families

Chapter 7 by James Parrott and Oliver Cooke and chapter 8 by Cordelia Reim-ers look at the effect of 9/11 on the labor market in New York City, particularly the impact on low-wage workers. Parrott and Cooke focus on the number of jobs as the key and most currently available indicator of the health of the local economy. They begin by noting the severity of the economic downturn faced by New York City in the 2000s. After a period during the late 1990s in which the rate of job growth in New York exceeded that for the nation, between 2001 and 2003 the city lost jobs at three times the national rate. Some 245,000 jobs, or 6.5 percent of its December 2000 peak level, disappeared. Though job growth has now resumed in New York, projections indicate that the number of jobs is not likely to regain its previous job peak until 2010.

Parrott and Cooke combine payroll employment data and an industry-occu-pation matrix with employment and earnings data from the Current Popula-tion Survey to estimate the effects of 9/11 on low-, middle-, and high-wage workers. To disentangle the particular effects of 9/11, the study combines the analysis of employment changes over the entire 2001 to 2003 recession with the findings of other studies to identify those occupational groups that sustained substantial adverse employment effects in the aftermath of 9/11.

Parrott and Cooke divide New York City's 2001 to 2003 recession into three phases: the pre-9/11 phase, dominated by the bursting of the Wall Street and dot-com bubbles; August 2001 to January 2002, when the 9/11 impact was most concentrated; and early 2002 to August 2003. The employment losses that occurred in late 2001 in the hotel, restaurant, arts, air transport, building services, and apparel manufacturing industries were primarily the result of 9/11. Although there has been a perception that high-wage workers bore the brunt of the 9/11 effects, Parrott and Cooke's occupational analysis shows comparable job declines for the three wage groups. They find that workers in low-wage occupations experienced serious but short-term dislocation effects (higher unemployment and reduced earnings) from 9/11. Mean weekly wage earnings for low-wage households declined by 7.9 percent in the fourth quarter of 2001 compared to the same quarter a year earlier, and they dropped by 18.2 percent in the first quarter of 2002 over the first quarter of 2001. Workers in middle- and high-wage occupations experienced less pronounced adverse effects in the immediate aftermath of 9/11, but as the recession wore on through late 2002 and 2003, these workers experienced greater increases in unemployment and greater proportionate declines in wage earnings.

In chapter 8, Cordelia Reimers evaluates the impacts of 9/11 on disadvantaged New York City residents—those who have low skills, are members of minority groups, or are recent immigrants. Using the 2000 to 2003 Current Population Survey, which provides data for the calendar years 1999 to 2002, she analyzes labor market outcomes—employment rates, weekly hours worked, weekly and annual earnings—and economic well-being, as measured by annual household income, including receipt of government transfer payments. She identifies the impact of the 9/11 attack through both before-and-after comparisons and other-city comparisons. The comparison cities are Boston, Chicago, San Francisco, Washington, and Los Angeles. The use of the CPS allows her to control for individual characteristics—particularly age and education—that are strongly correlated with employment outcomes.

Remarkably, Reimers finds that the annual earnings and household incomes of the combined disadvantaged groups declined less in New York City than in other big cities in 2002. In retrospect, this result is perhaps not too surprising, given the overall estimates of 50,000 to 75,000 lost jobs in the eight to twelve months following the attack. However, her results do differ somewhat depending on the particular group. She finds a short-term negative impact of 9/11 on employment for disadvantaged women, while for disadvantaged men the decreases in employment, hours worked, and earnings after September 2001 were more likely due to the recession. The exception to the general conclusion is for blacks, whose household incomes rose less in New York City than else-where. Medicaid coverage rose in New York relative to other cities, suggesting the importance of the social safety net in NYC.[5] More advantaged groups—those who are college-educated, white non-Hispanics, and not-recent immi-grants—fared as well in New York City as elsewhere in late 2001 and 2002, or even better. This finding reflects the underlying strength of New York's economy, as documented in chapters 2 through 4. Although these conclusions are relative to other big cities, a brief look at national outcomes suggests that they would not change if the comparison were with the rest of the nation. As emphasized by Parrott and Cooke, these conclusions should not be taken to imply that disadvantaged New Yorkers did "well" in any absolute sense in the post-9/11 period, but rather that the impact was not worse than elsewhere.

The argument was put forth after 9/11 that the terrorist attack could endur-ingly realign American values and priorities, leading to a "return to hearth and home." One possible manifestation of a renewed commitment to family life or a concern for children's mental and physical health would be an increase in home-based care of children. In chapter 9, Sanders Korenman asks whether, since September 11, 2001, parents have altered their child care arrangements so that children are cared for either by parents at home or by close substitutes for parents, such as nannies, babysitters, or relatives. There was widespread concern about the effects of the attack on children's mental health. One study found a significantly elevated prevalence of mental health problems such as depression, agoraphobia, and separation anxiety among New York City school-children in grades four through twelve six months after the WTC attack. Korenman gives special attention to the changes among children reporting physical or emotional damage from the 9/11 attack. The data for the child care study came from the 1999 and 2002 waves of the Columbia University New York Social Indicators Survey, a representative survey of the household popula-tion of New York City. There were just over 600 families with children under thirteen in each wave of the survey, for a combined sample size of 1,230.

The study finds little evidence that the attack on the World Trade Center affected the child care arrangements of New York families. Parents did not appear more likely after the attacks than before to provide care at or close to home in response to increased fear of terrorism or in order to cope with the problems for children that resulted from the terrorist attacks. Nor were par-ents who reported that their children had new emotional or health problems more likely to care for their children at home. Instead, these families were more likely to use out-of-home care. Restricting the analysis to those most likely to have the flexibility to change child care arrangements—families in which both parents work and education levels are high—did not alter these results.

What do these (non)results say about the change in values that was widely reported in the aftermath of 9/11? One possibility is that the study may have missed the very people most affected by the attack: those who moved out of the city and therefore were no longer in the sample. The more likely explanation is that families tended to resume their "normal" (previous) lives. If so, the purported change in values was more of a temporary phenomenon, as also evidenced by a brief spike in religious attendance, than a deep and long-lasting effect leading to real behavioral changes. The lack of any observable change in child care arrangements is consistent with the basic finding from other chapters in this volume: there is little evidence of a lasting effect of the attack on New York City.

In the last chapter, Howard Chernick considers the very substantial fiscal implications for New York City of September 11. As a result of the attack, many residents of New York City lost jobs and income. However, all faced higher tax rates and reduced public services. City government employment declined by at least 5 percent between fiscal year 2001 and fiscal year 2003. Medicaid enrollment went up by an additional 271,000 people, at a cost to the city of $130 million in additional Medicaid expenditures. Property, income, and sales taxes were all increased substantially. Overall, taxes as a fraction of personal income rose by almost a full percentage point, from an estimated 7.0 percent in 2002 to 7.9 percent in 2004. The increase in taxes exceeds the increase in the previous economic downturn. To cover current expenses the city had to draw on an extraordinary $2 billion in additional borrowing, creating future obligations of some $150 million to $180 million per year. As large as these adjustments have been, the underlying fiscal shortfalls were anticipated to be even greater. Fortunately, the city's strong real estate markets have yielded tax revenues substantially above original estimates. In fiscal year 2004, actual tax revenues were at least 6.4 percent higher than in the preliminary budget. The extra revenues have given the mayor the fiscal flexibility to rebate most of the property tax increase for homeowners, as well as stave off the most drastic cuts in city services.

Drawing on studies of the fiscal impacts that were prepared by various government agencies, Chernick assesses the overall dollar magnitude of the public-sector losses incurred from the attack and the cost per resident. The impact on the city's budget of the attack includes the effect of the additional expenditures required, the increase in transfer payments—mainly for Medicaid—and the loss in city and state tax revenues. The losses are then compared to the compensation paid to New York City through the federal 9/11 assistance package. Not including the cleanup costs at the World Trade Center site, the present discounted value of costs through 2003 is estimated to be about $3 billion. This equals $400 per capita, or about 0.8 percent of personal income. Total projected losses through 2010 equal $4.71 billion, or 1.35 percent of personal income. Federal compensation for general budgetary relief will offset between one-third and a little more than one-half of these public-sector costs.

(The higher federal offset takes into account the automatic federal cost sharing in Medicaid and the deductibility of state and local taxes.) New York City has been forced to make up a fiscal shortfall through tax increases, spending cuts, and additional borrowing that is equivalent to 4 to 8 percent of the current tax burden.

The distribution of the burden of tax hikes and spending cuts has on balance been slightly progressive—that is, the net burden has been borne more by higher- than by lower-income groups. New York State tax revenues were also severely affected by the fiscal crisis brought on by the 9/11 attack. Except for granting New York City permission to raise its tax rates and taking over a small share of the city's debt obligations, the state has done little to compensate New York City for the fiscal costs of 9/11.

CONCLUSION

If journalism is the first draft of history, the chapters in this volume are a second draft. The studies present a short- to medium-range assessment of the impact on New York City's economy of the devastating terrorist attack that occurred on September 11, 2001. A full assessment must await a somewhat longer time period. The theme that emerges from our work is that, despite the magnitude of the losses, the city is so large and its major industrial sectors so flexible in location of employees that the overall impact of the attack was relatively small. Continued strong demand for New York City locations indicates that the economic and social advantages that firms and residents derive from clustering together in dense geographic areas outweigh the heightened risks to cities that are part and parcel of global terrorism. This is reassuring, both for New York and for the nation.

There is, however, a danger that higher insurance costs as a result of 9/11 will weigh on the city's future competitiveness. Another terrorist attack on New York City would clearly raise the danger level for the city's economy dramatically. Effective national policies to reduce the risks of future attacks and fairly spread the costs of protection are therefore crucial.

NOTES

1. The employment rate—the employment-population ratio—for eighteen- to sixty-four-year-old residents of New York City had begun declining eight months earlier, in April 2000 (Reimers, this volume).
2. The findings from our volume are consistent with those of an earlier report on the September 11 attack. Bram and his colleagues (2002b) found that, despite significant temporary disruption, New York's concentration of high-growth industries—securities, business services, motion pictures, education—and its highly educated

workforce give cause to believe that the prospects for economic growth in New York City remain favorable.

3. One widely cited study finds that a doubling of employment density in a county increases average labor productivity by about 6 percent and that more than half of the variance of output per worker across states can be explained by differences in the density of economic activity (Ciccone and Hall 1996).

4. The Council of Economic Advisers (2005, 17) reports that the national economy lost almost 400,000 additional jobs in the three months after the 9/11 attacks.

5. The rise in Medicaid coverage after 9/11 is discussed by Howard Chernick in chapter 10 of this volume on the fiscal effect of 9/11.

REFERENCES

Bram, Jason. 2003. "New York City's Economy Before and After September 11." *Current Issues in Economics and Finance* (Federal Reserve Bank of New York) 9(2, February). Available at: www.newyorkfed.org/research/current_issues/ci9-2.html.

Bram, Jason, James Orr, and Carol Rapaport. 2002a. "Measuring the Effects of the September 11 Attack on New York City." *Economic Policy Review* (Federal Reserve Bank of New York) 8(2, November): 5–20.

Bram, Jason, Andrew Haughwout, and James Orr. 2002b. "Has September 11 Affected New York City's Growth Potential?" *Economic Policy Review* (Federal Reserve Bank of New York) 8(2, November): 81–96.

Chin, Margaret M. 2005. "Moving on: Chinese Garment Workers After 9/11." In *Wounded City: The Social Impact of 9/11*, edited by Nancy Foner. New York: Russell Sage Foundation.

Ciccone, Antonio, and Robert E. Hall. 1996. "Productivity and the Density of Economic Activity." *American Economic Review* 86(1): 54–70.

Comptroller, City of New York. 2002. "One Year Later: The Fiscal Impact of 9/11 on New York City." (September 4). Available at: http://www.comptroller.nyc.gov/bureaus/bud/reports/impact-9-11.

———. 2005. "William C. Thompson Jr.: December Unemployment Rate Increases to 6.2 Percent from 5.4 Percent." Press release PR05-01-008 (January 20). Available at: http://www.comptroller.nyc.gov.

Council of Economic Advisers. 2005. *Economic Report of the President*. Washington: U.S. Government Printing Office (February). Available at: http://www.whitehouse.gov/cea/erpcover2005.pdf.

Dolfman, Michael L., and Solidelle F. Wasser. 2004. "9/11 and the New York City Economy: A Borough-by-Borough Analysis." *Monthly Labor Review* 127(6, June): 3–33.

Fiscal Policy Institute. 2001. "World Trade Center Impacts Take a Heavy Toll on Low-Wage Workers." (November 5). Available at: http://www.fiscalpolicy.org/Nov5wtc report.prf.

Foner, Nancy. 2005. *Wounded City: The Social Impact of 9/11*. New York: Russell Sage Foundation.

Glaeser, Edward L., and Jesse M. Shapiro. 2002. "Cities and Warfare: The Impact of Terrorism on Urban Form." *Journal of Urban Economics* 51(2): 205–24.

Groshen, Erica L., Simon Potter, and Rebecca J. Sela. 2004. "Economic Restructuring in New York State." *Current Issues in Economics and Finance* (Federal Reserve Bank of New York) 10(7, June): 1–7. Available at: http://www.newyorkfed.org/research/current_issues/ci10-7.html.

Harrigan, James, and Philippe Martin. 2002. "Terrorism and the Resilience of Cities." *Economic Policy Review* (Federal Reserve Bank of New York) 8(2, November): 97–116. Available at http://www.newyorkfed.org/research/epr/02v08n2/0211harr.html.

Mollenkopf, John, ed. 2005. *Contentious City: The Politics of Recovery in New York City.* New York: Russell Sage Foundation.

Office of Management, City of New York. 2004. "Impact of 9/11 on New York City Tax Revenue." Mimeo. (September 15).

PART I

The Impact of 9/11 on
Economic Competitiveness

CHAPTER 2

Did 9/11 Change Manhattan and the New York Region as Places to Conduct Business?

Edward W. Hill and Iryna Lendel

MANHATTAN AND the New York region suffered three economic insults at the turn of the new century. First, the late 1990s saw the start of industrial restructuring, beginning with shifts in the telecommunications industry as customers moved from wired to wireless systems. The restructuring of the economic base continued when the technology and telecommunication stock bubbles burst. Although corrections in the financial markets were national economic events, the corporate finance industry is highly concentrated in the New York region, and the correction had disproportionately large regional effects, resulting in lower personal earnings. The economy took a second hit in 2001 when the collapse in technology stock valuations spread into a generalized national recession that had negative consequences for the publishing and advertising industries and the corporate headquarters business function.[1] Revenue and employment losses were substantial in New York because these industries and business functions are important employers in Manhattan and the region. Business losses spread from these key industries down their supply chains. A third traumatic event took place in September 2001—the terrorist attacks that killed nearly three thousand people at the World Trade Center (WTC). This tragedy pushed the already weakened visitors and trade show industries over the edge, causing layoffs in the air services, hotel, restaurant, and arts and entertainment industries. These three events—the restructuring of the technology sector, the collapse of technology stock valuations and the accompanying generalized recession, and the 9/11 terrorist attack—took place against a background of long-term structural shifts in New York's position on the global economic stage.

The purpose of this chapter is to determine whether the terrorist attack changed the competitive positions of Manhattan, New York City, and the New York metropolitan area in the spatial competition for jobs and as places to conduct business. The terrorist attack did not affect the locational calculus of businesses in isolation. The impact of the attack has to be considered against the backdrop of the size, structure, and cyclicality of the regional economy and the changes that were under way in the regional and national economies. The second set of contextual considerations is the start of the 2001 recession and the restructuring of some of New York's core industries that was under way before the attack took place. A third set of secular dynamics is the steady outward expansion of the metropolitan area and its impact on Manhattan's role in the regional business site location and employment markets. A final set of considerations is competition for economic activities with other regional economies at the top of America's urban hierarchy. The only way to determine whether the locational decisions of businesses were affected by 9/11 is to see how locational preferences are revealed in the site location market.

The first section of this chapter is an introduction to the interactions between the product markets, technology, and the way the economy uses geography in the New York region. The second section provides a general overview of New York City's performance in the competition for jobs since 1950.[2] A brief description of the current economic base of Manhattan and the region follows in the third section, which also probes the connection between employment trends in New York City and the performance of two stock market indices. The fourth section looks at Manhattan's market share of jobs and gross product (GP) in the region and at differences in a measure of productivity (the value of GP per job) in the different components of the New York metropolitan area.[3] We conclude with an examination of New York City and the New York consolidated metropolitan statistical area's (CMSA) market share of jobs and gross product among the six largest CMSAs, as measured by GP.

A BRIEF INDUSTRIAL HISTORY OF MANHATTAN

There is much that is unique about Manhattan as a place of production. Manhattan houses combinations of firms and skills that are difficult to replicate elsewhere; the result is localized ecologies of value creation and work that generate agglomeration economies (production cost savings and revenue opportunities triggered by the co-location of firms and locally dense labor markets). However, with the development of major financial centers in London,

Tokyo, and elsewhere in the United States, and with other major metropolitan areas such as Atlanta, Chicago, Dallas, Houston, Los Angeles, San Francisco, and Washington attracting headquarters of global firms, Manhattan's historic near-monopoly status in the markets for some types of business functions and business service production (known more formally as producer services) has weakened considerably since the 1960s. Despite this competition, New York's economy remains dynamic: the city's employment base has churned over the past fifty years, with old industries disappearing and new ones appearing. Employment has fluctuated within a wide band, resulting in dramatic changes in economic specialization and productivity.

Three major technological revolutions in transportation fundamentally changed Manhattan's economic base and purpose. The birth and completion of the interstate highway system exploded the size of the metropolitan area and opened up competitive business locations within the region. Air travel offered up global competitors for business, even as it expanded the global reach of enterprises located within the metropolitan area. Transportation deregulation and the containerization of freight resulted in competitors to New York's port, both within the region (New York City lost its port functions to New Jersey) and between regions. (The Port of New York competes with other East Coast ports, and with the increased volume of trade from the Pacific Rim, East Coast ports have lost market share to West Coast ports.)

Complementing the spatial impact of these transportation revolutions was a much more significant revolution in telecommunications. First analog and then digital telecommunications expanded the global reach of New York's businesses and reinforced the decentralization of business activity within the metropolitan area, giving rise to intraregional competitors for business locations. With the telecommunications revolution and the dispersion of the residences of business executives and highly skilled technical talent across the multistate New York consolidated metropolitan statistical area, Manhattan faces daily competition as a business address from within the metropolitan area.

We need look no further than at firms in the producer services industry—the armadas of business consultants, accountants, and highly specialized lawyers—with multiple offices within the region. Their suburban locations are rivals to those in midtown and downtown for clients. The suburbanization of producer or business services is nothing personal; these are simply businesses that follow the location of work and money.

The combined result of the technological changes in transportation and communication has been skyrocketing productivity growth from the businesses that remain in Manhattan, a narrower economic base in Manhattan and New York City than existed historically, the rise of intrametropolitan competitor business locations, and a change in the distribution of earnings from the jobs located in the city and region triggered by changes in the relative demand for specific occupations from the restructured economic base of Manhattan, New York City, and the region.

THE PATH OF EMPLOYMENT

New York City has experienced two long-term structural swings, or waves, in employment growth since 1950; each wave was interrupted at times by the local manifestations of national business cycles. The first wave ended in 1969, and the second began in 1977. A wave is triggered by a real microeconomic event that changes a region's product mix in some fundamental way; a business cycle fluctuation is associated with swings in aggregate demand and macroeconomic monetary phenomena that leave a region's economic base essentially unchanged.

Figure 2.1 contains a great deal of information about employment in New York City and its relationship to the national economy.[4] The nine post–World War II national economic recessions are marked with gray shading in the figure (see the note for their start and end dates).[5] The vertical dotted lines in the figure mark crashes in the stock market (see the note for the dates).[6] The average number of jobs in New York City over this long time period is nearly 3.5 million (3,491,900). The largest number of jobs was recorded in two months in 1969 (3,850,000), and the smallest was in January 1977 (3,133,500). The number of jobs in the city typically ranges between 3.2 million and 3.8 million (marked by the horizontal lines in the figure).

The first of these long waves began at the end of the Second World War and continued until city employment peaked at a bit more than 3.8 million jobs in 1969. Employment fluctuated within a band of 200,000 jobs over this time period, with the recovery from the 1962 stock market crash marking the start of a prolonged period of steady employment growth in the city. The economic spur of the Kennedy tax cuts, followed by the additional stimulus of wartime spending, was reflected in New York's employment growth. The growth of the 1960s was caused by the combination of the strength of New York's post–World War II manufacturing and distribution industries, the employment effects of the modern international equity and corporate debt markets concentrated in the city, and the impact of 106 months of national economic expansion on the stock market.[7] In economic terms, the jobs peak of 1969 marked an important transition in the structure of work in New York City; the decade that followed was just miserable.

A national recession started in December 1969, and the stock market crash four months later accelerated job declines in New York City. The subsequent national business cycle recovery skipped the city. Employment declines accel-

FIGURE 2.1   JOBS IN NEW YORK CITY FROM JANUARY 1950 TO JUNE 2004

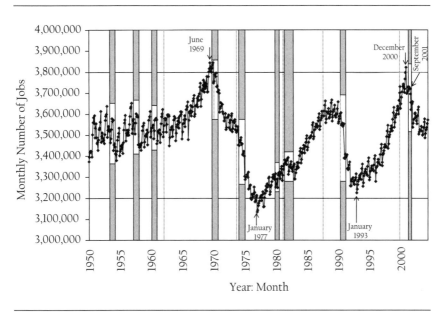

Source: U.S. Department of Labor, Bureau of Labor Statistics, Current Employment Survey.
Note: The gray shaded areas indicate the recessions that occurred between June 1953 and May 1954, August 1957 and April 1958, June 1960 and February 1961, December 1969 and November 1970, November 1973 and March 1975, January 1980 and July 1980, July 1981 and November 1982, July 1990 and March 1991, and March 2001 and November 2001. The dotted lines indicate the stock market crashes that occurred in March 1962, April 1970, October 1973, September 1987, July 1990, and March 2000.

erated with the October 1973 crash; a second national recession started a month after that crash.

The reason why New York's employment did not resume the cyclically influenced path of the previous two decades is that the city's economic base was restructured throughout the decade. The intensity of this process is marked by the fact that the number of jobs declined steadily from its June 1969 peak until bottoming out at 3.1 million in January 1977. The fall was not smooth: a large drop in jobs quickly followed the market crash in October 1973; New York lost over 100,000 jobs during the next year. At the end of the decade, an important part of New York City's traditional blue-collar employment base either died or moved out of town. The blue-collar portion of the city's economic base shifted from manufacturing to services, and the wholesale and distribution industry left the city for the suburbs.[8]

The 1970s marked the beginning of a difficult economic reality for New York City, and this reality, an outgrowth of New York's comparative advantage, grew sharper over the succeeding thirty years. The new economic reality is that the portfolio of industries that are part of New York's economic base narrowed throughout the latter half of the twentieth century. The city became more dependent on a single business function and industry—corporate finance and the equities markets. At the same time, finance has generated incomes and wealth to a degree that the world has never seen before.[9]

The number of jobs increased from 1977 through 1990, reaching a temporary plateau during the double-dip recessions of 1980 and 1983. The decade of job growth during the 1980s peaked over a two-year period from December 1987 to December 1989. Then a major decline set in with the July 1990 crash. The number of jobs slid in a cyclical fashion once again, hitting a trough of 3.2 million in January 1993 (see figure 2.2). A combination of growth in the equities markets, the rise of the NASDAQ as a competitive investment product, and the invention of new financial services products then drove a seven-year

FIGURE 2.2   JOBS IN NEW YORK CITY FROM JANUARY 1990 TO JUNE 2004

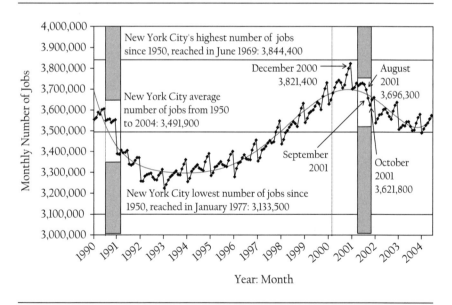

Source: U.S. Department of Labor, Bureau of Labor Statistics, Current Employment Survey.
Note: The gray shaded areas indicate the recessions that occurred between July 1990 and March 1991 and between March 2001 and November 2001. The dotted lines indicate the stock market crashes that occurred in July 1990 and March 2000.

expansion in the number of jobs in New York City that did not let up until employment peaked in December 2000 at 3.8 million. The next market crash was in March 2000, and the city's troubles became apparent soon thereafter.

Figure 2.2 offers detail on the number of jobs in New York City from January 1990 to June 2004. The decade-long swing in work from 1990 to 2000 was most likely the outcome of a regional business cycle fluctuation; the New York region is now subject to cyclical swings that are of longer duration than those experienced by the national economy.[10] The 1990 recession started in the same month in both the nation and in New York City; the pickup in employment started nationally in mid-1992, but started nearly a year later in the city. The most recent recession started in New York City in January 2001 and nationally in March 2001. The National Bureau of Economic Research (NBER) finds that the national recession ended in November 2001. Erica Groshen and her colleagues (2004) find that the recession ended in New York State in August 2003, almost two years after the national trough. Employment did not begin to recover until long after the business cycle trough was passed for the nation, state, and region.

The two stock market crashes that took place during the time period covered in figure 2.2 are marked by the vertical dotted lines. The months when the national economy was in recession are shaded in gray (see the note for the dates). In figure 2.2, the trend line that follows the monthly level of employment smoothes the actual data series; actual employment levels are presented along the line marked with diamonds.

New York City's job picture bottomed out at a bit over 3.2 million in 1993, and then a vigorous seven-year period of growth commenced. The number of jobs in the city reached a cyclical peak in December 2000 at 3,821,000, nearly matching the post-1950 high. However, two of the three catalytic economic events of the turn to the new century began to affect city employment soon after this peak was reached. The speculative technology and IPO (initial public offering) stock bubbles burst in March 2000, and the national economy entered a brief period of recession (as marked by GDP) a year later. Another important source of earnings in the city is merger and acquisitions finance, which peaked at more than $1.7 trillion in announced activity in 2000; this figure had fallen to less than $500 billion in 2002.[11] Based on the two earlier long waves, it is reasonable to suspect that the city embarked on another multiyear period of job decline as a critical and dominant part of the city's economic base contracted—the financial services sector. The job picture appeared to have stabilized in 2004. The terrorist attack came in the early stages of this downslide, in September 2001, and was the third catalytic event (September and October are marked by arrows in the figure). The number of jobs in August was about 3.7 million, and the October number was a bit above 3.6 million; the city lost 74,500 jobs over this two-month time period.[12] The figure indicates that the September employment figure was on the trend line; the post-attack employment numbers were below trend for about eight months; and then the trend was regained between eight and twelve months after the attack. The attack appears to have been catalytic, accelerating the movement of the city and the region into recession but not changing long-term economic forces.[13]

THE ECONOMIC BASE

Manhattan's economic base is composed of three large groupings of industries and business functions: financial services and corporate finance; cultural services and performing arts; and information, broadcast entertainment, and publishing.[14] This set of industries and business functions represent a unique specialization to Manhattan and are not shared with the economic base of the New York CMSA.[15]

The largest is financial services and corporate finance. This industry is composed of securities and commodity exchanges (NAICS 5232), activities related to credit intermediation (5223), other financial activities (5239), other investment pools and funds (5259), and their supply chains.

A second grouping of industries, the performing arts industry, forms a critical portion of Manhattan's base: it includes performing arts companies (7111), promoters of performing arts and sports (7113), and independent artists, writers, and performers (7115) and their related supply chains.

The third group comprises information, broadcast entertainment, and publishing industries: newspaper, periodical, book, and directory publishers (5111), motion picture and video industries (5121), sound recording industries (5122), and other information services (5191).

Lessors of nonfinancial intangible assets (except copyright work) (5331) are part of the base and are directly connected to Manhattan's headquarters function. This industry consists of establishments primarily engaged in assigning rights to assets, such as patents, trademarks, brand names, and franchise agreements, for which a royalty payment or licensing fee is paid to the asset holder. In other words, they are the portion of headquarters activities that licenses rights and collects fees from multistate and multinational business operations.

Other critical parts of Manhattan's economic base are shared with the larger regional economy. The headquarters and office business function is a regional specialization, not just a Manhattan specialization: it includes management of companies and enterprises (5511) and office administrative services (5611). Insurance carriers (5241) and depository credit intermediation services (5221) are CMSA specializations that join the Manhattan-based corporate financial services specialization. Wired telecommunications carriers (5171) are a specialization throughout the metropolitan area, while other telecommunications ser-

vices (5179) are a specialization in Manhattan. The cable and other subscrip-
tion programming industry (5152) is a regionwide specialization that joins
Manhattan's information and entertainment cluster. Agents and managers of
artists, entertainers, athletes, and other public figures (7114) join Manhattan's
performing arts cluster. The printing and related support activities industry
(3231) is a regional specialization with close ties to Manhattan's information
cluster. The biomedical industry is also a regional specialization and not
unique to Manhattan. The pharmaceutical and medicine industry (3254) is
regional, as is the hospital industry (6221). The performance of the base is
discussed in the fifth section of the chapter and in tables 2.3 and 2.4.

Two questions are frequently raised about these results: Where are the
lawyers? And where is the advertising industry? Both are prominent parts of
Manhattan's economic ecology and important users of Manhattan real estate.
Our answer has two parts. First, the cluster analysis–discriminant analysis
statistical technique did not identify either of these industries as economic
drivers of the New York regional economy or of Manhattan's economy. Given
the prominence of both industries, this is curious. The nature of the NAICS-
based GP data makes data error a possibility.[16] That leads us to the second
part of the answer, which is more convincing. Advertising and corporate law
are parts of the supply chains of other drivers of the economy, not independent
drivers of the economy. Corporate law firms work on a wide variety of legal
issues, but the heart of the New York practice is corporate finance in all of its
forms, from securities work to mergers and acquisitions. The advertising business is part of the supply chain of the information sector of the economy,
particularly publishing and broadcasting, but it is also critical to Internet-
related information dispersal. Our argument is that advertising talent, especially noncreative talent, follows the location of the information sector.

The Connection Between the Equities Markets and Employment in New York City

The equities markets play such a dominant role in Manhattan's economic base
that it is useful to compare the connection between the performance of the
equities markets and employment in New York City. A second reason for pay-
ing particular attention to that industry is that the 9/11 attack took place at
an important concentration of financial employment, lower Manhattan. Figure
2.3 can be used to compare the performance of two important indexes of the
public equities markets and employment in New York City. The percentage
change in the NASDAQ composite index and the percentage change in the
Standard & Poor's 500 index, both from January 1985, are plotted against the
left-hand vertical axis. (January 1985 was chosen as the starting point because
that is when the NASDAQ series available to us began.) The number of jobs

FIGURE 2.3   PERCENTAGE CHANGE IN THE NASDAQ COMPOSITE INDEX AND
STANDARD & POOR'S 500 AND NEW YORK CITY EMPLOYMENT
PERCENTAGE CHANGE FROM JANUARY 1985 BASE

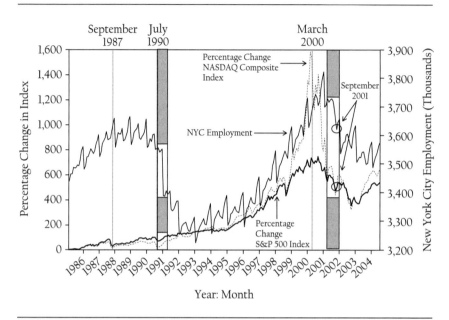

Source: Authors' compilation.

Note: Dotted lines represent the month of a stock market crash. Gray shaded areas indicate a national recession.

in New York City is plotted against the right-hand vertical axis. (These are the same data as used in figure 2.1.) All data series are monthly. The three stock market crashes over this time period are noted by the vertical dotted lines; gray shading marks the start and end points of the two recessions that took place over this time period; and the September 2001 data for the three series are circled in the figure.

A number of relationships are visible in the figure. First, the September 1987 market crash did not affect the number of jobs in the city. The number of jobs leveled out after the crash, and the large decline in the number of jobs did not begin until the July 1990 crash took place. Second, job recovery in the city during the middle 1990s tracked the growth in the value of the stock indexes, especially the NASDAQ. Third, each series peaked in 2000. The NASDAQ peaked in February, the Standard & Poor's 500 peaked in March—the month the crash was declared—and employment in New York City peaked in December with the holiday retailing season. Finally, the size of the speculative bubble in the NASDAQ is evident by looking at the gap between the percentage change in that index and the percentage change in the Standard and Poor's 500.

The terrorist attack occurred in the middle of September 2001. The stock data are based on the indexes on the last day of the month, and the employment data are for midmonth. The declines in the two market indexes are immediate, with a small rebound taking place over the next several months, and then the trend line that was in effect before the attack took place reasserts itself. Much the same can be said about the time series of jobs in New York City: the attack caused a sharp downward movement in the number of jobs, there was a brief recovery as the series moved back onto its trend, and then the cyclical decline reasserted itself. A conclusion that can be drawn from the figure is that the attack had a temporary negative effect on the labor market, catalyzing and accelerating labor market activities that were already under way; then, between three and six months after the attack, the overwhelming negative labor market trend that rested on the contraction in the national and regional business cycle reasserted itself.

Moving away from the horror of the attack and concentrating on the long-term economic position of New York City, it is tempting to take a macroeconomic view of the connection between the behavior of the equities markets, various forms of corporate finance and merger and acquisition activities, and New York City's labor market that links speculative excesses in the finance markets to the behavior of the city's labor and real estate markets. Federal Reserve Board chairman Alan Greenspan famously termed the bubble of the 1990s technology stock–fueled equities markets a period of "irrational exuberance." This exuberance had real employment effects in New York City because large numbers of those who produce and sell traded financial products work in New York City. The same can be said about the regional employment effects of the earlier junk-bond fever: speculative overshooting in the market resulted in a windfall of commissions and bonuses that were spent liberally in New York City, taking the city's property markets for a ride and generating spin-off employment as the creature comforts of the city's financial elite were sated. There is another microeconomic (and less moralistic and judgmental) explanation for the connection between the equities markets and the city's employment that is more satisfying. Employment and incomes in New York City are derived from the performance of the locally based financial markets. To understand movements in aggregate income and employment, the product life cycle of the goods that are sold (or traded) in those markets needs to be understood.

The financial markets are not just made up of two sets of unchanging generic products, stocks and bonds. Instead, the financial services industry is constantly inventing an array of financial instruments that are then sold to investors. Therefore, it is possible to think of New York City's path of employment as being partially, but importantly, connected to the life cycle of a portfo-lio of distinct financial services products that go through the same stages of growth, stagnation or product maturity, and decline as does any other product.

The product life cycle starts as an invention, or a financial technology, that is in search of consumers who find benefits in the product and are willing to purchase it. Once the new product is adopted by the marketplace, it experi-ences a tremendous growth rate and earns above-market rates of return as novel uses are exploited and the highest risk-adjusted rates of return are picked off. The high rates of return attract others into the market who knock off the product by either offering new features or producing it at lower cost. (As a financial services product matures and the market for it is saturated, there is frequently an incentive to sell the instrument to riskier borrowers or naive investors as a way of maintaining sales volumes, nominal returns, and commissions.) Finally, employment declines as fewer companies offer the now slower-growing product, riskier borrowers in the new product's portfolio de-fault, or expectations become more rational about the future revenue streams that will be derived from the instrument.

The invention of mutual funds, leveraged buyout (LBO) financing, flurries of merger and acquisitions activity, and the broadening of the IPO market all led to the rapid introduction of competing products, a supply of product that was not sustainable at the rates of return earned soon after each product was introduced, and a collapse in employment as the volume of new issues in these product groups slowed down and some of the specialist firms went out of business. A second phenomenon has also taken place in New York's financial services industry: as new financial products mature, innovation slows, product characteristics stabilize, competition intensifies, and operating margins de-cline. Then firms that sell the products become interested in operating costs and look for new, less expensive places to produce and manage the product, shifting employment (especially back-office employment) out of Manhattan and New York City. This commonly occurs in any number of industries. Em-ployment impacts from movements along the product cycle are regionally con-centrated because industries are concentrated, especially after the product ex-periences its initial major growth spurt due to agglomeration externalities (see Vernon 1966; Markusen 1985; Christensen 2003, 231, n. 2).[17]

Product cycle movements will not take the finance industry out of New York lock, stock, and barrel. Corporate finance will always be a customized business that relies on the concentration of talent in Manhattan. The global equities markets will maintain a presence in the New York region, and trading floors will always be present in the city. However, with the introduction of electronic trading, trading floors can either move or be started elsewhere in the region, nation, or globe (and have been). Back-office operations will diminish in number with the widespread adoption of paperless trading and record-keeping. Path dependencies built on reputation, interfirm and interpersonal contacts, and the deal volume required to support specialized niche firms will keep the iron hand of the product cycle from killing the corporate finance and equities markets in New York. But without innovation in financial services and corporate finance products, employment will tail off.

MARKET SHARE AND
PRODUCTIVITY DIFFERENCES

Determining how well New York City and Manhattan are doing in the market for business locations depends on the metrics used to gauge success or failure. Should the measure be market share within the metropolitan area or the nation? The answer is that both are important. The success of Manhattan and New York as places to do business should be measured against their competitors. Some business activities need to locate somewhere in the region so the relevant yardstick is the region. For other activities, the competitor locations are contained in a group of large regional economies, as is frequently true for headquarters business functions. Should the appropriate outcome measure be employment or gross product? Again, both measures are valid because they capture different aspects of economic success. Businesses do not exist to maximize employment—they maximize stock-owner return. And jobs are derived from product demand. GP is an approximation of value added in the production process and for return to the owners of the firm. The public, on the other hand, is not concerned with profits; individuals are worried about their jobs. We try to answer former mayor Edward Koch's famous question "How'm I doin'?" by looking at both outcomes. We look first at the market share of the metropolitan area's employment and then at its share of metropolitan-area GP. This section ends with an examination of an approximate measure of productivity: gross product per job.

Manhattan accounts for 63.6 percent of all jobs in New York City (up from a low of 62.1 percent in 1995) and 23.5 percent of the jobs in the CMSA. (Table 2.1 lists Manhattan's share of the annual number of jobs in the New York CMSA and in New York City from 1983 to 2004.)[18] The number of jobs in Manhattan peaked in 2000 at 2,437,600. Economy.com projected this number to be 2,320,900 in 2004, a drop of about 117,000 positions. Manhattan's share of jobs both within New York City and in the New York CMSA dropped continuously from 1983 until 1995. The borough then picked up substantial market share between 1995 and 2000 as the financial services markets strengthened. Manhattan's market share of jobs has declined since the 2001 recession and is projected to continue to decline throughout the recovery.

TABLE 2.1   JOBS, REAL GROSS PRODUCT, AND MARKET SHARE IN MANHATTAN, NEW YORK CITY, AND THE NEW YORK CMSA, 1983 TO 2004

| | | Manhattan (New York County) | | | | | Ratio: Manhattan's Share of GP to Share of Jobs | |
| | | Percentage of Jobs in | | | Percentage of GP | | | |
Year	Number of Jobs	New York City	CMSA	Real GP (Billion $1996)	New York City	CMSA	New York City	CMSA
1983	2,296,091	65.9	26.9	213.3	77.2	38.0	1.17	1.41
1984	2,336,252	65.6	26.3	225.5	77.7	37.7	1.18	1.43
1985	2,360,204	65.3	26.0	232.4	78.6	37.4	1.20	1.44
1986	2,381,042	65.1	25.7	236.6	77.6	36.5	1.19	1.42
1987	2,411,013	65.0	25.6	249.8	77.7	36.4	1.20	1.42
1988	2,378,561	64.1	25.0	254.8	77.7	35.5	1.21	1.42
1989	2,368,215	63.8	24.8	250.5	77.0	34.8	1.21	1.41
1990	2,341,151	63.8	24.9	250.4	76.6	34.7	1.20	1.39
1991	2,201,116	63.4	24.5	237.5	76.0	33.7	1.20	1.37
1992	2,110,851	62.4	24.0	245.7	75.9	34.1	1.22	1.42
1993	2,121,708	62.6	24.0	245.8	75.9	33.9	1.21	1.41
1994	2,136,498	62.6	23.9	252.6	75.9	34.2	1.21	1.43
1995	2,129,294	62.1	23.6	258.2	75.9	34.2	1.22	1.45
1996	2,155,406	62.3	23.6	278.5	77.2	35.2	1.24	1.49
1997	2,209,856	62.5	23.7	290.7	78.4	35.5	1.25	1.50
1998	2,284,953	63.1	24.0	320.4	79.5	36.8	1.26	1.53
1999	2,347,986	63.1	24.0	340.0	80.2	37.2	1.27	1.55
2000	2,440,138	63.9	24.4	382.8	81.8	38.7	1.28	1.59
2001	2,437,587	64.3	24.5	393.0	82.4	39.4	1.28	1.61
2002	2,351,291	63.9	23.9	391.1	81.9	38.5	1.28	1.61
2003	2,306,721	63.6	23.6	400.0	82.2	38.7	1.29	1.64
2004	2,320,929	63.6	23.5	414.2	82.3	38.7	1.29	1.64

Source: Economy.com, August 2004.

Manhattan's market share of New York City's job base has fluctuated between 63.0 percent and 63.9 percent and was projected to be at the middle of that range in 2003 and 2004. The borough's share of jobs in the CMSA was at 24.5 percent in 2001 and was projected to be at 23.5 percent in 2004.

The region is growing work outside of the city and the borough. Still, the number of jobs in Manhattan is in excess of 2.3 million and is 200,000 positions higher than it was in 1992 when the financial services boom began. Both the CES data for New York City and the Economy.com data for Manhattan indicate that the current employment swing reflects cyclical fluctuations, not structural change. The long wave that began in 1977 appears to be continuing. However, the forces of decentralization within the metropolitan area are also continuing.

Gross product produced in Manhattan from 1983 to 2004 is listed in billions of 1996 real dollars in table 2.1, along with Manhattan's share of New York City's GP and the region's GP. In 2004, it was projected that Manhattan produced over $400 billion in real GP and accounted for over 82 percent of New York City's real GP; the borough also accounted for nearly 38 percent of the CMSA's projected GP in 2004. As of 2004, Manhattan's share of regional GP had not yet recovered from the recession. The borough's share of regional GP was 39.4 percent at its 2001 peak and was projected to be at 38.7 percent in 2004.

Nationally, the 2001 recession continued the pattern observed in the 1990 to 1991 recession, when employment lagged the performance of the economy and GDP became the coincident indicator of the economy's position in the business cycle. Four reasons have been given for the lagging performance of job growth at the end of these two recessions: the uncertainty and volatility of health care costs; the increasing share of quasi-fixed cost benefits in total compensation packages, which makes employers hesitant to take on new workers until the recovery is well entrenched; the rarity of recalls because old jobs are destroyed during the downturn and new positions are not advertised until they are created, often when new capital equipment is in place (Groshen and Potter 2003); and the strength of the recovery was not clear in the early years of each cycle.

In both the nation and region, the number of jobs dropped rapidly during the two most recent recessions and continued to drop after the national recession ended (figure 2.2). During the 2001 recession, GP in Manhattan fell by 0.5 percent between 2000 and 2001 (table 2.1) and then was projected to grow by 2.3 percent and 3.6 percent, respectively, over the next two years. In contrast, the number of jobs fell by 3.5 percent from 2001 to 2002, fell another 1.9 percent from 2002 to 2003, and was projected to grow by only 0.6 percent from 2003 to 2004. Both the duration and depth of the recession look very different if measured by GP or by the number of jobs.

In figure 2.4, Manhattan's GP from 1983 to 2004 is plotted along the left-hand vertical axis with a dark solid line; Manhattan's average annual growth rate of GP, using 1983 as the base year, is plotted along the right-hand vertical axis using a lighter dotted line; and the average annual growth rate for the balance of the New York CMSA (the CMSA less Manhattan), using 1983 as

FIGURE 2.4 AVERAGE REAL ANNUAL GROWTH RATE OF GROSS PRODUCT IN MANHATTAN (BASE YEAR: 1983)

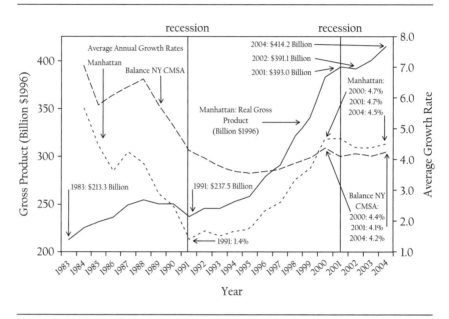

Source: Economy.com, August 2004 download, calculations by authors.

the base year, is plotted against the right-hand axis with a dark dashed line. The GP data are annual, so that movements in GP cannot be viewed with the same precision as movements in employment.

In real dollar terms, GP produced in Manhattan increased from $213 billion in 1983—the year following the end of the 1980 to 1982 double-dip recession—to over $400 billion twenty years later (in constant 1996 dollars). This is a compound annual growth rate of 3.4 percent. Manhattan's GP grew steadily from 1991 to 2004, leading employment growth with a very steep rate of increase from 1996 to the market peak in 2001. The impact of the 2001 recession on the borough's GP was modest, with growth picking up in 2002.

Are the movements in GP different in Manhattan when compared to the remainder of the New York CMSA? They are, and the suburbanization of GP is evident in figure 2.4. The average annual growth rate of GP in Manhattan is below that of the balance of the New York CMSA from 1983 to 1999, and it has been about 0.2 percentage points higher than in the balance of the CMSA in the years that followed. Measuring the average annual percentage change from the end of the double-dip recession in 1983 smoothes out annual percentage changes (or the annual growth rate) and is graphed in figure 2.4. We do not graph the annual percentage change in GP because it depicts an economic story that is similar to that told by the annual growth rate. The annual growth rate in GP in Manhattan is below that of the balance of the CMSA from 1984 to 1991; afterwards it is consistently higher than the balance of the CMSA from 1995 until the effects of the 2001 recession and terrorist attack were felt. Manhattan's growth rate dipped below that of the balance of the CMSA from 2001 to 2002 and was projected to track with the balance of the CMSA for the next two years. The higher growth rates in Manhattan coincide with a bull stock market.

The data in the last two columns of table 2.1 present the ratio of Manhattan's percentage share of New York City's GP to its percentage share of New York City's jobs (GP:Jobs); the same ratio is calculated between Manhattan and the New York CMSA in the last column. A ratio greater than one indicates that Manhattan has a greater share of GP than jobs; therefore it has higher than average GP per job—a proxy measure for productivity. The ratio demonstrates that Manhattan is and continues to be a center of high productivity work and productivity growth in the New York metropolitan region.

The GP:Jobs ratio between Manhattan and New York City increases over time, rising from 1.17 in 1983 to 1.29 in 2004. This implies that Manhattan's share of the city's GP is increasing relative to its market share of jobs. This ratio increased steadily over the time period covered and accelerated in the mid-1990s. The pattern is not the same between Manhattan and the CMSA. First, the ratio is much larger than in the previous series, meaning that Manhattan's share of GP in the region is much higher than its share of jobs. In 2004, the ratio was 1.64. Second, the ratio declined from 1983 to 1991 and then began to increase. The ratio of the share of GP to the share of jobs between Manhattan and the New York CMSA has either stayed the same or increased in every year since 1993. The current economic story of New York City and Manhattan is a story about productivity increase coupled with weak job generation.

Productivity Differences Within the New York Metropolitan Area

The only way real incomes can be increased in a sustainable fashion is by increasing productivity. Usually total factor productivity is thought of as people working smarter, harder, faster, or better (improved quality), with a liberal dose of capital equipment and improved management practices added to the mix, thereby lowering production costs. However, the most effective way of increasing worker productivity, which should be measured as value added per hour worked, is to increase the value of goods and services sold. When productivity increases are discussed casually, it is typically assumed that the product mix stays the same and that productivity is increased by squeezing the middle lines of the firm's income statement or by increasing the flow of product that is made each hour. However, the most direct way of increasing value added is to get a higher price for what is produced (assuming that competitors cannot get in the way of a price increase).

Figure 2.5 displays the approximation of productivity used in table 2.1, the value of real gross product per job. Data on the number of hours worked are not available at the subnational level, making it impossible to calculate value added per hour worked. Also, over time capital is continually added to the production process and the product mix changes, so GP per job is an approximation of total factor productivity. A final caution in the interpretation of these data is that the denominator is the total number of jobs that are in the economy; thus, a part-time job carries the same weight as a full-time job. Despite these limitations, real GP per job is used because it is the best approximation available for local area productivity.

FIGURE 2.5   GROSS PRODUCT PER JOB IN 1996 CONSTANT DOLLARS

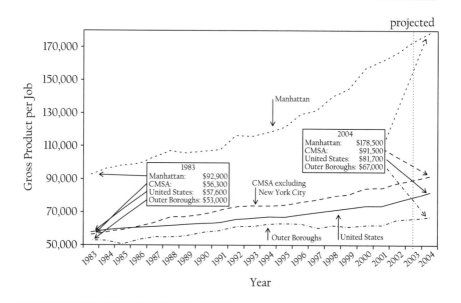

Source: Calculated from gross product and employment estimates from Economy.Com, August 2004.

Figure 2.5 shows the annual time trend of real gross product per job for Manhattan (New York County), the United States as a whole (to serve as a comparative benchmark), the outer boroughs of New York City, and the non–New York City portion of the CMSA. All dollar amounts are in 1996 real dollars. Gross product per job is given for each of these geographic units at the start of the time period (1983), concluding with projected data for 2003 and 2004. The trend for Manhattan is graphed using a dotted line at the top of the figure; the United States is the light solid line; GP per job for the outer boroughs of New York City is the dark dashed-dot line at the bottom of the figure; and the non–New York City portion of the CMSA is the dark dashed line. GP per job for the four geographic units in 1983 and 2004 is given in the text boxes. In 1983, Manhattan generated $92,900 (in 1996 dollars) in GP per job, while the three other geographical units were tightly bunched within a range of $4,600 per job. At the end of the time period, the range increased to $24,500. The outer boroughs of New York City had the lowest productivity per job at the beginning of the time period, and, surprisingly, the CMSA outside of New York City had a lower level of productivity per job than did the U.S. average. Twenty years later productivity in Manhattan skyrocketed to $178,500 per job, with no slowdown for recession or any other occurrence. Productivity in the balance of the CMSA outpaced the average level of productivity in the United States. Although productivity grew in the outer boroughs of New York City, it increased by only $14,000 per job—$10,000 less than the average increase in the United States. What is distressing is that most of the productivity gain in the outer boroughs took place either in the early 1990s or since 2001.

CHANGES IN MARKET SHARE AND NEW YORK CITY'S COMPETITIVE POSITION

How have New York City and the New York metropolitan area fared in the competition for jobs and as places of production? To help answer this question, we calculated New York City's share of jobs and GP within the CMSA and the city and the CMSA's market share among the nation's six largest CMSAs (as measured by their GP): New York, Los Angeles–Riverside–Orange County, San Francisco–Oakland–San Jose, Chicago-Kenosha, Washington-Baltimore, and Boston NECMA (New England county metropolitan area).[19]

Table 2.2 lists New York City's share of jobs in the CMSA and among the six largest CMSAs over a twenty-year period and then the New York CMSA's market share of jobs in the six largest CMSAs. The right half of the table repeats the calculations for GP.

The New York CMSA accounts for over one-third of the GP generated in the big six metropolitan areas and for about 30 percent of employment. What

TABLE 2.2   NEW YORK CITY AND THE NEW YORK CONSOLIDATED
METROPOLITAN STATISTICAL AREA'S (CMSA) MARKET SHARES
OF JOBS AND GROSS PRODUCT

	Market Share of Jobs			Market Share of Gross Product		
Year	NYC in NY CMSA	NYC in Six CMSAs	NY CMSA in Six CMSAs	NYC in NY CMSA	NYC in Six CMSAs	NY CMSA in Six CMSAs
1983	40.8%	13.7%	33.5%	49.2%	17.3%	35.2%
1984	40.1	13.4	33.3	48.5	17.1	35.3
1985	39.8	13.1	33.0	47.6	16.7	35.0
1986	39.6	13.0	32.9	47.0	16.5	35.1
1987	39.4	12.9	32.7	46.8	16.4	35.1
1988	39.0	12.6	32.3	45.7	15.9	34.9
1989	38.9	12.4	31.9	45.2	15.5	34.3
1990	39.0	12.3	31.5	45.3	15.4	34.1
1991	38.7	12.0	31.0	44.3	15.0	33.9
1992	38.5	11.9	30.9	44.9	15.4	34.4
1993	38.4	11.9	30.9	44.6	15.3	34.4
1994	38.2	11.8	30.9	45.0	15.4	34.3
1995	38.0	11.7	30.7	45.0	15.3	34.1
1996	37.9	11.6	30.5	45.6	15.7	34.3
1997	37.9	11.5	30.4	45.3	15.4	33.9
1998	38.0	11.5	30.3	46.2	15.7	34.0
1999	38.0	11.6	30.4	46.4	15.6	33.7
2000	38.2	11.6	30.3	47.3	16.0	33.8
2001	38.0	11.5	30.2	47.8	16.2	33.8
2002	37.4	11.3	30.2	46.9	15.9	33.8
2003	37.2	11.2	30.1	46.9	15.9	33.8

Source: Economy.com, October 2003.

is impressive is that while the region's share of employment among the big six metropolitan areas dropped by 3.4 percentage points, the drop in its market share of GP was 1.4 percentage points, or less than half. The decline in the region's market share of employment has been smooth, discrete, and continuous. (The loss was typically one-tenth of a percentage point a year, with larger drops occurring in the late 1980s.) The decline in GP is lumpy and occurred mainly in the mid-1980s, with market share gains from 1997 to 1999.

New York City accounts for 37.2 percent of the total number of jobs in its multistate CMSA, down from 40.8 percent in 1983. The city's share of the CMSA's GP dropped from 49.2 percent to 46.9 percent in the same period.

The market share of New York City among its competitor regions is more troubling than its intraregional decline. First, the decline in New York City's market share of jobs in the big six regions accounted for two-thirds of the decline of the entire metropolitan region and for the entire decline in the region's share of GP. New York City accounted for nearly 14 percent of all jobs in the big six in 1983, but it was projected to account for 11.2 percent in 2003. The city's share of GP has declined as well, but it is a full percentage point less. Although the city's market share of jobs has declined smoothly and continuously, the same cannot be said for its share of GP. The city's share of GP among the big six was lower from 1989 to 1999 than it was from 2000 to 2003. We conclude that:

- The productivity gains in Manhattan during the mid-1990s cushioned the rest of the city.

- Productivity is growing faster in the CMSA than in the outer boroughs of the city. (The city's market share decline in GP is larger than the CMSA's market share decline in GP.)

- The city's market share decline in jobs is greater than its market share decline in GP by at least a full percentage point.

- While the decline in job share has been continuous, the city regained market share in GP with the recovery in the equity markets.

- The source of the productivity and job loss in New York City is disproportionately located in the outer boroughs.

The data presented in table 2.3 show that in 2001 the New York CMSA was the market leader among the big six in most of New York's driver industries. This is partially due to the fact that the New York region was the largest in terms of employment. To see how the region's competitive position stands, we review information from tables 2.3 and 2.4 together for some of the New York region's driver industries, along with the data in figure 2.6.

Figure 2.6 displays recent data from the Quarterly Census on Employment and Wages (QCEW) for three professional services sectors that contain many of the New York regional economy's driver industries: information services, financial activities, and professional and business services. The data in the QCEW are more aggregated than the data used in the earlier parts of this chapter, so the material in table 2.4 and figure 2.6 are not directly comparable. The unit of observation in figure 2.6 is the newly defined New York metropoli-

(*Text continues on p. 50.*)

TABLE 2.3   MARKET SHARE OF EMPLOYMENT OF THE SIX LARGEST METROPOLITAN-AREA ECONOMIES IN 2001 FOR NEW YORK CITY'S DRIVER INDUSTRIES

NAICS: Industry	Employment Market Share Within Each Industry in 2001					
	New York	Los Angeles	San Francisco	Chicago	Washington	Boston
Total employment	30.2%	21.5%	11.2%	14.1%	13.0%	10.0%
Manufacturing[a]						
3231: Printing and related support activities	34.0	20.5	6.1	18.9	10.1	10.3
3254: Pharmaceutical and medicine manufacturing	46.0	17.2	10.1	13.8	4.3	8.6
3352: Household appliance manufacturing	18.1	46.5	2.4	22.6	0.0	10.4
4931: Warehousing and storage	26.0	25.4	7.4	25.4	10.0	5.7
Information[a]						
5111: Newspaper, periodical, book, and directory publishers	42.8	13.7	9.9	13.5	11.0	9.2
5112: Software publishers[b]	21.7	11.7	29.9	8.0	18.0	10.7
5121: Motion picture and video industries	22.3	61.6	4.9	4.4	4.5	2.3
5122: Sound recording industries	28.7	18.8	8.3	23.6	12.1	8.4
5151: Radio and television broadcasting[b]	28.0	29.2	12.4	9.0	13.5	7.8
5152: Cable and other subscription programming	53.8	15.5	7.6	5.0	11.2	7.0
5161: Internet publishing and broadcasting[b]	15.5	22.6	18.1	25.2	16.8	1.9
5171: Wired telecommunications carriers	33.9	17.9	11.6	12.0	16.4	8.1
5172: Wireless telecommunications carriers (except satellite)[b]	33.9	17.9	11.6	12.0	16.4	8.1
5179: Other telecommunications	29.4	8.0	6.7	7.2	48.4	0.2
5191: Other information services	24.6	23.0	18.9	11.4	12.4	9.7

Finance and insurance[a]					
5221: Depository credit intermediation	33.3	17.1	11.4	17.0	10.3	10.9
5222: Nondepository credit intermediation[b]	26.3	24.4	8.2	19.2	16.1	5.8
5223: Activities related to credit intermediation	36.9	22.0	7.1	14.6	7.3	12.0
5232: Securities and commodity exchanges	60.1	5.6	7.9	10.0	2.1	14.3
5239: Other financial investment activities	46.6	12.9	8.9	11.0	11.3	9.2
5241: Insurance carriers	36.2	16.8	7.0	16.8	11.4	11.8
5259: Other investment pools and funds	36.9	12.9	13.4	10.1	19.0	7.7
5331: Lessors of nonfinancial intangible assets (except copyrighted works)	44.7	14.5	15.3	10.7	8.2	6.6
Management[a]					
5511: Management of companies and enterprises	28.8	26.6	17.2	13.3	6.5	7.6
5611: Office administrative services	26.0	16.1	9.9	16.2	19.4	12.3
5612: Facilities support services	26.1	16.1	9.9	16.2	19.4	12.3
Performing arts, spectator sports, and related industries[a]					
7111: Performing arts companies	26.0	33.0	12.3	15.7	7.3	5.7
7113: Promoters of performing arts, sports, and similar events	26.3	31.1	13.2	13.4	9.9	6.1
7114: Agents and managers for artists, athletes, entertainers, and other public figures	21.1	33.3	12.2	20.0	7.8	5.6
7115: Independent artists, writers, and performers	21.1	42.4	8.1	15.9	8.8	3.8
7121: Museums, historical sites, and similar institutions[b]	39.2	12.2	8.2	18.8	10.6	11.0

Source: Economy.com, October 2003.

Note: Consolidated Metropolitan Statistical Areas in the table appear in the order of their economy size in 2001 as measured by gross regional product.

[a]The entire supersector [two-digit North American Industry Classification System (NAICS) industry] is not included. The list contains either drivers or close substitutes or complements.

[b]The industry was not identified as a driver. It is included because it is closely related to an identified driver industry.

TABLE 2.4 PERCENTAGE POINT CHANGE IN THE EMPLOYMENT MARKET SHARE OF THE SIX LARGEST METROPOLITAN-AREA ECONOMIES FOR NEW YORK CITY'S DRIVER INDUSTRIES, 1993 TO 2001

NAICS: Industry	Change in Employment Market Share 1993 to 2001					
	New York	Los Angeles	San Francisco	Chicago	Washington	Boston
Total employment	-0.7%	0.4%	0.4%	-0.3%	0.1%	0.2%
Manufacturing						
3231: Printing and related support activities	0.3	0.7	-0.8	-1.2	0.3	0.6
3254: Pharmaceutical and medicine manufacturing	-10.4	5.3	0.7	-1.7	1.3	4.9
3352: Household appliance manufacturing	-10.0	21.0	-0.1	-18.3	-0.1	7.5
4931: Warehousing and storage	-5.7	0.4	-1.1	7.9	-1.0	-0.5
Information[a]						
5111: Newspaper, periodical, book, and directory publishers	2.2	-0.9	0.3	-1.9	0.5	-0.3
5112: Software publishers[b]	-1.2	0.4	8.8	-2.8	-4.4	-0.8
5121: Motion picture and video industries	5.7	-2.3	0.1	-3.6	0.4	-0.3
5122: Sound recording industries	-2.5	-5.0	0.0	2.7	3.8	0.9
5151: Radio and television broadcasting[b]	-11.7	4.5	3.3	1.8	1.7	0.3
5152: Cable and other subscription programming	8.4	-6.2	-2.1	-1.9	2.9	-1.1
5161: Internet publishing and broadcasting[b]	-9.9	9.0	2.8	-0.3	1.5	-3.1
5171: Wired telecommunications carriers	-9.6	2.3	0.0	2.5	3.6	1.1
5172: Wireless telecommunications carriers (except satellite)[b]	-9.6	2.3	0.0	2.5	3.6	1.1
5179: Other telecommunications	17.0	-12.5	-5.9	-2.3	5.9	-2.2
5191: Other information services	-9.1	11.3	11.4	-6.9	-0.9	-5.7

Finance and insurance[a]

5221: Depository credit intermediation	-4.7	-1.6	0.4	3.3	1.6	1.1
5222: Nondepository credit intermediation[b]	-3.3	0.3	-1.5	3.1	1.9	-0.5
5223: Activities related to credit intermediation	-0.8	-2.6	-2.3	1.2	-1.9	6.4
5232: Securities and commodity exchanges	-3.5	-1.3	2.6	-1.7	-1.8	5.8
5239: Other financial investment activities	-1.1	0.1	1.5	-2.4	4.6	-2.7
5241: Insurance carriers	1.4	0.4	-0.8	-2.0	2.0	-1.0
5259: Other investment pools and funds	-1.3	-1.0	-1.5	-3.8	6.0	1.7
5331: Lessors of nonfinancial intangible assets (except copyrighted works)	-2.1	6.5	2.3	-6.4	-0.5	0.2

Management

5511: Management of companies and enterprises	-0.3	2.0	-0.7	-1.6	0.8	-0.2
5611: Office administrative services	1.9	-5.3	0.3	1.8	0.1	1.1
5612: Facilities support services	1.9	-5.3	0.3	1.8	0.1	1.1

Performing arts, spectator sports, and related industries[a]

7111: Performing arts companies	1.4	-5.8	-2.7	4.7	0.1	2.3
7113: Promoters of performing arts, sports, and similar events	2.6	-3.1	-1.7	1.9	-1.1	1.5
7114: Agents and managers for artists, athletes, entertainers, and other public figures	1.1	-3.8	-3.5	8.6	-3.7	1.3
7115: Independent artists, writers, and performers	1.0	1.8	-5.7	3.1	-0.7	0.6
7121: Museums, historical sites, and similar institutions[b]	-0.1	4.4	1.3	-1.2	-2.8	-1.6

Source: Economy.com, October 2003.

Note: Consolidated Metropolitan Statistical Areas in the table appear in the order of their economy size in 2001 as measured by gross regional product.

[a] The entire supersector [two-digit North American Industry Classification System (NAICS) industry] is not included. The list contains either drivers or close substitutes or complements.

[b] The industry was not identified as a driver. It is included because it is closely related to an identified driver industry.

FIGURE 2.6   LOCATION OF EMPLOYMENT IN THREE PROFESSIONAL SERVICES
SECTORS OF THE NEW YORK METROPOLITAN ECONOMY

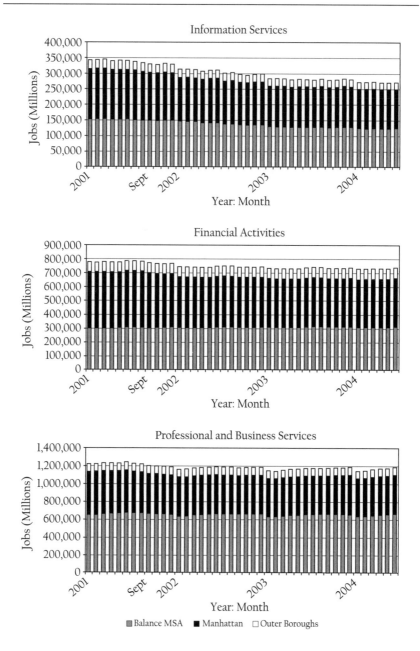

FIGURE 2.6   *CONTINUED*

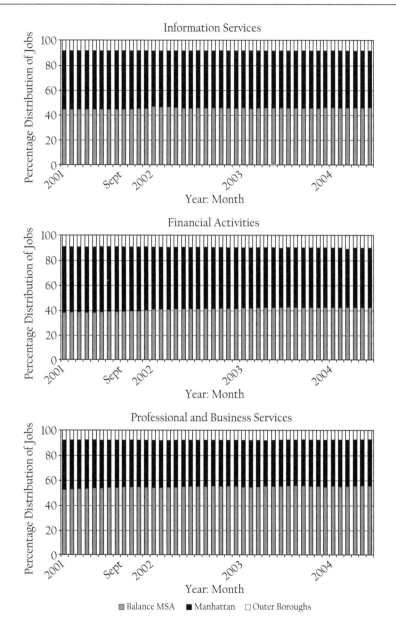

Source: Quarterly Census of Employment and Wages, U.S. Bureau of Labor Statistics.

tan statistical area (MSA) (Frey et al. 2004), which is larger than the old New York primary metropolitan statistical area (PMSA).[20] The regional GP and employment data we have been reporting up to now have been for the larger CMSA. The data in figure 2.6 allow for an improved understanding of the spatial competition for work in a critical portion of New York City's labor market. The figure reports on employment in Manhattan, the outer boroughs of the city, and the suburban balance of the MSA. The left column of the figure contains graphs of the number of jobs in each of the three producer services sectors, while the right side contains graphs of the percentage distribution of jobs between Manhattan, the outer boroughs, and the balance of the MSA in the three producer services sectors. The data are monthly from January 2000 to June 2004 (the 2004 data are preliminary).

Pharmaceuticals

The New York region had a 46 percent market share of employment in the pharmaceutical industry in 2001 among the big six regions; Los Angeles and Chicago occupied the second and third positions, with 17 percent and 13.8 percent market shares, respectively. New York's employment share dropped by 10.4 percentage points between 1993 and 2001, with Boston accounting for nearly half of New York's drop in share. Industry consolidation among big-pharma firms has boosted the region's market share nationally, but not among the big six. The New York region's competitive advantage in big-pharma lies in management, access to capital, and knowledge of the regulatory process. New York's competitor regions are building employment market share on the research and development activities of research-based biotech little-pharma.

Information

The information sector of the economy is a new way of organizing parts of the economy under the NAICS system and forms a critical portion of the economic base of the New York regional economy. Some of the industries in this sector have long been considered to be part of the region's base—publishing, printing, telephone, and broadcasting. Other portions of this sector are as new as the technologies that created them—cable television, wireless communications, and software publishing.

Publishing   The New York region retains its dominant position in book, magazine, newspaper, and directory publishing (a 42.8 percent share of employment among the big six), and the region has gained share as employment in this sector has suburbanized within the greater New York region (Groshen et al. 2004). New York holds second position in software publishing, following the

San Francisco–San Jose CMSA, with a small lead over the Washington-Baltimore region. New York's market share slipped by 1.2 percentage points from 1993 to 2001, while San Francisco's share increased by 8.8 percentage points.

Broadcasting and Visual Information   Los Angeles dominates the motion picture business, yet New York is in second place with an increased market share of employment. At the same time, its nearly 12-percentage-point decline in share of radio and television broadcasting employment gives Los Angeles first place in terms of share. What is interesting is to see the New York region's role in a new television medium—cable television programming. New York has over a 50 percent share of employment; Los Angeles is a distant second, and New York's share increased by 8.4 percentage points. In Internet publishing and broadcasting, a smaller portion of the information sector, Chicago is in first position, and New York's market share has dropped by nearly 10 percentage points.

Telephone Communications   The New York region has been the center of the U.S. telephone industry since Alexander Graham Bell invented the industry in its wired form. The cell phone industry owes its existence to chips, radio, and other technologies that rolled out of Bell Labs in Murray Hill, New Jersey, yet the New York region has not done well in the industry's transition from a regulated wired past to a competitive wireless present and future. Employment among wired carriers has plummeted while it has grown among wireless carriers. Despite this switch in technologies, the employment market shares of each metropolitan area are about the same in each technology (differing only at the second decimal place). From 1993 to 2001, New York's market share of employment in each branch of the telecommunications industry dropped by nearly 10 percentage points. Los Angeles has picked up most of the difference among wired carriers; the pickup in wireless telecommunications was spread among Los Angeles, Chicago, and Washington (with Washington-Baltimore gaining the most).

Intrametropolitan Shifts   The CEW data in figure 2.6 show that overall levels of employment in the information sector in the New York MSA dropped nearly 21 percent from January 2000 to June 2004. A bit over half (55 percent) of the loss is in Manhattan, where 36,000 jobs were lost, compared to 29,000 in the suburban portion of the MSA. The losses accelerated in September 2001, but continued on a steady downward pace afterward. The losses are concentrated in telecommunications and publishing.

Finance and Insurance

Finance is at the heart of New York City's economy and is a major pillar of the regional economy as well. This sector of the economy was the one most directly affected by the terrorist attack. It is also the sector that was subject to the other late-1990s shocks to the economy. The result is that both the city and its suburbs lost employment, while the suburbs have gained employment market share. The difference is that while Manhattan lost 14 percent of its finance employment, the suburban portion of the region lost 5 percent. Employment in the finance and insurance sector has dropped every month since September 2001, except for June 2004. The suburban portion of the New York MSA experienced employment losses of 39,000 jobs between January 2000 and June 2004. Over the same time period, Manhattan lost 56,000 jobs.

Both the depository (bank) and nondepository (nonbank) credit intermediation industries in the New York region have witnessed a declining market share among the big six, with Chicago earning market share gains.

Security and Commodity Exchanges   For the finance sector as a whole, declines in employment set in with the terrorist attack, but employment had begun declining in Manhattan's security and commodity exchanges earlier, in December 2000. In 2001, the New York region had 60 percent of the big six's employment in securities and commodities exchanges, Boston 14 percent, and Chicago 10 percent. Boston and San Francisco experienced gains in market share, while the other regions lost share. As mentioned earlier, the threat to New York City lies in the technological transformation of these industries as they move to an all-electronic system of exchange. There is little to choose from when faced with this technological threat—if New York's exchanges do not shift to a less costly, twenty-four-hour-a-day, seven day-a-week electronic global trading system, another exchange will eventually underprice the New York exchanges and start to steal their business. Electronic trading is also likely to shrink back-office employment and raises the prospect of placing back-office employment anywhere that has a sufficient workforce and telecommunications capacity. Groshen and her colleagues (2004) have documented the early stages of the trend to move financial services back-office operations to less costly locals.

Insurance Carriers   In 2001, insurance carriers provided 128,000 jobs, compared to 199,000 in the securities exchanges, in the New York region. The region had an employment market share of 36 percent among the big six, and that share increased a bit from 1993 to 2001. Financial returns in this industry declined when the stock market bubble burst and job losses corresponded to the decline in the industry's financial performance.

Management

New York has long been a headquarters town, and now it is a headquarters region. However, it shares that title with nearly all of the big six metropolitan regions. New York's market share of headquarters employment was 28.8 percent in 2001, Los Angeles trailed a bit with 26.6 percent, and San Francisco had a 17.2 percent share. New York, Los Angeles, Chicago, and Washington all had employment market shares for headquarters employment that were less than their share of total employment among the big six. The data also show that while the New York region has lost a bit of market share over the course of the expansionary phase of the business cycle (−0.3 percent), Los Angeles and Washington have gained employment market share. Chicago experienced the largest loss in share.

Closely related to headquarters employment is an industry within the finance sector: lessors of nonfinancial intangible assets (NAICS 5331). This industry leases intellectual property by assigning rights to assets, such as patents, trademarks, brand names, and/or franchise agreements for which royalty payments or licensing fees are paid to the asset holder. This includes brand-name licensing, trademark licensing, industrial design licenses, oil royalty agreements, and patent licensing, buying, and leasing. In an operating environment of global and multistate operations, this is a way in which headquarters operations assign value to their marks and intellectual property and transfer revenue to the home office. The New York region has 44 percent of the big six employment market share, although that share has declined since 1993 by 2.1 percentage points. Chicago experienced a larger loss in share, with the Los Angeles and San Francisco CMSAs gaining share.

Intrametropolitan Shifts   The CEW does not go down to the four-digit level of detail in the NAICS code, staying at the supersector level of aggregation. Figure 2.6 plots the data for professional and business services employment for the New York MSA and its components. Manhattan has lost 44,600 jobs in this sector since 2000—9.3 percent of the 2000 job level—and the suburban portion of the MSA has lost nearly as much, 33,700, which was only a loss of 2.8 percent.

CONCLUSIONS

What impact did the terrorist attack of September 11, 2001, have on New York City and Manhattan's position in the market for business locations? We conclude that the terrorist attack catalyzed cyclical trends in jobs and GP that were already well under way. There is no evidence that the city suffered permanent damage as a business location. This does not imply that the market for business locations will shrug off a second major attack.

Firms choose locations based on one of five factors related to their income statement: the location will generate higher revenue for the firm than other locations; the location is a low-cost production site; the location provides access to a pool of labor with particular skills that is deep (or thick) locally yet scarce (or thin) nationally or globally; the location is tied to a scarce but vital factor of production, such as a natural asset; or the location offers advantages in product development.[21] Since New York City has notoriously high operating costs and its harbor no longer provides a competitive advantage for production, firms now locate in the city because it provides advantages in generating revenue, in recruiting scarce labor, or in product development.[22] A large part of New York City's competitive advantage rests in the deep pool of human talent that invents new financial products, administers existing corporate financial products, or is employed as part of the supply chain that supports those products.

The data indicate that New York City's economy experiences spatial bifurcation, with jobs in the outer boroughs being much less productive than those in Manhattan or in the portions of the CMSA that lie outside the city's borders. Data on the number of jobs located in Manhattan and on the gross product that is generated by those workers indicate that Manhattan is a location of jobs that are extremely productive owing to the value of the product they generate. The productivity gap between Manhattan and the outer boroughs and between the outer boroughs and the balance of the CMSA has increased over the twenty-year period examined. New York needs to concentrate on the development of employment opportunities in the outer boroughs.

A second warning about the future of the economy of the city lies in the loss in intraregional employment market share in the information services, financial services, and professional and business services sectors coupled with absolute employment losses throughout the 2001 recession and the early stages of the national recovery from that recession. The suburban portions of the New York region are growing as competitors to Manhattan business addresses.

Of greater economic concern is the ability of the corporate finance and equities markets in the city to continue to generate new products and the city's ability to maintain its global market position in these markets. Although the city's economy is diversified, it is highly dependent on financial services, and is bifurcated in terms of the distribution of income-generating opportunities. What many analysts and academicians have interpreted as Manhattan's global position in producer services looks to be the supply chain of lawyers, accountants, and consultants who service the corporate finance and equities markets. If the city's firms stop innovating new financial products or if new centers of global finance arise that can rival New York, then the producer services industries that are the supply chain of the corporate finance industry and the equities markets in the city will suffer.

The city has benefited from new media production, from the renewed strength of the information industry, and from its unrivaled position in the arts and entertainment industry. But Manhattan faces substantial rivalry with its own suburbs for business headquarters functions and the producer services that supply those activities.

The data also indicate that, while Manhattan is an important location for businesses within the metropolitan area, it is far from a monopoly location. Manhattan's economy has produced an important contradiction. The base of the economy is diversified, yet at the same time New York's economy is highly dependent on the financial services and corporate finance industries. What appears to some analysts to be Manhattan's competitive advantage in producer services (especially law and advertising) is, to us, the supply chain of the corporate financial services industry and the supply chain to the information sector of the economy.

We appreciate comments provided by Howard Chernick, Hal Wolman, and an anonymous reviewer. Our work has also benefited greatly from the close interaction of the study team over the past three years.

NOTES

1. An industry is identified by the product, service, or good that is produced. A business function is an activity, or part of the production process, that cuts across industries.

2. For summaries of New York City's post-World War II employment performance see Benjamin Chinitz (1961) and Dick Netzer (1992).

3. In this chapter, the term gross domestic product (GDP) is used when referring to national-level data and gross product (GP) when referring to subnational data. GDP measures the value of goods and services produced by labor and property and is part of the National Income and Product Accounts (NIPA). Conceptually, GDP also exists for states and substate areas. The U.S. Bureau of Economic Analysis (BEA) produces estimates of gross state product (GSP). Substate estimates of GP are not yet produced by the BEA. We purchased the estimates used in this chapter from Economy.com. At the national level, GDP is calculated by adding personal consumption expenditures (C), gross private domestic investment (I), net exports of goods and services (XM for: Exports (X)–Imports (M)), and government consumption expenditures and gross investment. From an income perspective, GDP's equivalent is gross domestic income (GDI) and is equal to compensation plus taxes on production less subsidies, net operating surplus (profits and net earnings and the surplus from government enterprises), and consumption of fixed capital used in production (think of this as the physical depreciation of capital). The difference between GDI and GDP is known as the statistical discrepancy. GP estimates have more in common with GDI than GDP, owing to the data sources available (see Robinson and Smith 2004).

The GP data are based on the North American Industry Classification System (NAICS) and are estimated by Economy.com. At the time we acquired the data from Economy.com, the Bureau of Economic Analysis had GSP estimates available by the older Standard Industrial Classification (SIC) system. Economy.com used its SIC-NAICS conversion tables and data on earnings and employment to translate the SIC state-based GSP data into county-based NAICS data. This is done by "crosswalking" the data from SIC to NAICS and then "stepping the data down" from the state level to the county level. With the number of estimating steps, data errors are likely, and the smaller the unit of economy and the smaller the industry sector, the higher is the likelihood of error. The BEA released GSP data by two-digit NAICS supersector for the first time in December 2004, for 1998 to 2002; 2003 data are due to be released in June 2005. (The BEA is interested in estimating GP at the metropolitan-area level but has not yet committed to producing the data.) Economy.com will use the data released in December 2004 to estimate GP by county in a March 2005 data release, which will be superior to the data that we worked with in this chapter. The GP estimates will improve once again with the expected June 2005 BEA release of GSP data for 2003.

4. Figure 2.1 displays monthly job data by place of work from the Current Employment Survey (CES). The data are not seasonally adjusted. Because these data are collected by place of work, they count jobs, not the number of people employed. Data on the number of people employed are collected by residence. To minimize confusion the word *jobs* is used when discussing data collected by place of work and the term *employed* is used when the data are collected by place of residence. The number of jobs in an economy is greater than the number of people employed because some people work more than one job.

5. The dates of the recessions come from the National Bureau of Economic Research (NBER 2004).

6. The dates of the postwar stock market crashes are from Mishkin and White (2002).

7. John Steele Gordon (2004, 185) writes that Wall Street cemented its position as the financial center of the country in the 1850s. What has changed since is the speed of financial transactions and New York's increased global market share in the equities markets. Gordon stresses that the role of technology, especially the telegraph, was critical in connecting New York City to wider geographic markets. Its port made New York a center of the transatlantic trade in wheat and cotton, both of which required financial services. Wall Street was also the broker for the European capital that financed America's pre–Civil War infrastructure (154–58, 185). Wall Street's function as the nation's de facto central bank was demonstrated during the Civil War as the gold exchange was opened, various commodity exchanges were formed, and the Street became the location of the secondary market in government debt.

8. County business pattern (CBP) data for 1969 were compared to CBP data for 1980 to examine the shift in the structure of work over this time period. The data are from the mid-March pay period and avoid the July 1980 start date of the national recession. The number of jobs in New York City, as reported in the CBP

data, fell by 13.3 percent. Manufacturing jobs fell by 36.6 percent, the number of wholesale trade jobs dropped by 24.8 percent, and work in the personal services industry plummeted by 45 percent. The number of jobs in the securities and commodities industry fell by 20 percent. Gains were recorded by depository financial institutions (34.3 percent), nondepository financial institutions (68.4 percent), business services (16.4 percent), health services (37.6 percent), and legal services (53.6 percent). The trend in the outer boroughs was worse than for the city as a whole. The overall number of jobs dropped by 15.3 percent, with manufacturing plunging 38.7 percent, wholesale trade 14.8 percent, and personal services 48.5 percent; the number of jobs supported by insurance carriers fell by 50.6 percent. Construction work was down significantly both in Manhattan and in the outer boroughs, but that was an outcome of the general decline in New York City over the 1970s, not a structural change in demand. Also see Netzer (1992).

9.   This observation is also made by Bowles and Kotkin (2003).

10. Erica Groshen, Simon Potter, and Rebecca Sela (2004, 3) make the same observation about New York State: "New York's slowdowns of the 1970s and beginning of the 1990s lasted much longer than the corresponding national recession; they started earlier and ended later."

11. Data from a figure in Andrew Ross Sorkin, "Wall Street Designs on '05? A Boom in Merger Activity," *New York Times*, January 2, 2005. The original source of the data is a proprietary database maintained by Thomson Financial.

12. This is about the number of jobs that James Parrott and Oliver Cooke (this volume) estimate were directly lost because of the attack.

13. Groshen and her colleagues (2004, 1, 5) reach the same conclusion in their review of New York State's economic condition. They write that "the September 11 events ... [produced] purely temporary job losses that were reversed once the recovery began.... The employment effects of September 11 magnified the cyclical changes in New York State's most recent downturn."

14. The economic drivers of Manhattan and the New York region were identified with a two-stage, multidimensional statistical method. Variables were created using economic base theory as a point of departure.

Indicators of export specialization: The employment location quotient (LQ) in 2001, gross product LQ in 2001, and change in the GP LQ from 1993 to 1999 and from 2000 to 2001, to capture the amplitude of two portions of the business cycle using regional data to mark the start of the contraction phase of the cycle.

Indicators of current national competitiveness: Market share as measured by the share of the industry's 2001 national GP and change in market share over the two segments of the business cycle.

Indicators of current regional competitiveness: Industry's share of total regional gross product and change in share of regional gross product over the two phases of the cycle.

Future competitiveness: Productivity, as approximated by GP per job in 2001, change in this variable over the business cycle, relative earnings per job—relative to the national industry average in 2001—change in this ratio over the two parts of the cycle, and then relative regional earnings in 2001.

The first step in the analysis was to perform a mathematical cluster analysis to place industries that relate to the economy in similar ways into groups. These groups were then subjected to a statistical discriminant analysis to see why the groups held together and to interpret their relationship to the economy. Those that had a pattern of variation consistent with economic base theory were considered to be part of the economic base, or driver industries. Some industries were eliminated from the list of drivers because they reflect consumption patterns that are peculiar to the New York region. The technique is described in an economic development application similar to this in Hill and Brennan (2000). Edward Hill, John Brennan, and Harold Wolman (1998) describe the technique in building typologies in social science. James Held (2004) applied the technique to the regional economies of upstate New York, and Peters (2005) applied a variant of the technique to Missouri's regional economies. The technique has also been used in a number of regional science applications.

15. All data are at the four-digit level of the North American Industrial Classification System. NAICS is the successor to the Standard Industrial Classification, from which it differs substantially. The SIC was purely product-based, while the NAICS is a blend of products and business functions. Information on NAICS classifications can be found at: http://www.census.gov/epcd/www/naics.html.

16. See note 3.

17. Groshen and her colleagues (2004, 2) note that product cycle–induced movements of jobs that were observed in manufacturing and apparel are now evident in New York's financial services industry: "Many financial firms are moving their back-office operations out of New York—or even overseas—although they often keep their headquarters in the state." Jonathan Bowles and Joel Kotkin (2003, 10–12) make the same observation; however, they note that the movement may go beyond back-office jobs, and they see electronic exchanges challenging the very structure of the markets as they exist today.

18. The two most current years' data are projections provided by Economy.com. The jobs data provided by Economy.com are estimated from CES data and the quarterly Census of Employment and Wages (CEW), formerly known as the ES-202 program. ES-202 data are jobs data derived from unemployment compensation tax filings. The CES data reported in figure 2.1 were used because they cover a longer time period than we could obtain from Economy.com. We use Economy.com data from 1983 to 2004 on jobs, GP, and GP per job in the analytical portions of the chapter for two reasons. First, Economy.com estimates these variables by four-digit NAICS industry back to 1983 and estimates the data forward for a number of years. CEW data are available in NAICS format only from 2000 to 2004 monthly and annually. CEW data are available annually based on the SIC from 1997 to 2000. Second, we are interested in GP for Manhattan, New York, and the New York CMSA. Economy.com estimates GP by county by four-digit NAICS from 1983 to 2004 (see note 13). The data on GP and the number of jobs must be consistent.

19. There are three reasons why we use Los Angeles, San Francisco–San Jose, Chicago-Kenosha, Washington-Baltimore, and the Boston area as comparables. The first reason is statistical. The five rivals to the New York CMSA form a coherent set of regions as measured by their regional GPs. There is a major discontinuity, or a natural break, in the distribution of GP between Boston and the next largest CMSA or MSA. Second, each of these regions shares a portion of New York's economic base and is a potential rival. New York's portion of the financial services industry, with its supply chain in producer services, faces competition from Chicago and Boston. All five compete with New York in the information services industry and its supply chain. Los Angeles and New York are rivals in television and cable television production. New York and all five of its rivals compete in varying degrees in the arts and culture industry. Metropolitan Washington competes in telecommunications, government, third-sector activities, and corporate headquarters as the economy emphasizes telecommunications and defense. Chicago has targeted the headquarters business function as an economic development opportunity. Pharmaceuticals and biomedical products are important to northern New Jersey and are a competitive emerging industry in Boston, Chicago, San Francisco, and metropolitan Washington.

   The third reason is the global and national structure of the producer services industry. Peter Taylor and Robert Lang (2005) measure global connectivity within the producer services industry by tracking the global distribution of the offices of one hundred "leading advance services firms" and developing measures of the importance of each office to its firm. There were eighteen in accounting, fifteen in advertising, twenty-three in banking-finance, eleven in insurance, sixteen in law, and seventeen in management consulting. All had a presence in at least fifteen cities, including at least one each in North America, Western Europe, and along the Pacific Coast of Asia. These one hundred firms were present in a total of 315 cities worldwide. Taylor and Lang built a measure of the degree of connectedness for each of the 315 cities to all other cities. London sat at the top of the hierarchy, with New York in second place and Hong Kong in third. Taylor and Lang grouped the U.S. city-regions into ten strata based on breaks in their measure of relative global network connectedness. New York is alone in the first strata. Chicago and Los Angeles occupy the second; San Francisco, Miami, Atlanta, and Washington form the third; Boston leads the fourth and is joined by Dallas, Houston, and Seattle. Our top three competitor regions occupy the first two strata of Taylor and Lang's hierarchy, and we include two of the four regions in the third strata. (Miami and Atlanta have a greater presence in this list of one hundred producer services firms owing to their specialized geographical functions as gateways to South America [Miami] and to the rapidly growing U.S. Southeast [Atlanta].)

20. The CEW data are not available for the old PMSA and CMSA geography. The newly defined New York MSA is between the old PMSA and CMSA in size and is a better representation of the immediate labor market in which New York City competes. The new MSA has a population of 18.3 million out of 21.3 million, or 86 percent, of the old CMSA's population. The old PMSA covered 44 percent of the CMSA's population. The new MSA covers fifteen counties and is composed of the New York City–White Plains metropolitan division (New York City's

counties plus Putnam, Westchester, and Rockland), all of Long Island, and northern New Jersey stretching from Pike County in the west, to Hunterdon in the
south, to Ocean County. The exception is Mercer County, which is part of Tren-
ton, New Jersey's MSA (Frey et al. 2004, 12, 16–17).

21. Companies locate in the region for three reasons: competitors are located there,
and they need a watching position from which to monitor product development;
the technology used in the product is rapidly evolving, and the firm needs access
to suppliers; or it takes special knowledge to invest in the product, and financial
specialists are located in the region, making finance a critical part of the supply
chain.

22. New York's two international airports, coupled with its charter jet operations,
provide the necessary infrastructure component for managing an international or
national business. However, these advantages are shared with the rest of the metropolitan areas; Atlanta, Chicago, Washington, and other large metropolitan areas
have competing air travel resources.

REFERENCES

Bowles, Jonathan, and Joel Kotkin. 2003. *Engine Failure*. New York: Center for an Urban
Future. Available at: www.nycfuture.org.

Chinitz, Benjamin. 1961. "Contrasts in Agglomeration: New York and Pittsburgh." *American Economic Review* 51(2,May): 279–89.

Christensen, Clayton M. 2003. *The Innovator's Dilemma*. New York: HarperCollins.

Frey, William H., Jill H. Wilson, Alan Berube, and Audrey Singer. 2004. *Tracking Metropolitan America into the Twenty-first Century: A Field Guide to the New Metropolitan and
Micropolitan Definitions*, Living Cities Census Series. Washington, D.C.: Brookings
Institution, Center on Metropolitan Policy (November). Available at: http://www
.brookings.edu/metro/pubs/2004115_metrodefinitions.pdf.

Gordon, John Steele. 2004. *An Empire of Wealth*. New York: HarperCollins.

Groshen, Erica, and Simon Potter. 2003. "Has Structural Change Contributed to a Jobless Recovery?" *Current Issues in Economics and Finance* 9(8, August). Available at: http://
www.ny.frb.org/research/current_issues/2003.html.

Groshen, Erica, Simon Potter, and Rebecca J. Sela. 2004. "Economic Restructuring in
New York State." *Current Issues in Economics and Finance* 10(7, June). Available at: http://
www.ny.frb.org/research/current_issues/2004.html.

Held, James R. 2004. "Regional Variation and Economic Drivers: An Application of
the Hill and Brennan Methodology." *Economic Development Quarterly* 18(4, November):
384–405.

Hill, Edward W., and John F. Brennan. 2000. "A Methodology for Identifying the Drivers of Industrial Clusters: The Foundation of Competitive Advantage." *Economic Development Quarterly* 14(1, February): 65–96.

Hill, Edward W., John Brennan, and Harold Wolman. 1998. "What Is a Central City in
the United States? Applying a Statistical Technique for Developing Taxonomies."
Urban Studies 35: 1935–69.

Markusen, Ann R. 1985. *Profit Cycles*. Cambridge, Mass.: MIT Press.

Mishkin, Frederic S., and Eugene N. White. 2002. *U.S. Stock Market Crashes and Their Aftermath: Implications for Monetary Policy.* Working paper 8992. Cambridge, Mass.: National Bureau of Economic Research (June). Available at: www.nber.org/papers/w8992.

National Bureau of Economic Research. 2004. *Business Cycle Expansions and Contractions.* Cambridge, Mass.: National Bureau of Economic Research. Available at: www.nber.org/cycles/cyclesmain.html.

Netzer, Dick. 1992. "The Economy of the New York Metropolitan Region, Then and Now." *Urban Studies* 29(2): 251–58.

Peters, David J. 2005. "Using Labor-Based Industry Complexes for Workforce Development in Missouri." *Economic Development Quarterly* 19(2): 138–56.

Robinson, Brooks, and Shelly Smith. 2004. "Economic Statistics . . . from Theory to Practice." Presentation to the National Association of Business Economists (NABE) (May). Available at: http://www.bea.gov/bea/papers/NABEspeakernotes.pdf.

Taylor, Peter J., and Robert E. Lang. 2005. *U.S. Cities in the World City Network.* Survey Series. Washington, D.C.: Brookings Institution, Metropolitan Policy Program. Available at: http://www.brookings.edu/metro/pubs/20050222_worldcities.pdf.

Vernon, Raymond. 1966. "International Investment and International Trade in the Product Cycle." *Quarterly Journal of Economics* 80(2): 190–207.

CHAPTER 3

The Impact of 9/11 on the Manhattan Office Market

Franz Fuerst

THE SEPTEMBER 11 attack obliterated 13.4 million square feet of office space in the World Trade Center (WTC) complex and seriously damaged another 21.1 million square feet in 23 surrounding buildings, affecting approximately 34.5 million square feet, or 10 percent of the total stock of Manhattan office space. Nearly 100,000 office workers were subsequently dispersed to over 1,000 different destinations, many of them within Manhattan and a few as far away as London and Tokyo. The secondary consequences and potential economic ripple effects of the attack on lower Manhattan and New York City as a whole are more difficult to grasp than the immediate impact. Over the years since 9/11, it has become evident that initial speculation about a mass exodus of office companies from Manhattan has been unfounded. There are concerns nevertheless that the long-term effects of 9/11 will pose a continuing threat to lower Manhattan's economic health. The principal objective of this chapter is to elucidate the impact of the September 11 attack on the New York office market by using exploratory data analysis and an event study methodology to analyze market mechanisms in the wake of the destruction of the World Trade Center.

In the aftermath of the September 11 attack, a number of important studies have been published, documenting the damage and giving detailed accounts of the whereabouts of displaced tenants (see, for example, Kelly 2002). This chapter presents a reevaluation of the impact of 9/11 on the New York office market three years after the recovery process began.[1]

The first section describes the immediate impact of 9/11 on office inventory, absorption, vacancy rates, rent, and office employment by means of an exploratory data analysis. In the second section, I use an event study methodology to model the impact of 9/11 on the New York office market. Finally, these results are interpreted in the light of the discussion on rebuilding lower Manhattan and revitalizing New York City's economy.

THE IMMEDIATE IMPACT OF 9/11

Beyond the tragic loss of almost three thousand human lives, it is the physical destruction of the World Trade Center buildings that comes to mind when we think about the impact of the 9/11 attack. The New York City comptroller estimates the property damage at $34 billion for both the destroyed World Trade Center complex and the surrounding buildings that sustained serious damage. In a more comprehensive study conducted by the New York City Partnership and Chamber of Commerce (NYCPCC) (2001), a gross loss of $83 billion through 2003 is estimated as a consequence of the 9/11 attack, consisting of $30 billion in capital loss, $14 billion in cleanup costs, and a compound $39 billion loss of economic output. From these gross costs we deduct insurance payments and emergency funds managed by the Federal Emergency Management Agency (FEMA) and other federal agencies to estimate the net loss to the city's economy incurred by the attack. The federal funds are intended to defray the cost of cleanup and guide the economic recovery process. Although the amounts of the funds and compensation payments actually disbursed by insurance carriers and federal relief organizations are still not fully known, the NYCPCC estimates the overall net loss due to the 9/11 attack at $16 billion (4 percent of the gross annual output of Manhattan).

ESTIMATING THE EFFECTS OF 9/11 ON THE
OFFICE MARKET

Any attempt to measure the impact of 9/11 on the job market, on the stock market, or on fiscal revenues is faced with the difficulty of separating the effects of 9/11 from the impact of a wider economic recession and other simultaneous events influencing the market. In the case of the office market, disentangling and isolating the effects of 9/11 seems easier because of certain inherent characteristics of real estate markets. The impact on the supply of office space is clearly discernible thanks to available data on the World Trade Center buildings themselves and on the damaged buildings that were gradually returned to the market after restoration. Most of the data applied in this study were obtained from CoStar and Grubb & Ellis, two providers of real estate market intelligence. Beyond the information on displaced tenants, the analysis presented in this chapter draws on information from multiple sources at various aggregation levels.

The Basic Mechanisms of Commercial Real Estate Markets

Before we focus on assessing the observed and expected impact of the 9/11 attack on the New York office market in detail, it is helpful to review some basic mechanisms of office real estate markets.

In general, the office market can be considered a system of at least three interlinked markets: a space market (also called "user market"), a financial asset market, and a development market. The space market incorporates the demand for office space by tenants and the determination of rents. The amount of occupied space as the principal measure of demand for office space is a function of the number of office workers, the average space per office worker in a given market, and the output of office firms. While employment and output are major determinants of the absolute amount of required office space, the space per office worker depends on the level of rental rates (price elasticity of demand), in the sense that higher rents entail a more efficient space use and hence less space per worker. Typically, rental rates are a lagged variable, however, since short-run demand is relatively inelastic to changes in rental rates. Most equilibrium models of the office market assume that only a certain proportion of the adjustment toward the hypothetical steady state takes place each period. The net change in occupied space from one period to the next (called space absorption) is another example of only partial adjustment to a hypothetical equilibrium value caused by the imperfections inherent in the office market. Rental rates are determined in the space market as a function of the occupancy rate or its inverse, the vacancy rate. Similar to labor market economics and its concept of a "natural unemployment rate," real estate economics defines a "natural vacancy rate" as the market equilibrium at which rents remain stable. If the actual vacancy rate falls below the natural vacancy rate, rents will rise, and vice versa. Despite a number of theoretical problems associated with it, this concept has proved useful in many empirical studies (Rosen and Smith 1984; Shilling, Sirmans, and Corgel 1987). It originates from the observation that real estate markets do not conform to the basic economic theorem that equilibrium is reached when supply equals demand and markets clear completely. Frictions and imperfections as well as the need for a sufficiently large fluctuation reserve are frequently cited as factors that impede complete market clearing. The magnitude of the natural vacancy rate is not fixed, however, but varies across markets, owing to local market characteristics, and within a market over time, owing to long-run changes in local market characteristics (Wheaton and Torto 1988).

The stock of office space, albeit fixed in the short run, can be expanded in response to increasing demand for office space, thus linking the space market with the development market and in turn also with the financial asset market. According to investment theory, construction of new office space at a particular site becomes feasible when the expected asset price of the building exceeds its replacement cost. The asset price of the building is a function of the net operating income (NOI) of a building, or more accurately, the present discounted value of the expected future income stream (net of tax and expenses), which is mainly a function of rental rates. The three main components to use in estimating the asset price of a building are thus rent, vacancy, and the capitalization rate, which is determined by dividing the property's NOI by its purchase price. New construction is determined by all the factors making up the expected asset price as well as additional measures for estimating replacement cost. Variables used to estimate costs are typically the cost of capital (interest rates) and construction costs. Construction of new space is subject to particularly long lags, however, because assembling, financing, and permitting, along with actual construction, are all extremely time-consuming processes.

The effects of the 9/11 attack enter into this system simultaneously at various points: first, by reducing the total stock of office space; and second, by reducing the number of office workers and the amount of occupied space through movements of displaced tenants. These changes affect in turn the long-run equilibrium rent level (through the changed vacancy rate) and the overall feasibility of new space construction (through changes in rental rates and arguably also through higher construction costs because of additional security requirements for office buildings). The following sections analyze the effects of 9/11 on the various parts of the office market in more detail.

The Impact on Office Inventory

The total amount of office space affected by the 9/11 terrorist attack is estimated at 31.1 million square feet, of which 13.4 million were completely destroyed and 17.7 million were found to be severely damaged (table 3.1). Destroyed were the seven buildings of the World Trade Center, which included the two landmark towers with a total square footage of 4.7 million square feet of office space each, and five other buildings ranging from 600,000 to 2 million square feet in size. Also destroyed was the Deutsche Bank building at 130 Liberty Street. The building sustained damage that was eventually deemed too extensive to repair in an agreement between Deutsche Bank, four insurance carriers, and the Lower Manhattan Development Corporation (LMDC) in which the conclusion was reached to demolish and reconstruct the building.

To put the numbers in perspective, the destroyed space equals roughly the entire office stock of the city of Detroit. When the comparison is limited to

TABLE 3.1   NEW YORK OFFICE SPACE DESTROYED OR DAMAGED BY
9/11 TERRORIST ATTACK, BY OFFICE CLASSIFICATION

	Size (Square Feet)	Occupied (Square Feet)	Class
Destroyed buildings			
1 World Trade Center	4.761,416	4.507,467	A
2 World Trade Center	4,761,416	4,576,215	A
7 World Trade Center	2,000,000	2,000,000	A
5 World Trade Center	783,520	780,873	A
4 World Trade Center	576,000	561,491	A
6 World Trade Center	537,694	537,694	A
1 Bankers Trust Plaza	1,415,086	1,415,086	A
Destroyed total	13,420,046	12,963,740	
Damaged buildings			
130 Cedar	135,000	135,000	C
90 West	350,000	350,000	A
90 Church	950,000	950,000	B
140 West	1,171,540	1,171,540	B
101 Barclay	1,226,000	1,226,000	A
125 Barclay	273,900	273,900	C
22 Cortlandt	668,110	625,282	B
2 World Financial Center	2,591,244	2,006,577	A
100 Church	1,032,000	822,642	B
1 Liberty Plaza	2,121,437	1,874,584	A
4 World Financial Center	2,083,555	2,073,615	A
1 World Financial Center	1,461,365	702,999	A
3 World Financial Center	2,263,855	2,167,611	A
Damaged total	17,743,092	15,794,836	
Overall total	31,163,138	28,758,576	

Source: Grubb & Ellis (2002).

prime office space, the damaged and destroyed space equals the inventory of major office locations such as Atlanta and Miami (Jones Lang Lasalle 2001). In the New York City office market, however, because of its vast size, the affected space makes up approximately 10 percent of the total inventory of New York City, though roughly 60 percent of downtown's class A space.[2]

Often criticized as a white elephant of an office complex whose construction was clearly not justified by the demands of the marketplace, the World Trade Center remained largely vacant and unprofitable in the first years of its existence. The largest portion of the space was occupied by the Port Authority of New York and New Jersey and by various governmental institutions. Deriving its economic rationale from the principle known as Say's Law (supply creates its own demand), the World Trade Center was constructed with the intention of boosting the economic development of New York in a time of economic recession, weakening demand, and high vacancy rates. Because it was delivered to the market at an unfavorable time, however, the addition of more than 10 million square feet of office space to the existing inventory served to depress the market further. It took more than six years for the office market to adjust to the supply shock induced by the World Trade Center. During the 1980s, when the business climate in New York City became more favorable, the WTC complex developed a reputation as an attractive location for financial services companies with a need for large floorplates; eventually it achieved an estimated ratio of 90 percent to 10 percent private- versus public-sector tenants. The stock market crash of 1987 initiated a protracted period of decline for the lower Manhattan office market; vacancies soared to 25 percent and higher. By the end of the 1990s, however, the combined effect of the tech boom and exceptionally strong growth in the finance, insurance, and real estate (FIRE) industries had helped lower Manhattan to once again overcome the crisis and achieve historically high office occupancy rates and rents. At the end of 2000 the market began to soften gradually, but it was not until after September 11, 2001, that lower Manhattan experienced large-scale job losses and a severe office market recession.

In the wake of the 9/11 attack, a number of market analysts, predicting that the reduction in space would lead to extremely low vacancy rates, saw landlords as being "in the driver's seat" (Grubb & Ellis 2001) in the lease negotiation process. To the surprise of most market observers, however, demand for office space weakened significantly despite the large-scale loss of office space. Three reasons for the unexpected drop in demand can be identified: a pronounced decline in office jobs, owing to the combined effects of 9/11 and economic recession; the availability of large amounts of unused space at various locations throughout Manhattan not reported as vacant in the market statistics ("shadow space"); and reduced space per worker in higher-priced target submarkets and revised expectations for the future growth and space needs of office tenants.

The Impact on Leasing Activity and Absorption

The relocation patterns of larger private companies occupying at least 20,000 square feet of office space in the buildings destroyed or damaged on 9/11 have been recorded by the real estate services and brokerage firm Grubb & Ellis. This subset of displaced tenants accounts for roughly one third of the total occupied space of the affected buildings. The remaining two thirds of occupied space comprise large private companies with missing data, smaller private tenants, and government institutions. Hugh Kelly (2002, 26) tracked the movements of displaced public-sector tenants occupying 1.7 million square feet in all affected buildings and found that only 30 percent remained downtown; the rest relocated to midtown. Data are scarce on the approximately 500 small companies that occupied less than 10,000 square feet and the public tenants that accounted for about 8 million square feet in the WTC. Kelly, who was able to obtain and analyze a limited dataset of the smaller tenants, found that small companies displaced by the 9/11 attack were far more likely to remain in the downtown area than the large companies, thus accounting for about half of the overall space leased downtown to displaced tenants. This pattern could be explained by the fact that larger tenants typically require large floorplates and sizable amounts of contiguous space, which only a few buildings in lower Manhattan could provide on short notice after the destruction of the World Trade Center. The search process for suitable office space was arguably shorter for smaller companies since more matching possibilities existed within a short distance from the original location.

Kelly (2002, 25–29) reports that lower Manhattan retained about 50 percent of the large private-sector tenants. Taken together, the core markets of midtown and downtown Manhattan captured about 80 percent of the stream of displaced tenants through reoccupation of restored buildings, backfill, and new leases.[3] The nearby office agglomerations along the New Jersey waterfront, which had been developing into a back office market for Wall Street and lower Manhattan long before 9/11, managed to attract most of the relatively few tenants who opted to leave Manhattan. It is interesting to note that none of the other four boroughs of New York City outside of Manhattan was able to capture a significant percentage of displaced tenants especially when compared to the New Jersey waterfront.

As of September 2003, a number of large tenants of the buildings that were damaged in the 9/11 attacks returned to these buildings after they were restored (Newmark and Company Real Estate 2003). The remaining portion of office space damaged in the attack thus remained either vacant or was occupied by new tenants. According to a survey of Newmark and Company, more than half of the originally displaced tenants had returned to a downtown location during the first two years following the attacks and less than one fifth of the displaced tenants had decided to lease space permanently at a non-Manhattan location. These numbers are reassuring in terms of tenant retention in the restored damaged buildings and the downtown area as a whole, but it still remains to be seen whether tenants who have returned will opt to renew leases that expire in the next few years. Since some tenants were given the opportunity to break their leases after 9/11, owing to interruption-of-services clauses in their contracts, the percentage of tenants choosing to discontinue their lease later on is generally expected to be low. As far as the wider down-town area is concerned, however, the large number of leases expiring in 2004 and 2005 (36 million square feet, or roughly one-third of the inventory) poses a potential problem, especially since the process of rebuilding the World Trade Center and restoring the economic potential of the area will continue well beyond 2010. Given the fact that more than half of the downtown leases expire between 2004 and 2007 (Newmark & Company Real Estate 2003), around 200,000 jobs would be at risk of leaving the area. On the other hand, some factors work in favor of a recovery of lower Manhattan. The restoration of the transportation infrastructure, particularly of the PATH commuter train station, is expected to have a moderating impact on potential job losses since it facili-tates the movement of suburban workers into the city, thus enhancing lower Manhattan's profile as an attractive location and giving the area much-needed rapid access to a large pool of skilled labor. Moreover, an array of subsidies has been put in place to make the area more competitive. Tax deductions and accelerated depreciation benefits are available to businesses with fewer than 200 employees in the so-called Liberty Zone. Further support is available through the small-firm attraction and retention grant program. Certain com-mercial buildings are eligible for real estate tax abatements and rent tax elimi-nation or reduction for up to five years. The programs require that landlords pass on any benefits received under the auspices of these revitalization incen-tives to tenants by reducing rents proportionally.

Besides those tenants who chose to reoccupy previously damaged buildings, a number of new leases were signed in Manhattan, and in some cases in other locations, by tenants of destroyed buildings or tenants of restored buildings who were unwilling to return. Moreover, a considerable proportion of larger tenants of the space affected by 9/11 could be accommodated in excess space available at other locations of the same company. An estimated $341 million of rental income is lost due to backfilling displaced tenants into unused space at a different location (DRI-WEFA 2002, 37). The high percentage of unused space or shadow space among the larger multi-location tenants not accounted for in any market statistics revealed that vacancy and availability rates were generally understated. Therefore, displaced tenants who were accommodated within space that was rented but previously not used by the same company did not contribute to positive absorption in the market statistics.

Shadow space is widespread in office markets and is generally attributed to the inflexibilities arising from the long-term nature of office leases. Shadow space builds up when companies incorrectly estimate the number of employees and their space usage over the time of the lease term. Estimates of the amount of shadow space in Manhattan differ greatly since there are no reliable mea-surement methods available. Mitchell Stier, chairman of Julien Studley Inc., estimates 10 million to 14 million square feet of shadow office space in Manhattan in the fall of 2003 (quoted in Real Capital Analytics 2003), while other sources claim that if shadow space were accounted for, reported vacancy rates would have to be adjusted upward by 20 to 37 percent in some Manhattan submarkets (Holusha 2003).

Although more transparency is typically associated with a higher degree of market efficiency, some argue that the existence of shadow space generates positive effects as well. By being kept off the market, goes the argument, the vacant space does not exacerbate the downturn phase in the market cycle. Since this space is in fact excluded from the ratio of supply to demand that determines price, shadow space should work toward stabilizing the market. In other words, since shadow space is rented out and typically not offered on the market, such space, although de facto vacant, should not affect market conditions in a negative way. Two points have to be considered, however, regarding the validity of this argument. First, companies will fill up their shadow space before they lease any additional space. Consequently, shadow space does affect the office market indirectly by potentially delaying market recovery after a recession. Second, some of the unused space may indeed be available for sublease, even though it is not officially listed. Transactions of this kind are typically made when brokers possess insider knowledge of unofficially vacant space and approach the main tenant to find out whether the vacant space would be suitable for sublease to other companies.

More recently, changes to generally accepted accounting principles (GAAP) adopted in 2003 strictly require companies to record the write-off of unused space once a company has formally acknowledged that a certain percentage of its leased space is not being used.[4] The unintended consequence of this change is that office tenants have an additional incentive to keep unoccupied space off the market. Under previous regulations, office tenants were flexible with regard to both the definition of what constitutes unused space and the timing of the write-off in their accounting reports. While the previous accounting principles stipulated that companies do not have to take a charge against their earnings for rent payments made for unused space unless they adopt a formal "facility exit plan," the new regulations require a company to write off the cost of unused or underutilized office space as soon as the company terminates the lease or physically "ceases using" the space (Rich 2003). Offering space for sublease on the market is a clear indication of unused space in the definition of the GAAP. It is thus expected that many companies will avoid recording the write-offs, thereby aggravating the general problem of understated vacancy in office market space accounting. A quantitative analysis of the expected effect of the new GAAP is not, however, available to date.

Since there are no direct measures of the volume of shadow space, estimates must be inferred from other indicators. Typically, a large percentage of sublet

FIGURE 3.1   VACANT SPACE VERSUS SUBLET SPACE IN THE NEW YORK
OFFICE MARKET, FIRST QUARTER 1992 TO FIRST QUARTER 2004

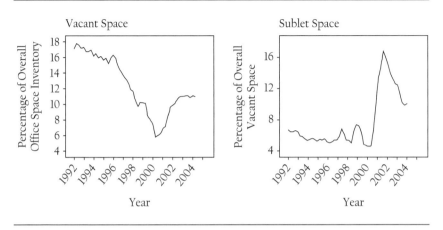

Source: Grubb & Ellis (2004).

space in a market is indicative of a related amount of shadow space, even though it is not possible to quantify the relationship accurately. Figure 3.1 illustrates that the share of sublet space rose dramatically in the second half of 2000 at a time when the direct vacancy rate was relatively low and asking rents still growing, indicating an impending shift in overall vacancy and rents. The progression of the indicators over time reveals that sublet space is a leading market indicator that captures the turning point in the market cycle three to four quarters prior to a change in rental rates.

The relationship between direct vacant space and sublet space is of particular relevance for understanding the market mechanisms of commercial real estate. It is noteworthy that the share of sublet space in total vacant space more than tripled within one year (from the third quarter of 2000 to the third quarter of 2001). In general, the more sudden and unexpected a recession is, the higher the amount of sublet space put on the market will be. This phenomenon became evident in the Manhattan office market at the end of a prolonged growth period. When the market unexpectedly started to soften at the end of 2000, many tenants realized that some of the space they had leased would not be required in the near future, and they made a large proportion of the excess space available for sublease. The third quarter of 2001 marks a peak in the percentage of sublet space. The additional amount of sublet space, however, not only is an indicator of weakened demand but also reflects the expectations of tenants with excess space that they would sublet some of it to displaced

World Trade Center tenants. Thus, tenants with unused space in their portfolio were more apt to offer sublet space on the market in the wake of the 9/11
attack than would have otherwise been the case.

In the following quarters, the percentage of sublet space decreased as leases
expired, direct vacancies increased, and tenants withdrew some of the available sublet space from the market.

Apart from the fact that displaced tenants were accommodated in a firm's
existing space portfolio, the strongly negative absorption in the aftermath of
9/11 was also caused by the fact that displaced companies rented less space
than they had occupied in the damaged or destroyed buildings. Table 3.2 demonstrates this phenomenon for a subset of 6.4 million square feet for which
both tenant and building information was available (Grubb & Ellis 2002).
Backfill is not considered in this subset. Grouped by submarkets, the data
show on average that companies rented only about 15 percent less space in the
new buildings than they originally held in the affected buildings.

A further reason for reduced space usage by displaced tenants at their new
locations is price elasticity of demand. The observed reduction in newly leased
space by displaced tenants was particularly strong in high-priced buildings
and submarkets, such as the Plaza District or Grand Central (table 3.2). Relatively high rents in some submarkets had an additional dampening effect on
the amount of space leased by displaced companies. In turn, the reduced space
usage contributed to higher vacancy rates and declining asking rents in the

TABLE 3.2   FORMER WORLD TRADE CENTER TENANTS, BY DESTINATION
SUBMARKET (NEW LEASES ONLY)

Submarket	Occupied Space Old (Square Feet)	Occupied Space New (Square Feet)	Difference (Percent)	Average Rent (Per Square Foot)	Typical Floorplate (Square Feet)
Plaza District	817,496	355,724	−56.49	39.87	22,294
Grand Central	619,470	481,733	−22.23	38.44	23,190
Hudson Square, Tribeca	60,000	80,000	33.33	33.00	65,828
Madison Square	1,142,482	923,911	−19.13	19.17	18,705
Midtown West	2,351,352	2,299,163	−2.22	19.75	19,578
Penn Station	578,800	472,000	−18.45	22.30	67,308
Wall Street	843,404	793,500	−5.92	25.38	10,881
Total	6,413,004	5,406,031	−15.70	32.22	25,981

Data source: Grubb & Ellis (2002), CoStar (2001)

following quarters. The aggregated demand elasticity of the World Trade Cen-ter tenants in the destination submarkets is −1.12.[5] Typically, demand for space is rather inelastic in the short run.[6] Owing to the particular circumstances of the 9/11 attack, displaced tenants were forced to sign new leases in the various submarkets during a macroeconomic recession, when price sensitivity is par-ticularly high. While it is difficult to separate the contribution to reduced space demand of recession-related employment layoffs from a "true" price elas-ticity effect, the cross-sectional data presented in table 3.2 suggest an inverse relationship between submarket prices and space reduction.

In summary, the most unanticipated effect in the aftermath of 9/11 has been the fact that the expected surge in additional space consumption attributable to the leasing activities of displaced tenants did not occur. Backfill of displaced tenants into existing leased space, employee layoffs, and reduced space usage per worker as evidenced by a relatively elastic demand for surrogate space are the three most important reasons for this. As a consequence, predictions of in-creasing rents and extreme space shortages did not come true because they were based on the simplistic calculation that constant demand after a 10 percent re-duction in supply would bring the vacancy rate down to almost zero. On bal-ance, however, absorption in the Manhattan market was overall negative because the wider economic recession and the indirect effects of 9/11 more than offset the positive absorption of space induced by displaced WTC tenants.

The Impact on Office Employment and Locational Behavior

The employment dynamics of office-based service industries are a main deter-minant of the demand for office space and an integral part of contemporary metropolitan economies. This is particularly true for Manhattan, where FIRE (finance, insurance, and real estate) and other office-using industries account for over 40 percent of total employment. In lower Manhattan, office jobs make up approximately 75 percent of all jobs. The importance of these jobs for the local economy, however, is even greater than the primary employment statis-tics suggest. When taking into account local multiplier linkages in the FIRE sector, one employee in the financial industry supports two further jobs in various types of economic activities, such as business services and restaurants (New York City Partnership and Chamber of Commerce 2001, 11).

To assess the dynamics of office employment in the context of 9/11 ade-quately, we analyze empirical datasets at three levels. First, we examine the regional context of office employment dynamics for spatial shifts of agglomera-tion economies. The second step is analyzing Manhattan office industries at the zip code level to determine which submarkets were hit hardest by the attack. Third, we trace the relocation patterns of the displaced World Trade

Center tenants. The observed relocation patterns of the displaced companies can provide valuable clues in our attempt to estimate the longer-term reverberations of the attack on the locational behavior of office companies. If the companies that were immediately affected by the attacks chose to remain within the office districts of Manhattan, there is reason to assume that the long-term negative impact of the 9/11 attack was not as powerful as it would be when displaced companies choose to disperse to peripheral locations.

Other analysts have disagreed on the implications of the attack for the future of Manhattan and particularly lower Manhattan. Some authors claim that 9/11 has had no significant lasting impact on the city (for example, Harrigan and Martin 2002), but others envisage a downward spiral that will eventually lead to the demise of lower Manhattan and some of the older inner-city office clusters. Those who take the latter view claim that even before the catastrophic events of September 11, 2001, New York's financial district was an "anachronism" whose economic viability could only be artificially maintained by massive government subsidies (Glaeser and Shapiro 2002). Arguing that the direct and indirect damage caused by the 9/11 attack created a need for even more subsidies to keep lower Manhattan alive, they conclude that it might not be justified to attempt saving the area at all because the public funds needed for this endeavor might be spent more efficiently elsewhere. On the other hand, lower Manhattan had experienced considerable economic growth in the years preceding the attack, thereby demonstrating that the area's structural problems are in principle curable. Before reliable conclusions on this highly controversial topic can be drawn, however, it is necessary to provide some background on the long-term locational behavior of service industries and office employment in the various parts of the New York metropolitan area in which the effects of the 9/11 attacks are embedded.

Spatially Disaggregated Analysis of Employment Impacts   Estimates of the total number of jobs lost because of the catastrophic events of September 11 differ considerably depending on the research methodology and time frame of the analysis. Jason Bram, James Orr, and Carol Rapaport (2002) applied an autoregressive forecasting model and arrived at an estimate of initial job losses in the amount of 38,000 to 46,000 in October 2001. Although the exact number of lost jobs is difficult to assess, it is clear that office-using industries were hit particularly hard by the attack.

This section explores the dynamics of office employment after September 11 in various Manhattan submarkets. Although almost all areas of Manhattan have been affected by the economic recession and subsequent declines in the number of office jobs, lower Manhattan has sustained particularly great losses because of the double impact of the 9/11 attack and the macroeconomic recession. The attacks of September 11 ended a period of sustained strong job growth in lower Manhattan, turning the overall balance from 2000 until 2003 negative. Figure 3.2 details the changing dynamics of office locations in Manhattan as a function of their share in overall office employment in the borough. Besides the World Trade Center area, the sharpest relative decline in office employment occurred in the neighborhoods formerly dubbed "Silicon Alley"— in particular Chelsea—as a consequence of the collapse of the dot-com boom. More surprisingly, the submarkets in the eastern section of the midtown market—including the Plaza District, which is the highest-priced area of Manhattan—saw their shares in Manhattan office employment diminish to varying degrees. In contrast, the western areas of midtown exhibited relative growth in office employment; a considerable part of Manhattan's new office space was built in the Times Square and Columbus Circle areas. In the downtown area, sharp losses in the World Trade Center area are juxtaposed with relative gains in the eastern financial district and north of the World Trade Center area in Tribeca. Although these areas have not been major recipients of displaced WTC tenants, it seems likely that temporary locational shifts of office companies away from the western area of lower Manhattan to the east and north contributed to their relative increase. Nevertheless, almost all areas of Manhattan lost office jobs in absolute terms. Since this happened to varying degrees, however, relative shares in overall office employment increased even if office employment in absolute numbers decreased.

The loss to lower Manhattan's economy as outlined in the previous sections becomes even clearer when considering the displaced tenants of the World Trade Center attacks. DRI-WEFA (2002, 36) estimates that approximately seventy thousand jobs were lost as a consequence of the attacks, whereof thirty thousand are estimated to be displaced permanently. Taking into account that each of these jobs supports other jobs, for example in the financial sector through economic linkages to the business and hospitality services sector, a complete economic recovery of lower Manhattan is bound to be a difficult long-term endeavor. The overall employment prospects may be more positive as these initial job loss assessments suggest, simply because new companies are attracted by the positive locational profile of lower Manhattan. Additional business incentives and tax benefits are available through a number of government programs, which enhance lower Manhattan's reputation as an attractive business location. Incoming new tenants attracted by lower rents and government incentives are bound to fill the vacancies created by those displaced tenants who are not returning to their original locations in lower Manhattan. It remains unclear, however, how long it will take to achieve a new market balance in the downtown area.

In the wake of the September 11 attack, some have argued that the collapse of the twin towers was definite proof that skyscrapers are "an experimental building topology that has failed" (Peirce 2001) and they have prophesied the

FIGURE 3.2   CHANGE OF SHARE IN MANHATTAN OFFICE EMPLOYMENT FOR
ZIP CODE AREAS, 2000 TO 2003 (PERCENTAGE POINTS OF
OVERALL SHARE)

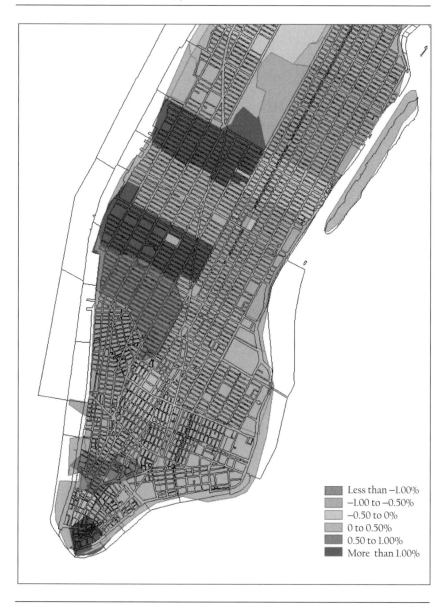

Less than −1.00%
−1.00 to −0.50%
−0.50 to 0%
0 to 0.50%
0.50 to 1.00%
More than 1.00%

Source: U.S. Department of Labor, Bureau of Labor Statistics.

eventual demise of dense central business districts characterized by office high-rises. Contrary to these predictions, the relocation patterns of displaced World Trade Center firms and other developments after 9/11 demonstrated that agglomeration economies, the underlying invisible forces that create and sustain dense urban environments like Manhattan's, are surprisingly resilient. Outside of lower Manhattan, companies displaced by the 9/11 attack relocated mainly in other high-density office submarkets in Manhattan. As outlined in the previous section, midtown Manhattan captured the majority of displaced tenants who moved away from lower Manhattan.

The Impact on Rents

As demonstrated by the data presented in the previous section, displaced tenants were not led merely by cost considerations in their relocation decisions. The aggregated dataset as well as anecdotal evidence suggest that companies did not simply migrate to areas where office space was readily available at the cheapest prices but gravitated toward existing agglomerations of their industry. The resiliency of agglomeration effects in the face of the 9/11 attack, which had nurtured concerns about a catalyzed dispersion of office firms to remote locations, bodes well for the ability of New York City to retain the industries that form its economic base.

Before estimating the impact of 9/11 on overall market rents and subsets of office buildings, we examine the spatial differentiation of Manhattan's submarkets over time. Being by far the largest office market in the United States, and arguably the second-largest office market in the world (after Tokyo), Manhattan's wide range of specialized business and financial services, as well as the array of building types and locations, generate effects in the submarkets that reflect the particular industry mix of tenants and building characteristics. Figure 3.3 shows a boxplot of the rental rates of the fifteen Manhattan submarkets in relation to overall aggregate market rents over a period of about twelve years. The horizontal reference line represents the average Manhattan rent and the vertical reference lines delineate the areas of midtown (left), midtown-south (center), and downtown (right). The boxplot shows the quartiles of the distribution for each submarket. The length of the box represents the difference between the twenty-fifth and seventy-fifth percentiles of the rent distribution relative to the Manhattan aggregate. It may seem surprising at first sight that the median values of all but three submarkets are below the Manhattan average. This can be explained, however, by the fact that about half of Manhattan's office space is concentrated in just three midtown submarkets with above-average values.

The height distribution of the columns in the boxplot resembles a longitudinal cross-section of Manhattan's built environment. This pattern is in line with

FIGURE 3.3   BOXPLOT OF SUBMARKET RENTS RELATIVE TO THE OVERALL
MANHATTAN OFFICE MARKET FROM THE FIRST QUARTER OF
1992 THROUGH THE FIRST QUARTER OF 2004

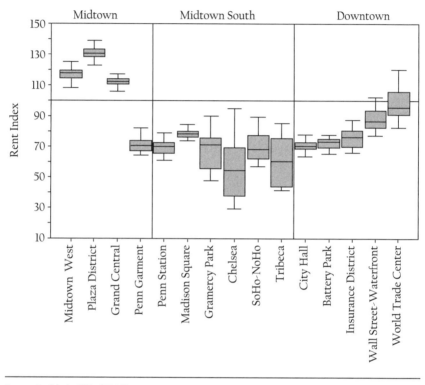

Source: Grubb & Ellis (2004).
Note: Manhattan = 100.

urban economic theory, which states that the physical density of the built
environment is a function of the bid rents in the area. Apart from the differences in median rent, the submarkets also differ in the volatility of rents over
time, as illustrated by the spread of the quartiles. In general, the established
midtown and downtown office core locations exhibit less variability in office
rent over time than the more peripheral locations of midtown-south. The
greater volatility of rents in Gramercy Park, Chelsea, Soho, and Tribeca can be
attributed to the dot-com boom of the late 1990s, when more than one thousand technology-related start-up companies settled in these hitherto peripheral
office locations. Soon after the precipitous fall of technology share prices and

the subsequent demise of many start-up companies in the district in the year 2000, rents also began to decline to previous levels, and few of these areas were able to retain a significant share of office companies.

Among the submarkets in the established office cores of midtown and downtown, the World Trade Center area (which today comprises about seventeen million square feet of office space in the World Financial Center and a number of other office buildings in the vicinity of the World Trade Center site) shows the greatest volatility. An analysis of the rent time series reveals that this volatility is attributable to a particularly steep decline in rents in the first half of the 1990s, possibly exacerbated by the first terrorist attack on the WTC building complex; a subsequent sharp increase in rents in the second half of the 1990s; and a dramatic decline in the wake of 9/11, with a partial recovery in more recent quarters.

Afraid of Heights? Tall Buildings Before and After 9/11   The 9/11 attacks had an unequal impact on various spatial submarkets, as the preceding section demonstrates. A further assumption to be investigated is that tenants would shun prominent skyscrapers in response to the 9/11 attack. The susceptibility of famous buildings and very tall buildings to terrorist attacks in the future might lead tenants in search of office space to move to low-height and "low-profile" buildings instead of the most prestigious and conspicuous buildings, which were favored locations before 9/11. Norman Miller and his colleagues (2003), along with Torto Wheaton Research (2002), postulate, however, that these so-called trophy buildings are still coveted by both tenants and investors and that there is no flight from tall buildings due to psychological reasons and fear of new attacks. By analyzing a set of seven high-profile trophy buildings, Torto Wheaton Research shows that these buildings exhibited below-average vacancy rates one year after the attack. Miller et al. (2003) envision, however, that adverse affects will harm the marketability of a few truly famous office buildings, such as the Empire State Building.

To test this assumption, it is important to distinguish between "trophy" buildings and "tall" buildings (despite a large overlap of the two categories). There are several buildings in Manhattan that are considered trophy, or "top-tier," but not all of these buildings are in the group of the thirty or even fifty tallest buildings in Manhattan. Conversely, not all of the thirty tallest office buildings in Manhattan are considered trophy. As far as a discounting of market values for fear of future terrorist attacks is concerned, it is simply the height of an office building that evokes concerns about being the target of another terrorist attack rather than the rating of a building by brokerage professionals or any measures of value and rental income. Figure 3.4 compares the vacancy rates of two sets of buildings (forty or more stories and fifty or more stories) extracted from the CoStar (2001) building database. (Samples are

FIGURE 3.4   VACANCY RATES IN OFFICE BUILDINGS OF VARIOUS HEIGHTS, MANHATTAN, FIRST QUARTER 1999 TO FIRST QUARTER 2004

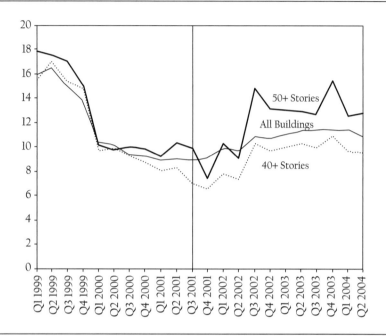

Source: CoStar (2004).

weighted by rentable building area.) The vacancy rate, which is a leading indicator and thus more appropriate to reveal trends than rental rates, shows that the tallest buildings (fifty or more stories) in particular recorded a sharp hike in vacancies after 9/11. Despite the fact that vacancy rates declined and approached the values of the average market in the following quarters, they still remain above market average and significantly above rates for buildings forty or more stories high. The difference becomes even more pronounced when fifty-story-or-higher buildings are eliminated from the forty-story-plus subset of buildings. The category of buildings between forty and forty-nine stories high shows significantly lower vacancies for these buildings. In general, it is evident that the expected flight of tenants from tall office buildings did not occur in the first three years following the attack. The data point to a potential problem for the tallest office buildings (fifty stories or higher), at least in the first three years following the attack. This might be attributed to a psychological effect among office tenants perceiving some of the tallest structures in the city as potential targets of terrorist attacks and seeking to avoid them, but the impact of this effect on overall vacancy in the affected buildings appears to be small and is likely to dissipate barring another incident involving tall office buildings.

Moreover, analyzing a list of displaced tenants (Grubb & Ellis, 2002) shows that most tenants in the database moved to buildings with more than twenty, but fewer than forty stories. A smaller percentage moved to buildings with forty to forty-nine stories, and a few large tenants decided to move to buildings with fifty or more stories. Overall, only a small share of the displaced tenants contained in the subsample moved to buildings with fewer than twenty stories. These findings underline the conclusion that there is no clear evidence of an aversion effect for either tenants in general or the group that was immediately affected by the attack.

The Impact on Building Values and Sales Transactions

Beyond the destruction of human lives, the September 11 attack also resulted in a massive destruction of capital values. The market value of the destroyed World Trade Center was assessed at $4 billion and the replacement cost estimated at $6 billion (not including excavation, infrastructure repair, environmental costs, internal finish, telecommunication, and other technological equipment). The total cost for restoring the damaged space in the World Financial Center and other affected buildings surrounding the World Trade Center is estimated at $2.2 billion (New York City Partnership and Chamber of Commerce 2001, 74).

One of the most remarkable and unexpected phenomena in the wake of 9/11 was the significant increase in sales prices per square foot, despite widespread speculations that falling rents, rising vacancies, and a growing aversion to working in high-rise office buildings would drive prices down dramatically. Simultaneously, average capitalization rates of Central Business District (CBD) office buildings (closed rates) continuously declined from about 9 percent in the third quarter of 2001 to 7.57 percent in the third quarter of 2004. Figure 3.5 shows the increase in sales prices after September 11, despite worsening market fundamentals and the overall economic recession. One particularly notable case is the sale of the General Motors Building in Manhattan in September 2003 for $1.4 billion ($764 per square foot), the highest price ever paid for an office building.

The rise in property values has been attributed to historically low interest rates and the fact that real estate is still considered a "safe haven" in times of economic and political uncertainty (Reis 2003). Large capital flows into office real estate and the sizable portion of international and domestic investors looking to purchase class A office buildings in prime locations put additional

FIGURE 3.5   AVERAGE SALES PRICE PER SQUARE FOOT FOR OFFICE
PROPERTIES IN MANHATTAN, THIRD QUARTER 2000
TO THIRD QUARTER 2003

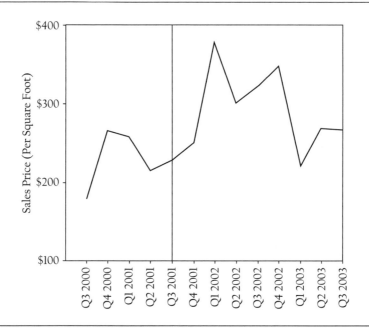

Source: Real Capital Analytics (2003).
Note: N = 183.

upward pressure on prices in the high-quality segment of inner-city office markets. It appears that the downward pressure on capitalization rates exerted by the extremely low level of interest rates was stronger than the upward pressure induced by weak market fundamentals (Torto Wheaton Research 2003). Although the complex interaction of interest rates, sales prices, and capitalization rates in the wake of 9/11 cannot be adequately considered in this chapter, the apparent disconnect between market fundamentals and sales prices deserves further investigation in order to arrive at a more comprehensive understanding of these effects.

THE EVENT STUDY

Following the exploratory analysis of the previous section, we proceed to investigate the impact of the 9/11 attack in more detail by utilizing an event study methodology. The event study approach was first laid out by Eugene Fama and his colleagues (1969) in a seminal paper and has since been applied to a wide variety of topics in economics and finance, typically with the objective of examining the impact of past occurrences on financial markets or particular industries and companies.

The basic assumption of the event study methodology is that markets are information-efficient so that any new information about changes in market conditions will be reflected in changing asset prices of the affected industries. The portion of the price change attributable to this specific event (for example, the announcement of a merger) is measured as an "abnormal return." In other words, the abnormal return is the difference between the expected future price of an asset prior to the event and the observed price including the event. The expected price can be derived by estimating the parameters of the statistical relationship between Manhattan and the overall national office market with OLS regression.[7]

The Definition of the Event Window

The first step of an event study is to define an estimation window and an event window. The estimation window is a sufficiently long time series of data before the onset of the event required to estimate the expected price of the asset. The occurrence of the event itself marks the end of the estimation window and the beginning of the event window. The sequence of data points that constitute the event window is determined either by a significance measure of abnormal changes for a specific event window or simply by the most recent available observation. In most event studies, the precise definition of the event window is plagued by the fact that information about an impending event— for example, a merger—can become available before the actual event, owing to news leaks. However, since the September 11 attack was a truly unpredictable event, the earliest possible beginning of the event window can be determined with great certainty. We therefore define the third quarter of 2001 as the first observation (T_1) and the fourth quarter of 2003 as the last observation (T_2) in the event window. The estimation window is specified as the quarterly time series from the first quarter of 1990 (T_0) through the second quarter of 2001, as shown in figure 3.6.

Estimation of Abnormal Changes and Cumulative Abnormal Changes

There are several ways to estimate the expected and abnormal changes of an asset (see MacKinlay 1997). To test the impact of the September 11 attack on the New York office market, we adopt here the *market model approach* because

FIGURE 3.6   TIMELINE FOR EVENT STUDY OF SEPTEMBER 11 ATTACK

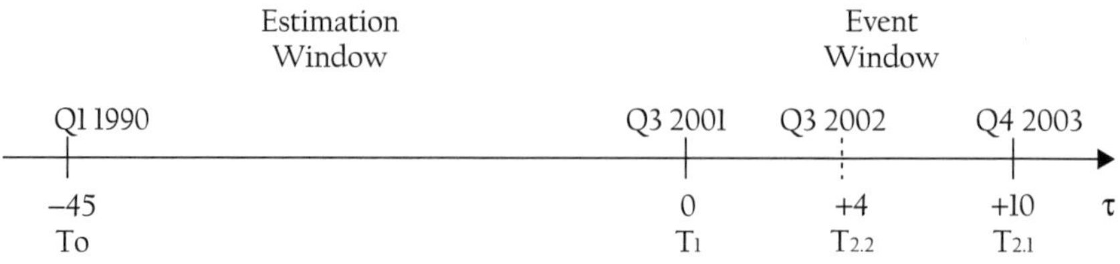

	Estimation Window			Event Window	

Q1 1990			Q3 2001	Q3 2002	Q4 2003
−45			0	+4	+10 τ
To			T_1	$T_{2.2}$	$T_{2.1}$

Source: Author's compilation.

it is more accurate than a long-run mean measure or approaches based on assumed identical change rates in submarkets and aggregated markets. The expected return or change rate is expressed as:

$$R_{it} = \alpha_i + \beta_i R_{mt} + \varepsilon_{it} \tag{3.1}$$

where R_{it} is the total return of asset i in period t, α_i is the baseline return of the asset in question, β_i is the coefficient for asset i in relation to R_{mt}, the overall market return, and ε_{it} is white noise, which is assumed to have a constant mean of zero and zero covariance. Conditional on the standard assumptions of OLS regression models, α_i and β_i are efficient estimators. In the context of this research, the market return rate R_{it} is proxied by the rental or vacancy rate of the Manhattan market or other submarkets, and R_{mt} is the corresponding rental or vacancy change rate of the overall U.S. office market. The abnormal change rate A_{it} is thus defined as:

$$A_{it} = R_{it} - \hat{\alpha}_i - \hat{\beta}_i R_{mt} \tag{3.2}$$

The abnormal change rate is the difference between the actual observed ex post return minus the expected return, as calculated in equation 3.1 with estimation window data.[8] In the present study, the abnormal change due to the 9/11 attack can be calculated through out-of-sample forecasting of the market model for all the periods constituting the event window (whose limits are denoted by T_1 and T_{2n}). Assuming efficient markets, the *null hypothesis* is consequently:

$$H_0 = CA(T_1, T_{2.n}) = 0 \tag{3.3}$$

If the 9/11 attack has generated no abnormal changes over the defined event window, the mean abnormal change rate and the cumulative abnormal change rate should be insignificantly different from zero. To test this hypothesis we define the average abnormal return as:

$$\bar{A}_i = \sum_{i=1}^{N} \hat{A}_{it} = \sum_{i=1}^{N} (R_{it} - \hat{\alpha}_i - \hat{\beta}_i R_{mt})$$ (3.4)

The total estimated impact or cumulative abnormal change over the defined period is calculated in the following manner:

$$CA(\tau_1, \tau_n) = \sum_{t=\tau_1}^{\tau_n} A_{it}$$ (3.5)

where τ_n are the time units (quarters) in the event window that are summed up to yield the cumulative abnormal change of the event. The variance of the cumulative abnormal change is calculated as:

$$\sigma_{CA_{it}}^2 = \frac{1}{N^2} \sum_{i=1}^{N} \sigma_i^2(T_i, T_{2n})$$ (3.6)

To test the null hypothesis, we apply a Z-test in the following form:

$$Z = \frac{CA(T_1, T_2)}{\sqrt{\sigma_{CA}^2}} \sim N(0,1)$$ (3.7)

If Z is significantly greater than zero, we reject the null hypothesis that the 9/11 attack had no significant effect on rents and vacancies in favor of the alternative hypothesis that the attack did have a significant impact. Since both A and CA are assumed to follow a normal distribution with zero mean and constant variance, the critical absolute test value for Z is 1.96 (for $p < .05$). If the absolute value of Z exceeds 2.58, the difference is also significant at the $p < .01$ level.

The measurement of abnormal changes in event studies is typically based on monetary units. In the case of the office market, however, using data on asking rents in the office market may not give an entirely accurate representation of the temporal reaction to the 9/11 effect, since asking rents are known to be "sticky" and do not adjust to new information with the same speed as, for example, stock prices. Therefore, we also examine vacancy levels (including sublet), which respond to market shocks with shorter delays.

It might be argued that the U.S. office market data utilized to estimate the expected values for the New York market were also subject to effects from the September 11 attack, thus introducing a possible bias into the estimators that could lead to underestimating the true impact of 9/11 on the New York office market. Although the overall direct impact of the attack on the aggregated U.S. market was considerably lower than its impact on the New York market, it is nevertheless important to keep in mind that any effects and abnormal changes reported here are specific local effects and in excess of the broader and indirect 9/11 impact on the U.S. market.

Empirical Results

The results of the analysis for the event window (T_1, T_{21}) are reported in table 3.3. The average abnormal changes (Å) and the cumulative abnormal changes (CA) demonstrate clear differences among the analyzed areas in the calculated impact of the 9/11 attack. As indicated by the R square and F statistics, significance values of the regressions decrease generally with the size of the geographic unit, giving rise to the assumption that smaller areas are more prone to idiosyncratic behavior over time than larger, aggregated markets. In the

TABLE 3.3   MODEL RESULTS AND ABNORMAL CHANGES DUE TO THE SEPTEMBER 11 ATTACK FOR EVENT WINDOW Q3 2001 THROUGH Q4 2003

	Average Abnormal Changes Å	Cumulative Abnormal Changes CA	Z Statistic	R Square	T of β_i	F	Durbin-Watson
Rent							
Manhattan	−0.64%	−6.94%	−1.81	0.517	7.023	37.410***	2.099
Midtown	−0.68	−6.81	−1.78	0.462	6.116	30.024***	2.158
Downtown	−1.15	−13.53	−3.89***	0.323	4.147	17.195***	1.651
World Trade Center submarket	−0.35	−3.46	−0.33	0.144	2.391	5.716*	1.402
Vacancy							
Manhattan	0.080	0.42	3.53***	0.291	3.606	13.004***	1.759
Midtown	0.18	1.77	2.63***	0.258	3.955	15.644***	2.101
Downtown	0.07	0.73	1.05	0.363	4.462	19.911***	1.943
World Trade Center submarket	0.49	4.93	2.46***	0.145	2.432	5.915*	1.425

Source: Grubb & Ellis (2004).
*p < .10; **p < .05; ***p < .01

TABLE 3.4   QUARTERLY ABNORMAL CHANGES IN VACANCY
RATES DUE TO THE SEPTEMBER 11 ATTACK

	Manhattan	Midtown	Downtown	WTC
Q3 2001	0.59	0.16	0.95	2.76
Q4 2001	−0.38	−0.09	−0.49	1.67
Q1 2002	−0.25	−0.18	0.00	2.96
Q2 2002	0.48	0.05	1.47	2.22
Q3 2002	−0.01	−0.07	0.44	−1.51
Q4 2002	−0.15	0.30	−1.09	−0.66
Q1 2003	0.07	0.63	−0.47	0.05
Q2 2003	0.13	0.37	−0.31	−0.40
Q3 2003	−0.10	0.00	−0.20	−0.96
Q4 2003	0.41	0.59	0.42	−1.21

Source: Grubb & Ellis (2004).

case of the World Trade Center submarket (which also comprises the World Financial Center and a number of other office buildings in the area), the regression is not significant at the 5 percent level, and therefore the reported abnormal changes have to be interpreted with caution.

In general, all the reported abnormal changes show the expected sign, a lower than predicted rent level and a higher than predicted vacancy rate. An intuitive assumption would be that the downtown and especially the World Trade Center submarkets exhibit higher abnormal changes than midtown or the overall Manhattan market. This is not unequivocally confirmed, however, by the results for the defined event window. Regarding rental values, the downtown market was indeed more strongly affected by the attack and is the only market where the null hypothesis of a nonsignificant impact can be rejected. In terms of vacancy rates, the opposite is the case. All markets exhibit a significant impact except downtown. Since the relationship between rents and vacancy rates is marked by significant lags, it seems advisable to inspect the quarterly changes after September 11, 2001, for both variables in more detail before redefining the event window.

Table 3.4 shows the quarterly abnormal changes for vacancy rates in the four examined areas. As expected, the initial impact in the third quarter of 2001 is highest in the downtown and WTC submarkets (see figure 3.7 for market boundaries). The abnormal change data suggests, however, that the pattern was reversed about one year after the attack when changes in the vacancy rate exhibited a more positive pattern than expected, which continued throughout the period. The reason for the unexpectedly positive developments downtown might be the effect of the massive subsidies and revitalization ef-

FIGURE 3.7   MANHATTAN SUBMARKETS AND LOCATIONS OF DISPLACED
WORLD TRADE CENTER TENANTS

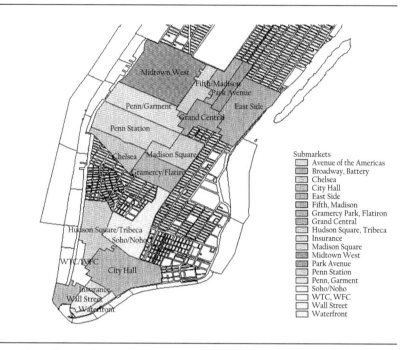

Submarkets
- Avenue of the Americas
- Broadway, Battery
- Chelsea
- City Hall
- East Side
- Fifth, Madison
- Gramercy Park, Flatiron
- Grand Central
- Hudson Square, Tribeca
- Insurance
- Madison Square
- Midtown West
- Park Avenue
- Penn Station
- Penn, Garment
- Soho/Noho
- WTC, WFC
- Wall Street
- Waterfront

Note: Grubb & Ellis (2004).

forts of multiple levels of government. An alternative explanation would be that this is simply a mean reversion effect, a counter movement to the jump in vacancy rates in the wake of September 11, 2001. The assumption underlying such an explanation is that markets tend to return to long-run equilibrium prices after a one-time, non-persisting shock event.

The rent data reported in table 3.5 seem to support this argument. While rents fell precipitously in the downtown and WTC submarkets in the first quarter following the September 11 attack (see figure 3.8), these submarkets achieved higher than predicted positive change rates as conditions in lower Manhattan gradually improved and buildings and critical infrastructure links were restored. This phenomenon is especially pronounced in the WTC market in the fourth quarter of 2001, when rental rates trended up toward previous levels as a result of the efforts to clean up the area and restore damaged buildings. The effect, however, dissipated in the medium run, hinting at a possible structural problem in the World Trade Center submarket that may not be

TABLE 3.5   QUARTERLY ABNORMAL CHANGES IN RENTAL
            RATES DUE TO THE SEPTEMBER 11 ATTACK, THIRD
            QUARTER 2001 TO FOURTH QUARTER 2003

	Manhattan	Midtown	Downtown	WTC
Q3 2001	0.36%	0.39%	−3.16%	−29.44%
Q4 2001	−1.32	−1.01	−4.81	31.69
Q1 2002	−1.01	−0.82	−0.68	0.58
Q2 2002	−1.65	−1.87	0.51	2.00
Q3 2002	0.94	1.31	0.86	3.81
Q4 2002	−1.72	−1.53	−2.62	−5.00
Q1 2003	−3.77	−3.78	−2.11	−6.93
Q2 2003	−1.48	−2.01	0.13	0.17
Q3 2003	−1.29	−1.41	−3.17	−1.48
Q4 2003	4.00	3.92	1.54	1.13

Source: Grubb & Ellis (2004).

completely remedied until the area has been fully rebuilt as a major office cluster and transportation hub.

To test the null hypothesis of insignificant cumulative abnormal changes from the September 11 attack for a shorter period, we redefine the event window. Table 3.6 shows the results for the event window ranging from the third quarter of 2001 through the third quarter of 2002 (T_1, T_{22} in figure 3.5). This time we find a more consistent pattern in the combination of rental and vacancy rates. Based on the statistical evidence for this event window, we reject the null hypothesis for the overall Manhattan and midtown markets but find a significant impact on the downtown market. The World Trade Center submarket exhibits highly significant results in terms of vacancies, but these results are not significant in terms of rents; this may be due to attempts by landlords to restore the previous levels of asking rents soon after 9/11 when in fact market conditions as reflected by vacancy rates were less favorable.

In summary, we find evidence of significant effects of the September 11 attack in the New York office market. These effects seem to be limited, however, in terms of their spatial and temporal impact. While the Manhattan office market as a whole has demonstrated remarkable resiliency in the wake of the attack (measured in reported rents and vacancy rates), the downtown market and particularly the World Trade Center submarket have been affected more clearly. Therefore, it is not surprising that rent levels are lower than expected and vacancy levels are higher than expected in these markets when compared to estimates derived from historic time-series data. Measured two years after the attack, however, cumulative abnormal changes in vacancy rates are moder-

FIGURE 3.8   RENTAL RATES OF THE SUBMARKETS ANALYZED IN THE EVENT
STUDY (CONSTANT DOLLARS), FIRST QUARTER 1992 TO FIRST
QUARTER 2004

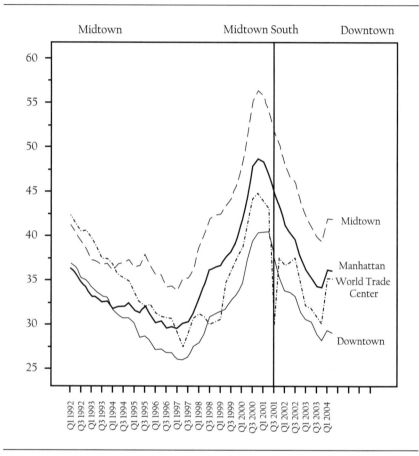

Source: Grubb & Ellis (2004).
Note: N = 183.

ate in the downtown submarket, indicating a much weaker medium-term impact of the attack than expected in its aftermath.

CONCLUSIONS AND FURTHER WORK

More than three years after 9/11, there is scant evidence that the attack will
have a long-lasting impact on the Manhattan office market. Particularly in the

TABLE 3.6   AVERAGE AND CUMULATIVE ABNORMAL CHANGES IN RENTS
AND VACANCY RATES FOR A SHORTER EVENT WINDOW
(Q3 2001 THROUGH Q3 2002)

	Average Abnormal Changes Â	Cumulative Abnormal Changes CA	Z Statistic
Rent			
Manhattan	−0.53%	−2.67%	−1.533
Midtown	−0.40	−2.00	−1.78
Downtown	−1.46	−7.29	−3.77***
World Trade Center submarket	−0.35	−3.46	0.56
Vacancy			
Manhattan	0.09	0.42	1.725
Midtown	−0.02	−0.12	−0.96
Downtown	0.48	2.37	3.100***
World Trade Center submarket	1.62	8.11	2.896***

Source: Grubb & Ellis (2004).
***p < .01.

submarkets of midtown Manhattan, no significant impact could be detected beyond the market adjustment process that took place in the two quarters following 9/11. Lower Manhattan, however, was more deeply affected by the attack and its various consequences.

The Manhattan office market as a whole does not show any signs of lasting economic damage. Of the companies that decided not to return to lower Manhattan after 9/11, the majority relocated to midtown Manhattan. An industry analysis demonstrated that both urbanization and localization economies were at play in the relocation process and that companies preferred to settle in preexisting large industry clusters in Manhattan. Taken together, the core markets of midtown and downtown Manhattan captured about 80 percent of the stream of displaced tenants after 9/11, while areas outside of these two core clusters captured only 20 percent, which bodes well for Manhattan's ability to remain a prime office location even in the face of a severe crisis.

To be sure, a more decentralized development of office space and a more dynamic increase in office workers in the wider CMSA region outside of Manhattan—processes that have been evolving for at least two decades—are likely to continue over the next years. Although security concerns are likely to accelerate this development at least temporarily as firms seek to create backup facilities and distribute key functions across various locations to protect their operations, preliminary analysis of the period after 9/11 shows that agglomeration economies and firm efficiency criteria are restraining and mitigating such dispersion tendencies in Manhattan. Moreover, Manhattan has clearly been able to retain a competitive productivity advantage in the office-using industries. In fact, Manhattan's productivity differential in the office-using industries over both the national and the regional average has continued to increase even since 9/11.

Three years after the attack, lower Manhattan has demonstrated considerable progress in overcoming this crisis both physically and economically. A total of 31.1 million square feet of office space were affected in lower Manhattan, of which 14.8 million were destroyed and 19.6 million damaged and eventually restored. The affected space makes up less than 10 percent of the total inventory of New York City but accounts for roughly 60 percent of downtown's class A space. The sudden loss of more than 100,000 jobs and a large portion of its office inventory sent lower Manhattan, which had been struggling for much of the last three decades, into a severe economic crisis.

However, the majority of businesses directly affected by the attack have opted to remain in the downtown area or have returned there after the damaged buildings were restored. The rebuilding process is well under way, and the first office tower to be rebuilt on the World Trade Center site, Building 7, with 52 stories and 1.7 million square feet of office space, is expected to open in early 2006. Rental rates and building vacancies seem to have stabilized after the lower Manhattan market weakened dramatically in the quarters following 9/11.

Despite the progress made to date, the lower Manhattan office market faces some serious challenges for the next few years. Office employment in the area is considerably lower than it was before the 9/11 attack, and it remains to be seen whether the losses can be fully recovered before the completion of the rebuilding process around 2015. Considering that the area has traditionally been more volatile owing to the dominance of finance and technology industries, a full recovery is possible once these key sectors demonstrate sustained job growth again. In the long run, however, it is critical that lower Manhattan diversify its economy and attract a broader cross-section of office-using industries to the area.

Both the exploratory data analysis and the event analysis demonstrate that markets reacted efficiently and predictably to the 9/11 attack. Among the most notable phenomena are the downward corrections in occupied space across Manhattan when displaced tenants had the choice of leasing new space after 9/11. On the aggregate, companies rented about 15 percent less space than they had occupied in the affected buildings. Space reduction was particularly pronounced in high-priced buildings and submarkets, such as Park Avenue and Grand Central. Moreover, the set of so-called trophy buildings proved to be less affected by the recession than the general market, a finding that runs counter to initial assumptions about the future of office high-rises. Only the tallest buildings in the city (fifty or more stories) exhibited slightly higher vacancies after 9/11, arguably because of an aversion to the very tallest and most famous structures in the city as potential targets of further terrorist attacks.

In addition to a drastic reduction in leased space, the accommodation of displaced tenants within the existing office space portfolio of large companies contributed further to lower occupancy rates than had been expected after the destruction of 10 percent of the inventory. This phenomenon, also known as backfill, caused overall absorption to be negative in the quarters following 9/11, since the positive demand created by displaced tenants was more than offset by losses incurred in the accelerated recession. Positive absorption of approximately 7 million square feet of office space in various submarkets of Manhattan can be attributed to tenants who were displaced by the 9/11 attack. This figure is much lower than expected given the square footage of the destroyed buildings. Approximately half of the anticipated demand dissipated through backfill into existing space, reduced staff, subleasing, and more economical space usage per office worker.

The full impact of the September 11 attack is still unknown after more than three years. The rent implications of 9/11-related factors such as increased security and insurance costs as well as government subsidies to New York City are not entirely clear at this point. Moreover, the recovery trajectory of the lower Manhattan market needs to be explored in detail with an econometric model, which could take into account a number of factors that influence supply and demand. Further research is required to answer these questions as longer time series of data become available to separate short-term adjustment processes from long-term impacts.

The author is grateful to Howard Chernick, Andrew Haughwout, Ned Hill, Joseph Pereira, James Parrott, Hugh F. Kelly, Sanders Korenman, Cordelia Reimers, and Leon Shilton for comments and suggestions on earlier versions of this chapter. The support of the CUNY Center for Urban Research in providing the infrastructure and software necessary to conduct this project is gratefully acknowledged.

NOTES

1. For an additional analysis of the impact of 9/11 on real estate markets, particularly the housing market, see Haughwout (this volume).
2. Figures for the total inventory of office space differ widely among providers of market data because of diverging definitions of geographic areas and types of build-

ings. Total inventory figures used in this study are based on the definitions and data provided by Grubb & Ellis (2001).

3. "Backfill" refers to displaced tenants being accommodated within the existing office space portfolio of a company without any additional new leasing.

4. Within a real-estate context, the two most significant among these are the Sarbanes-Oxley Act and FASB 146. The Sarbanes-Oxley Act, which aims at improving the accuracy and reliability of corporate disclosures was signed into law on July 31, 2002, with a gradual phasing in of compliance levels for companies until 2004. The Financial Accounting Standards Board issued FASB 146 effective January 1, 2003, which requires companies to write off the costs of unused space at the time the vacancy occurs rather than at the end of the lease.

5. The aggregate price elasticity of demand is calculated here as the quotient of the percentage change in rented space and the percentage change in average rental rates. Providing the basis of the comparison are the average rents paid at the original WTC location versus rental rates at new locations weighted by the amount of space the tenant held in the WTC.

6. For example, Wheaton (1999) and Wheaton, Torto, and Evans (1997) assume a general price elasticity of demand of −0.4 in the office market.

7. Since the number of independently estimated cross-sectional data is very limited in contrast to firm-level event studies, no further measures regarding cross-sectional heteroskedasticity and covariability are taken here.

8. James M. Patell (1976) suggests that the values obtained for the event window period have to be adjusted because they are bound to have a higher variance than the residuals of the estimation window. For the purpose of the present study, the values of abnormal returns are not standardized, since this does not change the results significantly (see Brown and Warner 1985).

REFERENCES

Bram, Jason, James Orr, and Carol Rapaport. 2002. "Measuring the Effects of the September 11 Attack on New York City." *Economic Policy Review* (Federal Reserve Bank of New York) 8(2, November): 5–20.

Brown, Stephen J., and Jerold B.. Warner. 1985. "Using Daily Stock Returns: The Case of Event Studies." *Journal of Financial Economics* 14(1): 3–31.

CoStar. 2001. *The CoStar Office Report: Year-end 2001. New York City Office Market.* Bethesda, Md.: CoStar.

DRI-WEFA. 2002. "Financial Impact of the World Trade Center Attack." Report prepared for the Prepared for the New York State Senate Finance Committee (January).

Fama III, Eugene F., Lawrence Fisher, Michael C. Jensen, and Richard Roll. 1969. "The Adjustment of Stock Prices to New Information." *International Economic Review* 10(1, February): 1–21.

Glaeser, Edward L., and Jesse M. Shapiro. 2002. "Cities and Warfare: The Impact of Terrorism on Urban Form." *Journal of Urban Economics* 51(2): 205–24.

Grubb & Ellis. 2001. "New York City's Office Market: Assessing the Damage." Market report (September).

———. 2002. "Where Permanently Displaced Tenants Have Landed." Table in"Permanently Displaced Firms Find New Homes." *New York Construction News* (September).

Harrigan, James, and Philippe Martin. 2002. "Terrorism and the Resilience of Cities." *Economic Policy Review* (Federal Reserve Bank of New York) 8(2, November): 97–116. Available at http://www.newyorkfed.org/research/epr/02v08n2/0211harr.html.

Holusha, John. 2003. "Some Best-Priced Space Isn't Even on the Market." *New York Times*, May 23.

Jones Lang Lasalle. 2001. "The Events of September 11: Impact and Implications for Corporate Real Estate Occupiers." *Global Insights* (second issue, 2001).

Kelly, Hugh F. 2002. *The New York Regional and Downtown Office Market: History and Prospects After 9/11*. Report prepared for the Civic Alliance. (August 9). Available at http://www.civic-alliance.org/pdf/econdev-book-kelly.pdf.

MacKinlay, A. Craig. 1997. "Event Studies in Economics and Finance." *Journal of Economic Literature* 35(1, March): 13–39.

Miller, Norman G., Sergey Markosyan, Andrew Florance, Brad Stevenson, and Hans Veld. 2003. "The Effects of 9/11 on Tall and Trophy Office Buildings." Paper presented to the nineteenth annual meeting of the American Real Estate Society (ARES). Monterey, Calif. (April 2–5).

Newmark & Company Real Estate. 2003. *Focus on Lower Manhattan*. Research report. New York: Newmark & Company Real Estate.

New York City Partnership and Chamber of Commerce (NYCPCC). 2001. *Economic Impact Analysis of the September 11 Attack on New York City: Working Together to Accelerate New York's Recovery*. Research report. New York: NYCPCC.

Partnership for New York City. 2003. *Transportation Choices and the Future of the New York City Economy*. Research report. New York: Partnership for New York.

Patell, James M. 1976. "Corporate Forecasts of Earnings per Share and Stock Price Behavior: Empirical Tests." *Journal of Accounting Research* (Autumn): 246–76.

Peirce, Neal R. 2001. "Skyscrapers: Has Their Era Ended?" Washington Post Writers Group, October 21.

Realtors Commercial Alliance (RCA). 2003. "The Specter of Shadow Space." *RCA Report* 4(4, Fall).

Reis. 2003. "Reis Insights: Trophy Building Sale Sets New Record" (October 10). Available at http://millercicero.comm/press/files-view.php?ViewNode=1066154585cVxrI.

Rich, Motoko. 2003. "How Companies Account for Vacant Space." *Wall Street Journal*, February 19.

Rosen, Kenneth T., and Lawrence B. Smith. 1984. "The Price Adjustment Process for Rental Housing and the Natural Vacancy Rate." *American Economic Review* 73: 779–86.

Shilling, James D., C. F. Sirmans, and John B. Corgel. 1987. "Price Adjustment Process for Rental Office Space." *Journal of Urban Economics* 22(1, July): 90–100.

Torto Wheaton Research. 2002. "Trophy Buildings in New York Fare Well One Year Later." *TWR About Real Estate* (November 22).

———. 2003. "The Cap Rate Outlook: Some Issues to Consider." *TWR About Real Estate* (May 19).

Wheaton, William. 1999. "Real Estate 'Cycles': Some Fundamentals." *Real Estate Economics* 27(2): 209–30.

Wheaton, William C., and Raymond G. Torto. 1988. "Vacancy Rates and the Future of Office Market Rents." *Journal of the American Real Estate and Urban Economics Association* 16(4): 419–30.

Wheaton, William C., Raymond G. Torto, and Peter Evans. 1997. "The Cyclic Behavior of the Greater London Office Market." *Journal of Real Estate Finance and Economics* 15(1): 77–92.

CHAPTER 4

Evidence from Real Estate Markets of the Long-Term Impact of 9/11 on the New York City Economy

Andrew F. Haughwout

NEW YORK'S economy in the late 1990s was booming by most measures. Between 1996 and 2000, private-sector employment in the city grew at a 2.6 percent annual rate, the strongest four-year run in more than four decades. Over those years the rate of job growth in the city exceeded that in the nation as a whole, a phenomenon that had not been seen since the national recession in 1982 to 1983. Private-sector wage and salary growth was also in excess of the national average over this period, rising 7 percent per year in real (inflation-adjusted) terms (Bram 2003). This economic strength was reflected in broader measures of activity as well. The city's index of coincident economic indicators (NYC CEI), a measure of the dynamics of city economic activity, reached its highest level ever (since 1965, when measurement began) in January 2000.[1] City housing values, which, as argued later in the chapter, are a good indicator of the long-run demand for a city residential location, were also strong in both absolute terms and relative to the nation as a whole (Bram, Haughwout, and Orr 2002). Real revenues from the city's four largest taxes reached an all-time high, in spite of rate reductions, in the fiscal year that ended June 30, 2001 (Edgerton, Haughwout, and Rosen 2004).

From 2001 to 2003, however, the city experienced an economic downturn. Private-sector jobs reversed their strong growth and during this period fell at a 2.1 percent annual rate. By November 2003, the NYC CEI had retreated nearly 10 percent from its peak value. Revenues from the city's four major taxes declined sharply in real terms during fiscal year 2002 and had yet to recover their 1999 level by fiscal year 2003.

The sources of this reversal in the city's fortunes are not controversial: the September 11, 2001, attack on the World Trade Center, the decline in the stock market, and the national recession all clearly played important roles in damaging the city's economy in the short run. In this chapter, we explore the relevance of the September 11 attack for the city's long-run economic future. New York's extremely strong growth in the 1990s and extremely weak performance since 2001 are probably both exaggerations of the underlying strength of its economy. Conditions in the national and local economies were extraordinarily conducive to strong short-run city growth in the 1990s, and some of these same conditions were rapidly reversed in the early 2000s, resulting in sharp short-term decline. Yet the data suggest that the city's long-run economic future was, and is, relatively healthy.

HOW SHOULD WE MEASURE GROWTH IN A MATURE CITY?

Figure 4.1 displays New York's total employment since 1965. Over that period city employment has exhibited essentially no trend, although it does show a pronounced cycle. These data, when coupled with the fact that the income and wealth of city residents have risen sharply over the same period, suggest that variations in aggregate city employment are not a good measure of long-term growth in New York. This follows from the fact that New York's borders have been fixed since the late nineteenth century. Since then, changes in the city's land area have been attributable to landfill, notably the expansion of lower Manhattan that accompanied excavation for the construction of the World Trade Center in the late 1960s and early 1970s.[2]

Employment and population growth in New York are likely to be significantly affected by the city's very low land supply elasticity. Significant increases in employment in the city require smaller offices, extensive conversion of residential land to commercial use, or increased density on previously commercial land. The last option would require such changes as taller office buildings, effected by changes to zoning regulations. Edward Glaeser, Joseph Gyourko, and Raven Saks (2003) argue that regulations on residential building have effectively limited the population growth of Manhattan since the 1950s. To the extent that fixed borders and land use regulation constrain the ability of developers to accommodate the expansion of a city's employment or population, these indicators provide a potentially misleading signal of a city's attractiveness as a place to live and work. Thus, the fact that New York's employment and population growth have been relatively slow, even over the long run, does not necessarily imply

FIGURE 4.1   EMPLOYMENT IN NEW YORK CITY, NOVEMBER 1965 TO
DECEMBER 2003

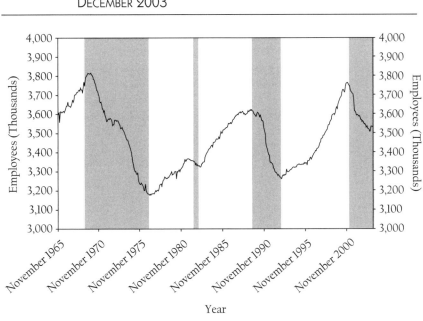

Source: U.S. Department of Labor, Bureau of Labor Statistics (seasonally adjusted).
Note: Shading reflects city downturns as defined by NYC CEI; see Figure 4.2.

that the city is unattractive to businesses and households. Indeed, even the fact that employment has been flat in New York is notable in light of well-documented declines in many other major northeastern cities.

In this chapter, we examine the health of the city's economy (and its future prospects) by examining its real estate markets.[3] Since land is inelastically supplied in a city with fixed boundaries, changes in its price reflect changes in demand. When the analyst can observe the price of unimproved (that is, vacant) land, this metric can provide useful guidance as to the value of un-traded local traits like tax rates, public services, climate, and safety. In the current context, the change in demand caused by the September 11 attack could be inferred from changes in the price of undeveloped land in New York.

Unfortunately, we do not observe prices of vacant land; rather, we must infer changes in demand for land from changes in prices (or rents) of improved properties—that is, residential dwellings and office buildings. In one of our analyses, our access to microdata enables us to control for the characteristics of the properties whose prices we observe, thus providing some confidence that the remaining variation is attributable to changes in the demand for land. In other analyses, however, our identification of demand shifts relies on looking at the short run, for which an assumption that the supply of capital is fixed seems plausible.[4] The exception is the office market, as we discuss later.

For a fixed supply of land, the supply of new buildings for office or residential use is determined by the price of capital (determined in national markets), local subsidies, regulations and fees placed on developers like building codes, taxes, and insurance, and expectations of these into the future. Local demand is determined by the costs and benefits of a New York City location, including taxes, amenities, and public goods like safety from death and injury, as well as the benefits of density. The interplay of these two sides of the market determines prices and rents. Note that in rental markets the period for which expected conditions are relevant is determined by the duration of the lease; prices reflect expectations of the value of the property in perpetuity.

9/11 AND PROPERTY MARKETS IN NEW YORK

The destruction of the World Trade Center had several potential effects on the demand for residential and office space in New York. First, and most horrific, the attack cost nearly 2,800 lives. In economic terms, this loss reduced the human capital stock for the entire metropolitan region, at least in the short run. In spite of the tragic consequences for the individuals and their families, however, the direct impact on the demand for space in New York, with over 3.5 million jobs and 8 million residents, was small.

Of much greater concern for the city's future is the possibility that this level of destruction produced a perception that being physically present in New York exposes people to high risks of injury or death relative to other places. Such a perception could lead to significant declines in both business and residence demands for New York locations. In addition, if agglomeration economies are very important, then the density of (especially high-skill) jobs in the city may provide productivity benefits to all city firms. In this situation, the dislocation of a relatively small number of jobs can expand into a much larger permanent loss, since the benefits of city locations decline with each job lost. Initially, these effects may be confined to relatively small geographic areas (Rosenthal and Strange 2003), but they may ultimately have repercussions over the entire metropolitan area (Haughwout and Inman 2002). While existing empirical evidence on the proposition that man-made disasters destroy the basis for large cities suggests that such effects are likely to be minor (Glaeser and Shapiro 2002; Davis and Weinstein 2002), it is the magnitude of these effects that we wish to estimate for New York. Note that we make no attempt to identify the channels through which these effects operate. Thus, if we observe demand reductions, they could be caused by increases in the perceived danger of locating in New York, increases in expected taxes required to protect the city from future terrorist attacks, or the expectation that others will flee New York, reducing the future density benefits offered by the city.

On the supply side, the 16 acres of the World Trade Center site housed approximately 13.4 million square feet of class A office space—nearly 30 percent of the downtown total.[5] This complex was destroyed, and several surrounding buildings were damaged when the towers fell. Although some residential space was damaged as well, it was reoccupied relatively quickly. As of this writing, the WTC site remains essentially vacant, although the reopened PATH station occupies a small portion of the area.

The loss of space available for economic activity, even for a short period of time, complicates the ability of the available (necessarily short-run) data to provide insights into the long-run economic prospects for New York. When supply is fixed, changes in the price of land result only from shifts in the demand for land. But when the supply of land falls, prices tend to rise, depending on the elasticity of demand for land. We should, however, note two characteristics of the WTC site: First, the amount of land left temporarily unusable by the attack (16 acres) represents about 0.01 percent of New York's total usable land area and about 0.15 percent of that available in Manhattan. Second, there can be little question that the great majority of the site, which has now been cleared and restored, will ultimately be reoccupied in some form. From these two facts we can conclude that the loss of usable land in the city was modest and is expected to be temporary.

The effect of the loss of the twin towers on the supply of office space in New York, on the other hand, was substantial. Since the space has yet to be rebuilt, and since long-run planning indicates that any redevelopment of the area is likely to include more residential and less office space, absent reductions in demand, the price of office space in lower Manhattan would be expected to rise. The price of residential space, whose current supply was unaffected and whose expected future supply is increased, is expected to fall unless this supply effect is offset by changes in demand.

We would thus expect to find that permanent negative shocks to the perceived benefits of a New York City residential location would be reflected in a relatively rapid reduction in city housing prices.[6] We first examine the effect of the attack on the city as a whole, and then turn to an analysis of particular neighborhoods. In neither case can we find evidence that the September 11 attack reduced the value of residing in New York.

Our second, and much briefer, analysis is of office markets; it can be seen as a complement to the analysis of Franz Fuerst (this volume). Here we compare trends in office rents and the prices of office buildings using aggregate time-series data on price indexes. This analysis does detect some evidence of a shift in the demand for office space from the downtown to the midtown market since 2001, presumptive evidence of at least a temporary effect of the terrorist attack.

SHIFTS IN MARKET FUNDAMENTALS: EVIDENCE FROM THE SHORT RUN

One of the most difficult aspects of determining the effect of the September 11 attack on the New York economy is defining a counterfactual: had there been no attack, what course would the city economy have followed? This task is always difficult, but especially so in the current circumstance: the attack oc-curred very near turning points in both the local business cycle and the stock market, an important determinant of the city's economic health. Indeed, as indicated in figure 4.2, the New York City Index of Coincident Economic Indicators peaked in January 2001, eight months before the terrorist attack and about four months after the NYSE composite index reached an all-time high in September 2000.

FIGURE 4.2   NEW YORK CITY INDEX OF COINCIDENT ECONOMIC INDICATORS, NOVEMBER 1965 TO DECEMBER 2003

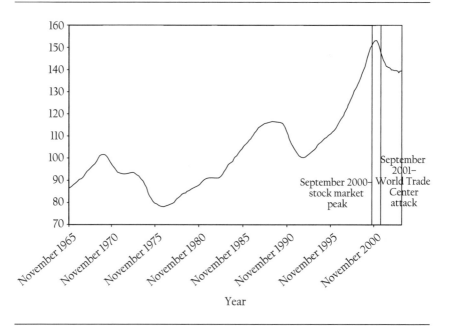

Source: Federal Reserve Bank of New York.

Defining a counterfactual for the attack is no easy matter, but it has important effects on the measurement of the short-term economic losses attributable to the attack. After exploring a variety of hypothetical trajectories for city employment in an attempt to establish a baseline, Jason Bram (2003) concludes that the economic impact of the attack was probably somewhat less than was estimated in its immediate aftermath.[7] Establishing the direct impact of the attack is important in identifying its effects on longer-run perceptions of the market. In addition, some models of cumulative causation might suggest that the loss of activity in the short run feeds through the economy and damages the economy in the long run as agglomeration benefits decline or fiscal stresses increase.

Given that the attack occurred during an ongoing downturn, one simple way of thinking about its short-term impact is to compare the severity of the current city downturn to those of previous cycles. If the attack's effect was very large, it might be expected to make the local recession worse than usual. Yet the downturn in the city from 2001 to 2003 was arguably less severe than previous recessions. Table 4.1 indicates that by August 2003 the NYC CEI had declined 5.9 percent since August 2001 (twenty-eight months) and 8.9 percent since it reached its cyclical peak in January 2001 (thirty-five months). In contrast, the CEI declined 14.2 percent in the forty-one months between April 1989 and September 1992, and by over 23 percent between October 1969 and October 1976.

Table 4.2 shows the largest one-, two-, and three-month percentage declines in NYC CEI's history. The shock caused (in large part) by the destruction of the World Trade Center helps September 2001 to rank as the fourth-largest one-month decline in the forty-year history of the index. Yet both the

TABLE 4.1   DECLINES IN NEW YORK CITY COINCIDENT ECONOMIC INDICATORS (CEI), CITY DOWNTURNS SINCE 1965

	City Downturns				
Peak month	October 1969	March 1982	April 1989	January 2001	August 2001[a]
Trough month	October 1976	October 1982	September 1992	August 2003	August 2003
Number of months	84	7	41	35	28
CEI change	−23.1%	−0.2%	−14.2%	−8.9%	−5.9%
Average monthly decline	−.31%	−.02%	−0.40%	−0.27%	−0.22%

Source: Author's compilation.
[a]Although August 2001 is not a peak month, it is used here to show 9/11 effects.

TABLE 4.2   LARGEST DECLINES IN NEW YORK CITY COINCIDENT ECONOMIC
INDICATORS SINCE 1965

One-Month Period		Two-Month Period		Three-Month Period	
Dates	Percentage Decline	Dates	Percentage Decline	Dates	Percentage Decline
1 January 1991	−1.13%	January–February 1975	−2.03%	December–February 1975	−3.04%
2 February 1975	−1.09	February–March 1975	−1.98	January–March 1975	−2.91
3 December 1974	−1.03	December 1974–January 1975	−1.97	November 1990–January 1991	−2.83
4 September 2001	−0.95	December 1990–January 1991	−1.92	November 1974–January 1975	−2.78
5 January 1975	−0.94	January–February 1991	−1.92	December 1990–February 1991	−2.70

Source: Author's compilation.

1970s and 1990s downturns recorded one-, two- and three-month declines that exceeded those of the latter part of 2001.

Although the aggregate data do not support the contention that the current downturn is more severe than recessions of the last four decades, this does not definitively establish that the September 11, 2001, attack did not have important consequences for the city economy, even in the short run. If the city were poised for a modest, short downturn (like the one it experienced in the early 1980s) but the attack prolonged it, then this would not be captured in tables 4.1 and 4.2. In addition, the NYC CEI is just one measure of local economic activity. Since the CEI is estimated over a long time period, it may under- or overestimate the extent of decline in any particular time period.

Nonetheless, the analysis suggests that the immediate impact of the attack was no larger than that of a typical cyclical downturn and that we can with some confidence interpret changes in city real estate prices as resulting from long-run considerations. We now turn to an analysis of real estate markets in order to draw these inferences.

DATA AND RESULTS

Housing Markets I: MSA-Level OFHEO Price Index

We analyze two types of housing market data: macrodata on the New York metropolitan statistical area (MSA) and the nation, and microdata on New

York housing prices and rents by broad neighborhood. The Office of Federal Housing Enterprise Oversight (OFHEO) produces the first of these, a repeat-sale price index series. The OFHEO measures the sales prices of single-family, detached housing units from data on mortgages and aggregates them into indexes for various metropolitan areas and for the nation as a whole.[8] Before turning to the data, several observations about the series and its construction are in order.

First, as noted, the data refer to single-family, detached houses with conforming mortgages, a relative rarity in Manhattan, although more common in the city's other boroughs and especially in the suburbs.[9] We thus interpret these data as indicating the strength of demand for the MSA as a whole and rely on other sources to help determine whether residential demands for those locations closest to the World Trade Center have changed since late 2001. This is important, since a possible effect of the attack would be reductions in demand for dense areas and increased suburbanization of the population.

Second, as the housing stock's characteristics change, the price of units can be expected to follow suit, even absent shifts in the demand for specific attributes or locations. The OFHEO index controls for this phenomenon by measuring repeat sales of the same unit at different points in time. This methodology presumably corrects some of the upward bias in house price measures that results from the fact that new units embody quality improvements, but it does not control for owners' investment in preexisting housing units. To the extent that such investments are both important and correlated with price appreciation, the OFHEO index may overstate the pure price appreciation of a given stock of housing capital. Joseph Gyourko and Joseph Tracy (2003) examine this issues in some detail, demonstrating that housing investment is both important and indeed reflects economic conditions. In our analysis, we confine ourselves to analysis of changes in the short run—one or two years—in an effort to minimize the chance that the price changes captured in the OFHEO index reflect significant investment in existing units.

Third, the key question we wish to address in this section is whether there is evidence of a change in the relative demand for residential locations in the New York metropolitan area. We must therefore control for housing demand nationwide. This may be particularly important in the current context, when debates about housing "bubbles" are swirling in both the popular press and academic journals (Ackman 2005; Herring and Wachter 2002). We attempt to clarify our interpretation of the results by examining the characteristics of the New York OFHEO index *relative to the nation as a whole*. Thus, we look for evidence that New York's residential prices have lagged the rest of the nation since September 2001.

As mentioned earlier, the attack resulted in the destruction of office space alone and had little effect on the actual supply of residential property. Indeed, if anything, proposals to increase the amount of residential space in lower

Manhattan might be expected to reduce the current price (although not necessarily rents) of existing housing. Significant reductions in demand resulting from diminished expectations of the benefits of a New York location should likewise reduce prices. Rents may fall if residents perceive the current environment in New York to be less beneficial than it was prior to the attack.

Results

The series depicted in figure 4.3 is the quarterly OFHEO single-family home price index for the New York metropolitan area, divided by the national index. Both indexes, and the resulting series, equal 100 in the second quarter of 1976, when the New York series began. Following its long, steep decline of the 1970s, the index began a steady rise in the first quarter of 1979. It peaked at about 210 in the first quarter of 1988, at which point New York house price appreciation since 1976 had been more than twice as fast as that in the nation. This peak gave way to a long-term decline beginning in 1989, and the index reached a trough (at 159) in 1997. Thereafter, the New York index again reversed

FIGURE 4.3   NEW YORK CITY–AREA HOUSE PRICES RELATIVE TO U.S.
              AVERAGE, 1976 QUARTER 2 TO 2003 QUARTER 3

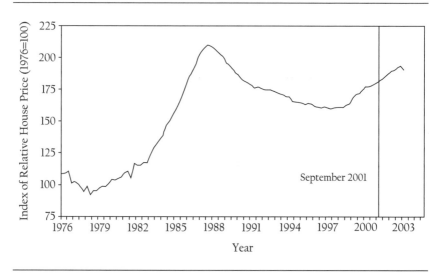

Source: Office of Federal Housing Enterprise Oversight; Federal Reserve Bank of New York Calculations.
Note: The index is based on the ratio of repeat-sales price measure for existing single-family homes in the New York City metropolitan area to that of the United States overall.

course, and New York prices rose sharply relative to the nation until the third quarter of 2003.

There is little evidence here that the September 11, 2001, attack on the World Trade Center reduced the demand for residential locations in the New York metropolitan area. The figure shows the date of the attack, which occurred during the third quarter of 2001. Repeat-sale house prices in the metropolitan area were rising faster than in the rest of the nation both before and after the attack, as shown by the steady rise in the index on both sides of the September 11 point. That is to say, the New York area's residential housing market *gained* ground on the rest of the nation immediately after the attack. Only two years later, in late 2003, was there any sign that housing prices in New York had faltered relative to the nation.

It is worth reemphasizing the limitations of this analysis before moving on. The data cover only single-family homes, which are presumably located primarily in the suburbs. Increased demand for single-family houses may reflect *reduced* demand for Manhattan locations and a decentralization of population from New York City proper. Such a result, for example, is consistent with Mills's (2002) early reflections on the implications of urban terrorism. To address this issue of urban form, we now turn to a detailed examination of the New York City housing market before and after the attack.

HOUSING MARKETS II: NEIGHBORHOOD-LEVEL MICRODATA

Our second housing market analysis is more restrictive in the sense that it focuses only on housing units in the city of New York. On the other hand, our data source for this analysis, the New York City Housing and Vacancy Survey (HVS), allows consideration of a much broader range of housing types, from rental apartments to condominiums to single-family homes, with the mix reflecting the actual housing consumption patterns of city households.

The HVS is conducted about every three years (the coverage here is 1991, 1993, 1996, 1999, and 2002). Each survey collects information on the structural and locational characteristics of about eighteen thousand housing units in the city. The structural characteristics include detailed items like the number of bedrooms, the presence of complete kitchen facilities, and the condition of exterior walls.[10] For the purposes of the survey, New York is divided into fifty-five sub-boroughs (see figure 4.4), and the location of each unit is identified in the public data to the sub-borough level.

Like the OFHEO data described earlier, the HVS data provide a limited view of changes in housing demand. In particular, the HVS complements the OFHEO index in the sense that it allows for a detailed look at those parts of

FIGURE 4.4   NEW YORK CITY SUB-BOROUGHS

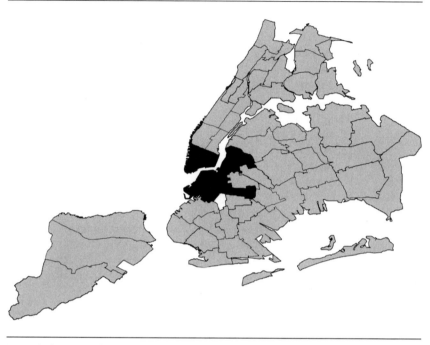

Source: Author's compilation.
Note: Areas defined in column 3 of table 4.4 are shaded.

the city that might be expected to have been most affected by the terrorist attack and the fear of future attacks.

To discern the effects of September 11 on the demand for housing in New York City, we estimate a set of regression equations of the form

$$V = V(t,N,H)$$

where V is a measure of unit value (expected sales price for owner-occupied units or gross rent for rental apartments), t indexes time, N indexes neighborhood, and H is a vector of housing capital measures. More specifically, we interact the fifty-five sub-borough measures with a set of five survey (year) dummies. Our test consists of looking for significant negative effects on the 2002 dummies in the city as a whole or in those sub-boroughs expected to have been most affected by the attack. The housing characteristics for which we control are described in table 4.3.[11] Our specification estimates average trait prices and looks for temporal variation in the relative value of particular neigh-

TABLE 4.3   HOUSING CAPITAL MEASURES

Trait	Measurement
Decade of construction	Dummies: 1900s to 1990s (including 2000 to 2002) = ten variables
Enumerator evaluation of the condition of the building	Dummy variables for broken exterior windows, cracks in exterior walls, holes in floors, dilapidated building exterior
Resident evaluation of the residential structures in the neighborhood	Dummy variables: Excellent, very good, good, and poor
Presence and functionality of kitchen	Dummy variables for complete kitchen facilities, available for exclusive use of this unit
Presence and functionality of plumbing facilities	Dummy variables for complete plumbing facilities, available for exclusive use of this unit
Number of rooms	Dummies: One to seven or more rooms = seven variables
Bedrooms	Dummies: Zero to seven or more bedrooms = eight variables
Enumerator evaluation of condition of windows	Dummy variables for broken, missing, rotten, loose, or boarded-up windows
Enumerator evaluation of condition of stairways	Dummy variables for loose, broken, or missing railings or steps
Enumerator evaluation of condition of floors	Dummy variables for sagging or sloping floors, deep wear, and holes
Overall deterioration of building	Dummy variable: Yes (building is deteriorating) or no (building is sound)
Visible broken windows in the neighborhood	Dummy variable: Yes or no
Condominium	Dummy variable: Yes or no
Co-op	Dummy variable: Yes or no
Condo or co-op maintenance fees	Fees were grouped into seventeen different levels up to $2,500 a month. Value is the midpoint of the level
Number of units in the building	The number of units was divided into twelve different levels up to one hundred units. Value is the midpoint of the level
Owner lives in building	Dummy variable: Yes or no

(Table continues on p. 110.)

TABLE 4.3   *CONTINUED*

Trait	Measurement
Stories in building	Stories were grouped into ten different levels up to forty. Value is the midpoint of the level
Presence of a passenger elevator	Dummy variable: Yes or no
Heating fuel	Dummy variables for oil, gas, electricity, or other fuel = four variables
Functionality of heating equipment	Dummy variable: Yes (breaks down) or no (equipment in working order)
Mice	Dummy variable: Yes or no
Exterminator	Dummy variable: Yes or no
Cracks in interior walls	Dummy variable: Yes or no
Holes in floors	Dummy variable: Yes or no
Broken plaster or peeling paint on ceiling or walls	Dummy variable: Yes or no
Water leakage	Dummy variable: Yes or no
Abandoned structures in neighborhood	Dummy variable: Yes or no
Sub-Borough	Fifty-five dummy variables for locations
Household weight	Final household weight

Interaction variables
  Mice × Exterminator
  Year × Sub-Borough	

Rental units only Rent stabilized	Dummy variable: Yes or no
Rent controlled	Dummy variable: Yes or no
Don't know rent regulation status	Dummy variable: Yes (don't know) or no (do know)
Year the resident moved to unit	Dummies: 1992 to 2002 and before 1992 = twelve variables
Length of lease	Dummies for five time lengths. Value is the midpoint of the time length
Owned units only Year the resident acquired unit	Dummies: 1992 to 2002 and before 1992 = twelve variables

Source: Author's compilation.

borhoods. If variations in traits whose prices are changing are correlated with neighborhood, then we may obtain biased estimates of neighborhood effects. We leave research on this topic to later work.

We experimented with several specifications of the basic relationships, including estimating the equation in level and semi-log forms, eliminating the top and bottom 5 percent of observations based on value, eliminating top-coded units, and augmenting the equation with information about financial arrangements and move-in or lease dates. Each of these specifications leads to the same qualitative conclusions.

Results

Table 4.4 reports the results of two sets of regressions designed to identify the effects of the September 11 terrorist attacks on the demand for residential locations in New York City. The figures in the table are the regression coefficients on year 2002 dummies either on their own, or interacted with dummies for particular sub-boroughs or groups of sub-boroughs. If the attack were to have broken the trend of price and rental growth in the city, we would expect negative coefficients to predominate in the table.

The first column of the table reports the overall, citywide, trends in prices and rents, controlling (as do all specifications reported here) for units' structural characteristics. In addition, we control for the year in which the owner acquired the unit (for owner-occupied units) or the year the occupant moved in (for rental units). The requirement that we have information for all of these variables reduces the sample size to the approximately 51,000 reported in the table. We present results from both the levels and semi-log specifications.

The results suggest that city residential prices and rents in 2002 were both higher than in 1999, the year of the previous survey. But when we subtract the national increase in shelter costs, 11.1 percent, only the price increase is statistically different from zero; rental increases were slower in New York City than in the nation as a whole.[12] Note, however, that we can reject the hypothesis that absolute rents and prices in New York fell on average; all four estimates in column 1 are positive and more than twice their standard errors.

The second column of table 4.4 reports the change in prices in Manhattan in 2002 relative to 1999, controlling for citywide time effects. These results reveal a pattern similar to that in the citywide estimates. Although the point estimate of 12 percent rental appreciation in Manhattan slightly exceeds the national average, the standard error of the estimated coefficient does not allow rejection of the hypothesis that the New York increase was the same as the nation's. Manhattan *prices*, meanwhile, grew much more rapidly than the national CPIU.

TABLE 4.4   2002 PRICE AND RENT EFFECTS IN NEW YORK AND SELECTED AREAS

			Coefficient and Standard Error Estimates on 2002 Prices Relative to 1999 Prices		
	Citywide	Manhattan	Lower Manhattan, Chinatown, Lower East Side, Western Brooklyn	Lower Manhattan, Chinatown, Lower East Side	Lower Manhattan
(N = 16,672)					
Prices ($)	**68,714**	**151,883**	**102,709**	**57,771**	**113,733**
	(3,732)	**(7,244)**	**(11,153)**	**(16,742)**	**(23,465)**
Prices (Log)	**0.78**	**1.30**	**1.03**	**1.23**	**2.01**
	(0.02)	**(0.07)**	**(0.10)**	**(0.15)**	**(0.22)**
(N = 34,586)					
Monthly rents ($)	39.6	169.1	91.1	161.0	**365.4**
	(5.8)	(8.0)	(12.2)	(6.8)	**(25.3)**
Monthly rents (Log)	0.05	0.12	0.02	0.12	**0.37**
	(0.01)	(0.01)	(0.02)	(0.03)	**(0.04)**

Source: Author's calculations.
Note: All regressions include controls for structural traits, survey year, rent control status, whether unit is a condominium or co-operative (price regressions), whether the owner lives in the building (rent regressions), and year acquired (price regressions) or year the current occupant moved in (rent regressions). Figures in bold represent increases that are significantly greater than national average increases in the shelter component of the Consumer Price Index between 1999 and June 2003 (11.1 percent).

Column 3 reports results for the two lower Manhattan sub-boroughs and three northwest Brooklyn sub-boroughs (see figure 4.4 for details). All of these areas benefit from direct accessibility to the lower Manhattan central business district, with housing units typically within a thirty-minute commute on public transportation.[13] We might thus expect the attack to have had a negative impact on residential markets in these areas. Again, the data provide little evidence for this conjecture, although rental increases are statistically indistinguishable from zero for these areas as a whole.

Since the attack occurred in lower Manhattan, we might expect that area to endure the most significant reductions in demand. Columns 4 and 5 address this issue, using two definitions. In column 4, we include the area that extends as far north and east as Chinatown, while the column 5 results are limited to the Financial District and Greenwich Village. Once again, the evidence suggests price *increases* relative to the nation in all these areas, as well as significant rent increases in the area closest to the World Trade Center.

Taken as a whole, there is no evidence here of any declines in prices or rents for residential property that could be attributed to the September 11 terrorist attack. Since the survey was conducted within a few months of the attack, it also seems unlikely that supply reductions are driving these results. Instead, we interpret these data as indicating that the demand for residential real estate in New York City, especially in lower Manhattan, strengthened, if anything, in the wake of the attack.

Our tests indicate that the demand for rental properties in New York was no stronger than that in the nation, and in some areas may have been weaker. Yet in lower Manhattan, the area most affected by the attack, rents grew strongly. The apparent divergence between rental markets in lower Manhattan and the rest of the city may be partially attributable to incentives for residents to locate in this area, part of the package of aid that the city received in the wake of the crisis. Under these programs, residents willing to make a two-year residential commitment to areas of lower Manhattan close to the site of the attack were eligible to receive grants of up to $12,000. Our estimated rental increase in lower Manhattan for 1999 to 2002 (column 5 of table 4.4), less that in the city as a whole, is about $325 per month, or about $7,800 over a two-year period. Unfortunately, we cannot identify which units received the subsidy, so a direct comparison of the rent with the value of the subsidy is not possible. However, since the majority of the units in lower Manhattan as we define it are eligible for smaller (or zero) subsidies, it seems most likely that our estimate of the rental increase in the area incorporates demand effects above and beyond those stimulated by the subsidy.

Given that the supply of downtown (and citywide) housing was little changed by the attack, we interpret these results as strong evidence that the demand for residential locations in New York remained very robust in the wake of the 9/11 attack.

Some Caveats

First, our analysis of the 2002 data is based on a comparison with 1999, the previous survey year. Because the 2002 survey was based on results from the 2000 decennial census, while the 1999 survey relied on the 1990 census, variations in the under- or overcount of housing units in the census could affect the results. This leads to biased estimates of the neighborhood effects only if changes in the housing characteristics of miscounted units are correlated with neighborhood. Such a bias would be likely to appear as a significant change in results when sampling weights, which takes into account the characteristics of the population of units. The results we describe here obtain whether the regression is estimated with or without the sampling weights, ameliorating this concern to some extent.

It is also possible that the prices and rents we observe in 2002, while higher than those in 1999, are lower than immediately before the attack, a period for which no data are available. We take some comfort in the fact that the analysis of annual MSA-wide trends produced conclusions broadly consistent with those advanced here.

Finally, the 2002 survey was conducted during the first half of the year, or in the immediate aftermath of the terrorist attack of late 2001. Since very little time had elapsed between the attack and the beginning of the survey, there is a potential for bias in the survey responses. This bias could be in either direction: respondents might not have had time to fully internalize the negative effect of the attack on their property values and might thus have provided an overly optimistic view of value. On the other hand, lower Manhattan in the first six months of 2002 was still very much in the throes of the turmoil created by the destruction of the WTC and a substantial amount of city infrastructure (roads, subways, and so on). Indeed, the fires that were ignited by the attack were extinguished only in late December 2001, and the cleanup of the site continued until late May 2002. In these circumstances, it seems unlikely that property owners would be overly optimistic about the value of their homes. Nonetheless, it is impossible to know for certain. Again, we take comfort in the fact that the results here are consistent with the analysis of the OFHEO price index described earlier.

OFFICE MARKETS

Our final analysis complements that of Fuerst (this volume). We examine trends in the market for office space in New York's two central business districts, downtown and midtown, using data from the National Real Estate Index.[14] These data are collected for class A office space in sixty markets across the nation. We focus on the two New York markets and, to control for prevailing national conditions, calculate indexes measuring appreciation in these markets relative to the nation as a whole. These indexes, which are based in the fourth quarter of 1985, are shown in figures 4.5 and 4.6.

Results

The attack destroyed or rendered temporarily or permanently unusable nearly 28 million square feet of class A office space, 13.4 million of which was in the WTC complex itself. If the demand for lower Manhattan location remained stable, we might expect to see a strong increase in office rents for the remaining downtown office space. There is little evidence of this in figure 4.5. Indeed,

FIGURE 4.5 OFFICE RENT INDEXES, CLASS A SPACE, MANHATTAN MARKETS
RELATIVE TO NATIONAL AVERAGE

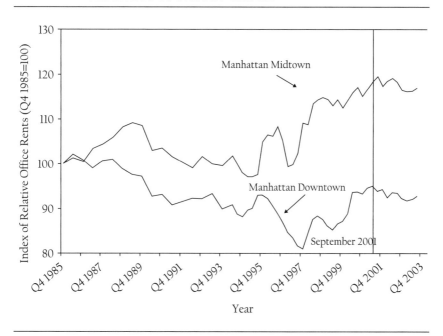

Source: Global Real Analytics, National Real Estate Index (available at: http://www.graglobal.com/index.php?section=products&page=aboutNREI); Federal Reserve Bank of New York calculations.
Note: Index is based on the ratio of office prices in Manhattan to those in the United States overall.

nominal class A office rents declined nearly 9 percent between the third quarter of 2001 and the third quarter of 2002, suggesting that demand fell at the same time as supply. A decline in demand is consistent with Edward Glaeser and Jesse Shapiro's (2002) view that the attack hastened the decline of lower Manhattan as a principal site for New York City office locations. Yet this decline was matched by an 8.5 percent decline in class A rents nationwide; as a result, both the downtown and midtown indexes depicted in figure 4.5 remained essentially flat, with perhaps a modest downward trend.

The price chart (figure 4.6) reveals an interesting pattern both before and after September 11, 2001. Between the fourth quarter of 1985 and the third quarter of 2003, downtown office building prices essentially held steady relative to the nation. Note, however, that downtown prices reached a trough in the first quarter of 1998 (at which point downtown had fallen over 10 percent relative to the nation since the end of 1985). From the second quarter of 1998

FIGURE 4.6   OFFICE PRICE INDEXES, CLASS A SPACE, MANHATTAN MARKETS
RELATIVE TO NATIONAL AVERAGE

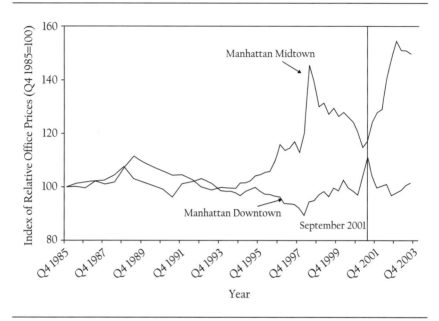

Source: Global Real Analytics, National Real Estate Index (available at: http://www.graglobal.com/
index.php?section=products&page=aboutNREI); Federal Reserve Bank of New York calculations.
Note: Index is based on the ratio of office prices in Manhattan to those in the United States overall.

to the second quarter of 2001 the downtown market rallied, and the relative
price index stood at 111.5 on the eve of September 2001. By the close of 2001,
the downtown market had given back all its gains relative to the nation, and
the index reached a recent low of 96.8 in the third quarter of 2002. There is
modest evidence here of a rally in the downtown market since that point: the
index rose back above the break-even point (at 101.6) by the third quarter of
2003.

The fact that the relative downtown office prices remain below the peak
they reached immediately prior to the September 11 attack might be taken as
evidence that the attack itself had a very substantial effect on office prices.
There are several points to make here. First, the peak of the office index (111.5)
in the second quarter of 2001 was anomalous in the sense that it represented
a sharply higher level than the previous quarter (103.7). Second, the pre-9/11
rise in the index as we measure it was the result of a modest decline in the

national index and a sharp uptick in the downtown index.[15] That is, the graph shows a sharp increase in part because of the national office market downturn. Third, the fact that the downtown office market stabilized in the subsequent two years provides some indication that demanders continue to find locations there attractive. By the end of the period, the relative downtown price index was about 3 percent higher than it had been three years earlier. On the other hand, there is some evidence, as suggested by Glaeser and Shapiro (2002), of a post-attack shift in demand to midtown, where prices have rallied strongly relative to both the nation and downtown since mid-2001.

Overall, the evidence from the office market suggests a post-attack weakening of demand in lower Manhattan relative to the rest of the nation, especially in light of the decline in the supply of space that accompanied the destruction of the World Trade Center. The most dramatic effects are seen in the price graph (figure 4.6), although an unusual spike just prior to the attack makes the data difficult to interpret. Nonetheless, it is clear that the dramatic increase in prices that occurred in midtown has not been experienced downtown. In rental markets there is some sign of weakening in both downtown and midtown, although there is also modest evidence of stabilization in both by the end of 2003. These data are consistent with a fairly benign view of the attack's effect on the demand for New York locations. As suggested by Glaeser and Shapiro (2002), it would appear that downtown's appeal to businesses has declined relative to that of midtown. On the other hand, downtown demand has held up reasonably well relative to the nation as a whole, especially given the temporary dislocations associated with the cleanup and redesign of the WTC site and surrounding areas.

For the city as a whole, we can calculate the weighted average price increase by applying the downtown and midtown shares of class A space as weights to the relevant price increases. That calculation yields a 12.6 percent *increase* in prices across the city.

CONCLUSION

This chapter has looked for evidence of a reduction in demand for New York City locations using a variety of data from real estate markets. In general, we find that demand for New York locations remains strong. One possible exception to this is the demand for downtown office space in the immediate aftermath of the September 11 attack. Although prices and rents for high-quality office space in lower Manhattan fell in the first year after the attack, there is some evidence that this deterioration had stabilized by the end of 2003.

These results shed light on some of the important issues regarding the effect of terrorism on cities and the demand for density. If firms and households view dense agglomerations of activity as potential targets of future attacks, we might expect this fear to result in substantially reduced demand for residential and business locations in the nation's densest centers. In New York, which had experienced attacks before 9/11 and is the densest of our cities, we see no evidence of such effects.

An alternative view is that terrorism works primarily on the supply side. Here we might expect that the fear of attack increases the cost of supplying space in targeted locations, since developers must make buildings less vulnerable, and insurers must charge high premiums (or refuse to provide terrorism coverage) to indemnify themselves against attack. In this case, reduced supply by itself could lead to stable or rising prices, in spite of stable or falling demand. We view this outcome as less likely, particularly in New York, where pre-attack expectations of supply increases were presumably modest in both residential and office markets.

In addition to assuaging potential concerns that New York and other cities were permanently and severely damaged by the attack, the analysis may provide some guidance for downtown reconstruction efforts. In particular, current plans call for a mixed residential-office development at the former World Trade Center site, suggesting that the supply of office (residential) space in lower Manhattan will be permanently lower (higher) than it was prior to the destruction of the twin towers. Such a development would be consistent with the price signals as we interpret them here.

The author is grateful to participants at the conference, particularly Jan Brueckner and two anonymous referees, for very helpful suggestions. Bess Rabin provided excellent research assistance in compiling, analyzing, and helping to interpret the various datasets described here. Howard Chernick, Edward Hill, Sanders Korenman, James Parrott, Cordelia Reimers, and Franz Fuerst provided helpful input in the early stages of this work. I also thank Christopher Mayer for valuable conversations and for suggesting the National Real Estate Index analysis. The views expressed here are those of the author and do not necessarily reflect those of the Federal Reserve Bank of New York or the Federal Reserve System.

NOTES

1. The NYC CEI is a broad-based, dynamic, single-factor measure of economic activity in New York City constructed following the methodology of Stock and Wat-

son (1989). The index is calculated from the common movements in four indicators tied to the city's labor market: payroll employment, the unemployment rate, average weekly hours worked in manufacturing, and real earnings. The NYC CEI is described more fully in Orr, Rich, and Rosen (1999).

2. This landfill extended Manhattan into the Hudson River, forming the basis for Battery Park City, a primarily residential development.

3. This approach is consistent with Edwin Mills's (2002) argument that the effect of terrorism on real estate markets is inseparable from its effect on urban form.

4. In a similar approach, Jan Brueckner (1982) argues that over short time horizons, housing prices likewise reflect the value of local traits.

5. For more information see http://www.buildings.com/Articles/detail.asp?ArticleID =341.

6. If markets are imperfect, especially if information on market conditions is not widely available, then these reductions may be somewhat slower. We address this issue to a limited extent later in the chapter.

7. See New York City Partnership (2001) for an early study of the effect of the attack on the city economy.

8. See Calhoun (1996) for details of the OFHEO methodology.

9. The metropolitan area defined here includes the five boroughs and Westchester, Putnam, and Rockland Counties.

10. A complete description is available from the New York City Housing and Vacancy Survey online at: http://www.census.gov/hhes/www/housing/nychvs/2002/nychvs02 .html.

11. Because of high correlations among the measures of unit quality, the specifications reported in table 4.4 exclude some of the variables reported in table 4.3. These exclusions have no effect on the coefficients of interest. R-squared values for the regressions range from 0.72 for the price equations to 0.85 for the rent equations. Detailed results are available from the author upon request.

12. All prices and rents are measured in nominal terms. The shelter component of the national CPIU increased 11.1 percent between 1999 and June 2002 (Council of Economic Advisers 2004, table B-61). Since the rental and owner's equivalent rent components grew at similar rates (12.3 versus 11.1 percent), we use the total as our benchmark; disaggregating would not affect our conclusions. Overall CPIU inflation over this time period was 8.0 percent.

13. Average commutes in New York City outside of Manhattan average over forty minutes, placing the four "outer boroughs" sixth, seventh, eighth, and ninth in the national ranking of longest commuting times.

14. Global Real Analytics, which produces the index, collects quarterly information on recently closed office building sales and average rents for class A office space. The index is available at: http://www.graglobal.com/index.php?section=products &page=aboutNREI.

15. The price for a square foot of class A office space in lower Manhattan rose from $307 in the first quarter of 2001 to $328 in the third quarter of 2001 (an all-time high), while the national average fell from $215 to $213. Comparing fourth-quarter prices, downtown prices were 4.8 percent higher in 2001 than in 2002.

REFERENCES

Ackman, Dan. 2005. "Fresh Pricks in Housing Bubble." *Forbes Online* (March 3). Available at: http://www.forbes.com/2005/03/02/cx_da_0302topnews.html.

Beardsell, Mark, and Vernon Henderson. 1999. "Spatial Evolution of the Computer Industry in the USA." *European Economic Review* 43(June): 431–56.

Bram, Jason. 2003. "New York City's Economy Before and After September 11." *Current Issues in Economics and Finance* 9(2, February). Available at: www.newyorkfed.org/research/current_issues/ci9–2.html.

Bram, Jason, Andrew Haughwout, and James Orr. 2002. "Has September 11 Affected New York City's Growth Potential?" *Economic Policy Review* 8(2, November): 81–96.

Brueckner, Jan. 1979. "Property Values, Local Public Expenditure, and Economic Efficiency." *Journal of Public Economics* 11: 223–45.

———. 1982. "A Test for Allocative Efficiency in the Local Public Sector." *Journal of Public Economics* 19: 311–31.

Calhoun, Charles A. 1996. *OFHEO House Price Indexes: HPI Technical Description*. Washington: Office of Federal Housing Enterprise Oversight (March). Available at: http://www.ofheo.gov/Media/Archive/house/hpi_tech.pdf.

Ciccone, Antonio, and Robert Hall. 1996. "Productivity and the Density of Economic Activity." *American Economic Review* 86(March): 54–70.

Council of Economic Advisers. 2004. *Economic Report of the President*. Washington: U.S. Government Printing Office.

Davis, Donald R., and David E. Weinstein. 2002. "Bones, Bombs, and Break Points: The Geography of Economic Activity." *American Economic Review* 92(5, December): 1269–89.

Edgerton, Jesse, Andrew Haughwout, and Raven E. Rosen. 2004. "Revenue Implications of New York City's Tax System." *Current Issues in Economics and Finance* 10(4, April).

Glaeser, Edward L., Joseph Gyourko, and Raven E. Saks. 2003. "Why Is Manhattan So Expensive? Regulation and the Rise in House Prices." Available at: http://post.economics.harvard.edu/faculty/glaeser/papers.html.

Glaeser, Edward L., and Jesse Shapiro. 2002. "Cities and Warfare: The Impact of Terrorism on Urban Form." *Journal of Urban Economics* 51: 205–24.

Gyourko, Joseph, and Joseph Tracy. 2003. "Using Home Maintenance and Repairs to Smooth Variable Earnings." Available at: http://www.newyorkfed.org/research/economists/tracy/papers.html.

Haughwout, Andrew. 1998. "Aggregate Production Functions, Interregional Equilibrium, and the Measurement of Infrastructure Productivity." *Journal of Urban Economics* 44(2, September): 216–27.

———. 2002. "Public Infrastructure Investment, Growth, and Welfare in Fixed Geographic Areas." *Journal of Public Economics* 83: 405–28.

Haughwout, Andrew F., and Robert P. Inman. 2002. "Should Suburbs Help Their Central City?" *Brookings-Wharton Papers on Urban Affairs*. Available at: http://ssrn.com/abstract=348980.

Herring, Richard, and Susan Wachter. 2002. "Bubbles in Real Estate Markets." Working paper 104. Philadelphia: University of Pennsylvania, Wharton School, Zell-Lurie Real Estate Center (March).

Mills, Edwin S. 2002. "Terrorism and U.S. Real Estate." *Journal of Urban Economics* 51: 198–204.

New York City Partnership. 2001. *The New York City Partnership's Economic Impact Analysis of the September 11 Attack on New York City*. New York: NYCP (November).

Orr, James, Robert Rich, and Rae Rosen. 1999. "Two New Indexes Offer a Broad View of Economic Activity in the New York–New Jersey Region." *Current Issues in Economics and Finance* 5(14, October)

Rosenthal, Stuart, and William Strange. 2003. "Geography, Industrial Organization, and Agglomeration." *Review of Economics and Statistics* 85(2): 377–93.

Stock, James H., and Mark W. Watson. 1989. "New Indexes of Coincident and Leading Economic Indicators." In *NBER Macroeconomics Annual*. Cambridge, Mass.: MIT Press.

CHAPTER 5

The Effects of 9/11 on New York's Publicly Traded Companies: A Brief Look at Financial Market Data

Sanders Korenman

WHY DO firms pay high rents and wages to locate in New York City? The standard answer is that the city provides some locational advantages, such as production spillovers and other economies of agglomeration (see, for example, Haughwout, this volume; Glaeser and Shapiro 2002; Beunza and Stark 2001). Did the attack on the World Trade Center (WTC) reduce the value of a New York location? If so, a decision taken before the attack to locate in New York would be revealed ex post facto to have been a less favorable economic decision. In this chapter, we investigate the hypothesis that investors believe that the locational advantages of New York have been reduced by the attack on the WTC. Specifically, we perform simple graphic before-after comparisons between the stock prices of firms that are headquartered in New York and other firms. In various models, "New York" is to be defined alternatively as:

- New York City
- New York State
- The tristate area of New York, New Jersey, and Connecticut

An effect on the stock prices of firms in New York should show up in a straightforward difference-in-differences estimate (after-before difference for New York companies minus after-before differences for companies located outside of New York). It is possible, however, that New York companies would have done worse after the attack on the WTC because of differences in industrial composition (for example, specialization in finance). Sectoral differences could bias difference-in-differences estimates of the effects of the WTC attack on the relative stock price of New York firms. Therefore, we also graph changes within individual sectors.

Our primary outcomes are the share prices and the value of outstanding shares (share price times number of shares). The value of a firm's shares should reflect the long-term profitability of the firm (the present value of expected future earnings). Sudden changes in the expected long-term profitability of a firm show up immediately as a decline in the relative value of the firm's shares. Similarly, unexpected costs affect short-term measures of profitability (such as net income) but have only small effects on the share prices if investors believe losses are temporary. In sum, this part of the chapter is intended to shed light on the question of whether investors expected the attack on the WTC to reduce the profitability of firms located in New York relative to firms located elsewhere.

Accounting information is also available (with a lag) in Standard & Poor's Compustat database, the source of our share-price data.[1] We prefer share prices because, as recent accounting scandals demonstrate, financial statements are subject to direct manipulation (some of which is intended to raise share prices) and can vary according to accounting conventions. Accountants may also raise a firm's true profitability, and hence its share price, by understating net income to the extent legal in order to reduce tax liability. A final advantage of share prices is that they become available quickly and, again, should reflect investor perceptions without a lag.

In the remainder of this chapter, we describe the methods and data used in our analysis of stock prices and financial data, and we present a series of figures. We first briefly address some theoretical issues.

CONCEPTUAL ISSUES

If asset markets are perfectly competitive, then a firm's share price should equal the present value of the expected (net of taxes) profit stream of the firm, adjusted for risk characteristics of the firm. Changes in investors' expectations of the firm's future performance should be reflected immediately in share prices. If the attack on the WTC was an unanticipated event (to the marginal investor), and if it was an event that revealed New York to be a more costly business environment than previously believed, then the advantages of locating a business in New York should not be as great after the attacks as before.

Even if these suppositions are true—that is, even if New York is costlier than had been believed and thus the locational advantages are expected to be lower—there remains the question of why such a change would affect firm profitability. In particular, the locational advantages might be entirely capitalized into land values. If so, the shock of the WTC attack to the New York economy might be borne by landowners in the form of reduced land prices and rents (Fuerst, this volume).

In this case, profits of New York firms could be reduced either because these firms own land in the city or because of imperfections in real estate markets. If rents and prices adjust only slowly (for example, because of long-term contracts or high transactions costs), then firm profits will fall below expectations, at least temporarily.

Another set of explanations does not rely on permanent changes in the locational advantages of New York. For lack of a better term, I refer to these as "incumbency" effects: a reduced profitability of firms located in New York on September 11, 2001, that does not affect the long-term locational advantages of New York. The productivity of workers may have been reduced by direct exposure to the terror of the events of that day, by the loss of friends, family, or business associates, and so forth. The effects of post-traumatic stress disorder associated with terrorist attacks have been found to be more profound and to last longer among the people most directly exposed to the attacks, those located closer to the attack (either at home or work), and those who lost friends or relatives in the attack. Although television, radio, and Internet coverage exposed the entire nation to the attacks, geographic proximity to the WTC and loss of family, friends, and neighbors were indisputably greater in the New York area than in other geographic areas (Curie 2002).[2] For example, there have been many reports of New Yorkers having emotional problems following the attack on the World Trade Center, including difficulty concentrating and sleep problems (see, for example, Garfinkel et al. 2003; Korenman, this volume). If these effects are generally greater for those employed in New York at the time of the attack, their productivity would be expected to fall relative to those employed outside New York, potentially lowering the performance of firms located in New York.

As explained later in the chapter, our geographic information is limited to the headquarters location. A more complete analysis would separate out those firms headquartered in New York that have smaller or larger portions of their operations in (or value added generated in) New York.[3] We address this concern to some degree by breaking down the data by industry. However, relatively large effects on a small number of firms whose operations are highly concentrated in New York may be diluted by our more highly aggregated sample, which includes firms with little operational presence.

Finally, the attack on the World Trade Center might raise the fear of attacks in other areas of dense economic activity. As such, differences between share prices of firms located in New York and those of firms located elsewhere would understate the effects of the attacks because some of the comparison locations would also be adversely affected by the attacks.

METHODS AND DATA

Our analysis samples consist of companies included in the S&P 1500 in 2001 drawn from the 2001 Compustat annual file and tracked between January 1997 and June 2002. The S&P 1500 includes companies in the S&P Industrial, S&P MidCap, and S&P SmallCap indexes. We created two main subsamples for analysis: an "inclusive" sample of the 2,083 companies that were included in the S&P 1500 at any time from 1997 to 2001, and a "consistent" sample of the 1,328 companies that were in the S&P 1500 in 2001 and for the entire period of observation from January 1997 to June 2002. Separate analyses were carried out for these two samples.[4] We present figures for the consistent sample. (Corresponding figures for the inclusive sample are similar and available upon request.) Appendix tables 5A.1 and 5A.2 present sample counts for the larger sample and the consistent sample, overall and by major industrial sector.

Our measure of the share price is the monthly closing price for shares of common stock. This abstracts from very short-run changes in expectations. We use an adjustment factor provided by Compustat to account for stock splits. To compute total valuation we multiply the adjusted close price by the number of common shares outstanding. However, for the second quarter of 2002 information on common shares outstanding was unavailable for about half the companies at the time we conducted this analysis. For these companies, we used the number of common shares outstanding at the end of 2001.[5]

Location

Compustat provides information on the location of each company's headquarters by state and county. (Companies in our samples did not change location over the analysis period.) We classified locations as follows: New York City (based on the five New York City counties); New York State; the tristate area (New York, New Jersey, and Connecticut); and outside the tristate area. For each month we calculated the average (across firms in a given area) of the adjusted close price, the total valuation, and the total valuation of all firms for each of the three geographic categories.

We also conducted separate analyses by eleven industry sectors (two-digit SIC code). We defined separate sectors for transportation and public utilities, which form one two-digit SIC, owing to concern about the impact of the WTC attack on transportation in particular.

We also examined quarterly sales as reported on firms' financial reports. We attempted to use net income from income statements. However, enormous write-downs of goodwill at times result in wild quarterly swings in this series. We therefore used a measure of net income on operations, before depreciation.

RESULTS

Share Prices and Company Valuations: Stock Market Data

Figure 5.1 shows the mean share price each month from January 1997 to June 2002. The figure shows a line for New York City (NYC), New York State (NYS), the tristate area, and the nation as a whole outside the tristate area. A guideline is drawn at September 2001 in all figures. Figure 5.1 clearly shows that share prices were in decline prior to 9/11 nationwide, took a sharp dip in September, and generally regained their pre-September levels by the end of November 2001.

Figure 5.2 shows the ratio of share prices of New York companies to those

FIGURE 5.1   MEAN CLOSE PRICES FOR NEW YORK FIRMS AND FOR ALL FIRMS OUTSIDE THE TRISTATE AREA, JANUARY 1997 TO JUNE 2002

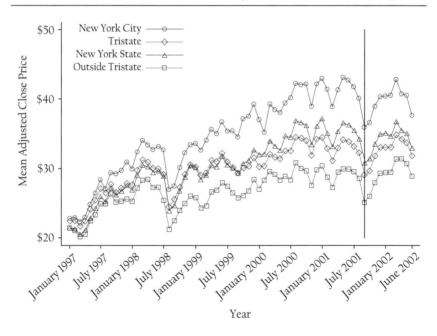

Source: Author's tabulations from Compustat database.

FIGURE 5.2   RATIOS OF MEAN CLOSE PRICES FOR NEW YORK CITY FIRMS
RELATIVE TO FIRMS OUTSIDE NEW YORK CITY, JANUARY 1997
TO JUNE 2002

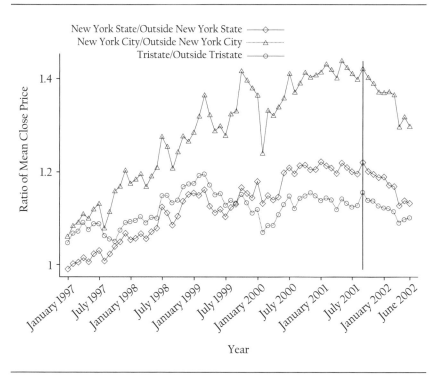

Source: Author's tabulations from Compustat database.

outside New York, for the three different definitions of New York (and outside New York). For example, in the ratio of New York City to outside New York City, the denominator is the average share price for all companies outside of the city. For the ratio of New York State to outside New York State, the denominator is the average share price for firms outside New York State. Figure 5.2 suggests a bit of decline in the relative value of shares of New York companies following September 11. Although the ratio of New York State and tristate companies fell relative to the rest of the nation, there was perhaps a more dramatic fall in New York City share prices. The ratio of the average share price in New York City to the average price of companies located outside New York City fell from nearly 1.4 around September 11 to about 1.3 by the middle of 2002. Nonetheless, this ratio was still far higher than it was at the beginning of the sample period (1997), and it had returned only to about its mid-1999 level by the end of the sample period.

The remaining figures on share prices show data for total valuations. The data are either sums of total valuation of shares (price multiplied by the number of shares) or the ratios of New York valuations to those outside New York. Figures 5.3, 5.4, and 5.5 show the basic pattern: there is a dip in the value of companies nationwide in September 2001 that is essentially erased by the end of November 2001. This dip and rise around September 2001 accounted for tens of billions of dollars but was only a small fraction of either the enormous run-up in valuation between 1997 and 2000 or the decline in valuation from midyear 2000 to midyear 2001.

Figure 5.6 shows more action in the ratios: here there is a perceptible dip in the value of New York firms relative to those outside New York. The decline is most noticeable for the tristate area as a whole, however, where the ratio falls by 0.04 from 0.45 to 0.41, or by about 10 percent. The larger decline in

FIGURE 5.3   TOTAL VALUATION FOR NEW YORK CITY FIRMS AND FOR FIRMS OUTSIDE NEW YORK CITY, JANUARY 1997 TO JUNE 2002

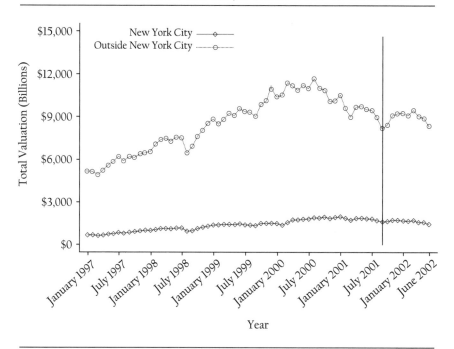

Source: Author's tabulations from Compustat database.

FIGURE 5.4   TOTAL VALUATION FOR NEW YORK STATE FIRMS AND
                FOR FIRMS OUTSIDE NEW YORK STATE, JANUARY 1997 TO
                JUNE 2002

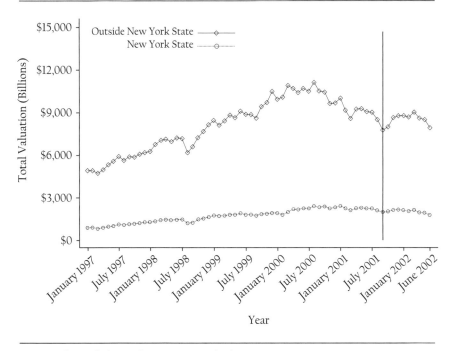

Source: Author's tabulations from Compustat database.

the tristate area as a whole as compared to New York City or New York State was not expected. For example, newspaper accounts describe partial relocation from New York City to Connecticut or New Jersey as a result of September 11. If headquarters actually relocated from the city to Connecticut or New Jersey, the decline in the value of New York City companies should be greater than the decline in Connecticut or New Jersey. Furthermore, even if firms headquartered in New York City simply relocated some activities to New Jersey or Connecticut as a result of the attack on the WTC, the relocation costs should have lowered the profitability of New York firms relative to New Jersey or Connecticut firms. The conclusion we are left with is that the entire tristate area fared worse than the country as a whole, but that New York City did not fall relative to the rest of the tristate area and New York State did not fall relative to New Jersey and Connecticut.

The next set of figures shows the valuations and ratios of valuations by

FIGURE 5.5   TOTAL VALUATION OF TRISTATE FIRMS AND OF FIRMS
OUTSIDE THE TRISTATE AREA, JANUARY 1997 TO JUNE 2002

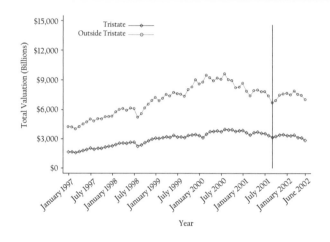

Source: Author's tabulations from Compustat database.

FIGURE 5.6   RATIOS OF TOTAL VALUATION OF NEW YORK CITY, NEW YORK
STATE, AND TRISTATE FIRMS RELATIVE TO FIRMS OUTSIDE THOSE
AREAS, JANUARY 1997 TO JUNE 2002

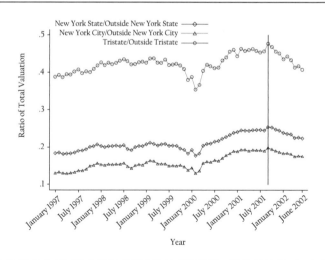

Source: Author's tabulations from Compustat database.

broad industry groups for industries with major representation in the New York area: manufacturing, transportation, public utilities, wholesale and retail trade, FIRE (finance, insurance, and real estate), and other services.

Tristate companies represent about 30 percent of valuation in manufacturing (among these publicly traded companies), and New York City makes up one-third to one-half of the tristate total (figures 5.7 and 5.8). There is little evidence of a 9/11 effect on the value of manufacturing firms, either nationally or in New York relative to the nation.

The tristate region has only a tiny fraction of transportation company valuation (less than .02), and it is difficult to see any region-specific devaluation (figures 5.9 and 5.10); the same is true for the wholesale and retail trade sector (figures 5.11 and 5.12), although the New York shares of total valuation are slightly larger.

Figures 5.13 and 5.14 suggest, if anything, an increasing valuation in New York public utility firms relative to the nation. After 9/11, the valuation of these shares for the nation as a whole continued a steady decline that had begun in

FIGURE 5.7   TOTAL VALUATION OF NEW YORK MANUFACTURING FIRMS, JANUARY 1997 TO JUNE 2002

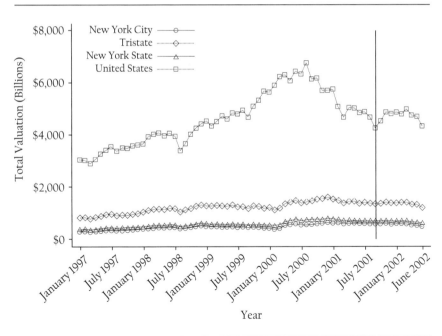

Source: Author's tabulations from Compustat database.

FIGURE 5.8   RATIOS OF TOTAL VALUATION OF NEW YORK MANUFACTURING
FIRMS, JANUARY 1997 TO JUNE 2002

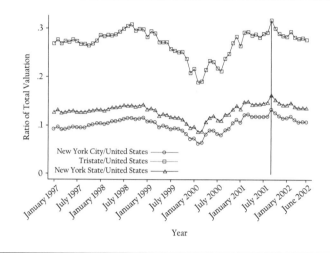

Source: Author's tabulations from Compustat database.

FIGURE 5.9   TOTAL VALUATION OF NEW YORK TRANSPORTATION FIRMS,
JANUARY 1997 TO JUNE 2002

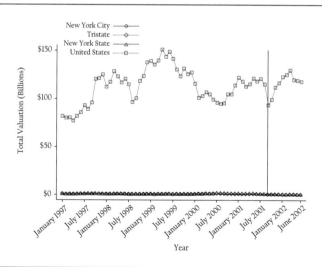

Source: Author's tabulations from Compustat database.

FIGURE 5.10   RATIOS OF TOTAL VALUATION OF NEW YORK
TRANSPORTATION FIRMS, JANUARY 1997 TO JUNE 2002

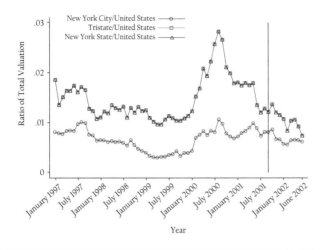

Source: Author's tabulations from Compustat database.

FIGURE 5.11   TOTAL VALUATION OF NEW YORK TRADE, RETAIL, AND
WHOLESALE FIRMS, JANUARY 1997 TO JUNE 2002

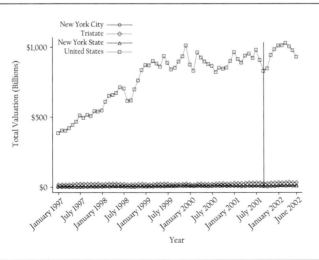

Source: Author's tabulations from Compustat database.

FIGURE 5.12   RATIOS OF TOTAL VALUATION OF NEW YORK TRADE, RETAIL,
AND WHOLESALE FIRMS, JANUARY 1997 TO JUNE 2002

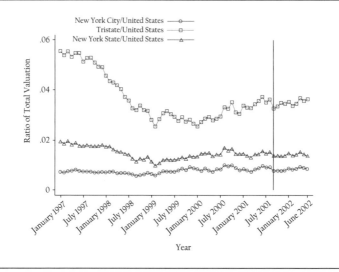

Source: Author's tabulations from Compustat database.

FIGURE 5.13   TOTAL VALUATION OF NEW YORK PUBLIC UTILITY FIRMS,
JANUARY 1997 TO JUNE 2002

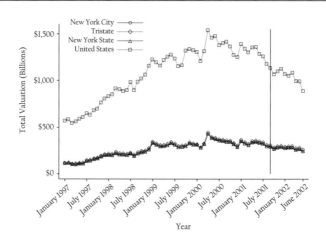

Source: Author's tabulations from Compustat database.

FIGURE 5.14   RATIOS OF TOTAL VALUATION OF NEW YORK PUBLIC UTILITY
FIRMS, JANUARY 1997 TO JUNE 2002

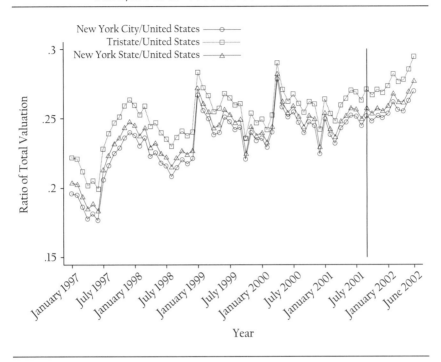

Source: Author's tabulations from Compustat database.

early 2000. Tristate firms account for about one-quarter of the valuation of these companies nationally.

The FIRE sector (figures 5.15 and 5.16) is considered the core of the region's economy, and New York is a prominent player, with New York City accounting for about 40 percent of national valuation in this sector. Figure 5.16 suggests that New York companies in the FIRE sector saw their valuation decline relative to the rest of the nation following 9/11. However, this decline in relative valuation had begun in mid-2000, and 9/11 is again a blip (down, then up) in a steady downward trend. Nonetheless, as of mid-2002, the ratio of city, state, or tristate company valuation remained about one-sixth higher than the 1997 ratio (about 3.5 versus about 3.0). At the peak, in mid-2000, area firms comprised nearly half the total valuation of this sector nationally!

Finally, there is little evidence that the value of publicly traded companies in "other services" located in the New York region has fallen relative to the rest of the nation.

FIGURE 5.15   TOTAL VALUATION OF NEW YORK FIRE, INSURANCE, AND
REAL ESTATE FIRMS, JANUARY 1997 TO JUNE 2002

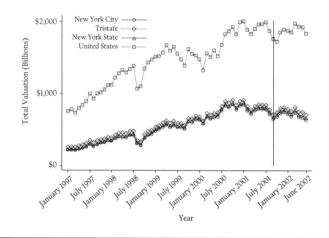

Source: Author's tabulations from Compustat database.

FIGURE 5.16   RATIOS OF TOTAL VALUATION OF NEW YORK FIRE,
INSURANCE, AND REAL ESTATE FIRMS, JANUARY 1997
TO JUNE 2002

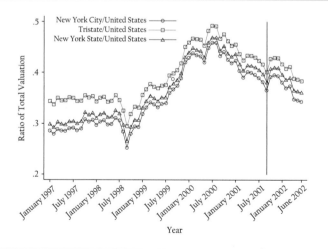

Source: Author's tabulations from Compustat database.

FIGURE 5.17   TOTAL VALUATION OF NEW YORK "OTHER SERVICES" FIRMS, JANUARY 1997 TO JUNE 2002

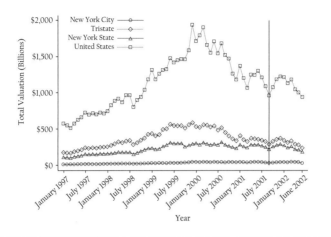

Source: Author's tabulations from Compustat database.

FIGURE 5.18   RATIOS OF TOTAL VALUATION OF NEW YORK "OTHER SERVICES" FIRMS, JANUARY 1997 TO JUNE 2002

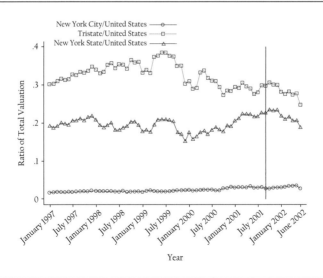

Source: Author's tabulations from Compustat database.

Sales and Net Income: Data from Financial Statements

Although we greatly prefer stock price data because they should indicate quickly what investors expect about the effects of the 9/11 attack on long-run profitability, as an alternative indicator we also present evidence on sales and net income. Figures 5.19 through 5.30 show monthly sales (based on quarterly reports) for a sample of publicly traded firms in New York City, New York State, the tristate area, and for the entire United States, from January 1998 through January 2002. The sample is the "consistent sample" described earlier. Quarterly figures are converted to monthly figures by assuming a uniform distribution of sales over the quarter. Figures 5.19 and 5.20 show sales for all companies in the sample, and figures 5.21 through 5.30 show data for the sectors described earlier. Finally, figures 5.19, 5.21, 5.23, 5.25, 5.27, and 5.29 show total sales, and figures 5.20, 5.22, 5.24, 5.26, 5.28, and 5.30 show New York sales as a fraction of U.S. sales.

Figure 5.19 shows that, after a tremendous run-up, sales flattened early in

FIGURE 5.19   TOTAL SALES FOR NEW YORK FIRMS AND FOR FIRMS
NATIONWIDE, JANUARY 1998 TO JANUARY 2002

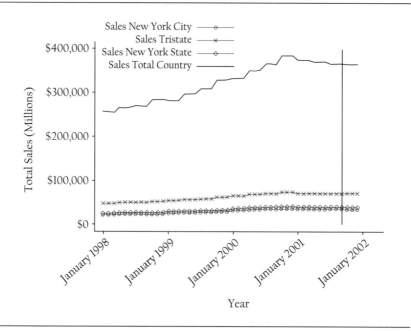

Source: Author's tabulations from Compustat database.

FIGURE 5.20   SHARES OF TOTAL SALES FOR NEW YORK FIRMS, JANUARY
1998 TO JANUARY 2002

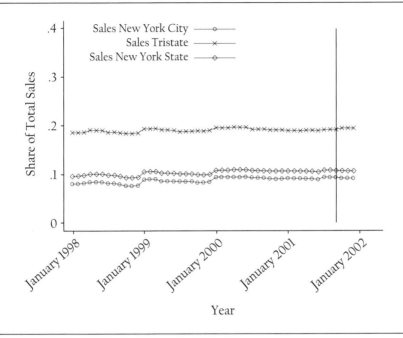

Source: Author's tabulations from Compustat database.

2001. Although there is limited data post-9/11, data through the end of 2001 suggest no noticeable decline in sales in the last quarter of 2001. There is also no evidence of a decline in the New York share of national sales (figure 5.20) for New York City, New York State, or the tristate area.

Figures 5.21 and 5.22 show total sales for the transportation sector; the New York shares are trivial and do not warrant further discussion. Figures 5.23 and 5.24 show sales and sales shares for the services sector; figures 5.25 and 5.26 represent public utilities. There is little evidence of changes in either sector following 9/11.

Sales by manufacturing firms have slowed since early 2001 (figure 5.27) but did not change noticeably after 9/11, and New York companies do not appear to have been affected adversely relative to companies nationally.

Finally, FIRE has seen a downturn since early 2001, but there appears to be no break in trend after 9/11 (figure 5.29). New York firms have also been losing sales shares since early 2001, but this decline did not accelerate after 9/11.

Figures 5.31 through 5.42 present the corresponding time series of net income from operations.

(Text continues on p. 151.)

FIGURE 5.21   TOTAL SALES FOR TRANSPORTATION FIRMS IN NEW YORK AND
NATIONWIDE, JANUARY 1998 TO JANUARY 2002

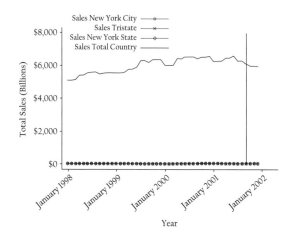

Source: Author's tabulations from Compustat database.

FIGURE 5.22   SHARES OF TOTAL SALES FOR NEW YORK TRANSPORTATION
FIRMS, JANUARY 1998 TO JANUARY 2002

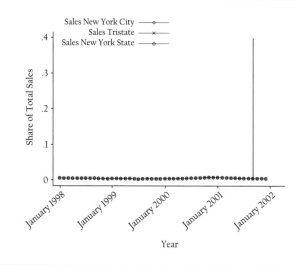

Source: Author's tabulations from Compustat database.

FIGURE 5.23   TOTAL SALES FOR SERVICES FIRMS IN NEW YORK AND
              NATIONWIDE, JANUARY 1998 TO JANUARY 2002

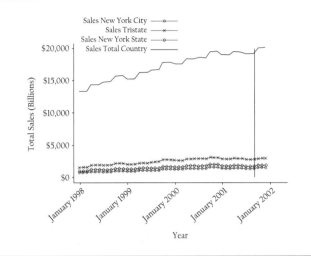

Source: Author's tabulations from Compustat database.

FIGURE 5.24   SHARES OF TOTAL SALES FOR NEW YORK SERVICES FIRMS,
              JANUARY 1998 TO JANUARY 2002

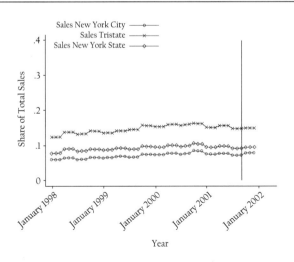

Source: Author's tabulations from Compustat database.

FIGURE 5.25   TOTAL SALES FOR PUBLIC UTILITY FIRMS IN NEW YORK AND
               NATIONWIDE, JANUARY 1998 TO JANUARY 2002

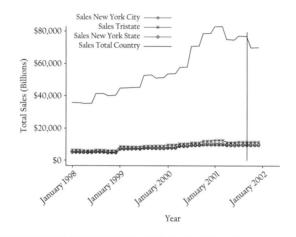

Source: Author's tabulations from Compustat database.

FIGURE 5.26   SHARES OF TOTAL SALES FOR NEW YORK PUBLIC UTILITY FIRMS
               JANUARY 1998 TO JANUARY 2002

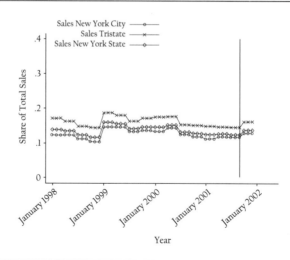

Source: Author's tabulations from Compustat database.

FIGURE 5.27   TOTAL SALES FOR MANUFACTURING FIRMS IN NEW YORK AND NATIONWIDE, JANUARY 1998 TO JANUARY 2002

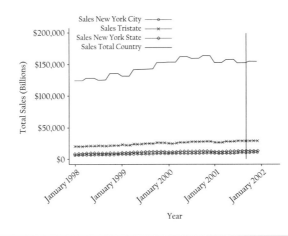

Source: Author's tabulations from Compustat database.

FIGURE 5.28   SHARES OF TOTAL SALES FOR NEW YORK MANUFACTURING FIRMS, JANUARY 1998 TO JANUARY 2002

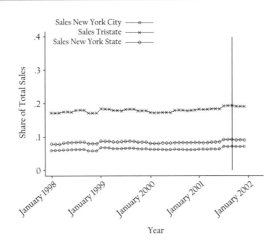

Source: Author's tabulations from Compustat database.

FIGURE 5.29   TOTAL SALES FOR FIRE, INSURANCE, AND REAL ESTATE FIRMS
IN NEW YORK AND NATIONWIDE, JANUARY 1998 TO
JANUARY 2002

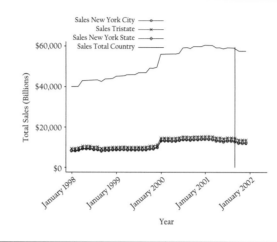

Source: Author's tabulations from Compustat database.

FIGURE 5.30   SHARES OF TOTAL SALES FOR NEW YORK FIRE, INSURANCE,
AND REAL ESTATE FIRMS, JANUARY 1998 TO JANUARY
2002

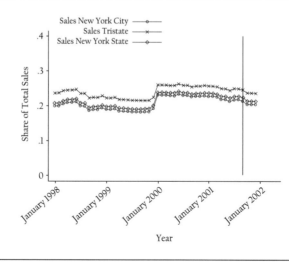

Source: Author's tabulations from Compustat database.

FIGURE 5.31   NET INCOME FOR FIRMS IN NEW YORK AND NATIONWIDE,
              JANUARY 1998 TO JANUARY 2002

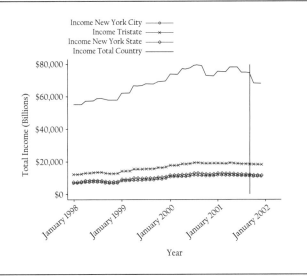

Source: Author's tabulations from Compustat database.

FIGURE 5.32   SHARES OF NET INCOME FOR NEW YORK FIRMS, JANUARY
              1998 TO JANUARY 2002

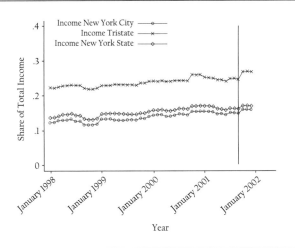

Source: Author's tabulations from Compustat database.

FIGURE 5.33   NET INCOME FOR TRANSPORTATION FIRMS IN NEW YORK
AND NATIONWIDE, JANUARY 1998 TO JANUARY 2002

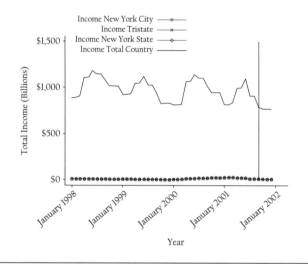

Source: Author's tabulations from Compustat database.

FIGURE 5.34   SHARES OF NET INCOME FOR NEW YORK TRANSPORTATION
FIRMS, JANUARY 1998 TO JANUARY 2002

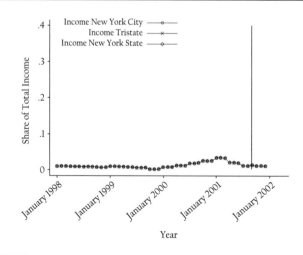

Source: Author's tabulations from Compustat database.

FIGURE 5.35   NET INCOME FOR SERVICES FIRMS IN NEW YORK AND
               NATIONWIDE, JANUARY 1998 TO JANUARY 2002

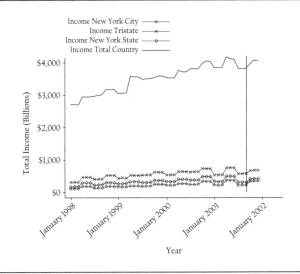

Source: Author's tabulations from Compustat database.

FIGURE 5.36   SHARES OF NET INCOME FOR NEW YORK SERVICES FIRMS,
               JANUARY 1998 TO JANUARY 2002

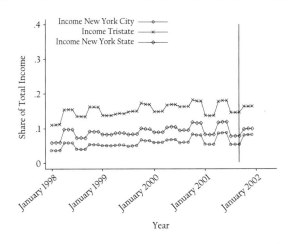

Source: Author's tabulations from Compustat database.

FIGURE 5.37   NET INCOME FOR PUBLIC UTILITY FIRMS IN NEW YORK AND
NATIONWIDE, JANUARY 1998 TO JANUARY 2002

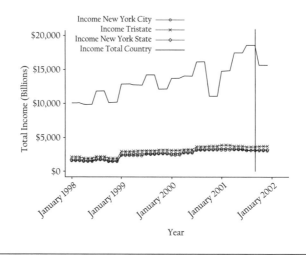

Source: Author's tabulations from Compustat database.

FIGURE 5.38   SHARES OF NET INCOME FOR NEW YORK PUBLIC UTILITY
FIRMS, JANUARY 1998 TO JANUARY 2002

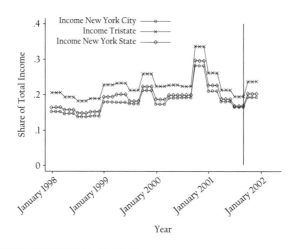

Source: Author's tabulations from Compustat database.

FIGURE 5.39 NET INCOME FOR MANUFACTURING FIRMS IN NEW YORK AND NATIONWIDE, JANUARY 1998 TO JANUARY 2002

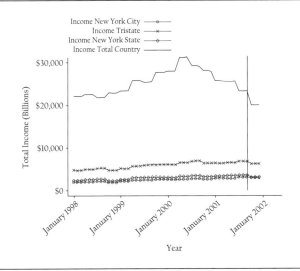

Source: Author's tabulations from Compustat database.

FIGURE 5.40 SHARES OF NET INCOME FOR NEW YORK MANUFACTURING FIRMS, JANUARY 1998 TO JANUARY 2002

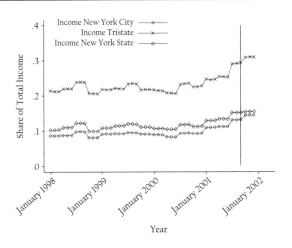

Source: Author's tabulations from Compustat database.

FIGURE 5.41   NET INCOME FOR FIRE, INSURANCE, AND REAL ESTATE FIRMS
IN NEW YORK AND NATIONWIDE, JANUARY 1998 TO
JANUARY 2002

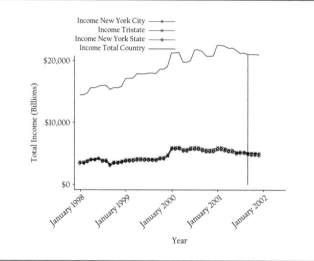

Source: Author's tabulations from Compustat database.

FIGURE 5.42   SHARES OF NET INCOME FOR NEW YORK FIRE, INSURANCE,
AND REAL ESTATE FIRMS, JANUARY 1998 TO JANUARY 2002

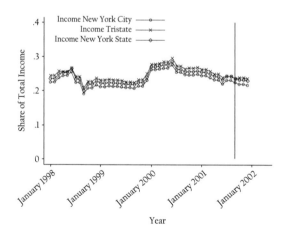

Source: Author's tabulations from Compustat database.

SUMMARY AND DISCUSSION

There is little in the data reviewed here to suggest that investors expected a major adverse impact on New York firms' profitability as a result of the 9/11 terrorist attack on the World Trade Center. That may not mean there has been no impact on firms. It may just mean that relative to the substantial swings in the stock market and, to a lesser extent, sales and net income, the impact of the terrorist attack is difficult to detect. Stock valuations and company sales were already in decline months before the attack, but the attack did not seem to cause major breaks from this trend.

The strongest evidence for an adverse impact is in figures 5.3 and 5.6, which show the share prices and market valuations of New York companies falling relative to those outside New York. However, we find no such dramatic evidence within industry sectors. This suggests that the decline in the overall series is being driven by a relative decline in the sectors in which New York is specialized (such as FIRE) rather than a decline of New York firms compared to other firms in the same sector.

Furthermore, figure 5.6 indicates that, if there are effects of the attack, they appear to be spread throughout the tristate area rather than focused on New York City. The decline in total valuation of companies is most apparent for the tristate area as a whole; the decline in New York City relative to the rest of the country (including the tristate area outside of the city) is very modest. Further research is needed to explore impacts on New Jersey and Connecticut.

This analysis has been graphic and descriptive. However, we doubt that deeper probing with time-series econometric methods would overturn the main conclusions. Perhaps a greater shortcoming is that geographic information is limited to headquarters location. More complete information on the New York presence of firms headquartered in New York would be useful.

If we assume that the "null" finding is correct, what are the larger lessons? One lesson might be that that the city and metropolitan-area economies have shown great resilience to the attack. Even if this is the appropriate conclusion for the metropolitan area as a whole, we may not want to conclude that there were essentially no adverse economic effects of the attack in the medium run, any more than we would conclude from the fact that only a tiny percentage of the population was killed that there were "no" human consequences. The distribution of costs clearly matters. In other words, some very large economic costs may have been concentrated on a small number of businesses, families, and individuals, and smaller losses may have been very widely diffused across the population.

I thank the Russell Sage Foundation for its generous support; the members of the working group on the economic effects of the 9/11 attack on the WTC; Alan Krueger and especially Howard Chernick for their comments. Ana Champeny and Baruch Feldman provided excellent research assistance. I am responsible for all errors.

APPENDIX

TABLE 5A.1   FIRM COUNTS BY S&P INDEX, GEOGRAPHIC AREA, AND SAMPLE

Geographic Area	S&P 500		S&P Mid Cap		S&P Small Cap		Total	
	LS	CS	LS	CS	LS	CS	LS	CS
New York City	43	31	27	12	24	12	94	55
New York State	57	41	45	25	62	41	164	107
Tristate area	99	70	75	43	133	81	307	194
Rest (not tristate)	430	296	485	328	861	510	1,776	1,134
Total	529	366	560	371	994	591	2,083	1,328

Source: Author's tabulations from Compustat database.

TABLE 5A.2   S&P 1,500 FIRM COUNT, BY GEOGRAPHIC AREA, SECTOR, AND SAMPLE

Sector	New York City		New York State		Tristate		Rest (not Tristate)		Total	
	LS	CS	LS	CS	LS	CS	LS	CS	LS	CS
Manufacturing	31	20	58	42	131	90	783	504	914	594
Transportation	1	1	2	2	4	2	52	34	56	36
Trade, retail, and wholesale	4	3	12	8	25	15	206	139	231	154
FIRE	36	18	49	28	65	36	214	147	279	183
Services	12	6	24	15	46	30	250	143	296	173
Public utilities	8	5	16	9	30	15	157	97	187	112
Total	92	53	161	104	301	188	1,662	1,064	1,963	1,252

Source: Author's tabulations from Compustat database.

NOTES

1. For information see www.compustat.com.
2. Of the 2,749 people who died in the terrorist attack on the WTC, 1,179 were

residents of New York City, 597 were residents of New York State outside the city, 679 were residents of New Jersey, and 64 were residents of Connecticut (New York City Department of Health and Mental Hygiene 2003).

3. I thank an anonymous referee for this observation.

4. Information from the quarterly Compustat file was merged with the annual file by company ticker symbol for fiscal years 1996 to 2002. Care was taken to assign fiscal year and month information to the appropriate calendar year and month. We included data from January 1997 through June 2002. The unit of analysis is the company month.

5. For the consistent sample, information on shares outstanding is missing, on average, for about 0.5 percent of companies each month from 1997 through March 2002. For the last quarter included in the sample, we used information on shares outstanding for either the first quarter of 2002 or the last quarter of 2001.

REFERENCES

Beunza, Daniel, and David Stark. 2001. "Trading Sites—Destroyed, Revealed, Restored." Essay in the "After September 11 Archive," Social Science Research Council. Available at: http://www.ssrc.org/sept11/essays/buenza.htm.

Curie, Charles G., administrator of the Substance Abuse and Mental Health Services Administration (SAMHSA). 2002. Testimony before U.S. Senate, Committee on Health, Education, Labor, and Pensions (June 10).

Garfinkel, Irwin, Neeraj Kaushal, Julien Tietler, and Sandra Garcia. 2003. *Vulnerability and Resilience: New Yorkers Respond to 9/11*. New York: Columbia University School of Social Work, Social Indicators Survey Center (September).

Glaeser, Edward L., and Jesse M. Shapiro. 2002. "Cities and Warfare: The Impact of Terrorism on Urban Form." *Journal of Urban Economics* 51(2): 205–24.

New York City Department of Health and Mental Hygiene. Bureau of Vital Statistics. 2003. *Summary of Vital Statistics 2002: The City of New York*. New York: New York City Department of Health and Mental Hygiene (December).

CHAPTER 6

Insurance Coverage for New York City in an Age of Terrorist Risk

Jonathan A. Schwabish and Joshua Chang

> The Congress finds that the ability of businesses and individuals to obtain property and casualty insurance at reasonable and predictable prices, in order to spread the risk of both routine and catastrophic loss, is critical to economic growth, urban development, and the construction and maintenance of public and private housing, as well as to the promotion of United States exports and foreign trade in an increasingly interconnected world.
>
> —Terrorism Risk Insurance Act of 2002
> (P.L. 107–297, sect. 101[a.1])

IN THE post-9/11 world, the insurance industry and the federal government are crucial players in ensuring the economic vitality of New York City and other cities across the country. Businesses in all sectors are dependent on the two players as the primary means of managing risk, which is essential to conducting daily operations and providing the environment for innovation and activity that keeps the city and the country performing as the global economic engine. Together, the insurance industry and the federal government played vital roles in spurring the recovery of New York City after 9/11. One study estimated that the 9/11 attack caused a loss of at least $83 billion in gross economic output to the New York City economy (Partnership for New York City 2001). Even after payment of insurance claims of about $47 billion and promised federal reimbursement for rescue, cleanup, and infrastructure repair costs of about

$20 billion, the net damage to the New York City economy was at least $16 billion (Partnership for New York City 2001).

Immediately following 9/11, the insurance market spiraled into a disequilib-rium that left businesses without affordable insurance to guard against poten-tial terrorist strikes. But even before the attacks, the insurance industry was in a period of financial difficulty. For more than a decade leading up to 2000, the nation's insurance industry had enjoyed a period of strong underwriting capacity and increased profits owing to large returns on investments. This "soft market" period resulted in increased competition that kept insurance premiums low. In the year preceding 9/11, however, the insurance industry underwent a severe decline in value and activity across the nation. The nation-wide recession, itself in part manifested by a significant decline in the stock market, had seriously undermined the portfolios of many of the major insur-ance companies, leading to a so-called hard market (New York City Comptrol-ler 2002; Scanlon 2004; Council of Insurance Agents and Brokers 2001a).[1]

The damage caused by 9/11 led to huge losses in the insurance industry. For the first time in history the U.S. property-casualty insurance industry reported a loss, reaching $7.9 billion in 2001 (Hartwig 2002a). After bearing the brunt of the losses, reinsurers began excluding acts of terrorism from their policies. In turn, primary insurers also excluded acts of terrorism from policies, leaving many businesses in high-risk areas to face the risk of terrorism with no cover-age, inadequate coverage, or coverage that could only be obtained at exorbitant prices. The federal government addressed this private market failure when Congress passed the Terrorism Risk Insurance Act (TRIA) of 2002. For the most part, this law has provided businesses with the option to purchase terror-ism insurance, and those options are more competitively priced than they were prior to TRIA.

TRIA provides an insurance backstop to insurers and covers 90 percent of all losses after the insurer meets its deductible. These deductibles are based on percentages of earned premium income and were set to increase annually from 7 percent in 2003 to 10 percent in 2004 to 15 percent in 2005. In its present form, the law sets an aggregate cap for liability at $100 billion for the government.[2] Insurers are covered under TRIA only if the secretary of the Trea-sury, the secretary of State, and the attorney general of the United States certify an event as a terrorist attack. To be certified under the terms of this law, the terrorist attack must cause aggregate damages of more than $5 million. Further, TRIA covers only a terrorist attack by "any foreign person or foreign interest"; hence, a domestic attack by a citizen—for example, the Oklahoma City bombing in 1995—would not be covered.

Throughout 2005 attention in Washington will focus on the possible exten-sion of TRIA, since it is set to expire at the end of the year. The nation's legislators have several options regarding government intervention in the insurance market, and five possibilities are discussed in this chapter. If TRIA is allowed to expire, businesses—both in New York City and in other parts of the country—may face an insurance market that is unwilling to provide an optimal level of terrorism coverage for the private sector. This may leave businesses vulnerable to greater financial risk in the event of a terrorist attack and may restrict their ability to borrow, expand, and engage in further development and construction. This issue is certainly timely, and policymakers and experts in the field should urge Congress and the White House to develop an optimal and fair level of protection for our nation's cities and business districts.

This chapter focuses on how 9/11 changed the insurance market for businesses in New York City. We begin with an examination of the theory behind terrorism insurance, followed by a discussion of how the private insurance market failed to provide optimal coverage following the 9/11 attacks. In the next section, we discuss the effect of 9/11 on the insurance market for New York City's private sector, assessing the city's risk factors, its relative risk in terms of insured losses, and outline the industry's recommended terrorism insurance rates. We conclude by laying out options for the future of terrorism insurance in the United States.

THE THEORY OF TERRORISM INSURANCE

Prior to 9/11, acknowledgment of the potential risk of a terrorist attack on the United States and ensuing economic losses was not widespread. Hence, terrorism insurance was essentially free and bundled with other types of insurance as an afterthought. Although it is similar to other lines of insurance, terrorism insurance invokes slightly different behavioral distortions and inefficiencies. This section presents a brief overview of the conceptual issues behind terrorism insurance, including moral hazard and adverse selection, the supply and demand of insurance, and the impacts of the 9/11 attacks on other lines of insurance.

Moral Hazard and Adverse Selection

Even in the face of the standard moral hazard dilemma, an insured party can take measures to reduce the likelihood of an event as well as the probability of loss should an event occur. For an individual homeowner, security systems, window and door locks, and smoke detectors help reduce the probability and impact of a break-in or fire. Those who live in coastal areas and are insured can mitigate effects from floods by raising structures or constructing barriers, and those who live close to geological fault lines can counter earthquakes by using flexible materials in construction. With respect to terrorism insurance, there are a few measures that policy holders can take, such as installing blast structures on windows and doors, adding redundancy in security and safety systems, or training building personnel to provide counterterrorism services. Few measures, however, can be taken by policy holders to protect buildings from attacks like those that occurred on 9/11.

Because a policy holder can do nothing to reduce the probability of an attack—or damage from an attack—the purchase of terrorism insurance has little impact on the policy holder's behavior. Hence, the terrorism insurance market is less concerned than other markets about the moral hazard dilemma. There are two more reasons why the purchase of terrorism insurance does not modify the policy holder's behavior: the inherent unpredictability of terrorist attacks and the private market's reliance on government actions (that is, security and other military activities). That being said, terrorism and terrorism insurance may distort the behavior of investors or real estate developers who choose not to invest in or construct a building, or choose to build elsewhere, if insurance cannot be obtained. These behavioral effects are made, however, *before* the insured facility exists; hence, the case of investors and developers is somewhat distinct from the classic case. Illustrating the classic case of the distorting effects of terrorism and terrorism insurance on individual behavior is the choice of tourists, residents, and workers to avoid visiting, living, or working in areas that are likely targets. In sum, because of the inherent inability to predict or protect against a terrorist attack, there are subtle differences between the moral hazard dilemma in the terrorism and other insurance markets.[3]

In addition to the subtle differences in moral hazard, terrorism insurance also introduces a distinction in adverse selection. Firms that view themselves as facing a higher risk of sustaining a terrorist attack are more likely to seek out terrorism insurance than those that do not. In such cases, there is a widening gap in demand between firms that purchase insurance and those that forgo the additional cost. Since insurers are then unable to spread the risk between high- and low-risk companies, terrorism insurance costs remain high. Thus, the adverse selection issue in the terrorism insurance market is not one of asymmetric information (since both parties are aware of the risk) but one in which the disparity between high- and low-risk properties creates a disequilibrium.

For New York City, adverse selection in the terrorism market is especially problematic since the city has a large number of assets that are terrorist targets and therefore require insurance. According to a July 2003 national survey by the Council of Insurance Agents and Brokers (CIAB), 72 percent of insurance brokers reported that their commercial clients were not purchasing terrorism risk coverage. Another survey by the insurance broker Kaye Insurance Associates Inc. found that 40 percent of real estate firms that were advised to buy terrorist risk coverage had not done so. Roughly 68 percent of respondents cited as their primary reason for not purchasing the recommended insurance their belief that they were not themselves a terrorism target (Muto 2003). Hence, because insurers are unable to spread the risk that terrorism presents across a pool of assets, or because the perceived risk is too high to offer insurance, property owners in New York City and across the country are largely unable to obtain or afford terrorism insurance.

Together, issues of moral hazard and adverse selection differ slightly from their counterparts in other insurance markets, yet empirical questions remain. One important question is whether the insurance market is able to sort out these various issues of risk and loss to reach an equilibrium where coverage can be provided so that firms are able to maintain their level of operation and profitability. The aftermath of the 9/11 attacks provides the clearest window for studying the gap between the supply and demand for terrorism insurance and is the focus of the next section.

Supply and Demand

In most markets, firms respond to sudden increases in demand by increasing production to take advantage of higher prices and higher profits. In the aftermath of 9/11, however, primary carriers quickly followed the reinsurance companies' lead by immediately excluding terrorism coverage from new and renewed policies. Aside from the determinants of risk—which include the visibility of the site, the businesses that are located in it, and the potential to incur substantial loss of property and life—insurers and reinsurers reduced or stopped providing insurance after 9/11 for three primary reasons. First, reinsurers bore the majority of the financial cost of the 9/11 terrorist attacks and were unwilling to bear the potential losses from another attack, which at the time seemed likely. Second, prior to 9/11, the insurance industry had entered a period of reduced capital reserves, owing to poor investment returns and the effects of several large natural catastrophes, such as Hurricane Andrew (1992) and the Northridge earthquake (1994) (see Cummins and Lewis 2003). Third, because foreign terrorist attacks in the United States have limited precedence (except for the 1993 bombing of the World Trade Center), insurers were unable to construct reliable risk models (Insurance Services Office 2003; Saxton 2002, 169–72 for a more detailed discussion).

In a simple supply-and-demand framework, if either the supply of or the demand for insurance was perfectly elastic or inelastic, the disequilibrium might not result in a change in price or quantity (although one or the other would change with a supply or demand shift). However, as Kenneth Froot and Paul O'Connell (1997) show, neither supply nor demand is perfectly elastic or inelastic.[4] This implies that the outward shift in demand and the inward shift in supply result in changes in both price and quantity.[5] An increase in the price of terrorism insurance and a decrease in the supply would be expected—a fact borne out in the statistics. In fact, both shifted so dramatically that offers of terrorism insurance were stopped altogether—an extreme version of panel C in figure 6.1.[6] However, with the passage of TRIA, the federal government mandated that insurers offer a minimum supply of terrorism insurance, which is pictured in panel D.

It is difficult to determine how the market will adjust over the long run. The market disequilibrium caused by the 9/11 attacks was more pronounced than after other catastrophic events (see Cummins and Lewis 2003), and there is no consensus on how long the market will need to reach a new equilibrium.[7] Compared to the period right after 9/11, when insurers were not offering terrorism insurance, we would expect the supply curve to shift outward, effectively increasing the quantity in the market. Since demand would shift outward as well, supply would then shift outward even further, resulting in an ambiguous price effect. Although it is difficult to determine what the price of separate terrorism insurance prior to 9/11 would have been, a logical conjecture is that the attacks gave insurers enough information to determine that the price after these supply and demand shifts was higher than what the (unknown) pre-9/11 price would have been.

Spillovers

Trends in other insurance markets may provide some clue to insurers' behavior in the aftermath of 9/11. Of course, there were other confounding events at the time—the anthrax attacks in the months after 9/11, the existing run-up in commercial coverage prices prior to 9/11 (Hillman 2002; Scanlon 2004), and the national recession, which had increased the unemployment rate by 0.8 percentage points over the previous year. All of these factors may have added to the changes taking place in other insurance markets. In fact, between 2001 and 2002, property and casualty losses from the 9/11 attacks, asbestos settlements, hurricanes, and so on, exceeded $50 billion, but capital losses from the global fall in equity values—over $180 billion—were far worse—over $180 billion (Boyle 2003).

The hard market that existed prior to 9/11 makes it difficult to attribute all of these price (premium) increases to the attacks. Anne Gron (1994) defines four stages of the insurance market's underwriting cycle. In the first, profitability is low, with low prices and an abundant supply of insurance. In the second, prices rise rapidly and quantity drops, increasing insurers' profitability. The third stage is characterized by continued high prices while the quantity supplied plateaus, so that profitability is stable. Finally, in the fourth stage, falling prices and abundant quantity translate into falling profitability. The 9/11 attacks no doubt affected capacity, capital, and subsequent pricing in the insur-

FIGURE 6.1   SHIFTS IN SUPPLY AND DEMAND IN THE TERRORISM INSURANCE
MARKET

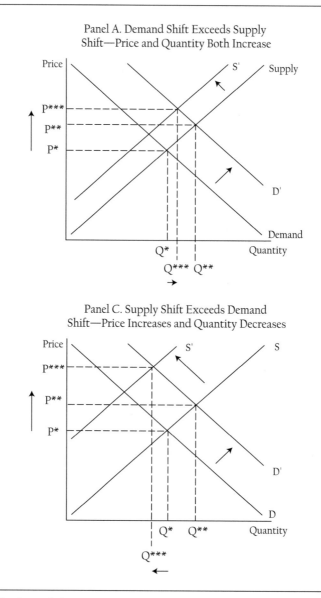

Panel A. Demand Shift Exceeds Supply
Shift—Price and Quantity Both Increase

Panel C. Supply Shift Exceeds Demand
Shift—Price Increases and Quantity Decreases

Source: Authors' compilation.
Notes: Panels A through D show that shifts in supply and demand in and for insurance result in
an increase in price (quantity returns only to its original level in panel B). Similar results would
hold if either or both supply and demand were elastic, or inelastic, but as Froot and O'Connell
(1997) show, that is unlikely. The most realistic depiction of the post-9/11 market is in panel C,

FIGURE 6.1   *CONTINUED*

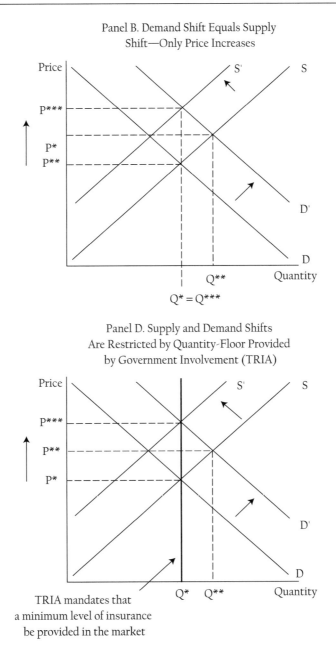

Panel B. Demand Shift Equals Supply
Shift—Only Price Increases

Panel D. Supply and Demand Shifts
Are Restricted by Quantity-Floor Provided
by Government Involvement (TRIA)

TRIA mandates that
a minimum level of insurance
be provided in the market

where the decrease in the supply of insurance being offered greatly outpaced the increase in demand. The effect of these shifts is to increase the price (more so than in panels A and B) and to decrease the available quantity of insurance. Panel D shows how TRIA's mandate that insurance be provided guarantees a minimum level of quantity while price still increases owing to shifts in supply and demand.

ance market, but it is important to realize that the price increases after the attacks here were not solely attributable to 9/11 and were driven at least in part by other trends in the economy.

The pricing cycle in one insurance market affects other lines of insurance. Clearly after 9/11 we would expect these spillover effects to be greatest in New York City, Washington, D.C., and elsewhere in the greater Northeast region. September 11 changed not only insurers' expectations for future attacks and subsequent pricing behavior in the terrorism insurance market but also the pricing and purchasing behavior of firms in other insurance markets, from commercial property to general liability. The next section turns from theory to the empirical evidence on the impact of 9/11 on the insurance industry and the implications for New York City.

THE EFFECT OF 9/11 ON INSURANCE COVERAGE FOR NEW YORK CITY

In this period of uncertainty, large cities around the country face increased risk. Although insurers do not insure cities, on the whole, assets in a city add to the level of risk, since a large concentration of probable targets raises the perceived risk for surrounding assets. Dense cities, such as New York City, provide large economies of agglomeration. These economies enhance productivity, reduce costs, and are the drivers of the U.S. economy. The shock and disruption that result from a terrorist attack in a dense city create greater economic loss and serve to undermine the economies of density realized in these urban economies.

This section focuses on the effect of the attacks of 9/11 on insurance coverage for New York City by first identifying the characteristics that make New York City a greater risk for a terrorist attack. We then describe the effects of these risks on the potential for insured losses and the increased cost of terrorism insurance and compare them to other cities. Finally, we present several anecdotes that relate the effects of 9/11 on the ability of business to obtain insurance.

A Risk Profile of New York City

New York City is at higher risk for insured losses than other cities for several reasons. First, Manhattan has a large concentration of symbolic and economic targets, including high-profile buildings, buildings that house U.S.-based global corporations, Wall Street, tourist attractions, and transportation hubs, all of which are appealing targets to terrorists. New York City's high concentration of tall buildings—sixty-seven of its buildings have fifty or more floors—is

TABLE 6.1   BUILDINGS WITH FIFTY FLOORS OR
MORE IN THE UNITED STATES

City	Buildings with Fifty Floors or More
New York	67
Chicago	39
Houston	11
Los Angeles	10
Dallas	10
Atlanta	8
Seattle	5
Philadelphia	5
Minneapolis	4
Denver	3
Boston	2
Cleveland	2
Miami	2
San Francisco	1
Charlotte	1

Source: Saxton (2002).

almost twice that of the next city, Chicago, and more than that of the next thirteen cities combined (table 6.1).

Second, terrorist attacks that occur in dense urban environments result in vastly higher losses than similar events that occur at targets in less dense cities, in suburbs, or in rural areas. New York City dwarfs other cities across America. Data from the 2000 U.S. Census make it possible to compute the population per square mile of every city and county in the United States. As table 6.2 shows, New York City is by far the densest city in the country, with over 26,000 people per square mile. New York County (Manhattan) drives this figure with a density of almost 67,000 people per square mile—four times as dense as all of San Francisco.

Third, New York City has already been attacked twice, and there have been several other foiled attempts in recent years. Not only has New York City endured the only two foreign terrorist attacks on American soil, but the two events rank among the world's top ten largest insured losses from terrorism. The 9/11 attacks rank as the costliest in the world at around $47 billion in insured losses (table 6.3).

TABLE 6.2   DENSITY OF U.S. CITIES AND COUNTIES, 2000

	Population	Land (Square Miles)	Population per Square Mile
Cities			
New York City	8,008,278	303.3	26,403
San Francisco	776,733	46.7	16,634
Chicago	2,896,016	227.1	12,750
Boston	589,141	48.4	12,166
Philadelphia	1,517,550	135.1	11,234
Washington	572,059	61.4	9,316
Baltimore	651,154	80.8	8,058
Los Angeles	3,694,820	469.1	7,877
Counties			
New York (N.Y.)	1,537,195	23.0	66,940
Kings (N.Y.)	2,465,326	70.6	34,917
Bronx (N.Y.)	1,332,650	42.0	31,709
Queens (N.Y.)	2,229,379	109.2	20,409
Hudson (N.J.)	608,975	46.7	13,044
Suffolk (Mass.)	689,807	58.5	11,788
San Juan (P.R.)	434,374	47.8	9,084
Richmond (N.Y.)	443,728	58.5	7,588

Source: Authors' calculations using the 2000 U.S. Census.

TABLE 6.3   LARGEST INSURED LOSSES FROM TERRORISM, 1970 TO 2001 (MILLIONS OF 2001 DOLLARS)

Event	Country	Number of Victims	Insured Loss
Attack on the World Trade Center (2001)	United States	2,823	$47,000
Bombing in city of London (1993)	United Kingdom	1	907
Bombing in Manchester (1996)	United Kingdom	0	744
World Trade Center bombing (1993)	United States	6	725
Bombing in London's financial district (1992)	United Kingdom	3	671
Suicide bombing in Colombo Airport (2001)	Sri Lanka	20	398
Bombing at London's South Key Docklands (1996)	United Kingdom	2	259
Oklahoma City bombing (1995)	United States	166	145
PanAm Boeing 747 explosion at Lockerbie (1988)	United Kingdom	270	138
Dynamiting of hijacked airplanes in Zarqa (1970)	Jordan	0	127

Source: Partnership for New York City (2001); Saxton (2002).

Potential Insured Losses for New York City Compared to Other U.S. Cities

After 9/11, major risk-modeling firms quickly developed probabilistic terrorism insurance models based on their catastrophe modeling of natural hazards such as earthquakes and hurricanes. These terrorism risk models rely on broad assumptions about targets and potential attacks. Unlike the natural catastrophe market, for which a substantial history exists to help determine trends, terrorist attacks lack any such history, being significantly less predictable and having occurred less frequently.

The models are designed to enable insurers to price and manage accumulated exposures to terrorism losses from various simulated attacks. The models estimate loss probability distributions, expected annual losses, and scenario losses for workers' compensation and property exposures. There are two main parts to calculating loss distributions from potential attacks. First, the models determine the type of terrorist attack, including a variety of conventional and nonconventional attacks with various types of weapons. Second, a list of likely terrorist targets is assembled, using the expertise of military and intelligence agencies. The models base the potential average annual loss figures for exposed values (human life, property, and interruption of business activity) on several factors, including the amount of insured loss and the probability and frequency of attack. These events are modeled at potential terrorist targets across the United States and include property, workers' compensation, and direct business interruption losses.

Based on an analysis from the risk-modeling firm Risk Management Solutions, Inc. (2002), approximately 50 percent of the nation's potential average annual insured loss due to terrorism is concentrated in New York City.[8] The size of this estimate is largely due to the city's density and large number of high-profile targets. While many large cities saw a slight increase in potential average annual insured loss from 2002 to 2003, New York City's share decreased from about 65 percent to 50 percent. This decrease stems mainly from international efforts to curb terrorism and domestic efforts—both nationally and locally—to reduce the probability of another attack. In 2004, RMS models show that New York City's share remained at about 50 percent. The city with the second highest share, Chicago, had about 15 percent of the country's potential average annual loss; San Francisco followed with 8 percent and Washington, D.C., with 5 percent (figure 6.2).

Relative Risk for Major Urban Counties

The risk-modeling firm AIR Worldwide Corporation (2003) calculates the relative risk (in terms of potential average annual insured loss, with Washington,

FIGURE 6.2   POTENTIAL AVERAGE ANNUAL INSURED LOSS FOR MAJOR U.S. CITIES, 2002 TO 2003

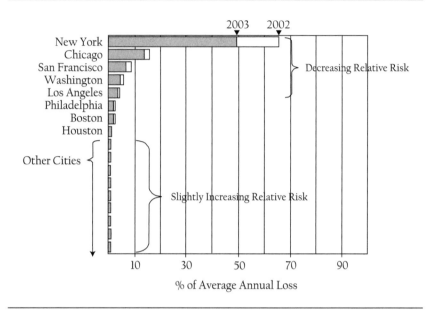

Source: Risk Management Solutions, Inc. (2002).

D.C., normalized to one) from terrorist attacks at the county level and finds that the potential average annual insured loss in Manhattan is thirteen times greater than in Washington, D.C., four times greater than in Los Angeles, and three times greater than in Chicago (see table 6.4).[9] When all five boroughs (counties) of New York City are analyzed, New York's relative risk in terms of potential average annual insured losses rises to 14.20. This elevated level of risk for the entire city reflects the potential impact of a terrorist attack on Manhattan on the four neighboring boroughs.

Terrorism Risk Exposure by City

The Terrorism Risk Insurance Act provided the necessary backstop for the insurance industry to begin covering terrorism risk. However, with a lack of loss cost data and experience in assessing terrorism risk, the insurance industry depended on the models cited here to determine the relative risk across the country. The Insurance Services Office (ISO), the insurance industry's technical support organization, is mandated by law to submit summaries of hun-

TABLE 6.4   RELATIVE RISK IN TERMS OF AVERAGE
            ANNUAL INSURED LOSSES FOR MAJOR
            U.S. COUNTIES

County	Relative Risk
New York County (Manhattan)	13.02
Cook County (Chicago)	4.12
Los Angeles County (Los Angeles)	3.01
San Francisco County (San Francisco)	1.24
Washington, D.C.	1.00
Harris County (Houston)	0.65
Suffolk County (Boston)	0.41
King County (Seattle)	0.40
Philadelphia County (Philadelphia)	0.30
Dallas County (Dallas)	0.30

Source: AIR Worldwide Corp. (2003).

dreds of millions of policies, including premiums and losses, to insurance regulators to help them evaluate the price of insurance in each state. ISO evaluated the output of the AIR terrorism model in determining three rating tiers across the country, which are shown in table 6.5. The tiers reflect a gradation in expected terrorism losses, from areas with highly concentrated property values and numerous attractive targets (tier 1), to areas with an elevated potential for

TABLE 6.5   ISO RECOMMENDED TERRORISM INSURANCE RATES FOR U.S. CITIES

Tier	Description	Cities	Terrorism Insurance Rate Recommendation
1	Areas with highly concentrated property values and numerous attractive targets	New York, Chicago, Washington, D.C., San Francisco	$0.03 per $100
2	Areas with an elevated potential for terrorist loss due to property concentration and available targets	Houston, Seattle, Los Angeles, Philadelphia, Boston	$0.018 per $100
3	Areas whose exposure to terrorist loss is small	Rest of the United States	$0.001 per $100

Source: Brady (2003).

terrorist loss due to property concentration and available targets (tier 2), to areas whose average exposure to terrorist loss is small (tier 3).[10]

In 2003, ISO modeled the risk left to the private insurance market under the provisions laid out by TRIA. Stratifying the country into three risk tiers (New York City is a member of tier 1, the highest-risk tier), ISO determined the proportion left to the private market. Nationwide, in year one of TRIA, the private market covers 47 percent of losses, 61 percent in year two, and 74 percent in year three. Similarly, in year one (2003) cities in tier 1 would cover 40 percent of losses, but tier 2 and tier 3 cities would cover 75 percent and 90 percent, respectively, of losses, since their risk is considerably less. In year two, the tiers would cover 55 percent, 85 percent, and 95 percent; and similarly in year three (70 percent, 95 percent, and 100 percent) as the TRIA-defined deductibles increase. Because of these issues of agglomeration and economies of scale, this recommendation appears to favor cities that are at greater risk of a terrorist strike than other areas of the country.

Evidence of the Insurance Effects of 9/11 Across the Country

The effects of 9/11 were not isolated to the terrorism insurance market. Price increases in other insurance markets, including commercial property, general liability, and umbrella coverage, increased across the country. Quarterly results from the Council of Insurance Agents and Brokers' Commercial Insurance Market Index Survey show a majority of firms were reporting a "somewhat hard" market in most lines of insurance in 2000 (see also New York City Comptroller 2002; Scanlon 2004) and price increases up to, and through, the 9/11 attacks.[11]

For most accounts, firms reported price increases in the third quarter of 2000, especially in the Northeast. Nationally, 49 percent of firms were reporting price increases that exceeded 10 percent. For medium and large accounts in the Northeast and the Midwest, over 60 percent of respondents were reporting price increases exceeding 10 percent. This contrasts sharply with the 40 to 50 percent of respondents reporting similar price increases in other parts of the country.

By the third quarter of 2001, in reaction to the 9/11 attacks, prices had increased dramatically for large accounts, with the brunt of the increases falling on businesses in the Northeast region. Nationally, 82 percent of the CIAB's members reported price increases exceeding 10 percent, while in the Northeast this proportion reached almost 90 percent (figure 6.3). By 2002 the share of firms continuing to see these large price increases had fallen to 75 percent, while the share remained steady in the Northeast. By the third quarter of 2003, the insurance market appeared to have settled down: only 18 percent of firms

FIGURE 6.3   PERCENTAGE OF RESPONDENTS REPORTING LARGE CHANGES
IN PREMIUM RATES: LARGE ACCOUNTS NATIONWIDE AND
IN THE NORTHEAST

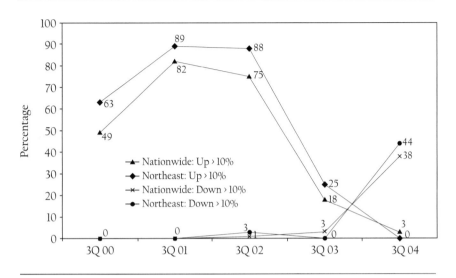

Source: CIAB (various years).
Note: Large changes are premium increases greater than 10 percent. Large accounts are firms with premiums greater than $100,000.

nationwide reported large price increases in large accounts. Price increases in the Northeast, however, remained higher than the national average at 25 percent. It is likely, though difficult to confirm quantitatively, that most of these price increases were driven by the New York City and Washington, D.C., insurance markets.

By the third quarter of 2004, pricing appeared to settle lower, with only 3 percent of firms nationwide reporting price increases greater than 10 percent. At the same time, the proportion of firms reporting significant price *decreases* had increased to 44 percent in the Northeast and 38 percent nationwide (see figure 6.3). Although the CIAB survey does not allow for a further decomposition, which would make it possible to examine the experience in specific cities, the trends are illustrative of the impact that 9/11 had on insurance pricing behavior in the Northeast for a wide range of insurance lines.

Marsh Inc. (2004b) also provides evidence that terrorism insurance prices were beginning to fall nationally in late 2003, owing, at least in part, to increases in take-up rates. Take-up rates are defined as the percentage of businesses purchasing insurance at a specified time or during a specified interval.

For the last three quarters of 2003, Marsh Inc. (2004b) found that the take-up rate for terrorism insurance rose from 23.5 percent in the second quarter to 26.0 percent in the third quarter to 32.7 percent in the fourth quarter. On average over the three quarters, the take-up rate was 27.3 percent. The June 2004 update shows that take-up rates increased even further in the first quarter of 2004, to over 40 percent. In analyzing take-up rates by region, Marsh Inc. found that the Northeast has a higher take-up rate (30.3 percent) than the other regions of the country (figure 6.4) in 2003. The report concludes that "the fact that the Northeast ranks highest ... must reflect, to some unquantifiable degree, the fact that the September 11 attacks took place in New York City and Washington, D.C."

Further evidence from Marsh Inc. (2004a) points to increases in take-up rates in terrorism insurance over the latter part of 2003 and the first quarter of 2004. Between the second quarter of 2003 and the first quarter of 2004, terrorism insurance take-up rates increased from 23.5 percent to 26.0 percent to 32.7 percent to 44.2 percent—a remarkable 20.7-percentage-point increase in less than a year. The increase in take-up rates was balanced across industry and firm value and may reflect a better economy, since decreasing premiums for other lines of insurance enable firms to fill gaps in their insurance coverage.

FIGURE 6.4   TERRORISM TAKE-UP RATES BY REGIONAL MARSH OFFICE, 2003

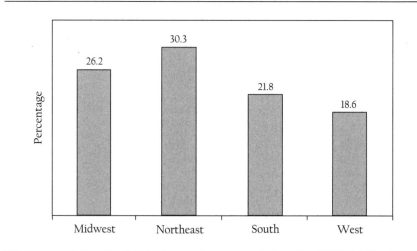

Source: Marsh (2004b).

Evidence of the Insurance Effects of 9/11 on New York City

The economic importance of terrorism insurance is well established.[12] In the post-9/11 world, the absence and high cost of terrorism insurance were drags on business activity. Low coverage limits left large exposures for businesses, and many firms could not proceed with normal activity. Ratings agencies lowered debt ratings for potential projects that were unable to obtain terrorism insurance. In turn, the absence of terrorism insurance and the lower ratings issued by the ratings agencies led many banks not to proceed with the funding of construction projects and real estate transactions.[13] A wealth of anecdotal evidence supports this point; we cite six representative examples here:

- Moody's Investors Service cut the AAA ratings on eleven separate issues of commercial mortgage–backed securities totaling $4.5 billion. The trigger for the downgrades was the inability of the owners of the underlying properties to obtain full terrorism insurance cover. Asset-backed securities deals offer greater security than most loans, so the downgrades increased market anxiety. The commercial assets that were downgraded included 280 Park Avenue, 1211 Avenue of the Americas, 1251 Avenue of the Americas, and Four Times Square Trust (Cohen 2002).

- The Empire State Building carried more than $600 million of property and liability insurance prior to 9/11, with an annual premium of approximately $1 million. After the attacks, the Empire State Building obtained substantially less coverage for property and liability, including terrorism insurance, for a premium of $9 million—nine times the premium prior to 9/11 (Malkin 2004).

- A plan to build a thirty-story residential building that would have employed approximately five hundred workers was stopped. The project was put on hold because the builder was unable to find the terrorism insurance required by the bank financing it (Saxton 2002).

- Prior to 9/11, the prospective buyer of a trophy property was close to securing $200 million in financing. After the attacks, the deal was halted because the prospective buyer was unable to find terrorism insurance, as required by the lender, that would cover the replacement value of the property (Saxton 2002).

- Fleet Bank put two large loans on hold owing to lack of terrorism insurance. The loans would have gone to a $300 million real estate purchase and a $100 million construction project (Saxton 2002).

- In 2001 the Metropolitan Transportation Authority (MTA) paid $6 million for a $1.5 billion policy. In 2002 the MTA paid $18 million for a $500 million policy that excludes terrorism losses. A separate terrorism policy was obtained, but it provides just $70 million in coverage at a cost of $7.5 million (Saxton 2002).

The New York City comptroller's office conducted a survey of insurance agents and brokers serving businesses located throughout New York City. The survey asked respondents to report rate increases and availability for nine lines of property and casualty coverage in the year before and the year following 9/11. The survey found that premiums for all business sizes increased dramatically following 9/11. For large accounts (more than $1 million in premiums), the average premium increase jumped from 11.4 percent to 73.3 percent (see figure 6.5). In 2002 premium increases in accounts across the country rose by 20 percent, roughly one-third of the rate of premium increase in New York City. About half of the national rate increase was related to the terrorist attack (Hartwig 2002b).

The comptroller's survey also found a decline in the availability of insurance for all accounts. For large accounts in New York City, those survey respon-

FIGURE 6.5   AVERAGE PREMIUM INCREASES BY ACCOUNT SIZE IN
              NEW YORK CITY

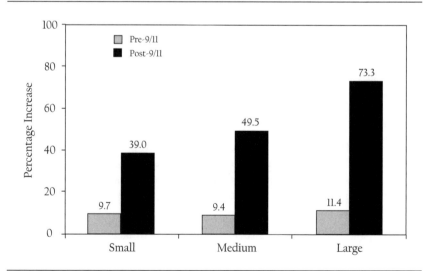

Source: New York City Comptroller (2002).

FIGURE 6.6   AVAILABILITY OF INSURANCE BY ACCOUNT SIZE: PERCENTAGE
OF RESPONDENTS RATING INSURANCE AS BEING "READILY
AVAILABLE" OR "SOMEWHAT AVAILABLE" IN NEW YORK CITY

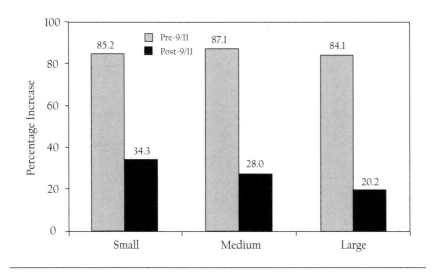

Source: New York City Comptroller (2002).

dents who rated insurance as being "readily available" or "somewhat available" fell from 84.1 percent to 20.2 percent (figure 6.6). These trends—a substantial decline in availability coupled with an increase in the average premium—lead to the intuitive conclusion that insurance costs rose much faster in New York City than in the rest of the country.

OPTIONS FOR FEDERAL ACTION

Following the 9/11 attacks, the private insurance market effectively broke down—terrorism insurance was rarely offered in new or renewed contracts, and the insurance that was being offered was so costly that few companies could afford to purchase it. The attacks exacerbated a market situation that was already undergoing a substantial shift in its value as portfolios and investments declined with the U.S. economy. Using TRIA as a backup, the market found its footing, although private market premiums are still extraordinarily high in some parts of the country.

Unless it is renewed, TRIA will expire at the end of 2005. Key members of Congress are waiting for the June 2005 Treasury Department report evaluating the effectiveness of TRIA before making a decision on TRIA renewal. Even if it is renewed, the law is considered an interim solution for managing terrorism risk and assumes that the private terrorism insurance market will stabilize in a few years. During that time, property and casualty insurers will work to develop reliable models for pricing this insurance. When the Treasury secretary ruled on June 18, 2004, to extend the "make available" provision of TRIA for an additional year in advance of the September 2004 deadline, the federal government sent a clear signal that acting in advance of the provision's expiration would help avoid market disruptions (U.S. Department of the Treasury 2004).[14]

Would the gap between the supply and demand of insurance have extended further had the government not intervened? Trends in profit margins along with acknowledged risk and difficulty in assessing that risk make that question difficult to answer (although with time an answer should become clearer). Cummins and Lewis (2003) show that the market value of insurance companies fell noticeably right after 9/11 and that the effects lingered for a full month after the attacks, with only small signs of subsiding, although these effects differed by firm rating.[15] Sanders Korenman (this volume) shows that New York City–based firms saw no appreciable drop in their stock price owing to 9/11 compared to companies elsewhere in the United States. To date, no research has shown that the terrorism insurance market would have adjusted to a new equilibrium in the months and years after 9/11. However, given the change since 9/11 in how insurers (and the insured) view terrorism on domestic soil, there is little reason to believe that the terrorism insurance market would have adjusted to affordable levels. In fact, in the absence of government intervention, the terrorism insurance market may never feature actuarially fair prices or high participation because of the inherent unpredictability of the terrorist risk.

Given these shifts in supply and demand and the government's response to the terrorist attacks in the insurance market, is it advisable to create a permanent federal terrorism insurance program?[16] If the government were to extend TRIA (or something similar) indefinitely, distortions in the insurance market would certainly ensue. It is not clear whether these distortions would manifest themselves in pricing and capital allocation in the insurance industry or in an increase in the nation's deadweight loss by changes in tax rates, or both. What is also clear is that New York City, because of its higher density and risk profile, would witness a significant increase in its average business costs—disproportionate to other low-risk areas of the country—as insurance rates rise. However, a permanent government terrorism insurance subsidy could be welfare-improving if other related costs are lowered and other distorting behavior is minimized.

TRIA has enabled businesses to obtain valuable insurance that would probably not be otherwise available. It has helped maintain a positive environment for borrowing, expansion, development, and construction and indirectly may have helped the nation avoid plunging into a deeper recession. The early extension of the "make available" provision demonstrates the importance that policymakers see in making early TRIA-related extension decisions. As the debate over the law's extension continues, we can only hope that the cooperation between business and government will continue (see also Kunreuther and Michel-Kerjan 2004).

The key question going forward is, what role, if any, will the government play in the provision of terrorism insurance? Delayed action by the government puts business's ability to make insurance and other investment decisions at risk. To prevent either of these possibilities from becoming a reality, the private sector and Washington have at least five options to consider. One option, or a combination of these options, may work effectively. With input from members of the business community and the insurance industry, the federal government should act early and expeditiously to reach a consensus on the most workable option, a set of options, or a temporary extension of TRIA if the parties are unable to reach a consensus. Without action on a new approach or an extension of TRIA, businesses in high-risk areas like New York will face reduced access to coverage and higher terrorism insurance premiums for the coverage they do obtain. Inaction in Washington will create a drag on economic growth in New York and other large cities.

Option 1: Allow TRIA to Expire

When TRIA was originally passed in November 2002, many hoped that by the time it was set to expire the insurance industry would be able to assess the risk of terrorism and model the costs and subsequent prices. The market does seem to be settling as prices have fallen slightly through late 2003 and 2004 (Marsh Inc. 2004b; CIAB, various years), but much uncertainty remains. Given these trends, some believe that TRIA should be allowed to expire, while others have called for a temporary extension to give the industry more time to adjust (Ayer 2004). A two-year extension has been proposed by members of the insurance industry and seems to enjoy some support in Congress (U.S. Senate 2004); such an extension might give the industry much needed time to achieve the goals set out in 2002. The obvious question, of course, is whether a two-year extension granted in 2005 will lead to other extension requests in the future, effectively making TRIA a permanent government program.

In an April 2004 report, the Consumer Federation of America (CFA) (Hunter 2004) posits three reasons why TRIA is no longer needed. First, the high deductible levels under TRIA minimize its overall impact. Second, the insurance industry is fundamentally sound and the private market will find ways to provide coverage. And third, taxpayers should not be responsible for providing a backstop to only a few high-risk areas; instead, the private market should—and it is believed will—ultimately provide terrorism insurance.[17] A recent Congressional Budget Office (2005) report agrees with CFA and concludes that TRIA has served its purpose over the first two years of enactment and that the expiration of TRIA would not have negative effects on the country but would spur the private sector to find its own solution while absolving the nation's taxpayers of the burden.

Although profitability in the insurance market may now be on the rise, it is clear that the private market failure after 9/11 exposed gaps in the industry and the perception of terrorism insurance. It is not clear whether the industry has filled these holes, but competition in the marketplace should help.

Additionally, the fact that the risk of terrorist attack extends to only a few areas of the country should not negate the need for a federal role. These high-risk areas represent over 11 percent of the nation's population, and part of an overall public goods argument should be that a nation provides protection for *all* its citizens, regardless of location and subsequent risk. This public goods argument rests on the claim that everyone in the nation "consumes" an efficiently insured dense-urban-areas policy, regardless of whether they actually live in such an urban center. A 2004 study by R. Glenn Hubbard and Bruce Deal (2004) discussed the economic effects of extending TRIA and calculated that in the absence of TRIA U.S. gross domestic product (GDP) may be $53 billion lower and that roughly 326,000 fewer jobs may be created. As Christopher Nassetta, CEO of Marriott Hotels, testified in May 2004 before a Senate hearing: "To suggest that terrorism insurance is relevant to only nine U.S. urban areas is ludicrous."

Its high deductible and aggregate cap may keep TRIA from being of any particular value to the insurance industry. Conceptually, perhaps the federal government should not play the role of insurer to the nation's businesses (see, for example, Gron and Sykes 2002; O'Neill 2001; McCool 2001). Overall, it remains to be seen what would happen in the private market without a government backstop; further research should help assess the market's ability to provide terrorism insurance without government intervention.

Option 2: Extend TRIA Permanently

There is little doubt that the insurance industry viewed TRIA favorably—federally backed support to the entire industry would no doubt be viewed positively by any industry (see Oster 2001).[18] Should it be the federal government's job to provide a permanent backstop to terrorism insurance permanently? Is a long-term TRIA program viable—both politically and economically—in the United States?

Between unemployment insurance, workers' compensation, the trade adjustment assistance program for workers who lose their jobs to overseas competition, and other programs, the federal government has several programs in place to provide a backstop for workers in the labor market. But should the federal government be in the business of providing insurance to all firms when a private market—though perhaps overpriced—does in fact exist? It is not just a theoretical question: in the terrorism insurance market the government's potential liability of up to $100 billion (as laid out in TRIA) exceeds most rational expectations of loss.

In recent decades, the federal government has stepped in to provide insurance or financial support to industries that have been unable to obtain coverage from insurers in the private sector. The level of federal government involvement ranges from no government subsidies (Pension Benefit Guaranty Corporation insurance)[19] to partial government subsidies (the National Insurance Development Program)[20] to full government subsidies (federal crop insurance and national flood insurance) (U.S. General Accountability Office 2001).

Left to the market, terrorism insurance may induce inefficiencies, distortions, and crowding-out; it is arguable how these would compare to government-provided insurance (see Brown, Kroszner, and Jenn 2002). Under the current TRIA legislation, the federal government is responsible for losses up to a maximum of $100 billion, but revisions to the legislation might lower that limit. Other possible modifications include limiting taxpayer support to attacks that include weapons of mass destruction, such as chemical, biological, and nuclear weapons, or further limiting the government's role in both regulation and financial liability (see also Hunter 2004).

Option 3: Create an Insurance Pool to Be Run Privately

When a series of terrorist attacks in Great Britain in 1992 led insurers to refuse to offer terrorism coverage, government intervention was immediately necessary. In 1993 the Pool Reinsurance Company Ltd. ("Pool Re") was formed, a mutual insurance company funded by private insurers with the British government acting as the reinsurer of last resort (Astre 2004; Barnes 2004). In the United States, before the passage of TRIA in November 2002, the insurance industry proposed a similar organization as part of the Insurance Stabilization and Availability Act of 2001.[21] Some in Congress opposed the proposal, in part out of concern that the government would be left administering the program, while others criticized various elements of the proposal, including the apparent override of antitrust laws and changes in tort reform. It also allowed individual companies to opt in or out of the program (see Hunter 2001; McCool 2001; Sebelius 2001). Several other nations, including Israel, Italy, Spain, France, Germany, and South Africa, have national terrorism insurance and reinsurance programs with varying degrees of federal government involvement (Hartwig 2002a; Meder 2004).

Going forward, a privately maintained insurance pool may be a way for the insurance industry to pool both funds and risk in order to keep premiums down and the number of businesses insured up. Of the many reasons why terrorism insurance premiums are so high, the most important two include insurers' inability to confidently assess the terrorist risk and the potential liability is high. A pooled insurance fund would enable insurers to create a singular methodology to assess terrorism risk *and* share the risk across firms. However, it does not appear that the proposal put forth in 2001 would now garner congressional support.

Option 4: Mandate a Level of Terrorism Insurance and Reinsurance

The federal government could mandate a level of terrorism insurance and reinsurance for all commercial property owners and businesses with a certain number of employees.[22] If insurance coverage were made mandatory, insurers would be better able to spread the risk and provide more insurance. However, this begs the question of whether it is fair to require businesses that have almost no risk of attack to incur this additional cost even though the threat of terrorism affects the entire country regardless of individual location.

Mandatory terrorism insurance would be similar to mandatory car insurance. Car insurance is mandated since accidents by their nature are difficult to predict and individual drivers have unobservable driving behaviors. The car insurance mandate blunts the effect of adverse selection. It spreads the risk of accidents across the entire pool of drivers, thus lowering the cost of insurance and making it available to everyone.

Mandating terrorism insurance would have a similar effect. Because terrorist attack locations are difficult to predict and commercial property owners are located near many of the nation's important assets, mandating terrorism insurance would serve to pool risk and lower premiums. Moreover, individual property owners' lack of perfect information concerning their individual risk of attack inhibits their ability to assess risk and determine whether to purchase terrorism insurance. Before the September 11 attack, for instance, very few people, including tenants in commercial buildings, knew that there were reserve fuel tanks in 7 World Trade Center, which, unbeknownst to those property owners, increased the risk of loss.

Option 5: Reform Homeland Security Funding for High-Risk Urban Areas

The federal government has played a significant role in not only alleviating the financial burden of declared natural disasters but mitigating the financial burden of future disasters. The Federal Emergency Management Agency (FEMA) provides hazard mitigation funding to communities that develop mitigation plans. Hazard mitigation refers to sustained measures taken to reduce or eliminate long-term risk to people and property from natural hazards and their effects. In the long term, mitigation measures reduce personal loss, save lives, and reduce the cost to the nation of responding to and recovering from disasters.

A significant part of managing risk in natural disasters is preparation through preventative actions. Hazard mitigation funding goes toward measures such as elevating structures or relocating them outside of a hazardous zone, rehabilitating existing structures seismically, or strengthening existing structures. In some cases the funds allow communities to purchase and demolish damaged structures so as to use the land as open space in perpetuity. There are two important aspects of hazard mitigation funding—the funding goes to areas that have the greatest risk of natural disasters and the funding goes to states that have mitigation plans.

By contrast, the measures that individual property owners can take to prevent damage from a terrorist attack are limited. And outside of deserting high-threat areas, individual property owners can only do so much to limit the effects of future attacks. High-threat areas are highly dependent in many ways on the government to provide intelligence and law enforcement to prevent attacks and to mitigate the effects of future attacks through preparation and training.

The federal government has taken action in this area by forming the Department of Homeland Security (DHS) and funding a variety of programs to prepare for future attacks. However, the current funding system is flawed. An April 2004 report released by Representative Christopher Cox (R-Calif.), chairman of the House Select Committee on Homeland Security, found that "DHS awarded homeland security grant funds to States . . . without any real assessment of need or risk (except for the Urban Area Security Initiative)." The report also found that "there were no Federal terrorism preparedness standards or goals to guide expenditure of funds at the state and local levels, leading to numerous examples of questionable spending" (U.S. House of Representatives 2004). In recent months the department has shifted a larger share of its antiterrorism grants to the nation's largest cities (Lipton 2004). However, the department must take steps to depoliticize the funding system and change the funding formulas to reflect the risk of attack.

In the insurance industry, steps can be taken by those who are insured to manage risk and lower insurance premiums as a result. In the case of terrorism insurance, policy holders are highly dependent on the government to take actions to prevent and plan for terrorist attacks. Because the current federal government system does not appropriately account for the needs of high-threat areas that face the greatest risk of attack, terrorism insurance costs in those areas have increased significantly. The federal government should consider homeland security funding initiatives based on need and risk.

CONCLUSION

One of the important effects of the 9/11 attack was the structural change in the insurance industry. Prior to 9/11, terrorism insurance was essentially an afterthought; it was bundled with other forms of property and casualty insurance, since neither insurers nor policy holders considered a terrorist attack on U.S. soil a significant risk. After 9/11, insurers realized that the risk of an attack on domestic soil was real; they also realized the potentially enormous financial impact a terrorist could have on their financial viability, especially in light of the billions of dollars at stake in the World Trade Center liability case involving Larry Silverstein (Levitt 2004). In response, insurance companies restricted coverage, and as a result any available coverage was offered at such high rates that the premiums became prohibitively high for everyday business operations. On the other side, private firms realized that their potential liabilities from a terrorist attack lay in the billions—not millions—of dollars; when they sought more insurance, they found its supply restricted and often priced out of range.

The combination of these two effects was a failure of the entire private insurance market. In response, the federal government passed the Terrorism Risk Insurance Act of 2002 to provide a valuable backstop to the insurance market in the case of another terrorist attack. That law is slated to expire on December 31, 2005. The role of the federal government in the insurance market continues to be discussed as policymakers work with experts in the industry to determine the appropriate course of action in a new age of terrorism risk.

Predicting a terrorist attack and the losses that would result is understandably difficult. Given the rarity of such attacks in the United States so far, the insurance industry is just beginning to derive ways in which to quantify these risks. However, certain commonsense assumptions can be made. Terrorists prefer targets that are easily recognized by people all over the world or that have the highest probability of causing catastrophic losses of life and property. For the most part, large, dense cities typify this type of target, and New York City is the best example of a large, dense city. New York City businesses are at exceptional risk for a terrorist attack, and there are a limited number of steps that private firms can take to reduce the probability of attack or reduce the devastation resulting from an attack. Yet the cost structure of businesses has been irrevocably changed as the market for terrorism insurance introduces significant risks and costs.

As the country continues its war on terrorism and involvement in Iraq, policymakers will be confronted with related domestic issues. One of the im-

portant consequences of these wars will be the impact on the insurance industry. Will the market be able to provide insurance after the expiration of TRIA
in 2005? Is it the government's responsibility to provide terrorism insurance
akin to crop insurance for the agricultural market? Are there combined public-
private programs that could perhaps meet the needs of the market? These are
some of the many questions that policymakers will need to resolve before
TRIA expires at the end of 2005. To reach a decision, the federal government
should work together with businesses and the insurance industry to achieve a
reasonable resolution on terrorism insurance for the entire nation.

The views expressed here are those of the authors and do not necessarily reflect the views of the Partnership for New York City.
The authors wish to thank Tim Brady, Howard Chernick, Jill Dal-
ton, Jerry Downing, Al Modugno, John Rodgers, Rosemary Scanlon,
Ernest Tollerson, George Zanjani, and individuals at RMS and AIR
for offering their comments and expertise.

NOTES

1. In a "soft market," many companies are writing insurance (strong capacity and
   competition) and premiums are low because of reduced losses and/or a strong return on investment for insurance companies. In a "hard market," few companies are
   writing insurance (weak capacity and competition) and premiums are high because
   of greater losses and/or weak return on investment for insurance companies.
2. Estimates of total insured losses from 9/11 range from a low of $25 billion
   (Moody's 2002) to a high of $70 billion (Woodward 2002). Most analysts esti-
   mate the total losses at between $40 billion and $50 billion (Partnership for New
   York City 2001; Marsh Inc. 2004a; Hartwig 2002a; Saxton 2002; Hillman 2002),
   although more recent estimates put the figure at between $30 billion and $35
   billion (U.S. Senate 2004).
3. See also George Lakdawalla and Darius Zanjani (2003), who present a modeling
   approach to terrorism insurance and moral hazard.
4. Froot and O'Connell (1997) examine the reinsurance market and find that average
   premiums on catastrophe insurance exceed their estimates of actuarial value and
   that prices and quantities are negatively correlated. Both facts suggest that the
   supply of insurance is not perfectly elastic. Furthermore, they show that higher
   prices right after a catastrophe are driven by both an increase in demand *and* a
   decrease in the supply of reinsurance. See also Neil Doherty and Clifford Smith
   (1993), who show that insurance markets are less competitive when prices are
   high, and Anne Gron (1994), who shows that the short-run industry supply curve
   is upward-sloping.
5. Unless, of course, both shift by the same amount, in which case the supply of

insurance could remain unchanged but not the price, which would still necessarily increase.

6. It is possible that the supply curve becomes more inelastic over time; this would exacerbate the price and quantity shifts seen in figure 6.1.

7. David Cummins and Christopher Lewis (2003) also show that the price of insurance settled down after natural catastrophes such as Hurricane Andrew and the Northridge Earthquake. Because there is a historical pattern to natural catastrophes, it is easier for researchers and the insurance industry to model their impacts. There have been no events analogous to 9/11 that enable similar types of modeling. There is a literature on business and government reactions to natural catastrophes, an issue not approached in detail here (see Moss 1999, 2002).

8. These numbers produced by RMS are based on a model that quantifies the impact of 78,000 potential terrorist events that range from the use of conventional weapons to chemical, biological, radiological, or nuclear attacks.

9. The AIR analysis is based on possible attacks by both conventional weapons and weapons of mass destruction on more than 300,000 potential terrorist targets across the United States. The analysis considers both international and domestic terrorist threats and includes property, workers' compensation, and direct business interruption losses. Both the AIR and RMS models factor in only privately insured buildings and workers covered by workers' compensation. Government buildings, which are not privately insured, are not included in the analyses. Although Washington, D.C., and New York City face a similar likelihood of attack, a large share of Washington's buildings are government-owned and hence not privately insured.

10. The area in Manhattan south of Fifty-ninth Street qualifies as tier 1. The rest of New York City qualifies as tier 2, and the rest of New York State is in tier 3. Note that these are *recommended* rates and that it is possible for rates to vary within each tier.

11. The CIAB asks its roughly 250 member firms about the pricing and underwriting trends in the market by commercial account and line of business for the entire nation and by region. Commercial accounts are defined by size: small, less than $25,000; medium, $25,000 to $100,000; and large, greater than $100,000. Lines of business include auto, workers' compensation, property, general liability, umbrella, and reinsurance. The CIAB uses five regions of the country: the Northeast, Southeast, Southwest, Midwest, and Pacific Northwest.

12. Although insurance premiums account for only 0.25 to 0.50 percent of total business costs, as James Harrigan and Philippe Martin (2002) argue, the vitality of cities is threatened only under unique circumstances. One of those circumstances, firms being unable to buy private insurance, occurred directly after 9/11.

13. This is, of course, the missing counterfactual that cannot be quantified—projects that were slated to begin but were not undertaken because of prohibitively high insurance costs.

14. The "make available" provision requires insurers to make coverage for insured losses available in all property and casualty insurance policies and to not allow that coverage to differ materially from the coverage applicable to losses from events other than acts of terrorism.

15. Cummins and Lewis (2003) divide their sample into three financial ratings based on A. M. Best's rating guides. Some of these effects may be confounded by the anthrax attacks in the months following 9/11.

16. In a recent paper, Kent Smetters (2005) argues that if there is any failure in the private insurance market, it rests with government accounting, tax, and regulatory policies. Correcting these policies would help the insurance industry cover terrorism-related risks without government intervention.

17. Robert Hunter (2004) refers to the ISO/AIR methodology discussed earlier, which identifies nine high-risk cities: New York City, Washington, D.C., San Francisco County, Cook County (Chicago), Suffolk County (Boston), King County (Seattle), Los Angeles County, Harris County (Houston), and Philadelphia County.

18. Jeffrey Brown and his colleagues (2003) show, however, that firms in the industries most likely to be affected by TRIA (banking, construction, insurance, real estate investment trusts, transportation, and public utilities) saw their stock prices fall in the thirteen months prior to the signing of the act into law.

19. The Pension Benefit Guaranty Corporation was established by federal law in 1974 to insure the retirement benefits of workers and beneficiaries covered by private sector–defined benefit pension plans. This agency is financed by premiums paid by employers on behalf of their employees.

20. The National Insurance Development Program insures against property losses due to riot and civil disorder. This program is financed by insurer premiums with a federal reinsurance mechanism.

21. The proposal was also similar to the Homeowners' Insurance Availability Act of 1999 (H.R. 21), which set up a reinsurance pool relating to natural disasters.

22. Of course, insurance and reinsurance companies would be required to offer terrorism insurance akin to TRIA's "make available" provision.

REFERENCES

AIR Worldwide. 2003. *The AIR Terrorism Loss Estimation Model*. Boston: AIR Worldwide Corp.

Astre (a division of the Scor Group). 2004. *Provisions of Terrorism and Riot Coverage in Different Countries*. Available at: http://astre.scor.com/astrehelp/en/Assur/inc/extensionuk/terrorism.htm#Terrorism.

Ayer, Ramani. 2004. "Extend the Terrorism Risk Insurance Act." *Hartford Courant*, July 4.

Barnes, Lee. 2004. "A Closer Look at Britain's Pool Re." *Risk Management* (May): 18–23.

Boyle, Charles E. 2003. "The Reinsurance World 2003—Capacity, Profitability, and 'the Cycle.'" *Insurance Journal* (November 3): 44–46.

Brady, Diane. 2003. "Terrorism: Put the Money Where the Danger Is." *BusinessWeek* (April 14): 40.

Brown, Jeffrey R., J. David Cummins, Christopher M. Lewis, and Ran Wei. 2003. "An Empirical Analysis of the Economic Impact of Federal Terrorism Reinsurance." Working paper 10388. Cambridge, Mass.: National Bureau of Economic Research (November).

Brown, Jeffrey R., Randall S. Kroszner, and Brian H. Jenn. 2002. "Federal Terrorism

Risk Insurance." Working paper 9271. Cambridge, Mass.: National Bureau of Economic Research (October).

Cohen, Norma. 2002. "The High Costs of Terrorism." *Financial Times*, October 4.

Congressional Budget Office. 2005. "Federal Terrorism Reinsurance: An Update." Washington: CBO (January).

Council of Insurance Agents and Brokers (CIAB). 2000. *Property/Casualty Market Survey* (third quarter market index). Available at: http://www.ciab.com.

———. 2001a. *Property/Casualty Market Survey* (third quarter market index). Available at: http://www.ciab.com.

———. 2001b. *Property/Casualty Market Survey* (fourth quarter market index). Available at: http://www.ciab.com.

———. 2002. *Property/Casualty Market Survey* (third quarter market index). Available at: http://www.ciab.com.

———. 2003. *Property/Casualty Market Survey* (third quarter market index). Available at: http://www.ciab.com.

———. 2004a. *Property/Casualty Market Survey* (first quarter market index). Available at: http://www.ciab.com.

———. 2004b. *Property/Casualty Market Survey* (third quarter market index). Available at: http://www.ciab.com.

Cummins, J. David, and Christopher M. Lewis. 2003. "Catastrophic Events, Parameter Uncertainty, and the Breakdown of Implicit Long-Term Contracting: The Case of Terrorism Insurance." *Journal of Risk and Uncertainty* 26(2–3): 153–78.

Doherty, Neil A., and Clifford W. Smith Jr. 1993. "Corporate Insurance Strategy: The Case of British Petroleum." *Journal of Applied Corporate Finance* 6(3, Fall): 4–15.

Froot, Kenneth A., and Paul G. J. O'Connell. 1997. "On the Pricing of Intermediated Risks: Theory and Application to Catastrophe Insurance." Working paper 6011. Cambridge, Mass.: National Bureau of Economic Research (April).

Gron, Anne. 1994. "Capacity Constraints and Cycles in Property-Casualty Insurance Markets." *RAND Journal of Economics* 25(1, Spring): 110–27.

Gron, Anne, and Alan O. Sykes. 2002. "Terrorism and Insurance Markets: A Role for the Government as Insurer?" John M. Olin Law and Economics working paper 155. Chicago: University of Chicago Law School.

Harrigan, James, and Philippe Martin. 2002. "Terrorism and the Resilience of Cities." *Economic Policy Review* (Federal Reserve Bank of New York) (November): 97–116.

Hartwig, Robert P. 2002a. "The Impact of the September 11 Attacks on the American Insurance Industry." In *Insurance and September 11: One Year After*, edited by Patrick M. Leidtke and Christopher Courbage. Geneva, Switz.: International Association for the Study of Insurance Economics ("Geneva Association") (August): 10–42.

———. 2002b. *September 11, 2001: The First Year; One Hundred Minutes of Terror That Changed the Global Insurance Industry Forever*. New York: Insurance Information Institute (September). Available at: http://www.bnet.com/abstract.aspx?scid=1701&docid=65779.

Hillman, Richard J. 2002. "Rising Uninsured Exposure to Attacks Heightens Potential Economic Vulnerabilities." Testimony before U.S. House of Representatives, Committee on Financial Services, Subcommittee on Oversight and Investigations (February 27).

Hubbard, R. Glenn, and Bruce Deal. 2004. *The Economic Effects of Federal Participation in Terrorism Risk.*: Analysis Group (September 14). Available at: http://www.analysisgroup .com.

Hunter, J. Robert. 2001. Testimony before U.S. Senate, Committee on Banking, Housing, and Urban Affairs (October 4).

———. 2004. "The Terrorism Risk Insurance Act: Should It Be Renewed?" Washington, D.C.: Consumer Federation of America (April).

Insurance Services Office (ISO). 2003. "Loss Costs/Rules—Implementation" Circular LI-BM-2003–043/LI-CF-2003–024/LI-CM-2003–007/LI-CR-2003–008 (February 20).

Kunreuther, Howard, and Erwann Michel-Kerjan. 2004. "Challenges for Terrorism Risk Insurance in the United States." *Journal of Economic Perspectives* 18(4, Fall): 201–14.

Lakdawalla, Darius, and George Zanjani. 2003. "Insurance, Self-protection, and the Economics of Terrorism." Working paper. Santa Monica, Calif.: RAND Institute for Civil Justice (December).

Levitt, David M. 2004. "Trade Center Jury Says Insurers Liable on Two Attacks." Bloomberg News Service, December 6.

Lipton, Eric. 2004. "Big Cities Will Get More in Antiterrorism Grants." *New York Times*, December 22.

Malkin, Peter L. 2004. Letter to Kathy Wylde, President and CEO, Partnership for New York City (February 3).

Marsh Inc. 2004a. "Marketwatch: Property Terrorism Insurance Update—First Quarter 2004." Research report. New York: Marsh Inc. (June).

———. 2004b. "Marketwatch: Property Terrorism Insurance 2004." Research report. New York: Marsh Inc. (April).

McCool, Thomas J. 2001. Testimony before U.S. Senate, Committee on Banking, Housing, and Urban Affairs (October 4).

Meder, Robert C. 2004. "Global Solutions to Terrorism Coverage." *Risk Management* (May): 10–15.

Moody's Investors Service. 2002. "CMBS: Moody's Approach to Terrorism Insurance for U.S. Commercial Real Estate." Structured finance special report. New York: Moody's Investor Service (March 1).

Moss, David. 1999. "Courting Disaster? The Transformation of Federal Disaster Policy Since 1803." In *The Financing of Catastrophe Risk*, edited by Kenneth Froot. Chicago: University of Chicago Press.

———. 2002. *When All Else Fails: Government as the Ultimate Risk Manager*. Cambridge, Mass.: Harvard University Press.

Muto, Sheila. 2003. "No Truce in Sight in Battle for Currituck Lighthouse." *Wall Street Journal*, October 8.

Nassetta, Christopher. 2004. Testimony before U.S. Senate, Committee on Banking, Housing, and Urban Affairs (May 18).

New York City Comptroller. 2002. "One Year Later: The Effects of 9/11 on Commercial Insurance Rates and Availability in New York City." New York: New York City Comptroller's Office (November 13).

O'Neill, Paul H. 2001. Testimony before U.S. Senate, Committee on Banking, Housing, and Urban Affairs (October 4).

Oster, Christopher. 2001. "Bouncing Back: Insurance Companies Benefit from September 11, Still Seek Federal Aid—Marsh & McLennan Starts New Units; Others Raise Some Premiums by 100%—Turning Away Eager Investors." *Wall Street Journal*, November 15.

Partnership for New York City. 2001. "Economic Impact Analysis of the September 11 Attack on New York City." New York: Partnership for New York City (November).

Risk Management Solutions Inc. (RMS). 2002. "Understanding and Managing Terrorism Risk." Newark, Calif.: RMS.

Saxton, Jim. 2002. "Economic Perspectives on Terrorism Insurance." Joint Economic Committee report to U.S. Congress (May).

Scanlon, Rosemary. 2004. "The Impact of Insurance Industry Issues on New York City's Construction Industry." Report to the New York Building Congress (March).

Sebelius, Kathleen. 2001. Testimony before U.S. Senate, Committee on Banking, Housing, and Urban Affairs (October 4).

Smetters, Kent. 2005. "Insuring Against Terrorism: The Policy Challenge." Working paper 11038. Cambridge, Mass.: National Bureau of Economic Research (January).

U.S. Department of the Treasury. 2004. "Treasury Announces Decision to Extend the 'Make Available' Provisions of the Terrorism Risk Insurance Act into 2005" (press release). June 18.

U.S. General Accountability Office. 2001. "Terrorism Insurance: Alternative Programs for Protecting Insurance Consumers." Statement of Thomas J. McCool (October 24).

U.S. House of Representatives. House Select Committee on Homeland Security. 2004. "An Analysis of First Responder Grant Funding." Washington: U.S. House of Representatives (April 27).

U.S. Senate. Committee on Banking, Housing and Urban Affairs. 2004. "Oversight of the Terrorism Risk Insurance Program" (May 18).

Woodward, W. Jeffrey. 2002. "The ISO Terrorism Exclusions: Background and Analysis." *IRMI Insights* (February). Available at: http://www.irmi.com/Insights/Articles/2002/Woodward02.aspx.

PART II

The Impact of 9/11 on Labor Markets and Families

CHAPTER 7

The Economic Impact of 9/11 on New York City's Low-Wage Workers and Households

James A. Parrott and Oliver D. Cooke

BOTH 9/11 and the 2001 to 2003 recession exacted heavy tolls on many of New York City's workers and their families. It is important to consider whether these events differentially affected subgroups of the city's workforce and, if so, how. Besides being important in their own right, answers to these questions should prove valuable in helping to inform policies designed to redress the economic losses suffered by workers during future economic downturns and catastrophic events that entail significant economic dislocation.

This chapter explores the effects of these events on various wage strata of the workforce during three phases of the 2001 to 2003 recession: the pre-9/11 recession, the immediate 9/11 impact period, and the post-9/11 recession. Two analytical lenses are used to examine and compare these effects: an *industry* lens, the most common approach to analyzing local and regional economies, and an *occupational* lens. An occupational perspective is important because workers' wages tend to be closely related to their occupations. One analysis uses an industry-occupation matrix to translate industry employment changes over the period into occupational employment changes. The second analytical method utilizes the Current Population Survey (CPS) to categorize workers into three occupational wage groups. This analysis then examines their employment and unemployment status and wage and household earnings over the 2001 to 2003 period.

The principal findings are that workers in low-wage occupations experienced serious but relatively short-term dislocation effects—higher unemployment and reduced earnings—from 9/11. Although workers in middle- and high-wage occupations experienced less pronounced adverse effects *in the immediate aftermath* of 9/11, as the recession wore on through late 2002 and 2003 these workers experienced greater increases in unemployment and greater proportionate declines in household wage earnings. These differential labor market outcomes across occupational wage groups in the immediate post-9/11 period often reflected the post-9/11 constraints and operating environment of each group's *employer*. In many cases, these factors appear to have heightened the likelihood that workers in low-wage occupations would experience periods of unemployment and/or reduced working hours in the immediate post-9/11 period. This in turn resulted in declines in these workers' earnings.

9/11 IN THE CONTEXT OF THE 2001 TO 2003 RECESSION

The attack on the World Trade Center (WTC) came at a time when the New York City and national economies were already in recession (see figure 7.1). At the national level, the National Bureau of Economic Research (NBER) business cycle dating committee determined that the recession began in March 2001 and ended in November 2001. In an unprecedented development, national employment continued to decline for another twenty-two months—until August 2003—following the official "end" of the national recession. The timing of local recessions is usually determined based on the seasonally adjusted employment peak and trough months. The peak month for employment for New York City occurred in December 2000, nine months prior to the September 2001 World Trade Center attack. Similar to the nation, New York City's employment finally bottomed out in August 2003.

During New York City's thirty-two-month 2001 to 2003 recession, the city lost 245,000 jobs, or 6.5 percent of its December 2000 peak level. This pace of job decline was three times the national job decline. Given the tepid 1.1 percent job growth (37,300 jobs) in the first sixteen months after the August 2003 trough and the current projections for job growth over the next few years, it is likely to take five to six years for New York City to recoup job losses from the 2001 to 2003 recession.

Any study of the labor market effects of 9/11 has to grapple with disentangling the effects of the ongoing recession from the economic effects of the 9/11 attack. How long did the 9/11 impact last? Would some of the workers displaced by 9/11 have lost their jobs because of the ongoing recession anyway? Did 9/11 prolong the recession by checking the return of consumer and business confidence? The challenge of isolating 9/11's effects from those of the ongo-

FIGURE 7.1   EMPLOYMENT LEVELS IN NEW YORK CITY AND THE
UNITED STATES, FEBRUARY 2001 TO DECEMBER 2003

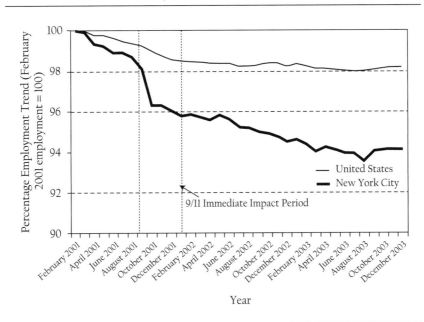

Source: New York State Department of Labor and U.S. Bureau of Labor Statistics. New York City data seasonally adjusted by authors.

ing recession makes such questions difficult to answer. New York City's economy, which had already lost 52,000 jobs prior to 9/11, would probably have continued to deteriorate for some time even if the attack had not taken place. At the same time, 9/11 clearly altered the recession's course and may have prolonged it by checking the return of consumer and business confidence. In 2002 and 2003, the wave of corporate scandals, the buildup to the Iraq War, and then the actual fighting also affected the recession's post-9/11 trajectory because of the effects these developments had on Wall Street and consumer and business confidence.

This study offers no easy answers to these difficult questions. We combine an analysis of changes in industry and occupational employment over the course of the 2001 to 2003 recession period with the findings of sociological and other studies to make an informed approximation of the jobs that appear to have been those most directly affected by the attack. This approach permits us to identify groups of workers who experienced adverse labor market effects in the immediate aftermath of 9/11. We find that, because 9/11 had differential effects across industries and occupations, and because the recession did not unfold in a linear fashion, low-, mid-, and high-wage workers were affected in different ways at different points over the course of the 2001 to 2003 recession.

AN INDUSTRY PERSPECTIVE ON 9/11 AND THE 2001 TO 2003 RECESSION

Because the industry perspective is by far the most familiar approach that has been used to analyze the effects of 9/11 and the recession (and thus has tended to shape impressions and interpretations of the 9/11 impact and the recession's effects), this chapter begins with an assessment of the 2001 to 2003 period from that perspective.

The city's 2001 to 2003 recession can be divided into three phases: the pre-9/11 phase, dominated by the bursting of the Wall Street and dot-com bubbles; the period from August 2001 to January 2002, when the 9/11 impact was most concentrated; and a third phase from early 2002 to August 2003 that included continued downsizing on Wall Street, influenced in part by a series of corporate financial scandals and then by the buildup to the Iraq War and the onset of combat operations. Employment in New York City continued to decline through August 2003. Thus, the overall 2001 to 2003 recession period in New York City spans thirty-two months, divided into the eight-month pre-9/11 period, the five-month 9/11 impact period, and the nineteen-month post-9/11 recession period.

The September 11, 2001, attack on the World Trade Center resulted in two types of job loss for New York City: the relocation (either temporary or permanent) out of New York City of jobs previously located in the WTC or the immediate vicinity, and the loss of jobs in industries that suffered from the economic fallout of the attack. The latter category, which was by far the greater of the two, extends beyond the immediate vicinity of the WTC and includes sizable job effects among businesses that were bound to the WTC (such as the Windows on the World restaurant or building services), industries such as tourism (a sector encompassing hotels, restaurants, retail trade, culture, and entertainment) and air transport, and businesses, including apparel manufacturing, in the Chinatown community a few blocks from the WTC. In addition, the immediate and sharp blow to consumer spending that resulted from the attack reduced employment in wholesale and retail trade and consumer services.

Table 7.1 presents New York City payroll employment change by industry for each of the three phases of the 2001 to 2003 recession. To analyze how different wage strata of the workforce were affected during the 2001 to 2003 period, we have grouped the industries into low-, mid-, and high-wage categories based on average wages for the middle year, 2002.[1]

TABLE 7.1 Employment Change in New York City, by Industry and Wage Group, During 2001 to 2003 Recession

Wage Group and Industry	Employment (Thousands) December 2000	Pre-9/11 Recession December 2000 to August 2001		9/11 Immediate Impact August 2001 to January 2002		Post-9/11 Recession January 2002 to August 2003		Peak to Trough December 2000 to August 2003		Annual Average Wage 2002
		# Change	% Change	# Change	% Change	# Change	% Change	# Change	% Change	
Low-wage industries										
Educational services	132	2	1.6	0	0.0	8	5.9	10	7.7	$37,452
Other services	149	0	0.0	-1	-0.5	-1	-0.6	-2	-1.1	32,559
Accommodation and food service	205	3	1.3	-15	-7.3	9	4.7	-4	-1.7	23,758
Administrative services	216	-2	-0.8	-11	-5.0	-14	-6.7	-26	-12.1	35,100
Retail trade	284	-12	-4.1	-7	-2.7	2	0.8	-17	-5.9	29,519
Health care and social assistance	499	-5	-0.9	6	1.1	17	3.5	18	3.7	37,415
Total	1,485	-13	-0.9	-28	-1.9	22	1.5	-20	-1.3	
Share of employment	39.5%									
Share of wage group's peak-to-trough job loss		66.9%		145.2%		-112.1%		100%		
Share of period's total job loss		25.5%		22.9%		-31.9%				
Mid-wage Industries										
Arts, entertainment, and recreation	58	-1	-1.8	-2	-2.8	-1	-1.7	-4	-6.2	50,815
Transportation and warehousing	119	-3	-2.6	-11	-9.7	-1	-1.2	-15	-13.1	41,935
Real estate, rental and lease	120	-3	-2.6	-3	-2.3	1	0.7	-5	-4.2	46,666
Construction	125	-5	-3.7	-2	-1.6	-6	-5.1	-13	-10.1	55,978
Wholesale trade	155	0	0.1	-4	-2.8	-4	-2.7	-8	-5.4	61,910
Manufacturing	171	-17	-10.2	-9	-6.1	-21	-14.6	-48	-28.0	40,332
Government	564	15	2.6	-10	-1.7	-15	-2.7	-11	-1.9	46,848
Total	1,311	-15	-1.1	-41	-3.2	-48	-3.8	-103	-7.9	

(Table continues on p. 194.)

TABLE 7.1 CONTINUED

Wage Group and Industry	Employment (Thousands) December 2000	Pre-9/11 Recession December 2000 to August 2001		9/11 Immediate Impact August 2001 to January 2002		Post-9/11 Recession January 2002 to August 2003		Peak to Trough December 2000 to August 2003		Annual Average Wage 2002
		# Change	% Change	# Change	% Change	# Change	% Change	# Change	% Change	
Share of employment	34.9%									
Share of wage group's peak-to-trough job loss		14.1%		39.7%		46.3%		100%		
Share of period's total job loss		28.2%		33.0%		69.3%				
High-wage industries										
Utilities	15	0	-1.9	0	0.9	0	-0.3	0	-1.3	80,212
Management of companies	52	4	8.0	1	2.5	1	2.4	7	13.3	133,634
Other finance and insurance	73	-2	-2.9	-2	-2.8	-1	-1.4	-5	-7.0	95,500
Banking	100	-2	-1.6	-3	-3.2	-4	-4.7	-9	-9.2	105,755
Information	195	3	1.7	-17	-8.8	-16	-8.7	-30	-15.3	78,248
Securities	199	-7	-3.6	-17	-8.9	-14	-8.2	-38	-19.3	225,493
Professional, scientific, and technical services	331	-20	-6.1	-17	-5.4	-9	-3.1	-46	-13.9	82,841
Total	964	-24	-2.5	-55	-5.8	-43	-4.9	-122	-12.6	
Share of employment	25.6%									
Share of wage group's peak-to-trough job loss		19.6%		45.0%		35.4%		100%		
Share of period's total job loss		46.4%		44.1%		62.6%				
Total, three wage groups	3,760	-52	-1.4	-124	-3.4	-69	-1.9	-245	-6.5	

Sources: New York State Department of Labor (NYSDOL) 790 (establishment) employment data and authors' calculations. Employment data seasonally adjusted by authors. Annual average wage data from NYSDOL ES-202 (Covered Employment and Wages) program.

Phase 1: Pre-9/11 Recession   The main reason New York City exceeded the nation's job growth rate in 1999 and 2000 was the prolonged run-up in stock prices on Wall Street and the frenzied pace of expansion of dot-com firms. The city was led into recession when Wall Street and the dot-coms started cutting jobs following the bursting of the speculative financial market bubble in mid-2000. Following the December 2000 peak month for New York City's total employment, securities employment fell by 7,200 over the next eight months. Employment in computer system design and related services—the Labor Department industry in which many dot-com companies were classified—and in the broader professional and business services sector that had also grown rapidly during the late 1990s began to decline as well. Employment in computer systems design, advertising, employment services, and accounting declined by a combined total of 21,500 during the pre-9/11 recession period. Manufacturing (17,000 jobs lost) and retail trade (12,000 jobs lost) were the two other sectors contributing substantially to the net loss of 52,000 jobs in New York City prior to 9/11.

Phase 2: Immediate 9/11 Impact Period   New York City lost a total of 124,000 jobs between August 2001 and January 2002. This number exceeds the 75,000 to 100,000 range for estimates of the 9/11-related job loss since it includes job losses that are more appropriately considered recession-related.[2] In addition to the jobs lost related to 9/11, sizable employment declines continued in computers, advertising, and employment services. In a development related to the prior years' overexpansion rather than to 9/11, telecommunications industry employment fell by 10 percent (nearly 4,000 jobs) in this period. The number of Wall Street jobs reported in the city plummeted by 25,000 between August and December 2001. However, many of these finance-sector jobs were relocated outside the city by firms whose lower Manhattan office space had been destroyed or damaged in the attack. A Bureau of Labor Statistics (BLS) report indicated that by the end of October 2001, over 17,000 jobs, more than 80 percent of which were in finance, had relocated to New Jersey. By the end of that year, all but 5,200 of these jobs had reappeared in the city's employment numbers as operations were moved back to New York City—in some cases to space in other facilities downtown or in midtown where there had been recession-related layoffs (Dolfman and Wasser 2004).

Phase 3: Post-9/11 Recession   The period of the immediate 9/11 economic shock appears to have wound down by around January 2002. By mid-2002, half of the hotel job loss during the immediate 9/11 period had been recovered, and one-third of affected restaurant jobs were restored. Air transport–related employment stabilized in the first half of 2002. Because of Chinatown's proximity to the World Trade Center, its reliance on tourism, and the disruptions created for its apparel manufacturing sector by street closures in the weeks after 9/11, that community suffered a significant economic impact as a result of 9/11 (Asian American Federation of New York 2002a).[3] In a year-later report, Chinatown was still reeling from the 9/11 economic fallout (Asian American Federation of New York 2002b).

Although the city's overall employment level stabilized through the first half of 2002, the ongoing recession caused noticeable job losses in many individual industries. However, these losses were numerically offset by job growth in more recession-resistant fields, led by education, health, and social services.

For a time during the spring of 2002 there was optimism that the national economy was poised for a rebound from what would have been a fairly brief recession. That optimism proved short-lived as investor confidence then suffered in the wake of a series of corporate accounting scandals and reports of questionable corporate research by Wall Street firms.[4] Consumer confidence began to erode in mid-2002 as the employment outlook failed to brighten and the prospect arose of heightened military action in the Middle East.

Job losses in the post-9/11 recession period largely occurred between September 2002 and April 2003, during the buildup to the Iraq War and the period of intense military action through the fall of Baghdad. New York City lost a net total of 51,000 jobs during this time. Overall, for the post-9/11 recession period from January 2002 through August 2003, the city lost 69,000 jobs on net. These job losses were concentrated in manufacturing, securities, information, professional services, administrative services, and government. Education, health, and social services added 25,000 jobs during this time. Retail trade employment—which had declined by 12,000 in the pre-9/11 recession phase—increased by 2,000 in the post-9/11 recession phase. This resiliency in retail employment during a recession was reflected at the national level in consumer spending boosted by low interest rates, extensive mortgage refinancings and rising home values, and substantial federal income tax cuts.

Interpreting the Industry Employment Data

This analysis of industry employment changes during the three phases of the 2001 to 2003 period, coupled with considerable anecdotal evidence, does allow us to identify and make an informed approximation of the number of jobs likely to have been *directly* affected by the 9/11 attack.[5] The employment losses that occurred in late 2001 in the hotel, restaurant, arts, air transport, building services, and apparel manufacturing industries were primarily the result of 9/11. The employment losses in the first four of these industries reflected the dramatic falloff in business that the city's hospitality and tourism industries experienced in the months immediately following 9/11. The decline in building services employment reflected the destruction of the World Trade Center and the damage to many buildings in lower Manhattan that were rendered uninhabitable. The job declines in apparel manufacturing reflected the industry's significant presence in Chinatown, which, because of its proximity to Ground Zero, experienced a significant and lengthy period of business disruption.

The securities industry and the professional and technical services industry were also affected by 9/11, owing to their significant presence in lower Manhattan. These two industries lost 34,000 jobs between August 2001 and January 2002—27 percent of all jobs lost in the period (compared to their 14 percent share of all jobs). Unlike the industries mentioned earlier, however, which experienced more modest employment losses prior to 9/11, these two industries had already recorded significant job losses (27,000 jobs) *prior* to 9/11. As detailed already, after 9/11 the finance industry in particular moved several thousand jobs out of New York City, and pre-9/11 job declines primarily reflected the bursting of the Wall Street and dot-com bubbles and the recession's onset. Although there were obviously layoffs in these industries following 9/11, it is more difficult to link them directly to 9/11's fallout. It seems more probable that 9/11's effect on the securities industry and on professional and technical services was to exacerbate, intensify, and concentrate ongoing industry-specific and recession-related trends. The significant decline in the information sector (mainly publishing and broadcasting) in the wake of 9/11 was in part a reflection of similar factors.

As table 7.1 shows, employment in high-wage industries declined by 5.8 percent in the immediate impact period. This decline was considerably greater than the 3.2 percent decline in employment experienced in mid-wage industries in this period, and *three times* the job loss experienced in low-wage industries. These facts, in conjunction with the securities industry's significant and well-known presence in lower Manhattan and at the World Trade Center towers, have contributed to a general impression that the attack was absorbed principally by the securities and related industries. Further, the vast majority of all jobs lost during New York City's 2001 to 2003 recession period did occur in mid- and high-wage industries. High-wage industries accounted for 50 percent of all lost jobs during the recession, nearly twice their share of December 2000 employment. This industry-oriented perspective on 9/11 and the 2001 to 2003 recession, however, masks the ways in which these events affected New York City's *workers*. Looking more closely at the 9/11 economic dislocations provides considerable evidence that the city's *low-wage workers* also suffered greatly as a result of the attack.[6]

Indeed, there are good reasons to expect that whatever dislocations did occur in the aftermath of 9/11, those among low-wage workers resulted in disproportionately adverse labor market outcomes for them, for example, in unemployment and reduced earnings.[7] Several of the industries that suffered the largest job losses in the immediate impact period and had significant concentrations of employment in low-wage occupations—such as hotels, restaurants, retail, administrative support (which includes security guards and janitors), and apparel manufacturing—experienced considerably longer periods of business disruption or downtime than many other industries affected by 9/11, such as securities. In part, these differences reflected the constraints faced by enterprises in different industries. For example, many larger corporations that were displaced as a result of 9/11, especially those in the finance industries, were considerably less location- and capital-constrained relative to many smaller employers located in lower Manhattan, such as restaurateurs, hoteliers, and retailers. As is well known, many securities and banking firms either secured new office space for their displaced lower Manhattan employees and operations (in midtown, New Jersey, Westchester, and Long Island, among other places) or transferred these employees and operations to existing but underutilized space elsewhere within weeks of 9/11. As a result of such actions, the total business disruption and downtime experienced by many of these types of enterprises was often relatively short.

In contrast, other employers (including restaurants, hotels, and retailers)—especially those located within close proximity to the World Trade Center and those whose physical spaces suffered structural or fallout-related damage—were often more location- and capital-constrained than larger corporations and therefore suffered longer periods of business interruption. These factors necessarily placed these industries' employees—who, owing to these industries' occupational structures, tended to be employed in low-wage occupations—at greater risk of layoff or termination.[8] Several examples from "the frozen zone" provide evidence of this:

- Business operations in Chinatown were severely disrupted in the aftermath of 9/11 (Asian American Federation of New York 2002b). While Chinatown businesses (like all businesses in the so-called frozen zone) were effectively shut down in the first two weeks following 9/11, heightened security measures in lower Manhattan, restricted public and surface transportation access, reduced subway and bus services, and severed power and phone lines continued to plague the area's business community for several months following 9/11. During the three months following 9/11, an estimated forty garment factories closed down, while an additional twenty-five closed between January and November 2002. Although several factors contributed to these manufacturers' decisions to close (or relocate), it is undeniable that these closings further reduced pedestrian and patronage traffic for other neighborhood businesses and thereby further exacerbated an already poor operating environment.[9]

- The major discount department store retailer, Century 21, which had about one thousand employees, suffered extensive damage as a result of 9/11 and was forced to close for a period of several months while the store was repaired. Many of the employees who were laid off, such as cashiers and stock clerks, worked in low-wage occupations.

- The Millenium Hilton Hotel, located directly across the street from Ground Zero, was forced to close for nineteen months while the building under-went repair (Rogers 2003). According to one report, over 90 percent of the Millenium's 340 workers were unable to secure alternative employment during this period. The occupational structure of the accommodations in-dustry suggests that approximately two-thirds of these workers would have been employed in low-wage occupations.

- In addition to the loss of the World Trade Center towers, many other buildings in the vicinity of Ground Zero suffered structural or internal damage. To the extent that these buildings underwent repairs and cleaning in the months following 9/11, many building services–related employees (janitors, cleaners, security guards) would have been adversely affected.

- For security reasons, the city banned driving alone into Manhattan at the Lincoln, Holland, and Queens-Midtown Tunnels during the morning rush hour (6:00 to 10:00 A.M.). As a result, parking garages—especially those located downtown and in midtown—suffered significant drops in busi-ness. According to one garage workers' representative, at least three hun-dred downtown garage workers lost their jobs largely as a result of the ban, while thousands more saw their hours reduced (Bagli 2001).

These sorts of 9/11 effects suggest that the layoffs that did occur in several industries in lower Manhattan took a significant toll on workers in several low-wage occupations. These workers may have been more likely to experi-ence unemployment than workers in higher-paying occupations. This may have been especially true for low-wage workers, such as displaced Chinese apparel workers, with characteristics such as limited formal education, few transfer-able skills, and limited English-language capability.[10]

At a minimum, the fact that workers in many low-wage occupations are often paid hourly or on the basis of production (especially garment workers and taxi and livery drivers) suggests that the dislocations and disruptions that occurred in the aftermath of 9/11 would have resulted in significant declines in earnings. This would have been the case regardless of whether or not these workers experienced periods of official unemployment.[11]

The impact of 9/11 on low-wage workers was not restricted to the frozen zone. Employment in the city's accommodations industry declined 10 percent (4,000 jobs) between August 2001 and January 2002. Based on the industry's occupational makeup, 65 percent of its employees work in low-wage occupations. Although there were several hotels located in lower Manhattan that were affected by 9/11 (including the Millenium Hilton), the significant drop-off in business and tourism traffic in the city in the months following 9/11 exacted a considerable toll on the city's entire accommodations industry. The city's hotel occupancy rate plummeted to 62 percent in September 2001, from 77 percent in August.

After coming to a virtual standstill immediately following 9/11 and then undergoing several subsequent months of reduced air travel, the city's air transportation industry lost 7,000 jobs (a decline of 22 percent) between August 2001 and January 2002. Based on the industry's occupational makeup, nearly one-quarter of its employees work in low-wage occupations such as baggage porters.

This evidence, in conjunction with the fact that intra-occupational wage differentials tend to be narrower than intra-industry wage differences, suggests that switching from an industry perspective to an occupational perspective may provide a better handle on the nature of the effects of 9/11 and the broader 2001 to 2003 recession on various wage strata of the city's workforce.[12]

TRANSLATING EMPLOYMENT CHANGES BY INDUSTRY INTO EMPLOYMENT CHANGES BY OCCUPATION

One way to make the switch from an industry perspective to an occupational perspective is to use an industry-occupation matrix, which provides information on the occupational structure of industries and thus can facilitate the transformation of the industry employment data analyzed here into occupational employment data.[13] The resultant data reveal how the changes in industry employment would have translated into occupational employment changes *had job losses cascaded across the occupational spectrum in proportion to occupational cohorts' respective shares of industry employment.* Given this, the following industry-occupation analysis should be interpreted as offering a hypothetical benchmark against which additional occupation-oriented analysis of these events can be assessed.[14]

To clarify the relationship between industry employment data and its occupational analogue, table 7.2 shows how job losses in the air transportation industry in the immediate impact period might have translated into occupational job losses. As shown, 90 percent of the industry's job losses during the immediate impact period were concentrated in four occupational groups: office and administrative support; transportation and materials moving; personal care and service; and installation, maintenance, and repair. The office and administrative group includes reservation and ticket agents; the transportation and materials group includes pilots, cargo handlers, parking lot attendants, and taxi drivers; the personal care and service group includes flight attendants and

TABLE 7.2   THE OCCUPATIONAL DISTRIBUTION OF JOB LOSSES IN NEW YORK CITY
IN THE AIR TRANSPORTATION INDUSTRY IN THE IMMEDIATE 9/11 IMPACT
PERIOD

Occupational Group	Jobs Lost in Immediate Impact Period August 2001 to January 2002 (Thousands)	Job Losses Tied to Air Transportation Industry (Thousands)	Air Transport's Share of Group's Losses	Group's Share of Air Transport's Job Losses
Office and administrative support	−28.5	−2.3	8.0%	32.3%
Transportation and material moving	−9.3	−1.6	17.2	22.5
Personal care and service	−2.3	−1.5	67.4	21.8
Installation, maintenance, and repair	−5.5	−0.9	17.2	13.4
Business and financial operations	−7.4	−0.2	2.8	2.9
Management	−8.2	−0.2	2.1	2.4
High-wage sales	−10.5	−0.1	0.8	1.2
Architecture and engineering	−1.4	−0.1	5.7	1.1
Computer and mathematical	−9.5	−0.1	0.6	0.8
All other occupational groups	−40.8	−0.1	0.3	1.6
Total	−123.3	−7.1		100.0

Sources: New York State Department of Labor (NYSDOL) 790 (establishment) employment data and authors'
calculations. Employment data seasonally adjusted by authors.

baggage porters; and the installation and maintenance repair occupational
group includes aviation mechanics. It should be noted that over two-thirds of
the jobs lost in the personal care and service occupational group during the
immediate impact period were attributable to the air transport industry.

Following the construction of the twenty-three occupational employment
series, each series was allocated to one of three wage categories: low-, mid-,
and high-wage.[15] Each occupational group's classification was based on its median and mean hourly wage rates. The three wage groups were separated at
the major breaks in the occupational wage (both mean and median) ranking
for New York City. Because the relative rankings of occupations by median
and mean wages are very similar and there are clear breaking points dividing
the three wage groups, there would be few, although undoubtedly some, instances of individual workers who are misclassified by wage group. That is, a
few workers in a given occupation might be in a different wage group than
that of their occupational cohorts. Table 7.3 shows the allocation of occupa-

TABLE 7.3 OCCUPATIONAL GROUPS' DISTRIBUTION AND WAGES (FOURTH-QUARTER 2003 DOLLARS), NEW YORK CITY, 1999 TO 2003

Wage Group and Occupational Group	Hourly Median Wage	Hourly Mean Wage	NY PMSA Employment	NYC Nonfarm 1999 to 2003	December 2000 Employment (Thousands)
Low-wage occupations					
Food preparation and service	$9.11	$10.75	5.5%	6.0%	216
Personal care and service	9.68	11.55	3.8	3.2	117
Farming, fishing, and forestry	10.42	12.85	0.0	0.2	6
Production	11.29	13.55	3.8	4.4	180
Health care support	12.00	12.15	3.5	2.7	98
Building and grounds cleaning and maintenance	13.67	13.55	3.5	3.4	125
Low-wage sales	6.73 to 17.27	8.26 to 22.99	n.a.[a]	5.8	220
Total			20.2	25.8	962
Mid-wage Occupations					
Transportation and material moving	14.36	16.46	4.9	5.8	219
Office and administrative support	15.41	16.53	20.9	21.8	819
Protective services	16.46	17.90	3.8	3.7	136
Community and social services	17.27	19.97	1.9	2.1	73

Installation, maintenance, and repair	19.44	19.58	3.4	3.5	131
Arts, design, entertainment, sports, and media	22.24	27.20	2.8	2.2	85
Education, training, and library[b]	23.87	26.84	7.5	3.9	137
Construction and extraction	24.36	25.09	3.3	3.5	129
Total			48.4	46.5	1,730
High-wage occupations					
Health care practitioners and technical	27.57	32.85	5.2	5.2	184
Life, physical, and social science	27.84	31.63	0.8	1.0	37
Business and financial	29.15	34.17	4.9	5.6	214
Architecture and engineering	29.55	32.50	1.0	1.3	49
Computer and mathematical	33.42	35.05	2.4	2.8	112
Legal	41.51	52.80	1.6	1.7	61
Management	49.89	56.44	5.4	6.1	228
High-wage sales	24.95 to 61.68	30.71 to 66.16	n.a.[a]	4.2	156
Total			21.4	27.8	1,041
Total	17.50	23.10	90.1[a]	100	3,733

Source: U.S. Bureau of Labor Statistics, Occupational Employment Statistics (OES), July 8, 2004, release for NY PMSA (New York City plus Westchester, Putnam, and Rockland Counties). n.a. = not available.

[a] All sales and related occupations account for 9.9 percent of NY PMSA employment.

[b] The discrepancy between the PMSA and New York City share of employment represented by educational services primarily reflects the greater relative importance (as an employment source) of primary and secondary schools in the northern suburbs of the city.

tional groups into these three wage categories. As shown, this classification scheme resulted in 28 percent of the city's nonfarm workforce being classified as high-wage, 46 percent as mid-wage, and 26 percent as low-wage. The median wage for the low-wage group was roughly $11 in 2003, an hourly level that represents about 150 percent of the three-person federal poverty threshold.

Following the construction of the occupationally based employment time series, we generated the occupational analogue to table 7.1. Table 7.4 shows the employment changes in the three occupational wage groups during the three phases of the 2001 to 2003 recession period. Again, it should be noted that this occupational picture reflects the critical assumption implicit in the use of the industry-occupation matrix—namely, that industry job losses (gains) translated into occupational job losses (gains) in proportion to each occupational group's respective shares of industry employment.

While all three occupational wage groups suffered job losses in the pre-9/11 period, the low-wage occupational group lost a disproportionate number of jobs prior to 9/11. Low-wage occupations lost jobs at a 1.8 percent pace compared to a 1.3 percent overall job loss between December 2000 and August 2001. Low-wage job loss was largely concentrated among production and low-wage sales occupations. High-wage occupations lost jobs at the same 1.3 percent pace as the overall job loss, while mid-wage occupations lost jobs at a slightly slower pace, 1.1 percent.

More important, however, is *the change in interpretation* that results from the switch to an occupational perspective from an industry perspective. In particular, in the immediate impact period, job losses in the low-wage occupational group were proportional to the overall decline (both declined 3.3 percent from August 2001 to January 2002). Thus, the low-wage *occupational* story is different from the low-wage *industry* story produced by the industry-based analysis, which shows that low-wage industries' employment loss in the immediate impact period (a 1.9 percent decline in jobs) was considerably *less than* the 3.4 percent overall decline, and only one-third of the 5.8 percent decline in high-wage industries.[16] (See table 7.5, which brings together the relevant data from tables 7.1 and 7.4.)

During the immediate impact period, steep declines in three low-wage and three middle-wage occupations were far more pronounced than either before or after the 9/11 impact period. Declines in these occupations were consistent with the pattern of industry-based 9/11 job losses noted earlier. Within low-wage occupations, food preparation and serving occupations lost 5 percent of that occupation's jobs, and building cleaning and maintenance occupations and personal care service occupations lost jobs at a much faster pace than in either the pre- or post-9/11 phases.

Meanwhile, high-wage occupations lost jobs at a faster rate (3.8 percent) than the 3.3 percent overall rate, while job decline among mid-wage occupa-

TABLE 7.4 EMPLOYMENT CHANGE IN NEW YORK CITY BY OCCUPATION AND WAGE RANGE, DURING 2001 TO 2003 RECESSION

Wage Group and Major Occupational Group	Employment (Thousands) December 2000	Pre-9/11 Recession December 2000 to August 2001		Immediate Impact August 2001 to January 2002		Post-9/11 Recession January 2002 to August 2003		Peak to Trough December 2000 to August 2003	
		# Change (Thousands)	% Change	# Change (Thousands)	% Change	# Change (Thousands)	% Change	# Change (Thousands)	% Change
Low-wage occupations									
Farming, fishing, and forestry	6	0	-0.7	0	-3.4	0	-3.1	0	-7.0
Health care support	98	-1	-0.5	1	0.5	2	2.4	2	2.4
Personal care and service	117	0	0.1	-2	-1.9	0	0.4	-2	-1.5
Building and grounds cleaning and maintenance	125	-1	-0.9	-4	-3.0	-2	-1.7	-7	-5.6
Production	181	-11	-6.3	-9	-5.1	-15	-9.4	-35	-19.4
Food preparation and service	216	4	1.6	-11	-5.0	6	2.9	-1	-0.6
Low-wage sales	220	-8	-3.6	-6	-3.0	0	0.0	-14	-6.5
Total	964	-17	-1.8	-32	-3.3	-9	-0.9	-57	-6.0
Share of December 2000 employment	25.7%								
Share of wage group's peak-to-trough job loss		30.0%		55.1%		14.9%		100%	
Share of period's total job loss		34.2%		25.7%		12.4%			
Mid-wage occupations									
Community and social services	73	0	0.3	0	0.7	1	0.7	1	1.7
Arts, design, entertainment, sports, and media	85	-2	-1.8	-5	-5.7	-2	-3.1	-9	-10.3
Construction and extraction	129	-3	-2.3	-3	-2.0	-5	-4.4	-11	-8.5
Installation, maintenance, and repair	132	-2	-1.5	-5	-4.2	-4	-3.3	-12	-8.8
Protective service	136	2	1.6	-3	-2.1	-4	-2.8	-5	-3.3
Education, training, and library	137	1	0.5	1	0.4	5	3.6	6	4.5

(*Table continues on p. 206.*)

TABLE 7.4 *Continued*

Wage Group and Major Occupational Group	Employment (Thousands) December 2000	Pre-9/11 Recession December 2000 to August 2001 # Change (Thousands)	% Change	Immediate Impact August 2001 to January 2002 # Change (Thousands)	% Change	Post-9/11 Recession January 2002 to August 2003 # Change (Thousands)	% Change	Peak to Trough December 2000 to August 2003 # Change (Thousands)	% Change
Transportation and material moving	221	−4	−2.0	−9	−4.3	−5	−2.6	−19	−8.7
Office and administrative support	823	−12	−1.4	−28	−3.5	−20	−2.5	−60	−7.2
Total	1,737	−20	−1.1	−52	−3.1	−35	−2.1	−107	−6.2
Share of December 2000 employment	46.3%								
Share of wage group's peak-to-trough job loss		18.3%		48.9%		32.9%		100%	
Share of period's total job loss		38.9%		42.5%		51.0%			
High-wage occupations									
Life, physical, and social science	37	0	0.0	−1	−2.5	−1	−2.4	−2	−4.8
Architecture and engineering	50	0	−0.2	−1	−2.9	−2	−5.0	−4	−7.9
Legal	61	0	−0.1	−1	−1.3	0	−0.6	−1	−2.0
Computer and mathematical	112	−4	−3.5	−9	−8.7	−6	−5.7	−19	−16.9
High-wage sales	164	−2	−1.4	−10	−6.5	−8	−5.5	−21	−12.9
Health care practitioners and technical	185	0	−0.2	−1	−0.3	4	2.4	3	1.8
Business and financial operations	214	−3	−1.6	−7	−3.5	−7	−3.3	−18	−8.2
Management	229	−3	−1.4	−8	−3.6	−5	−2.5	−17	−7.3
Total	1,051	−14	−1.3	−39	−3.8	−25	−2.5	−78	−7.4
Share of December 2000 employment	28.0%								
Share of wage group's peak-to-trough job loss		17.4%		50.2%		32.4%		100%	
Share of period's total job loss		26.9%		31.8%		36.7%			
Total	3,751	−50	−1.3	−123	−3.3	−69	−1.9	−243	−6.5

Source: New York State Department of Labor (NYSDOL) 790 (establishment) employment data seasonally adjusted by authors.

TABLE 7.5   INDUSTRY VERSUS OCCUPATIONAL PERSPECTIVES ON 9/11 AND THE 2001 TO 2003 RECESSION IN NEW YORK CITY

Perspective	Pre-9/11 Recession December 2000 to August 2001		Immediate 9/11 Impact August 2001 to January 2002		Post-9/11 Recession January 2002 to August 2003	
	# Change	% Change	# Change	% Change	# Change	% Change
Industry						
Low-wage industries	−13,100	−0.9	−28,500	−1.9	22,000	1.5
Mid-wage industries	−14,500	−1.1	−41,000	−3.2	−47,800	−3.8
High-wage industries	−23,900	−2.5	−54,800	−5.8	−43,200	−4.9
Total	−51,500	−1.4	−124,300	−3.4	−69,000	−1.9
Occupational						
Low-wage occupations	−17,200	−1.8	−31,700	−3.3	−8,500	−0.9
Mid-wage occupations	−19,600	−1.1	−52,400	−3.1	−35,200	−2.1
High-wage occupations	−13,600	−1.3	−39,200	−3.8	−25,300	−2.5
Total	−50,400	−1.3	−123,300	−3.3	−69,000	−1.9

Sources: New York State Department of Labor (NYSDOL) 790 (establishment) employment data and authors' calculations. Employment data seasonally adjusted by authors.

tions again trailed the overall pace of decline. It should be noted once again that the switch from an industry to an occupational perspective produces a different interpretation of the immediate impact of 9/11 on high-wage occupations. In particular, the rate of job loss among high-wage *occupations* was considerably less (3.8 percent) than the rate of job loss in high-wage *industries* (5.8 percent).

Within the mid-wage group, the arts, design, entertainment, and media field, the transportation field, and installation, maintenance, and repair occupations all lost jobs during the immediate impact period at a pace well above the pre- or post-9/11 phases, and indeed, at a pace exceeding the overall 3.3 percent job decline in this period.

Between January 2002 and August 2003, the post-9/11 recession period, job losses in the high-wage occupational group again led the other occupational groups in job loss, with a 2.5 percent decline compared to 1.9 percent overall job loss. Job losses in computer and high-wage sales occupations continued to lead high-wage job declines. Construction occupations in the mid-wage category and architecture and engineering occupations in the high-wage category both lost jobs at a pace well ahead of the overall 1.9 percent job decline during this period. Although jobs among low-wage occupations were lost at their slowest pace overall during this third phase of the 2001 to 2003 recession, declining by only 0.9 percent, production occupations declined by 9.4 percent, the highest rate for any individual occupation for any of the three periods from 2001 to 2003. Food preparation jobs, which had been hit hard during the immediate impact period, bounced back quickly in the post-9/11 period and registered a 2.9 percent increase.

Figure 7.2, which indexes employment to a December 2000 starting point, shows the respective employment trajectories, by month, for these low-, mid-, and high-wage occupational groups over the 2001 to 2003 period. The figure illustrates the sharp drop in jobs in low-wage occupations in the immediate aftermath of 9/11. Moreover, as figure 7.2 makes clear, employment in the low-wage occupational group, unlike that in the mid- and high-wage groups, stabilized in mid- to late 2002 before beginning to decline again in 2003. This was not the case for the other two occupational wage groups, which continued to experience job losses.

Based on this analysis, it would appear that workers in the low-wage occu-

FIGURE 7.2　EMPLOYMENT TRENDS IN NEW YORK CITY, BY OCCUPATIONAL WAGE GROUPS, DECEMBER 2000 TO DECEMBER 2003

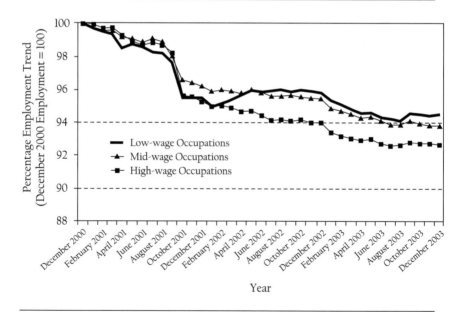

Sources: New York State Department of Labor (NYSDOL) 790 (establishment) employment data, seasonally adjusted by authors, and industry-occupation matrix.

pational group did *not* suffer disproportionate job losses during the immediate 9/11 impact period.[17] At the same time, it should be recognized that this occupational analysis reflects the assumption implicit in the use of the industry-occupation matrix—namely, that occupational job losses in the wake of 9/11 occurred in proportion to *occupational cohorts' respective shares of industry employment*. This may or may not have been the case. At the same time, even if this assumption is valid, it does not rule out the possibility that 9/11-induced job displacement and business disruption resulted in a higher incidence of official unemployment for workers in low-wage occupations. This could have been the case owing to the differential constraints and operating environment these workers' *employers* faced in the immediate post-9/11 period. Indeed, it would seem that there are good reasons to suspect that whatever dislocations did occur in the aftermath of 9/11, those among workers in low-wage occupations resulted in disproportionately adverse labor market outcomes for them, such as unemployment and reduced earnings. Further, it should be underscored that these estimates of the extent of occupational *job* loss do not reflect the extent of underemployment entailing *earnings* losses for those workers (such as garment workers and taxi drivers) who may have retained their jobs but were forced to work fewer hours or experienced reduced production-related pay.

Also, it should be kept in mind that this industry-occupation analysis is based on payroll employment for jobs in New York City, not on the city's resident labor force. Because city residents are more likely to hold the low-paying restaurant and hotel jobs in New York and suburban commuters are more highly represented in high-paying Wall Street jobs, an analysis based on city residents might be expected to reveal a larger proportional 9/11 impact on workers in low-wage occupations.

With this payroll-based industry-occupational analysis serving as a backdrop, the next section develops a different occupational perspective on 9/11 and the 2001 to 2003 recession. In particular, we use the Current Population Survey (CPS) to try to hone in on the question of whether different wage strata of the city's workforce experienced different labor market outcomes in the wake of 9/11. Using the same occupation-based wage stratification scheme employed earlier, unemployment and household earnings for three groups of New York City resident workers (low-, mid-, and high-wage) are derived and considered in light of the industry and industry-occupation analyses set out here.

AN OCCUPATIONAL PERSPECTIVE ON 9/11 BASED ON THE CURRENT POPULATION SURVEY

To examine the post-9/11 labor market outcomes—unemployment and household earnings—of workers in each wage stratum, we used the outgoing rotation group (ORG) subsample of the monthly CPS, since it provides earnings-related information. The CPS—the monthly household survey conducted by the Census Bureau and the Bureau of Labor Statistics—is used to derive all official labor force data. The survey's limited sample size for New York City limits our ability to draw inferences regarding any single occupational group's labor market outcomes.[18]

We assigned all workers in the labor force to one of three wage categories based on occupation. (The CPS indicates occupation for unemployed workers.) To address the small sizes of individual occupational cohorts, we used the same wage stratification scheme we used in the industry-occupation matrix analysis. That is, we aggregated the existing CPS occupational cohorts into three occupational groups based on median and mean hourly wage rates in the BLS Occupational Employment Statistics (OES) report.

Table 7.6 shows the mean and median hourly wages for the occupational groups from the ORG file. (Note that these wages are slightly different from the occupational wages based on the OES shown in table 7.3.) Table 7.6 also shows each group's share of New York City resident employment. The low-wage group is 31.3 percent of the total, a higher share than for the low-wage group's share of New York City payroll employment. As previously noted, because New York City residents tend to be concentrated in lower-wage jobs and because nonresident commuters are more likely to hold high-paying New York City jobs and some mid-wage jobs, both the mid-wage and high-wage groups' shares of resident employment are less than their respective shares of New York City payroll employment.

Table 7.7 shows several demographic characteristics for the three wage strata generated using the CPS. As the table shows, low-wage workers are more likely to be female, Hispanic, and less educated than middle- and high-wage workers.

TABLE 7.6   HOURLY WAGES IN NEW YORK CITY BY OCCUPATIONAL WAGE GROUP, 2000 TO 2003 (FOURTH-QUARTER 2003 DOLLARS)

Wage Group	Mean	Median	Group's Share of Total
Low-wage	$11.26	$9.36	31.3%
Mid-wage	17.13	14.30	43.4
High-wage	27.76	22.40	25.2

Source: Current Population Survey outgoing rotation group files for New York City, 2000 to 2003 pooled data.

TABLE 7.7 DEMOGRAPHIC CHARACTERISTICS OF OCCUPATIONAL WAGE GROUPS IN NEW YORK CITY, 2000 TO 2003

Wage Group	Gender		Race-Ethnicity				Educational Attainment				Age (mean)	Full-Time Status
	Male	Female	Non-Hispanic White	Non-Hispanic Black	Hispanic	Asian and All Other Non-Hispanic	Less Than High School	High School	Some College	B.A. and Higher		
Low	46%	54%	23%	25%	37%	16%	33%	37%	19%	12%	38.9	76%
Mid	56	44	39	27	24	10	14	30	25	30	38.8	80
High	55	45	58	16	12	14	3	12	17	68	40.7	89
Total	53	47	39	24	25	13	17	28	21	34	39.3	81

Source: Current Population Survey outgoing rotation group files for New York City, 2000 to 2003 pooled data.

UNEMPLOYMENT AMONG OCCUPATIONAL
WAGE GROUPS IN THE AFTERMATH OF 9/11

As a first step in the analysis of the CPS data, we derived quarterly unemployment rates for New York City from the ORG sample and compared them, on a two-quarter moving average basis, to the official seasonally adjusted Local Area Unemployment Statistics (LAUS) unemployment rate (see figure 7.3). Although the unadjusted quarterly unemployment rate unsurprisingly exhibits greater volatility than the official seasonally adjusted rate, it nevertheless tends to closely track movements in the official rate. Seasonally adjusted data are generally used to compare quarter-to-quarter movements in unemployment rates, but all ORG-derived unemployment rates in this analysis are presented in an unadjusted form. This decision was dictated by changes made to the CPS occupational classification scheme implemented in January 2003. Had this classification issue not existed, longer time series for each occupational wage group could have been derived and seasonal adjustments performed. At the

FIGURE 7.3   UNEMPLOYMENT RATE IN NEW YORK CITY, JUNE 1989 TO DECEMBER 2003 (TWO-QUARTER MOVING AVERAGE)

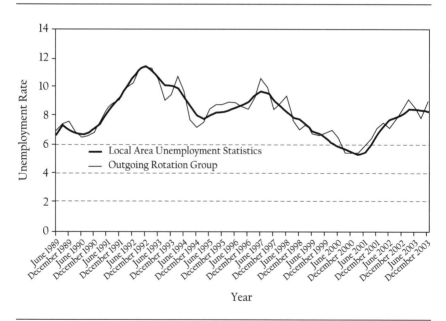

Source: Authors' calculations from Current Population Survey outgoing rotation group files and U.S. Bureau of Labor Statistics.

FIGURE 7.4   UNEMPLOYMENT RATE IN NEW YORK CITY, BY WAGE
GROUP, JUNE 2000 TO DECEMBER 2003 (TWO-QUARTER
MOVING AVERAGE)

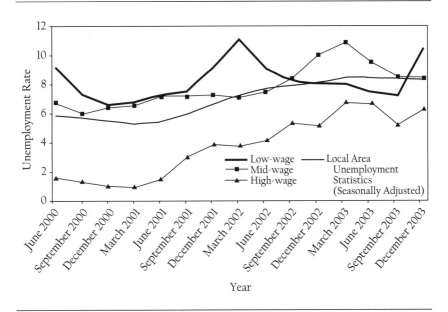

Source: Authors' calculations from Current Population Survey outgoing rotation group files and U.S. Bureau of Labor Statistics.

same time, comparisons between the BLS seasonally adjusted New York City quarterly unemployment rate and the unadjusted rate suggest that seasonal adjustment would not have substantially altered the principal finding detailed later in the chapter.

Figure 7.4 shows quarterly unemployment rates—smoothed via a two-quarter moving average—for the three occupational wage groups, along with the BLS seasonally adjusted New York City unemployment rate. Reflecting the onset of the national recession in early 2001, the unemployment rate for all three occupational wage groups began trending up in early 2001.

Figure 7.4 clearly shows a marked increase in unemployment among workers in the low-wage occupational group in the fourth quarter of 2001—the first three months following 9/11. On a two-quarter moving average basis, the increase in the number of unemployed in the city between the third quarter of 2001 and the first quarter of 2002 was 61,000, based on the ORG sample.

This compares to an increase of 63,000 over this period based on the LAUS unadjusted series and 49,000 for the adjusted series. Of this 61,000, 77 percent were classified as workers in low-wage occupations, 7 percent as workers in mid-wage occupations, and 16 percent as workers in high-wage occupations. Figure 7.4 also indicates that unemployment among workers in the low-wage occupational group began to decline rather quickly following the apparent 9/11-related increase, suggesting that 9/11's unemployment effect on these workers was relatively short-lived. (It appears to have lasted approximately two quarters.) In contrast, unemployment among workers in the mid- and high-wage groups began to trend steadily upward through much of 2002.

This suggests that there were differences in unemployment experiences among the three occupational wage groups in the aftermath of 9/11. These unemployment trends support the hypothesis that the 9/11-related displacements and business disruptions experienced by several low-wage workers' *employers* (especially those located in lower Manhattan) resulted in a higher incidence of unemployment among low-wage workers compared to workers in the mid- and high-wage occupational groups. In part, these divergent unemployment experiences among workers in different wage strata reflected differences in affected employers' abilities to restart, reorganize, and relocate their lower Manhattan operations and employees in the aftermath of 9/11. Further, several industries that were severely affected by 9/11 (such as those in the tourism and hospitality area), despite being less physically concentrated or anchored in lower Manhattan than other industries that were significantly affected, such as securities, experienced dramatic falloffs in business in the months that followed 9/11. This forced many to lay off personnel.

We do not mean to suggest that workers across the occupational wage spectrum were unaffected by 9/11—they undoubtedly were. Many of the industries located in Lower Manhattan and those experiencing the most significant 9/11 disruptions had high concentrations of workers in low-wage occupations. Thus, low-wage workers faced a greater likelihood of being laid off or suffering reduced earnings from under-employment. This disproportionate unemployment or underemployment of low-wage workers does not seem to be largely derivative of increased high-wage unemployment. Although the decline in retail and low-wage sales occupations in the pre-9/11 period may reflect reduced incomes and consumer expenditures among high-wage workers, the distinct pattern of 9/11-related job loss in food preparation, transportation, building cleaning, and arts and design occupations does not appear to be derivative of losses sustained among high-wage workers. Neither does the loss of low-wage production jobs that occurred throughout the 2001 to 2003 period. Undoubtedly, some low-wage service and retail sales jobs rise and fall with the relative prosperity of high-wage industries and occupations, but most low-wage jobs depend heavily on broader developments.

HOUSEHOLD EARNINGS

To gauge the effect of unemployment and underemployment on wage earnings in the wake of 9/11, we derived weekly household wage earnings for the three wage groups using the ORG sample. Since households may have workers from different wage strata, low-wage households were defined as those containing workers belonging only to low-wage occupations (as defined earlier), high-wage households as those with at least one member belonging to a high-wage occupation, and mid-wage households as the remainder. On this basis, approximately 22 percent of households were low-wage households, 45 percent were mid-wage households, and 33 percent were high-wage households. It should be noted that weekly household wage earnings include only wage and salary earnings and omit all other forms of income.

Table 7.8 shows mean and median weekly household wage earnings, by quarter, for each of the three wage groups for the first quarter of 2000 through the fourth quarter of 2003. Figure 7.5 shows the mean weekly household earnings from table 7.8 for the three types of households over the 2000 to 2003 period (graphed on a two-quarter moving average basis to smooth out fluctuations).

As table 7.8 and figure 7.5 indicate, low-wage households suffered a significant decline in their household earnings in the last quarter of 2001 and the first quarter of 2002. Mean weekly wage earnings for low-wage households declined by 7.9 percent in the fourth quarter of 2001 compared to the same quarter a year earlier, and they dropped by 18.2 percent in the first quarter of 2002 over the first quarter of 2001. This pattern of low-wage households' weekly earnings suggests that the higher incidence of 9/11-induced unemployment and underemployment among workers in low-wage occupations had a significantly adverse impact on household earnings. As with any sizable group, substantial changes in broad measures such as mean and median earnings mask the fact that some individual households had gains while others had declines much steeper than the figures show for the group as a whole.

Household earnings for mid-wage workers also appeared to be adversely affected but less severely than for low-wage workers, while the earnings of high-wage workers did not decline appreciably until about a year later. For mid-wage workers, mean weekly household earnings declined by 2.2 percent, and median earnings dropped by 11.6 percent in the fourth quarter of 2001. (Mean and median household wage earnings for mid-wage households had dropped by over 10 percent at the very start of the recession in the first quarter of 2001.)

The earnings of low-wage households fared slightly better through the remainder of 2002, with mean earnings up by slight amounts while median wages fell by single digits during the last two quarters of 2002 over the same

TABLE 7.8   REAL WEEKLY HOUSEHOLD EARNINGS IN NEW YORK CITY, 2000 TO 2003 (FOURTH-QUARTER 2003 DOLLARS)

	Mean				Median			
	Low-Wage Households	Mid-Wage Households	High-Wage Households	All Households	Low-Wage Households	Mid-Wage Households	High-Wage Households	All Households
Weekly household earnings								
Q1 2000	$602	$965	$1,502	$1,059	$489	$836	$1,275	$842
Q2 2000	$538	$925	$1,618	$1,107	$431	$725	$1,364	$862
Q3 2000	$608	$903	$1,542	$1,044	$493	$748	$1,209	$831
Q4 2000	$587	$942	$1,476	$1,026	$424	$815	$1,308	$848
Q1 2001	$630	$865	$1,583	$1,087	$511	$748	$1,374	$868
Q2 2001	$563	$913	$1,545	$1,064	$428	$795	$1,330	$845
Q3 2001	$588	$909	$1,524	$1,041	$442	$780	$1,301	$812
Q4 2001	$540	$921	$1,614	$1,063	$443	$721	$1,385	$801
Q1 2002	$515	$992	$1,701	$1,148	$363	$781	$1,549	$898
Q2 2002	$577	$917	$1,527	$1,068	$453	$791	$1,364	$854
Q3 2002	$598	$912	$1,644	$1,074	$409	$748	$1,389	$819
Q4 2002	$541	$878	$1,437	$998	$415	$744	$1,273	$783

Q1 2003	$588	$877	$1,743	$1,088	$484	$767	$1,534	$807
Q2 2003	$521	$919	$1,509	$1,057	$403	$744	$1,260	$863
Q3 2003	$589	$866	$1,466	$998	$451	$701	$1,230	$752
Q4 2003	$543	$910	$1,432	$1,010	$440	$750	$1,188	$800
Year-on-year change								
Q1 2001	4.6%	−10.3%	5.4%	2.6%	4.5%	−10.5%	7.8%	3.0%
Q2 2001	4.7	−1.2	−4.5	−3.9	−0.8	9.6	−2.5	−2.0
Q3 2001	−3.2	0.6	−1.2	−0.3	−10.3	4.4	7.6	−2.4
Q4 2001	−7.9	−2.2	9.3	3.6	4.4	−11.6	5.9	−5.6
Q1 2002	−18.2	14.6	7.5	5.6	−28.9	4.4	12.7	3.5
Q2 2002	2.4	0.3	−1.1	0.4	5.9	−0.5	2.6	1.1
Q3 2002	1.7	0.4	7.9	3.2	−7.4	−4.2	6.8	0.9
Q4 2002	0.1	−4.6	−11.0	−6.1	−6.3	3.2	−8.1	−2.2
Q1 2003	14.2	−11.6	2.5	−5.2	33.3	−1.8	−1.0	−10.1
Q2 2003	−9.7	0.3	−1.2	−1.0	−10.9	−6.0	−7.7	1.1
Q3 2003	−1.6	−5.1	−10.8	−7.1	10.1	−6.2	−11.4	−8.2
Q4 2003	0.4	3.6	−0.3	1.2	6.1	0.8	−6.7	2.1

Source: Authors' calculations from Current Population Survey outgoing rotation group files.

FIGURE 7.5   MEAN HOUSEHOLD WEEKLY WAGE EARNINGS IN NEW YORK
CITY, FIRST QUARTER OF 2000 TO FOURTH QUARTER OF 2003

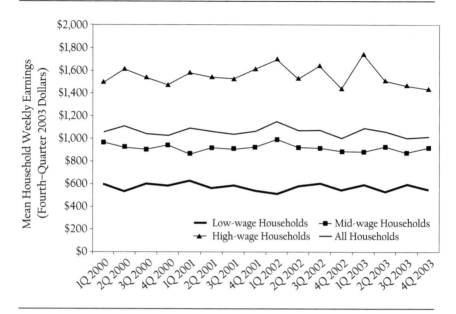

Source: Authors' calculations from Current Population Survey outgoing rotation group files.

quarters the year before. Low-wage household wage earnings improved significantly during the first quarter of 2003 over the year before, but then both mean and median wages dropped by about 10 percent in the second quarter of 2003.

Wages faltered for both mid-wage and high-wage households during the last four quarters of the 2001 to 2003 recession (through the third quarter of 2003). As table 7.9 shows, the dramatic decline in low-wage households' earnings in the first part of 2002 resulted in these households' average earnings declining by 3.5 percent in 2002, with medium earnings falling 11.5 percent. In contrast, mid- and high-wage households' average earnings increased slightly in 2002 before declining in 2003. This differential pattern in household earnings among the three types of households appears to be consistent with each group's unemployment experiences during 2002. Both mid- and high-wage households were spared significant wage erosion in the immediate aftermath of 9/11 but experienced earnings declines as the recession wore on in late 2002 and into 2003.

Overall, for the 2001 to 2003 recession, the weekly earnings of low- and

TABLE 7.9 REAL WEEKLY HOUSEHOLD EARNINGS IN NEW YORK CITY, 2000 TO 2003 (FOURTH-QUARTER 2003 DOLLARS)

	Mean				Median			
	Low-Wage Households	Mid-Wage Households	High-Wage Households	All Households	Low-Wage Households	Mid-Wage Households	High-Wage Households	All Households
Weekly household earnings								
2000	$585	$934	$1,539	$1,060	$458	$797	$1,293	$842
2001	$578	$902	$1,567	$1,064	$469	$765	$1,353	$832
2002	$558	$928	$1,574	$1,073	$415	$774	$1,378	$831
2003	$563	$893	$1,535	$1,038	$440	$731	$1,281	$798
Year-on-year change								
2001	-1.1%	-3.4%	1.9%	0.4%	2.4%	-4.1%	4.6%	-1.2%
2002	-3.5	2.9	0.5	0.8	-11.5	1.2	1.9	-0.2
2003	0.9	-3.7	-2.5	-3.3	6.1	-5.6	-7.1	-4.0

Source: Authors' calculations from Current Population Survey outgoing rotation group files.

mid-wage households declined, as table 7.9 shows, with median mid-wage household earnings ($731) 8.3 percent lower than in 2000 ($797). The mean weekly earnings for low-wage households dropped by 3.8 percent, from $585 in 2000 to $563 in 2003, with median earnings falling by about the same percentage, to $440, in 2003. Although high-wage households experienced mean and median declines in 2003, their wage earnings were only very slightly lower in 2003 compared to 2000, the last year of the economic expansion. The earnings for these households continued to rise in 2001 and 2002.[19]

POST-9/11 AID AND RELIEF PROGRAMS AND POLICIES

As part of the massive relief effort that followed the attack, various forms of government and private charitable financial assistance were provided to workers dislocated by the attack. This study does not attempt to gauge the extent to which any 9/11-related decline in household earnings may have been offset by specially targeted 9/11 government or private relief programs. The 9/11 United Services Group, established by a consortium of thirteen larger private relief agencies, estimated in the spring of 2002 that 45,000 workers whose jobs were affected by the attack continued to suffer an income loss of more than 25 percent. Most of these workers were still unemployed at the time of the survey (McKinsey & Co. 2002). No subsequent studies attempted to identify and track individual displaced workers. The data needed to make such an assessment do not exist. Available evidence does suggest the following observations regarding specially targeted 9/11 aid.

The relief response to dislocated workers was ad hoc and very unsystematic, largely because federal disaster relief programs provided by the Federal Emergency Management Agency (FEMA) usually focus on economic loss associated with property damage and not on broader economic impacts such as worker dislocation.

Financial assistance generally took the form of small cash grants or short-term mortgage and rental assistance. Workers were also aided in applying for unemployment insurance or searching for reemployment. Special outreach efforts increased the likelihood that unemployed low-income workers applied for and received unemployment insurance benefits. At the same time, low-wage workers were much less likely to receive benefits than higher-wage workers (Bernhardt and Rubin 2003). Some were provided with vocational training or English-as-a-second-language instruction to aid their reemployment. And in an effort to maintain employment opportunities, wage subsidies were provided to a few employers in a program run by the Consortium for Worker Education.

Assistance programs by major private charitable organizations helped fill some of the gaps left by governmental assistance, particularly in the area of income assistance, but usually only on a very short-term basis. Generally, since the city's public assistance caseload continued to decline through at least the end of 2002, it is unlikely that the city's safety net aided many low-income households adversely affected by the World Trade Center attack.[20]

Some of the workers who were not able to qualify for regular unemployment insurance or food stamps were assisted under special disaster unemployment or disaster food stamp programs. Generally, only workers whose jobs were located in lower Manhattan were eligible for 9/11-related financial assistance.[21] As a result, thousands of workers whose jobs happened to be in midtown hotels, at the airports, or elsewhere outside of lower Manhattan received limited assistance. Several months after the attack, at the end of June 2002, FEMA's Mortgage and Rental Assistance Program was expanded to all of Manhattan and to those who worked for businesses that had an "economically dependent business relationship" with a Manhattan business.

Disaster Relief Medicaid, which dramatically expanded the Medicaid rolls after 9/11, was the exception in not restricting eligibility by geographic area within the city. Disaster Relief Medicaid aided tens of thousands in the wake of 9/11 when the federal government allowed New York City to ease traditional eligibility and recertification requirements for Medicaid for four months (Chernick, ch. 10, this volume).

Compared to the scale of federal reconstruction aid provided to New York City and New York State, the financial assistance flowing to dislocated workers was minimal. Post-9/11 federal aid committed to New York totaled $20.7 billion, and private charitable assistance totaled $2.8 billion. Aside from the regular unemployment insurance system and Medicaid and Disaster Relief Medicaid, assistance to dislocated workers totaled roughly $700 million to $750 million. About 70 percent of this was in the form of cash assistance, mainly from FEMA's Mortgage and Rental Assistance Program, the September 11 Fund, and the Red Cross. A little over $200 million in aid took the form of employment and training assistance under programs funded by the September 11 Fund as the lead private charitable conduit or with federal funds under the Consortium for Worker Education's Emergency Employment Clearinghouse and the New York State Labor Department's National Emergency Grant.[22]

Although special 9/11-related public and private employment and training assistance enabled some workers to increase their employability and, through partial wage subsidies, aided some employers in retaining workers, very little of the billions in federal economic development assistance was used to stimulate job creation in order to ameliorate the high unemployment (especially among workers in low-wage occupations) that persisted in the wake of the 9/11 attack.

CONCLUSION

Both 9/11 and the 2001 to 2003 recession exacted heavy tolls on many of New York City's workers and their families. The analysis developed here suggests, however, that these events differentially affected various wage strata of New York City's workforce. This analysis yields the following conclusions.

- The 9/11 attack on the World Trade Center had serious short-term dislocation effects on New York City workers in low-wage occupations. These effects resulted in sharp increases in unemployment and underemployment among these workers and subsequent declines in their household earnings during the last quarter of 2001 and the first quarter of 2002.

- Although dislocation effects in the immediate 9/11 impact period among higher-wage groups appear not to have resulted in labor market outcomes as stark as those for workers in low-wage occupations, as the recession wore on into late 2002 and 2003 unemployment rose and household earnings fell for workers in middle- and high-wage groups.

- The differences in labor market outcomes experienced by workers in low-wage and higher-wage occupations reflected the occupational makeup of those industries most directly affected by 9/11 and its aftermath, as well as the ramifications of this aftermath for these workers' employers. It was often the case that employers of workers in low-wage occupations faced considerably longer periods of business disruption and downtime than employers of higher-paid workers. This partly reflected differences in these employers' location and capital constraints.

- All three occupational wage groups experienced substantial job declines between the December 2000 New York City employment peak and the August 2003 trough. The high-wage group experienced (slightly) disproportionate employment losses over this period. For the analyses based on payroll employment industry data—jobs located in New York City whether held by residents or commuters—the *occupational* analysis shows much more comparable job declines for the three wage groups than the *industry* analysis, which shows disproportionately high job declines in industries with high average wages and much lower employment declines in industries with low average wages.

- Overall, for the 2001 to 2003 period, weekly wages for low- and middle-wage households fell by much more than for high-wage households, since high-wage households continued to experience strong real wage earnings gains in 2001. For low-wage households, earnings declines sustained during the immediate aftermath of 9/11 were much more of a factor in accounting for the earnings declines these households experienced over the entire 2001 to 2003 period. For high-wage households, the bulk of the earnings declines sustained over the entire period were concentrated in the latter phase of the recession, while for mid-wage households earnings declines were experienced at various points over the 2001 to 2003 period, with the sharpest declines coming at the very beginning of the recession and in the last year of the recession.

NOTES

1. Monthly New York City payroll employment data were seasonally adjusted by the authors at a detailed industry level based on the March 2003 benchmark current employment survey series.
2. The Fiscal Policy Institute (FPI) concluded in a report six months after the attack that approximately 75,000 jobs were lost in New York City during the fourth quarter of 2001 as a fairly immediate result of the attack and that another 13,000 jobs (primarily in the finance sector) had been relocated outside the city. These estimates were slightly below those developed by several governmental and private organizations in late 2001 that put the New York City employment effect in the neighborhood of 100,000 jobs (Parrott 2002a). See New York City Partnership and Chamber of Commerce(2001/2002), Comptroller, City of New York (2001), New York Governor and State Division of the Budget (2001), New York State Senate Finance Committee Staff (2002), and New York State Assembly Ways and Means Committee Staff (2002). For a review of these studies, see U.S. Government Accounting Office (2002).
3. According to Asian American Federation of New York (2002a), 23 percent of the Chinatown workforce was laid off in the three months after 9/11. Garment workers suffered a 46 percent reduction in their average weekly wages after 9/11, and restaurant workers experienced an 80 percent decrease in weekly wages.
4. For an analysis of the effect of corporate scandals on New York City and New York State budgets and pension systems, see Comptroller, State of New York (2003).
5. The methodology employed by the FPI to make the job loss estimates referred to in note 2 included extensive interviews with representatives of business, industry, and labor; the use of an input-output model to estimate indirect and induced effects; and evaluation of preliminary estimates against published Labor Department payroll employment data. These estimates factored out a portion of fourth-quarter job losses that could be attributed to the ongoing recession by adjusting the job loss for selected industries for the average monthly employment decline sustained in the period from December 2000 through August 2001 (Parrott 2002a).
6. The FPI's November 2001 report was the only analysis of 9/11-related economic impacts conducted within the first year after the attack to examine the question of the impact on different wage strata. In that report, the FPI estimated that 60 percent of the workers likely to have lost their jobs as a direct result of the attack worked in what could be considered low-wage occupations: the average wage was $11 an hour or less (Parrott and Nowakowski 2001).

7. A Federal Reserve Bank of New York study takes the contrary view. Jason Bram, James Orr, and Carol Rapaport (2002, 9) cite the example of workers in general merchandise stores (low-wage) and in legal settings (high-wage) to suggest that it "does not support the hypothesis that the 9/11 attack caused disproportionate job losses in low-wage industries." However, neither of these industries was among the industries most heavily affected, and the authors do not look at the wage levels for workers in the major industries affected by the 9/11 attack.

8. In addition, many of the smaller businesses in lower Manhattan (especially those in Chinatown) that faced significant periods of business disruption in the aftermath of 9/11 were cash-based businesses, had very small profit margins, and relied heavily on volume. These factors undoubtedly increased the likelihood that these businesses had to resort to layoffs in the face of the significant reductions in patronage they experienced in the months following 9/11 (Asian American Federation of New York 2002b).

9. There were an estimated 14,000 to 15,000 garment workers employed in Chinatown prior to 9/11. Thus, garment workers employed in Chinatown's apparel factories accounted for around 30 percent of the city's apparel manufacturing industry employment (New York State Department of Labor).

10. The FPI estimated that 56 percent of the workers displaced by 9/11 were immigrants. Additionally, because of their significant presence in certain heavily affected industries, particularly restaurants and apparel manufacturing, undocumented immigrant workers accounted for an estimated 10 percent of all 9/11 job dislocation (Parrott 2002b).

11. The FPI's November 2001 report estimated that 76,000 workers in three industries—taxis, apparel manufacturing, and graphic arts—remained "employed" but suffered reduced earnings through loss of work (Parrott and Nowakowski 2001).

12. Consider that the health care and social assistance sector's average annual wage of $37,400 places it in the group of low-wage industries, according to table 7.1. The sector's occupational makeup, however, makes clear that the health care industry has two distinct sets of employees—one with high wages and one with low wages. The predominant classification of workers in the social assistance industries largely in community and social service occupations places them in the mid-wage occupational category (See table 7.4).

13. Since the New York State Department of Labor no longer makes available a New York City industry-occupation matrix, we used the national industry-occupation matrix for 2003. The occupational analysis performed by the FPI in the fall of 2001 used a late 1990s New York City industry-occupation matrix (see note 6).

14. The occupational distribution by industry was applied at a NAICS (North American Industry Classification System) industry level equivalent to a three-digit industry level in the Standard Industrial Classification (SIC) system. Given the fairly detailed level at which the industry-occupation matrix was applied, it is likely that New York City's occupational distribution closely tracks the national occupational distribution for most industries.

15. Because workers in the sales occupational group have a bimodal wage distribution—particularly in New York City, where there are many low-wage cashiers

and sales workers at one end and many very highly paid securities brokers at the high end—the sales occupation was divided in two on the basis of wages.

16. The difference between the two perspectives is a function of the fact that our low-wage industries' share of the nonfarm employment base is larger than low-wage occupations' share. The low-wage classification is based on wage data in both instances, however. This point merely underscores the potential import of the definition of "low-wage" workers and the value of considering both industry- and occupation-based distributions.

17. It should be noted that while the majority of jobs lost during the entire 2001 to 2003 period (December 2000 to August 2003) occurred in the immediate impact period for all three occupational wage groups, the low-wage occupational group lost 55 percent of all the jobs it lost between 2001 and 2003 during the immediate impact period. Both the high- and mid-wage occupational groups sustained about half of their 2001 to 2003 job loss during the 9/11 immediate impact period (see table 7.4).

18. The ORG sample we used represents one-quarter of the monthly New York City CPS sample. Monthly CPS data were grouped into calendar quarters. For the period from the first quarter of 2000 to the fourth quarter of 2003, quarterly sample sizes averaged 970. Classification of cases into three occupational wage groups resulted in sample sizes of approximately 290 low-wage workers, 420 mid-wage workers, and 260 high-wage workers. These sample sizes limit the precision of the labor market time series derived in this analysis. The CPS, however, represents the best source of information available for exploring the labor market effects of 9/11 on different wage strata of the workforce.

19. Cordelia Reimers (this volume) reaches somewhat different, but not necessarily contradictory, conclusions. She uses the CPS to analyze labor market effects for disadvantaged workers, comparing New York City with five other large cities to try to separate out 9/11 effects from the impact of the ongoing recession. She finds a short-term negative impact of 9/11 on the employment of disadvantaged women in New York City, but for disadvantaged men, her analysis suggests, the recession was more likely the proximate cause of labor market effects. Although this chapter does not examine labor market effects based on demographic characteristics, the low-wage grouping used here was more heavily female (54 percent) than the mid-wage (44 percent) or high-wage (45 percent) groups. Also, the technique followed in this chapter to identify 9/11-affected industries and occupations pointed to industries such as accommodations and air transport and occupations such as food service and transportation. As Reimer notes, these industries are likely to have been affected in some degree in the other large cities as well, but her method focuses on differentials between New York City and other cities.

20. In an examination of trends in New York City's public assistance caseload, the city's Independent Budget Office noted that, while the number of family public assistance cases continued to decline in 2001 and 2002, the percentage of applications that were rejected increased. Both caseloads and the number and rate of rejections increased in 2003 (New York City Independent Budget Office 2004).

21. In their assessments of the lessons learned from the philanthropic and government

9/11 relief efforts, Melcher (2003, 10) and Dixon and Stern (2004, 101) note that arbitrary geographic boundaries hindered the provision of relief to dislocated workers.

22. The $20.7 billion federal aid figure does not include the more than $5 billion disbursed under the Victim Compensation Fund. The $700 million to $750 million estimate for cash and employment and training assistance to dislocated workers includes the small amounts under Disaster Unemployment Assistance and Disaster Food Stamps but does not include another $700 million to $750 million provided to workers under regular unemployment assistance or provided on behalf of dislocated workers covered under Disaster Relief Medicaid. (Regular unemployment insurance is funded through a payroll tax.) See also Dixon and Stern (2004, ch. 6).

REFERENCES

Asian American Federation of New York. 2002a. *Chinatown After September 11: An Economic Impact Study.* New York: AAFNY (April 4).

———. 2002b. *Chinatown One Year After September 11: An Economic Impact Study.* New York: AAFNY (November).

Bagli, Charles V. 2001. "Parking Garages Suffering from Manhattan's Single-Driver Restrictions." *New York Times,* November 26.

Bernhardt, Annette, and Kate Rubin. 2003. *Recession and 9/11: Economic Hardship and the Failure of the Safety Net for Unemployed Workers in New York City.* New York: New York University Law School, Brennan Center for Justice (August).

Bram, Jason, James Orr, and Carol Rapaport. 2002. "Measuring the Effects of the September 11 Attack on New York City." *Economic Policy Review* (Federal Reserve Bank of New York) 8(2, November): 9.

Comptroller, City of New York. 2001. "The Impact of the September 11 World Trade Center Attack on New York City's Economy and City Revenues." (October 4).

Comptroller, State of New York. Office of the State Deputy Comptroller. 2003. *Impact of the Corporate Scandals on New York State.* New York: Office of the State Deputy Comptroller for New York City (August).

Dixon, Lloyd, and Rachel Kaganoff Stern. 2004. *Compensation for Losses from the 9/11 Attacks.* Santa Monica, Calif.: RAND Corporation, 2004.

Dolfman, Michael L., and Solidelle F. Wasser. 2004. "9/11 and the New York City Economy: A Borough-by-Borough Analysis." *Monthly Labor Review* (June): 3–33.

McKinsey & Co. 2002. *A Study of the Ongoing Needs of People Affected by the World Trade Center Disaster: Key Findings and Recommendations.* New York: 9/11 United Services Group (June 27).

Melcher, Michael F. 2003. *The Philanthropic Response to 9/11: A Practical Analysis and Recommendations.* New York: Simpson Thacher & Bartlett LLP (December).

New York City Independent Budget Office. 2004. "Despite Recession, Welfare Reform and Labor Market Changes Limit Public Assistance Growth." Fiscal brief (August).

New York City Partnership and Chamber of Commerce. 2001/2002. "Economic Impact of the September 11th Attack on New York City." (November 2001; rev. February 11, 2002).

New York Governor and State Division of the Budget. 2001. "Rebuild New York—Renew America: The World Trade Center Attacks; Current Estimated Cost." (October 9).

New York State Assembly Ways and Means Committee Staff. 2002. "New York State Economic Report." (March).

New York State Senate Finance Committee Staff. 2002. "Financial Impact of the World Trade Center Impact, Prepared by DRI-WEFA." (January).

Parrott, James. 2002a. *The Employment Impact of the September 11 World Trade Center Attack: Updated Estimates Based on the Benchmarked Employment Data.* New York: Fiscal Policy Institute (March 8).

———. 2002b. *Immigrant Workers Displaced by the September 11 World Trade Center Attacks.* New York: Fiscal Policy Institute (June 5).

Parrott, James, and Zofia Nowakowski. 2001. *World Trade Center Job Impacts Take a Heavy Toll on Low-Wage Workers: Occupational and Wage Implications of Job Losses Related to the September 11 World Trade Center Attack.* New York: Fiscal Policy Institute (November 5).

Rogers, Josh. 2003. "Beginning to Put Downtown's Plans in Place." *Downtown Express,* April 9. Available online at: http://www.zwire.com/site/news.cfm?BRD=1841&dept_id=513522&newsid=7660376&PAG=461&rfi=9.

U.S. Government Accounting Office (GAO). 2002. *Review of Studies of the Economic Impact of the September 11, 2001, Terrorist Attacks on the World Trade Center.* Washington: GAO (May 29).

CHAPTER 8

The Impact of 9/11 on Low-Skilled, Minority, and Immigrant Workers in New York City

Cordelia W. Reimers

THIS CHAPTER describes the effect of the September 11, 2001, attacks on workers who live in New York City. It differs from other studies of the effects of 9/11 on New York City's labor market in that it focuses on what happened to residents of New York City rather than on jobs located in New York City, many of which are held by commuters who live in the suburbs. The chapter focuses on those New York City residents who are disadvantaged by virtue of lack of education, minority status, or recent arrival in the United States. In most economic downturns these segments of the workforce lose more than "advantaged" workers. However, because the 9/11 attack hit the financial district in lower Manhattan so hard, and because many highly educated whites work in the financial services industry, this generalization may not hold in this case.

As described in other chapters in this volume and other volumes in this series, the destruction of the World Trade Center (WTC) disrupted economic activity in New York City both directly and indirectly. The destruction and damage to buildings, transportation, and communications in lower Manhattan and the consequent relocation of many offices had a ripple effect on the businesses in that area that had provided goods and services for the office workers. Street closings also disrupted activity in lower Manhattan, preventing residents, visitors, and workers from moving freely. This relative immobility further reduced business for manufacturers and other suppliers of goods and services in the area. Beyond the financial district, Chinatown's garment manufacturers, restaurants, and shops were hard hit by lack of telephone service and barriers to motor vehicles. Beyond lower Manhattan, the hard hit suffered by New York City's tourism industry due to the decline in air travel after 9/11 affected the hotel, restaurant, and entertainment industries as well as the airline industry and airports. In their chapter in this volume, James Parrott and Oliver Cooke document the job losses in the industries that were particularly affected by the 9/11 attacks.

Most of these business disruptions were temporary, lasting only a few weeks or months. Some firms relocated inside New York City, creating new employment and therefore business for shops and restaurants in other neighborhoods, such as midtown Manhattan, Sunset Park in Brooklyn, and Flushing in Queens. Others relocated outside New York City, and some marginal firms went out of business. Consequently, many workers in New York City lost work time and income, and some lost their jobs, as a result of the World Trade Center attack.

It is difficult if not impossible to disentangle the effects of 9/11 from the effects of the recession that began earlier in 2001. According to the Federal Reserve Bank of New York, New York City's recession began in January 2001, two months before the national recession officially began in March (Bram 2003). The employment rate (that is, the employment-population ratio) for eighteen- to sixty-four-year-old residents of New York City, as measured by the Current Population Survey (CPS), had actually begun declining nine months earlier, in April 2000 (author's tabulation). Since then, recovery from the recession has been very sluggish nationwide, especially in the labor market. Because job creation has not kept pace with labor force growth, employment rates have continued to decline. It would be difficult enough to identify the effects of 9/11 statistically because they coincided with the aftermath of the recession. But there is a deeper conceptual problem: the reaction to 9/11 exacerbated and prolonged the recession, and its depressing effects on travel-related industries hindered recovery from the recession.

So where do we draw the line between effects due to the recession and effects due to 9/11? I offer no complete solution to this puzzle but attempt to control for the effects of the nationwide recession by comparing New York City with five other U.S. cities that are its main competitors in its key industries. However, because 9/11 affected transportation and tourism all over the country (indeed, the world), this is an imperfect control. At best, it isolates the direct effects on New York City of the destruction of the World Trade Center from the more diffuse effects of the reaction to 9/11 on the national and world economies.

Most analyses of job loss in New York City due to the recession and 9/11 have used data from employers that trace the number of jobs located in New

York City or Manhattan, including those held by commuters, and these employers' average monthly payrolls. My analysis uses household survey data instead to trace the employment, hours worked, and earnings of New York City residents, including those who work in the suburbs or are self-employed. The results could differ. My results do not include jobs lost by suburbanites or jobs held by New York City residents that were simply relocated from Manhattan to other boroughs or the suburbs. Because commuters are more likely than New York City residents to be well-educated, white non-Hispanics and less likely to be recent immigrants, this focus on New York City residents is more likely than other approaches to capture disadvantaged workers. My employment rates also take account of changes in the working-age population of New York City and whether the number of jobs has kept up with population growth. Indeed, as noted earlier, the downturn in New York City residents' employment-population ratio occurred nine months before the city's recession began.

This chapter uses CPS microdata to provide a descriptive analysis of the labor market outcomes, household incomes, and Medicaid receipt of New York City residents before and after September 11, 2001, by education level, race or Hispanic origin, recency of immigration, and gender. The labor market outcomes investigated are weekly employment rates and hours worked, weekly earnings, and annual earnings. As a "bottom-line" summary of what happened to the economic well-being of New York City's disadvantaged residents, changes in household income—including the value of in-kind benefits other than Medicaid—and Medicaid coverage are also described. The next section describes the data used, and the third section explains the methods of smoothing the monthly time series and adjusting for changes in the composition of the samples by education and age. Results are presented in the following section, and conclusions are in the final section.

DATA

The data for this chapter are drawn from the Current Population Survey. This is the monthly household survey that is used to measure official unemployment rates and poverty rates. It is the only monthly or annual survey that identifies workers' characteristics. Most other studies of the effects of 9/11 on New York City's labor market (Bram 2003; Bram, Orr, and Rapaport 2002; Dolfman and Wasser 2004; Fiscal Policy Institute 2001, 2002a, 2002b; Parrott and Cooke, this volume) have been based on the monthly Current Employment Survey (CES) of employers or on unemployment insurance covered wages and employment data.[1] These employer data measure employment and payrolls by the employer's location and detailed industry, but they have no information on workers' characteristics or place of residence. The New York City employment numbers in these data include jobs in New York City held by suburban commuters and exclude self-employed workers. The employment measure based on the CPS household survey, on the other hand, includes all jobs held by New York City residents, including the self-employed and those whose jobs are located outside New York City.

I use three sets of CPS microdata files: the monthly basic files for 2000 to 2003 to investigate weekly employment and hours worked; the outgoing rotation group (ORG) files for 2000 to 2003 to investigate weekly earnings; and the annual demographic supplement files for March 1996 to 2003 to investigate annual earnings, household income, the value of in-kind benefits, and Medicaid receipt. The samples for employment, hours, and earnings consist of persons age eighteen to sixty-four who live within the city limits of New York City or the five cities chosen for comparison because they are New York's main competitors in its key industries: Los Angeles County, San Francisco, Chicago, Washington, D.C., and Boston.

The CPS is the only available dataset that identifies workers' demographic characteristics and is collected frequently; the sample is rather small, however, and the questions are worded so that they do not measure temporary effects on employment or earnings. For the demographic groups that are the focus of this study, average sample sizes in New York City for the employment and hours analyses range from 180 to 280 observations per month, since they include everyone age eighteen to sixty-four in the monthly basic file. Samples for annual earnings from the March CPS are a little larger, ranging from 230 to 540 observations per year. Samples for weekly earnings are considerably smaller (only 19 to 45 observations per month, depending on the group), since they include only wage and salary employees in the ORGs, which are only one-quarter of the monthly CPS sample. The samples from the March CPS for household income and Medicaid receipt are limited to household heads age eighteen to sixty-four living in these same locations and range in size from 300 to 460 observations.[2] With such small samples, random sampling variation may mask changes affecting a small portion of the population.

The exact wording of the CPS questions also limits what we can learn from these data. The monthly questions ask about labor force activity "last week." Anyone who answers yes to either of the following two questions is classified as "employed":

"Last week, did you do any work for either pay or profit (including any unpaid work in a family business or farm)?"

"Last week, ... did you have a job either full- or part-time? Include any job from which you were temporarily absent."

Weekly hours worked are the sum of the answers to two questions:

"Last week, how many hours did you actually work at your (main) job?"

"Last week, how many hours did you actually work at your other job(s)?"

Usual weekly earnings are measured by a question that is asked only of wage and salary earners:

"(Including overtime pay, tips, and commissions), what are your usual weekly earnings on your *main* job, before taxes or other deductions?"

The CPS survey is conducted in the third week of each month. Thus, by coincidence, the September 2001 survey was conducted the week after 9/11 and asked about the very week of the attacks. It asked whether the respondent had a job the week of 9/11, and if so, how many hours she or he actually worked that week and how much she or he "usually" earns per week on his or her "main" job. As we shall see, the time series of weekly hours worked shows a dramatic "hit" in September 2001. However, the September 2001 survey could not capture effects of the 9/11 attack on employment or earnings. Because the attack occurred on a Tuesday and anyone who had a job on the Monday of that week would correctly answer yes to the employment question—whether or not that person worked at all that week and even if she or he lost that job on Tuesday morning—the CPS would miss transitory employment effects that lasted less than a month. Longer-term employment effects would not show up until October. The earnings question asks, "What are X's *usual* weekly earnings on his/her *main* job?" (emphasis added). By its very wording the question refers to a "normal" week and avoids measuring transitory effects of 9/11 in September. It also omits the self-employed. Whereas measured weekly hours include temporary variations and all jobs, measured earnings include only usual earnings on the main job for wage and salary workers—a much less sensitive measure. Therefore, in contrast to hours worked, the time series of employment rates and earnings would not be expected to show a "hit" in September. Moreover, if low-wage workers disproportionately lose jobs, average weekly earnings may rise owing to selectivity (and vice versa). Despite these drawbacks, it is worth investigating the patterns in the CPS data to see whether there is evidence of negative effects of 9/11 on New York City's disadvantaged workers.

METHODS

As mentioned earlier, this chapter traces labor market outcomes and household incomes of New York City and comparison-city residents age eighteen to sixty-four before and after September 11, 2001, by education level, race or Hispanic origin, recency of immigration, and gender. Four labor market outcomes are investigated: the likelihood of being employed during the survey week (either working or with a job but not at work); weekly hours worked (including zeroes for those not employed); usual weekly earnings on the main job for wage and salary workers; and annual earnings (including zeroes). I analyze the first three outcomes using monthly CPS data for 2000 to 2003. To analyze annual earnings, household income, and Medicaid coverage for 2000 to 2002, I use data from the March CPS for 1996 to 2003, which report income in the previous calendar year. All data are weighted, using the CPS final weights for the monthly data and the March supplement weights for the annual data.

The likelihood of being employed reflects both labor force participation and unemployment rates and thus takes account of discouraged workers as well as those officially classified as unemployed. Changes in weekly hours worked, including zeroes, reflect changes in employment as well as changes in hours actually worked. Weekly hours conditional on being employed are not analyzed separately because of the small sample sizes. However, results for usual weekly earnings are presented despite the reduced sample size of wage and salary employees in the outgoing rotation groups because that is the only available evidence on weekly earnings. For salaried workers, this captures changes in salary, expressed on a weekly basis. For hourly wage earners, changes in weekly earnings reflect changes in *usual* hours worked on the person's main job as well as in wage rates. Annual earnings are actual earnings from all jobs, including self-employment; therefore, they may move differently from usual weekly earnings of wage and salary workers.

I also analyze changes in annual household income and Medicaid coverage from 2000 to 2002 for households whose head is of working age (eighteen to sixty-four), measuring both money income and income including the value of in-kind benefits (other than Medicaid) received by any member of the household.[3]

I attempt to disentangle the direct effects of the World Trade Center destruction in New York City from the effects of the nationwide recession and the more diffuse effects of the reaction to 9/11 nationally by comparing labor market outcomes in New York City with those in five other cities taken as a group: Los Angeles County, San Francisco, Chicago, Washington, D.C., and Boston. Although it is difficult to find other cities in the United States that are directly comparable to New York in economic structure, these five metropolitan areas have been identified by Edward Hill and Iryna Lendel (this volume) as New York's main competitors for the following reasons: First, they are the next five largest metropolitan areas after the New York consolidated metropolitan statistical area (CMSA), as measured by gross product (GP), and there is a major discontinuity in size between Boston and the next largest metropolitan region. Second, each of these regions has sectors of its economy that compete with New York either in product markets or as a North American location for business activity. New York's portion of the financial services industry, with its supply chain in producer services, faces competition from businesses in Chicago and Boston. All five compete with New York in the information services industry. Los Angeles and New York are rivals in television and cable television production. Metropolitan Washington competes in telecommunications, government, third-sector activities, and corporate headquarters as the economy emphasizes telecommunications and defense. Chicago has targeted the headquarters business function as an economic development opportunity. Pharmaceuticals and biomedical products are important to northern New Jersey and constitute a competitive emerging industry in Boston, Chicago, San Francisco, and metropolitan Washington. (The structure of these competitive relationships is the subject of the concluding section of Hill and Lendel's chapter.)

Because they are New York's main competitors in its key industries, we infer that these five metropolitan areas would be affected similarly to New York by the nationwide recession but not by 9/11.[4] Because I am investigating the effects of 9/11 on residents of New York City, I confine the comparison group to residents of the central cities of these metropolitan areas—that is, Los Angeles County, San Francisco, Chicago, Washington, D.C., and Boston. A comparison of employment rates in these five cities with the nation as a whole indicates that the decline started later, but then (in 2002 and 2003) was slightly more severe in these five cities than nationally. The differences, however, are very small: only 0.3 percentage points in October to December 2001 and 0.6 points in 2002. A relatively small and temporary effect of 9/11 in New York City compared with the national recession is evident, regardless of whether New York is compared with these five cities or with the nation as a whole.

The limited CPS sample size for New York City prevents us from analyzing demographic groups in great detail lest the cell sizes become too small. I therefore focus on broad markers of disadvantage in the labor market, without detailed cross-classification, by first examining two education levels: high school dropouts and high school graduates who did not go to college. Because high school dropouts and graduates are concentrated in different industries and occupations, 9/11 may have affected them differently. Separately, I examine three minority groups: African Americans, Hispanics, and Asians. My colleague Howard Chernick and I have found that Hispanics and blacks in New York City were affected differently by welfare reform in the 1990s, with Hispanics' employment rates rising more than blacks' (Chernick and Reimers 2004). This indicates a difference in their positions in the labor market that may be reflected in the impact of 9/11 as well as in the impact of welfare reform. Unfortunately, the samples of Puerto Ricans, Dominicans, and "other Spanish" are too small for reliable analysis; thus, I do not analyze these Hispanic groups individually.[5]

In a third set of analyses, I classify persons by nativity and recency of arrival in the United States and examine immigrants who have been in the United States less than fifteen years. I chose this dividing line on both theoretical and practical grounds. Fifteen years is about how long it takes an immigrant to adapt to the U.S. labor market, learn the language and other U.S.-specific skills, acquire citizenship and occupational licenses, and otherwise compete on a more or less equal footing with those born in the United States who have a similar level of education. It also yields a large enough sample of "recent" immigrants in New York City for reliable analysis. For comparison, I examine "advantaged" New Yorkers—that is, white non-Hispanics who attended college and are not recent immigrants.[6] In all cases the outcomes for men and women are analyzed separately because they are concentrated in different occupations and industries that may have been affected differently by 9/11.

Even with such broad demographic categories, the monthly CPS samples are not large. Therefore, the monthly time series of labor market outcomes are very volatile and need smoothing in order to detect the patterns in the data. I employ a model that includes dummy variables for the periods April to December 2000, January to August 2001, September 2001 itself, October 2001 to December 2001, the year 2002, and the year 2003. The starting point is April 2000 because employment rates in New York City peaked in that month. Complete interactions with a dummy variable indicating residence in New York City are included in the model. Thus, this model estimates average outcomes for two pre-9/11 periods and three post-9/11 periods in New York City compared with the other five cities combined.

It is possible that the comparisons of mean outcomes over time, and particularly between New York City and the comparison cities, are affected by differences in the composition of the cross-section samples by education levels and age. All the models (except Medicaid receipt) therefore include an adjustment for education and potential experience. Specifically, the models include quartic functions of years of schooling and potential experience since age sixteen.[7]

Thus, for each demographic group I use the monthly CPS data for 2000 to 2003 to estimate a linear probability model indicating whether the person was employed in the previous week and regression models of hours worked in the previous week and usual real weekly earnings (in 2002 dollars). All three models are estimated by ordinary least squares (OLS). The independent variables are quartic functions of years of schooling and potential experience since age sixteen, the time-period and New York City dummy variables described earlier, and interactions of the New York City and time-period dummy variables.

In the annual data from the March CPS, only one year's income after 9/11 (2002) is available at this time.[8] The models of annual earnings and income are estimated on a pooled sample from the March CPS for 1996 to 2003, with year and New York City dummies and interaction terms in addition to the quartic functions of years of schooling and potential experience. This allows us to compare mean annual earnings, household incomes, and Medicaid receipt in 2000, 2001, and 2002 for New York City with the other five cities combined.

RESULTS

The results for employment rates, weekly hours, and usual weekly earnings are presented in the form of graphs (figures 8.1 through 8.8) that show the adjusted outcomes in New York City and the difference in outcomes, relative to January to August 2001, between New York City and the comparison cities. The results are summarized in tables 8.1 through 8.4, which show the direction and statistical significance of the effect of 9/11 in New York City (the "first differences") and of the effects for New York City versus the comparison cities (the "difference-in-differences"). The direction of the effect in New York City is measured for both the short term, by the sign of the change in New York City from the period January to August 2001 to the period October to December 2001, and the medium term, by the sign of the change from the period January to August 2001 to the year 2002. A negative sign indicates a decline in the outcome in New York City, owing to the combined effects of the recession and 9/11. The sign of the difference-in-differences effect is shown for the same time periods. Because the difference-in-differences effect is the change in New York City minus the change in the comparison cities, its sign is negative if the outcome fell more, or rose less, in New York City than elsewhere. This is intended to measure the effect in New York City of 9/11 alone. Tables 8.1 through 8.4 also show the direction of the changes in annual earnings, household income, and Medicaid coverage from 2001 to 2002 in New York City and the difference-in-differences. The detailed results underlying the figures and tables are presented on the worldwide web (see notes 9 and 12 for website address).

The results (except for Medicaid receipt) are adjusted for education and age.[9] Predicted outcomes for a thirty-year-old are presented for each education level.[10] For each race and Hispanic origin and nativity-time in the U.S. category, predicted outcomes are presented for a thirty-year-old high school graduate (that is, someone with twelve years of schooling and twelve years of potential experience). All dollar values are adjusted for inflation and expressed in 2002 dollars. Because of the limited sample sizes for New York City, the changes and difference-in-differences are imprecisely measured and often are not statistically significant, but this is the best information available that gives a quantitative picture of the effects of the 9/11 attacks on New York City's disadvantaged workers.

We begin by examining the results for all disadvantaged groups combined, in figure 8.1 and table 8.1. Because the sample sizes are much larger than for the individual groups, changes in outcomes can be measured more precisely. Employment rates and weekly work hours of disadvantaged men in New York City eroded steadily from 2000 through 2003. Employment rates of both disadvantaged men and women in New York City were significantly lower after September 2001 than before, and they remained significantly below the pre-9/11 rates in 2002. For disadvantaged women, the drop in employment in the period October to December 2001 (compared with January to August 2001) was significantly greater in New York City than in comparable cities. The estimated size of the drop was also greater, but not significantly so, in New York City than in the comparison cities for disadvantaged women in 2002 and for disadvantaged men in October to December 2001. For disadvantaged men in 2002, the drop was the same in New York City and the other cities.

Weekly hours worked were also lower in New York City after 9/11 than before. The drop was statistically significant for New York City's disadvantaged men in 2002; however, this drop was significantly *smaller* than in the other cities. The estimated drop in hours worked was also smaller (though not significantly so) in New York City than in the other cities for disadvantaged men in the period October to December 2001 and for disadvantaged women in 2002. It was greater (though not significantly so) for disadvantaged women in late 2001.

Usual weekly earnings of disadvantaged men in New York City were virtually the same in 2002 as in 2001 before 9/11, in both New York City and the comparison cities. Surprisingly, usual weekly earnings of disadvantaged men in New York City are estimated to have been *higher* in September and the period October to December 2001 than before 9/11, despite the estimated drop in employment and weekly hours worked. We should not make too much of this apparent paradox, however, because the changes in earnings are not statistically significant, even at the 10 percent level. The samples for September and for October to December 2001 are much smaller than the samples for the longer time periods, and the samples for weekly earnings are much smaller than the samples for employment and hours.[11] Therefore, the "blips" in earnings of disadvantaged men may be caused by sampling variability.

Estimated annual earnings of disadvantaged men (but not women) in New York City declined from 2001 to 2002, as did the income of households with disadvantaged heads. However, these declines were smaller than in the comparison cities and were not statistically significant at the 10 percent level. The fraction of disadvantaged households in New York City in which someone was covered by Medicaid increased by one percentage point in 2002, but this was also not statistically significant.

In sum, disadvantaged men and women in New York City lost employment and worked less per week after 9/11, but with the significant exception of disadvantaged women in the period October to December 2001, the employ-

FIGURE 8.1   EMPLOYMENT RATES, WEEKLY HOURS WORKED, AND
USUAL WEEKLY EARNINGS ON MAIN JOB, ADJUSTED FOR
POTENTIAL EXPERIENCE: COMBINED DISADVANTAGED GROUPS
AGE EIGHTEEN TO SIXTY-FOUR IN NEW YORK CITY AND
COMPARISON CITIES, BY GENDER, APRIL 2000 TO
DECEMBER 2003

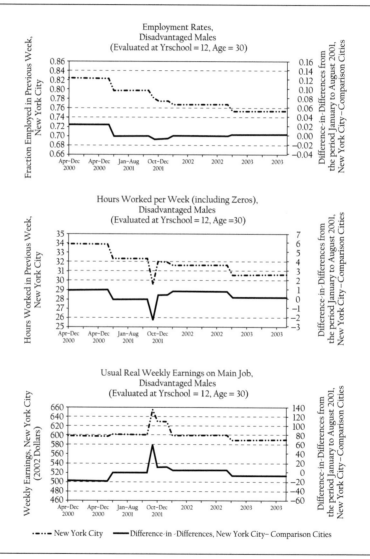

Source: Current Population Survey monthly basic files, 2000 to 2003.

FIGURE 8.1   CONTINUED

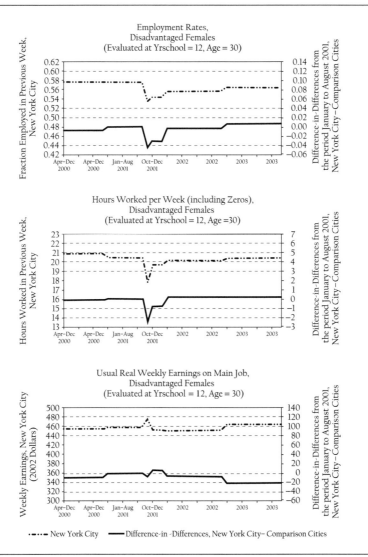

·─·─· New York City   ───── Difference-in-Differences, New York City– Comparison Cities

TABLE 8.1 Signs of Changes in New York City from the Period January to August 2001 and Difference-in-Differences, New York City–Comparison Cities, Disadvantaged versus Advantaged Groups

	Disadvantaged Groups Combined				Advantaged Group			
	Jan–Aug 2001 to Oct–Dec 2001		Jan–Aug 2001 to Year 2002		Jan–Aug 2001 to Oct–Dec 2001		Jan–Aug 2001 to Year 2002	
	New York City Change	Diff-in-Diff	New York City Change	Diff-in-Diff	New York City Change	Diff-in-Diff	New York City Change	Diff-in-Diff
Males								
Employment	sig —	—	sig —	0	—	+	sig —	—
Weekly hours worked	—	+	sig —	sig +	+	sig +	—	+
Usual weekly earnings	+	+	—	+	sig +	sig +	+	+
Annual earnings, 2002–2001			—	+			—	—
Females								
Employment	sig —	sig —	sig —	—	+	+	sig +	sig +
Weekly hours worked	—	—	—	+	—	+	+	sig +
Usual weekly earnings	—	+	+	—	+	+	+	+
Annual earnings, 2002–2001			+	+			—	+
Households								
Annual income, 2002–2001, money plus in-kind income			—	+			—	—
Medicaid receipt, 2002–2001			+	+			sig —	sig —

Source: Author's calculations from the Current Population Survey.

Notes: "Disadvantaged groups combined" includes all nonwhites, Hispanics, recent immigrants, and those with no more than a high school education. "Advantaged group" is white non-Hispanics who are not recent immigrants and who attended college. "+" signs in the "New York City Change" columns indicate an increase in New York City after 9/11; "—" signs indicate a decrease. "+" signs in the "Diff-in-Diff" columns indicate a larger increase or smaller decrease in New York City than in the comparison cities after 9/11. "—" signs in the "Diff-in-Diff" columns indicate a smaller increase or larger decrease in New York City than in the comparison cities after 9/11. "sig +" and "sig —" indicate that the change or difference-in-difference is significant at the 10 percent level.

ment losses in New York City were not significantly greater than in the comparison cities, and the hours lost were fewer—significantly so for disadvantaged men in 2002. These employment and hours changes were reflected in lower male annual earnings and annual household incomes in New York City, but the declines were not statistically significant and were not as large as in the comparison cities. Usual weekly earnings on the main job also did not change significantly. Thus, the evidence suggests that the losses for disadvantaged men were due to the recession rather than to 9/11, whereas 9/11 had a short-term negative impact on the employment of disadvantaged women.

Looking behind the changes for disadvantaged workers overall in New York City, in figures 8.2 through 8.7 and tables 8.2 through 8.4 we find that the significant losses of employment after 9/11 occurred among high school graduates, blacks, Hispanic females, and recent immigrants, with the employment losses of female high school graduates, female Hispanics, and female recent immigrants in the period October to December 2001 (and the female recent immigrants' loss in 2002) being significant relative to the comparison cities. The significant drops in weekly work hours in New York City occurred among female high school graduates, black men, Asian women, and female recent immigrants, though these drops were not significantly different from the comparison cities. Hispanic women's hours were slightly lower in New York City in October to December 2001 than in January to August 2001, whereas they went up in the comparison cities, so that their hours went down significantly more in New York City than in the comparison cities. On the other hand, male high school dropouts and Hispanic men worked significantly *more* hours in New York City in October to December 2001 than before 9/11. The increase in Hispanic men's hours was significantly greater than in the comparison cities in both October to December 2001 and the year 2002, but the increase in male dropouts' hours was not. Hispanic men also experienced a significant increase in annual earnings from 2001 to 2002, both in New York City and relative to the other cities. Usual weekly earnings were significantly higher among black men in New York City in October to December 2001 than before 9/11, but their annual earnings dropped significantly relative to the comparison cities from 2001 to 2002.

Thus, a comparison of the changes in New York City and similar cities suggests that female high school graduates, black men, Hispanic women, and recent immigrant women were adversely affected by the 9/11 attacks, since their subsequent drops in employment, hours, or annual earnings were significantly larger in New York City than in the other cities. Other groups—male high school graduates, black women, Asian women, and recent immigrant men—experienced significant declines in employment and/or hours in New York City that were not significantly larger than in the comparison cities, which suggests that these declines were due to the ongoing nationwide reces-

(*Text continues on p. 255.*)

FIGURE 8.2   EMPLOYMENT RATES, WEEKLY HOURS WORKED, AND USUAL
WEEKLY EARNINGS ON MAIN JOB, ADJUSTED FOR POTENTIAL
EXPERIENCE: HIGH SCHOOL DROPOUTS AGE EIGHTEEN TO
SIXTY-FOUR IN NEW YORK CITY AND COMPARISON CITIES, BY
GENDER, APRIL 2000 TO DECEMBER 2003

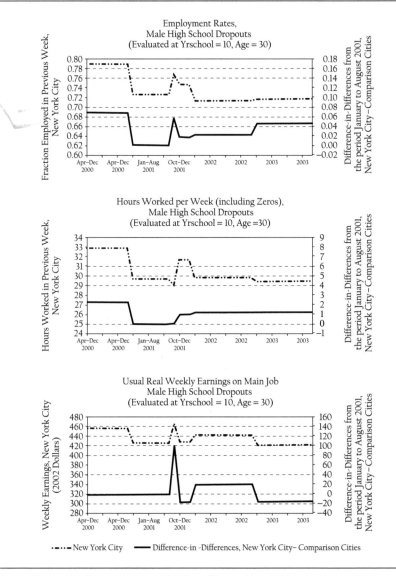

FIGURE 8.2   CONTINUED

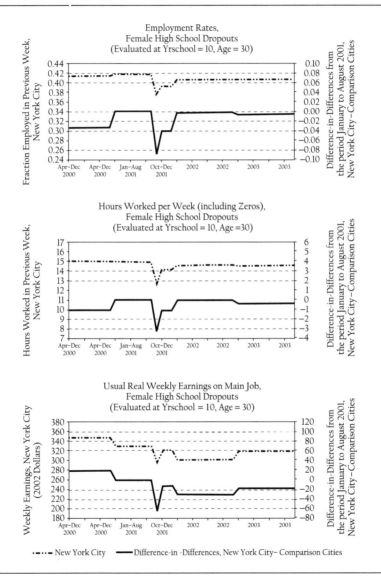

..—.. New York City   ——— Difference-in-Differences, New York City– Comparison Cities

FIGURE 8.3   EMPLOYMENT RATES, WEEKLY HOURS WORKED, AND USUAL
WEEKLY EARNINGS ON MAIN JOB, ADJUSTED FOR POTENTIAL
EXPERIENCE: HIGH SCHOOL GRADUATES AGE EIGHTEEN TO
SIXTY-FOUR IN NEW YORK CITY AND COMPARISON CITIES, BY
GENDER, APRIL 2000 TO DECEMBER 2003

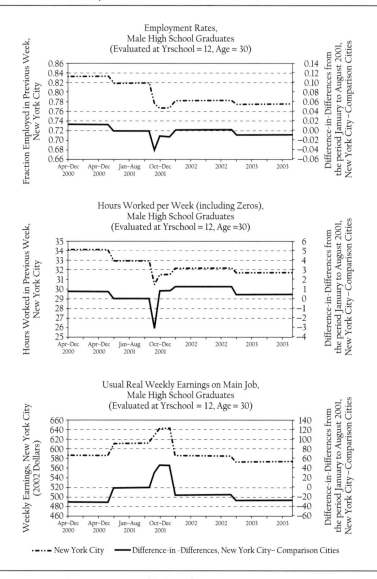

Source: Current Population Survey monthly basic files, 2000 to 2003.

FIGURE 8.3   CONTINUED

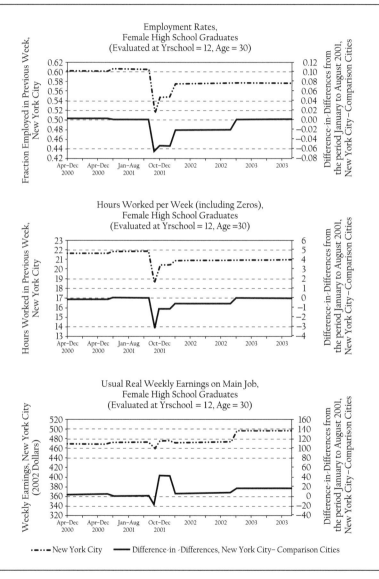

FIGURE 8.4   EMPLOYMENT RATES, WEEKLY HOURS WORKED, AND USUAL
WEEKLY EARNINGS ON MAIN JOB, ADJUSTED FOR EDUCATION
AND POTENTIAL EXPERIENCE: BLACK NON-HISPANICS
AGE EIGHTEEN TO SIXTY-FOUR IN NEW YORK CITY AND
COMPARISON CITIES, BY GENDER, APRIL 2000 TO
DECEMBER 2003

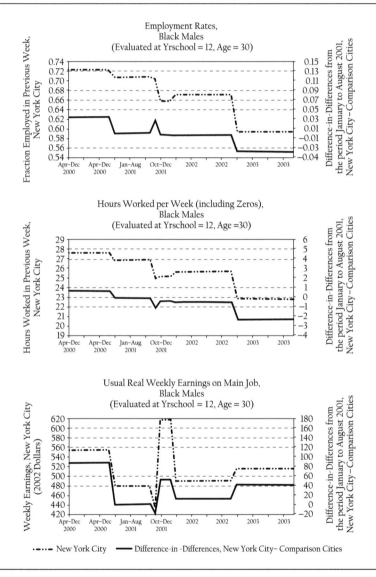

Source: Current Population Survey monthly basic files, 2000 to 2003.

FIGURE 8.4   *CONTINUED*

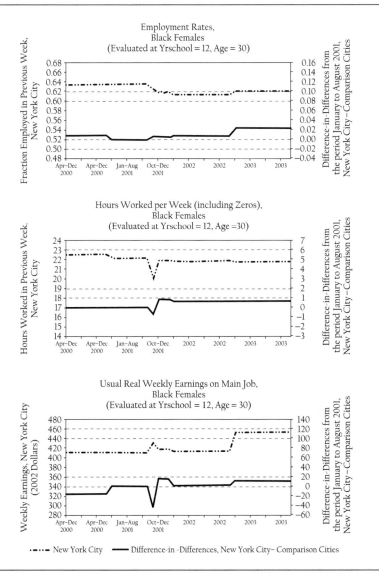

FIGURE 8.5   EMPLOYMENT RATES, WEEKLY HOURS WORKED, AND USUAL
WEEKLY EARNINGS ON MAIN JOB, ADJUSTED FOR EDUCATION
AND POTENTIAL EXPERIENCE: HISPANICS AGE EIGHTEEN TO
SIXTY-FOUR IN NEW YORK CITY AND COMPARISON CITIES, BY
GENDER, APRIL 2000 TO DECEMBER 2003

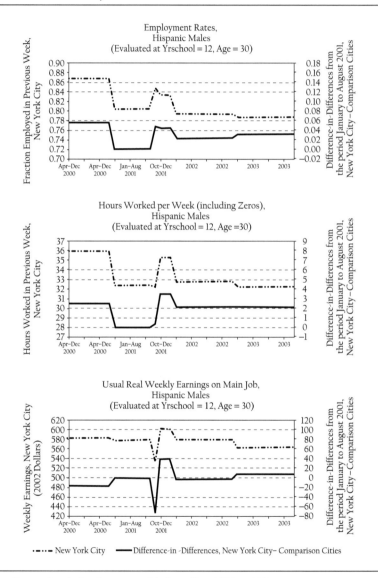

Source: Current Population Survey monthly basic files, 2000 to 2003.

FIGURE 8.5   CONTINUED

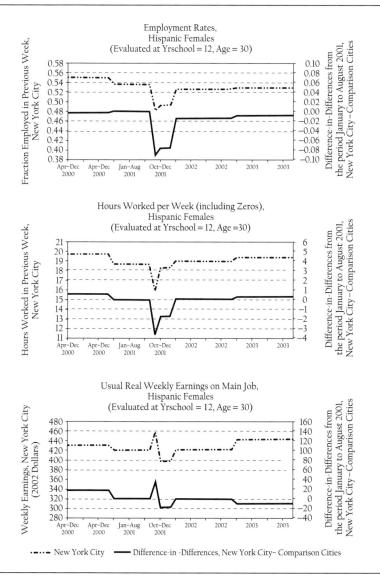

FIGURE 8.6   EMPLOYMENT RATES, WEEKLY HOURS WORKED, AND USUAL
               WEEKLY EARNINGS ON MAIN JOB, ADJUSTED FOR EDUCATION
               AND POTENTIAL EXPERIENCE: ASIAN AND PACIFIC ISLANDERS
               AGE EIGHTEEN TO SIXTY-FOUR IN NEW YORK CITY AND
               COMPARISON CITIES, BY GENDER, APRIL 2000 TO DECEMBER
               2003

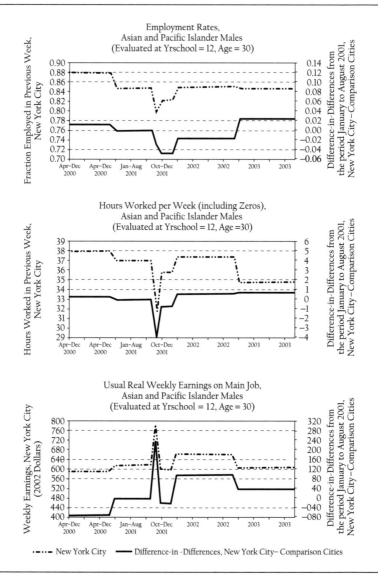

Source: Current Population Survey monthly basic files, 2000 to 2003.

FIGURE 8.6   CONTINUED

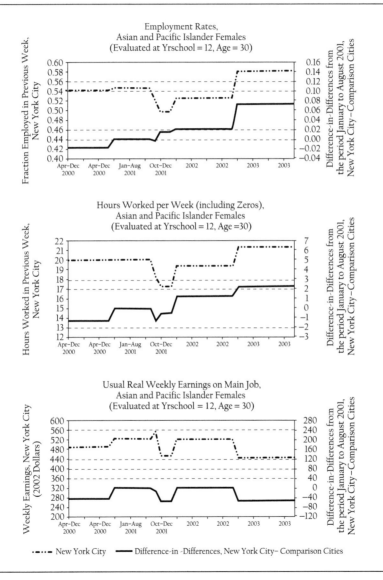

Employment Rates,
Asian and Pacific Islander Females
(Evaluated at Yrschool = 12, Age = 30)

Hours Worked per Week (including Zeros),
Asian and Pacific Islander Females
(Evaluated at Yrschool = 12, Age =30)

Usual Real Weekly Earnings on Main Job,
Asian and Pacific Islander Females
(Evaluated at Yrschool = 12, Age = 30)

·—··— New York City   ——— Difference-in -Differences, New York City– Comparison Cities

FIGURE 8.7   EMPLOYMENT RATES, WEEKLY HOURS WORKED, AND USUAL WEEKLY EARNINGS ON MAIN JOB, ADJUSTED FOR EDUCATION AND POTENTIAL EXPERIENCE: FOREIGN-BORN MALES AND FEMALES IN THE UNITED STATES LESS THAN FIFTEEN YEARS, AGE EIGHTEEN TO SIXTY-FOUR IN NEW YORK CITY AND COMPARISON CITIES, BY GENDER, APRIL 2000 TO DECEMBER 2003

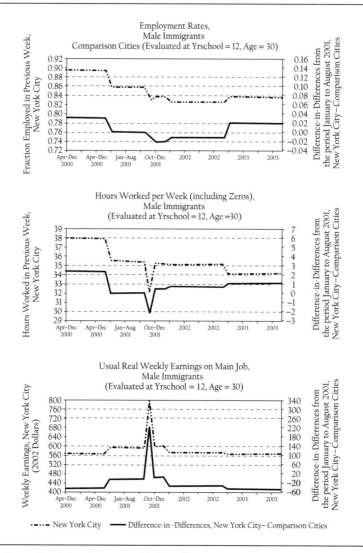

FIGURE 8.7 *CONTINUED*

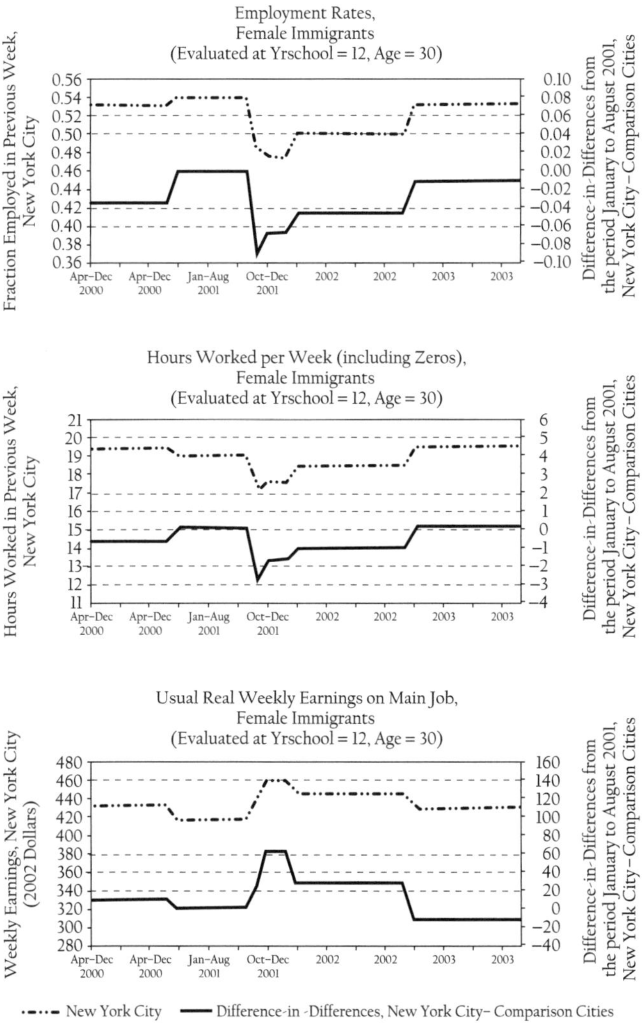

TABLE 8.2   SIGNS OF CHANGES IN NEW YORK CITY FROM THE PERIOD JANUARY TO AUGUST 2001 AND DIFFERENCE-IN-DIFFERENCES, NEW YORK CITY–COMPARISON CITIES, BY EDUCATIONAL LEVEL

	High School Dropouts				High School Graduates			
	Jan–Aug 2001 to Oct–Dec 2001		Jan–Aug 2001 to Year 2002		Jan–Aug 2001 to Oct–Dec 2001		Jan–Aug 2001 to Year 2002	
	New York City Change	Diff-in-Diff	New York City Change	Diff-in-Diff	New York City Change	Diff-in-Diff	New York City Change	Diff-in-Diff
Males								
Employment	+	+	—	+	sig —	—	sig —	~0
Weekly hours worked	sig +	+	+	+	—	+	—	+
Usual weekly earnings	~0	—	+	+	+	+	—	—
Annual earnings, 2002–2001			—	+			+	—
Females								
Employment	—	—	—	~0	sig —	sig —	sig —	—
Weekly hours worked	—	—	—	—	sig —	—	sig —	—
Usual weekly earnings	—	—	—	—	~0	+	~0	+
Annual earnings, 2002–2001			+	—			+	+
Households								
Annual income, 2002–2001, money plus in-kind income			~0	+			—	~0
Medicaid receipt, 2002–2001			+	+			—	~0

Source: Author's calculations from the Current Population Survey.

Notes: "+" signs in the "New York City Change" columns indicate an increase in New York City after 9/11; "—" signs indicate a decrease. "+" signs in the "Diff-in-Diff" columns indicate a larger increase or smaller decrease in New York City than in the comparison cities after 9/11. "—" signs in the "Diff-in-Diff" columns indicate a smaller increase or larger decrease in New York City than in the comparison cities after 9/11. "sig +" and "sig —" indicate that the change or difference-in-difference is significant at the 10 percent level.

sion. The signs of the relative changes suggest that 9/11 may have had a small negative impact on the labor market outcomes of female high school dropouts and Asian men in New York City, but the estimated effects are not statistically significant.

On the other hand, there is no sign that the 9/11 attack had a negative labor market impact on Hispanic men in New York City. Indeed, quite the contrary is true: Hispanic men did significantly better after 9/11, relative to the period January to August 2001, in New York City than in the comparison cities. This may reflect differences between the labor market positions of Puerto Ricans and Dominicans, on the one hand, and Mexicans and Central Americans, on the other, rather than effects of the World Trade Center disaster in New York City versus national economic conditions. In any case, the annual income of Hispanic households rose in New York City more than elsewhere, though this change is not statistically significant.

Male high school dropouts' outcomes also mainly improved after 9/11 in New York City relative to the comparison cities, though not significantly. The signs of the "difference-in-differences" suggest that household incomes of high school dropouts, Asians, and recent immigrants in New York City also improved in 2002, relative to the comparison cities, while those of blacks declined and those of high school graduates remained the same in relative terms. None of these income changes was significant, however.

For comparison, we investigate what happened to "advantaged" men and women in New York City—that is, white non-Hispanics who have been in the United States at least fifteen years (or were born here) and who attended college. For advantaged men in New York City, figure 8.8 and table 8.1 show that employment was significantly lower in 2002 than in January to August 2001, but the drop was no different than the drop in the comparison cities. Weekly hours worked in New York City bounced back after the "hit" in September 2001; from October 2001 onward, weekly hours did not differ significantly from before 9/11. However, weekly hours in the other cities did not bounce back in the October to December 2001 period, so that the relative change in hours in New York City was significantly positive. Usual weekly earnings on the main job were higher in New York City in September and in October to December 2001 than in January to August 2001—significantly so in October to December. Meanwhile, usual weekly earnings declined in the other cities, so that the increase in New York City relative to the other cities was statistically significant both in September and in October to December 2001. Annual earnings of advantaged men and household income were lower in 2002 than in 2001 in New York City and relative to the other cities, but the changes were not statistically significant. At the same time, Medicaid receipt did decline significantly in New York City and relative to the other cities.

Advantaged women, on the other hand, had significantly *higher* employment

TABLE 8.3   SIGNS OF CHANGES IN NEW YORK CITY FROM THE PERIOD
JANUARY TO AUGUST 2001 AND DIFFERENCE-IN-DIFFERENCES,
NEW YORK CITY–COMPARISON CITIES, BY RACE AND
HISPANIC ORIGIN

| | Black Non-Hispanics | | | |
| | Jan–Aug 2001 to Oct–Dec 2001 | | Jan–Aug 2001 to Year 2002 | |
	New York City Change	Diff-in-Diff	New York City Change	Diff-in-Diff
Males				
Employment	sig —	~0	sig —	~0
Weekly hours worked	sig —	—	sig —	—
Usual weekly earnings	sig +	+	+	+
Annual earnings, 2002–2001			—	sig —
Females				
Employment	—	~0	sig —	~0
Weekly hours worked	—	+	—	+
Usual weekly earnings	+	+	~0	~0
Annual earnings, 2002–2001			+	+
Households				
Annual income, 2002–2001, money plus in-kind income			+	—
Medicaid receipt, 2002–2001			~0	0

Source: Author's calculations from the Current Population Survey.
Notes: "+" signs in the "New York City Change" columns indicate an increase in New York City after 9/11; "—" signs indicate a decrease. "+" signs in the "Diff-in-Diff" columns indicate a larger increase or smaller decrease in New York City than in the comparison cities after 9/11. "—"

rates in 2002 than in January to August 2001, both in New York City and relative to the other cities. Their average weekly hours went up (insignificantly) in New York City but down in the other cities, so that weekly hours were significantly higher in 2002 than before 9/11 in New York City relative to the other cities. Nevertheless, advantaged women's usual weekly earnings and annual earnings did not change significantly (though they fell less from 2001 to 2002 in New York City than in the other cities).

The results show the importance of the exact wording of the CPS questions and the timing of the CPS interviews. The fact that hours worked in the

| Hispanics | | | | Asian and Pacific Islander Non-Hispanics | | | |
| Jan–Aug 2001 to Oct–Dec 2001 | | Jan–Aug 2001 to Year 2002 | | Jan–Aug 2001 to Oct–Dec 2001 | | Jan–Aug 2001 to Year 2002 | |
New York City Change	Diff-in-Diff	New York City Change	Diff-in-Diff	New York City Change	Diff-in-Diff	New York City Change	Diff-in-Diff
+	sig +	—	+	—	—	~0	—
sig +	sig +	+	sig +	—	—	+	+
+	+	~0	~0	—	—	+	+
		sig +	sig +			—	+
sig —	sig —	—	—	—	+	—	+
—	sig —	+	0	sig —	—	—	+
—	—	0	~0	—	—	~0	~0
		—	—			—	—
		+	+			+	+
		+	+			+	+

signs in the "Diff-in-Diff" columns indicate a smaller increase or larger decrease in New York City than in the comparison cities after 9/11. "sig +" and "sig —" indicate that the change or difference-in-difference is significant at the 10 percent level.

previous week show a significant drop in September 2001 for most groups in New York City is to be expected, because the survey was conducted the week after 9/11 and asked how many hours the respondent worked in the previous week.[12] But employment rates dropped significantly in September 2001 in New York City in only a handful of groups (all disadvantaged females combined, female high school graduates, Hispanic females, recent female immigrants, women born in the United States, and white men) and the estimated changes are actually positive (though insignificant) in five groups. Recall that the employment question asks whether the respondent had a job at all in the previous week, even if he or she was absent from that job. Anyone who had a job on

TABLE 8.4   SIGNS OF CHANGES IN NEW YORK CITY FROM THE PERIOD JANUARY TO AUGUST 2001 AND DIFFERENCE-IN-DIFFERENCES, NEW YORK CITY–COMPARISON CITIES, IMMIGRANTS IN THE UNITED STATES LESS THAN FIFTEEN YEARS

	Jan–Aug 2001 to Oct–Dec 2001		Jan–Aug 2001 to Year 2002	
	New York City Change	Diff-in-Diff	New York City Change	Diff-in-Diff
Males				
Employment	—	—	sig —	—
Weekly hours worked	—	+	—	+
Usual weekly earnings	~0	+	—	—
Annual earnings, 2002–2001			—	+
Females				
Employment	sig —	sig —	sig —	sig —
Weekly hours worked	sig —	—	—	—
Usual weekly earnings	+	+	+	+
Annual earnings, 2002–2001			~0	—
Households				
Annual income, 2002–2001, money plus in-kind income			—	+
Medicaid receipt, 2002–2001			—	+

Source: Author's calculations from the Current Population Survey.
Notes: "+" signs in the "New York City Change" columns indicate an increase in New York City after 9/11; "—" signs indicate a decrease. "+" signs in the "Diff-in-Diff" columns indicate a larger increase or smaller decrease in New York City than in the comparison cities after 9/11. "—" signs in the "Diff-in-Diff" columns indicate a smaller increase or larger decrease in New York City than in the comparison cities after 9/11. "sig +" and "sig —" indicate that the change or difference-in-difference is significant at the 10 percent level.

Monday, September 10, 2001, would correctly answer yes to the employment question in the September 2001 CPS. Therefore, the recession, rather than 9/11, must account for the declines in reported employment in September. Because the sample sizes for a single month are small, only those groups that were hardest hit—certain groups of women and white men—would show significant declines in that month.

Most of the cases in which usual weekly earnings on the main job differ significantly from their level in January to August 2001, either in New York

FIGURE 8.8   EMPLOYMENT RATES, WEEKLY HOURS WORKED, AND USUAL
WEEKLY EARNINGS ON MAIN JOB, ADJUSTED FOR EDUCATION
AND POTENTIAL EXPERIENCE: ADVANTAGED GROUP AGE
EIGHTEEN TO SIXTY-FOUR IN NEW YORK CITY AND
COMPARISON CITIES, BY GENDER, APRIL 2000 TO DECEMBER
2003

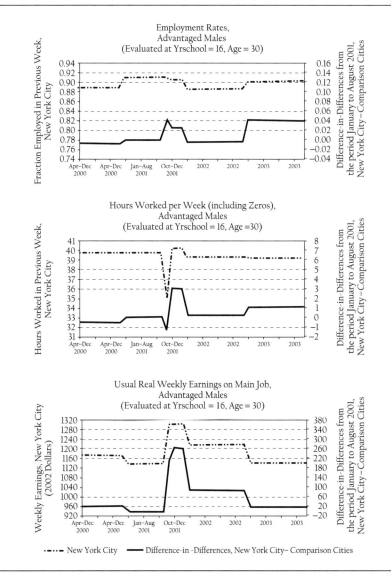

Source: Current Population Survey monthly basic files, 2000 to 2003.

FIGURE 8.8   *CONTINUED*

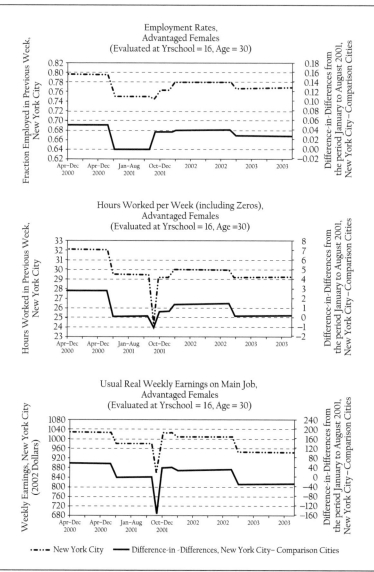

·—·—· New York City   **——** Difference-in -Differences, New York City– Comparison Cities

City or in New York City relative to the comparison cities, show *increases* in weekly earnings for men, mainly in September and/or in October to December 2001.[13] This might seem to imply that wages rose after 9/11, since average weekly hours worked per adult declined in all but one of these cases.[14] However, it should be kept in mind that the earnings measure is *usual* (not actual) weekly earnings, which would not vary automatically with hours actually worked in the previous week. Moreover, hours and earnings are measured for different universes. Usual weekly earnings are collected only for wage and salary employees. Thus, the self-employed and the secondary jobs of those working multiple jobs (as well as the non-employed) are included in average weekly hours, but not in usual weekly earnings. If these jobs are lost, employment and hours could decline without affecting measured weekly earnings. Furthermore, average usual weekly earnings on a worker's main job could rise while employment and actual hours worked per week fell if the loss of employment was selectively among the lower-paid.

SUMMARY AND CONCLUSIONS

This chapter has analyzed the labor market outcomes and economic well-being of New York City residents before and after September 11, 2001: employment rates, weekly hours worked, usual weekly earnings of wage and salary earners, annual earnings, annual household income—both cash and the value of in-kind benefits—and rates of Medicaid coverage. It has focused on the most disadvantaged groups in the labor market: high school dropouts, high school graduates who did not attend college, blacks, Hispanics, Asians, and recent immigrants who have been in the United States less than fifteen years. By comparing the period after the 9/11 attacks with the period before and comparing New York City with five other cities that are its main competitors in its key industries, this study has tried to distinguish the impact of the destruction of the World Trade Center in New York City from the effects of the recession and more diffuse nationwide aftereffects of the attacks. The estimates are adjusted for differences in education and potential experience over time and among cities.

I find that for disadvantaged men overall, the decreases in employment, hours, and earnings in New York City after September 2001 were the same or smaller than in the other cities and so were probably due to the recession, not 9/11. I do find evidence of a short-term negative impact of 9/11 on the employment and hours of disadvantaged women overall in New York City relative to other cities in the period October to December 2001, but it disappeared in 2002. Annual earnings and household incomes of the combined disadvantaged groups declined less in New York City than elsewhere in 2002. The "advantaged" group (that is, college-educated, white non-Hispanics who are not recent immigrants) fared better in New York City than elsewhere in late 2001 compared with the months before 9/11; women in this advantaged group also fared significantly better than elsewhere in 2002, while advantaged men fared no worse.[15]

The labor market effects were not uniform among disadvantaged groups. Female high school graduates, black men, Hispanic women, and recent immigrant women in New York City appear to have been adversely affected by the World Trade Center disaster, as distinct from the recession. In contrast, there is little or no evidence of a more negative effect in New York City than in the other cities for high school dropouts, male high school graduates, black women, Hispanic men, Asians, or recent immigrant men. In future research, it would be useful to investigate the industrial distributions of these demographic groups in New York City before September 2001 to see whether the groups that were adversely affected were more likely to be employed in the industries that were hit hardest by 9/11, such as financial services, air transportation, hotels, restaurants, entertainment, and garment manufacturing.

In the face of adverse labor market experiences, household income may be cushioned by the earnings of other members of the household and by transfer payments and in-kind benefits, so that overall economic well-being is insulated to some degree. Unfortunately, the March CPS samples are too small to measure changes in annual income and Medicaid coverage precisely, and none of the estimated changes from 2001 to 2002 is statistically significant. If we use the signs as evidence of what happened to annual household income, we find that, owing to the improved earnings of Hispanic men, Hispanic New Yorkers' household income rose despite the negative impact on Hispanic women, while that of Hispanics in the other cities fell. The household income of high school dropouts held steady in New York City while it declined elsewhere. Rates of Medicaid coverage increased for Hispanics and high school dropouts in New York City, but not in the other cities. Recent immigrants and high school graduates who did not go on to college did lose household income and Medicaid coverage in New York City in 2002, but to slightly smaller degrees than in the other cities. This suggests that the lingering effects of the recession and welfare reform, rather than 9/11, were responsible for the decline in income of these groups in New York City. Blacks are the only disadvantaged group whose household income fell relative to the other cities, because their income rose less in New York City than elsewhere. If our comparison-group strategy is valid, we may attribute this lag for blacks in New York City to the effect of 9/11. Their rate of Medicaid receipt was flat.

With the important exception of blacks, and despite its adverse effects on the employment, hours, and/or weekly earnings of some other groups, 9/11 does not appear to have had a negative impact of its own on the annual income of the average low-skilled, Hispanic, or recent immigrant household in New York.

Incomes of disadvantaged households overall did not deteriorate as much in New York City in 2002 as in other comparable cities. This attests to the size and flexibility of New York's labor and capital markets. New York City's economy was already declining before September 2001. Disastrous as it was, the destruction of life and property in the World Trade Center attack nevertheless represented only a small fraction of New York's workers, firms, and buildings. Flexible capital and labor markets enabled the affected firms and workers to relocate or find other jobs, thus dampening the multiplier effects of the attacks. Case studies reveal that there were severe impacts on specific groups that live or work in lower Manhattan, but these impacts were too small relative to the city as a whole to be detected in the available household survey data, given the limited CPS sample size. For example, we know there were adverse effects on Asians in Manhattan's Chinatown neighborhood, which was severely affected by disruptions of telephone service, motor vehicle traffic, and parking for months after 9/11 (Asian American Federation of New York 2002; Chin 2005), but we cannot measure them reliably. We conclude that apart from the effects of the recession, the New York City labor market and benefit safety net performed relatively well in cushioning the impact of 9/11, especially when compared with its major "rival" cities. The ongoing recession had a much more negative impact than 9/11 on New York City's workers, disadvantaged and otherwise.

Many thanks to Kat Morgan for making many more tables and charts than could be included here and to David Howell and Howard Chernick for helpful comments.

NOTES

1. One exception is Parrott and Cooke (this volume), who use CPS data to track unemployment rates and weekly household earnings for New York City residents in low-, medium-, and high-wage occupations. Another exception, the study by Hotchkiss and Pavlova (2004), uses CPS data to estimate a labor supply function with a possible shift after 9/11. They find no significant change in hours worked among residents of New York City through December 2002, after controlling for the national industry unemployment rate.

2. The samples for household income and Medicaid receipt are larger than the samples for annual earnings because the latter are analyzed for men and women separately, whereas the former combine male- and female-headed households.

3. The valuation of Medicaid benefits in the March CPS is problematic because this value does not represent actual services received by the household but resembles an imputed insurance premium whose value is large relative to the income of eligible households. Since low-income households would be unlikely to spend so

much of their limited income on health insurance, the valuation of Medicaid coverage by recipients is probably considerably less than the value in the March CPS. I therefore exclude the value of Medicaid from household in-kind income and instead tabulate receipt of Medicaid coverage by anyone in the household.

4. The attack on the Pentagon on 9/11 did not affect the economy of Washington the way the destruction of the World Trade Center affected New York City. The Pentagon is outside Washington, across the Potomac River; it was damaged, not completely destroyed; and most importantly, it is a federal government building, not a private-sector office building. Pentagon workers are federal employees whose jobs were not jeopardized by the attack. Moreover, if employers (or workers) believe that skyscraper office buildings are more vulnerable to future attacks than low-rise buildings, jobs may shift out of New York City, whereas no such belief would be likely to take hold in the District of Columbia since it has no skyscrapers.

5. The comparison-group strategy may not control well for the effects of the recession on Hispanics in New York City when they are aggregated into a single ethnic category. The composition of the Hispanic population in the other cities is very different from that in New York City. Puerto Ricans and Dominicans are the largest Hispanic groups in New York City, whereas Mexicans and Central Americans dominate the Hispanic population in the other cities (except Boston). These national-origin groups occupy different positions in the labor market and so might be expected to fare differently than Hispanic New Yorkers during a recession.

6. Results are available from the author for detailed groups not discussed in the text: persons with some college education but less than a bachelor's degree, those with a bachelor's or higher degree, non-Hispanic whites, those who have been in the United States fifteen years or more, and those born in the United States.

7. Potential experience is defined as $max(age - max(ed + 6, 16), 0)$. The quartic function of years of schooling is omitted when the sample is stratified by education level. A linear term in schooling and a quartic in potential experience are included for "advantaged" workers.

8. The March 2004 CPS, containing income data for 2003, was released in September 2004 after this chapter was completed.

9. The "raw" unadjusted outcomes for January to August 2001 in the monthly data and for 2000, 2001, and 2002 in the annual data are also presented in the additional tables available at: www.rsage.org/publications/050519.227994/.

10. High school dropouts are assumed to have ten years of schooling, so that potential experience equals fourteen at age thirty; high school graduates have twelve years of schooling, so potential experience equals twelve at age thirty; those with some college education are assumed to have fourteen years of schooling, so potential experience equals ten at age thirty; and those with a bachelor's or higher degree are assumed to have sixteen years of schooling, so potential experience equals eight at age thirty.

11. Recall that the earnings question is asked only of wage and salary workers in the ORGs. The ORGs are only one-quarter of the CPS sample, and excluding those without jobs and the self-employed reduces the sample even further.

12. Significance levels for the changes in September 2001 are shown in the additional tables available at www.rsage.org/publications/050519.227994/. The groups for whom

the drops in September are not statistically significant also show declines in hours in that month.

13. These are male high school dropouts, males with a B.A. degree or higher, and white non-Hispanic, Asian, and recent immigrant men in September 2001; advantaged, black, white non-Hispanic, and U.S.-born men in October to December 2001; and U.S.-born men in 2002. The exceptions are female immigrants who had been in the United States for fifteen years or more in 2002 and females with a B.A. degree or higher in 2003.

14. Hours were greater for advantaged males in New York City in October to December 2001 than in January to August 2001, but not significantly so.

15. These results are broadly consistent with those of Parrott and Cooke (this volume), who find that workers in low-wage occupations experienced serious but short-term dislocation from 9/11, while the short-term effects on workers in higher-wage occupations were less adverse.

REFERENCES

Asian American Federation of New York. 2002. *Chinatown After September 11: An Economic Impact Study.* New York: AAFNY (April 4).

Bram, Jason. 2003. "New York City's Economy Before and After September 11." *Current Issues in Economics and Finance* (Federal Reserve Bank of New York) 9(2, February): 1–6.

Bram, Jason, James Orr, and Carol Rapaport. 2002. "Measuring the Effects of the September 11 Attack on New York City." *Economic Policy Review* (Federal Reserve Bank of New York) 8(2, November): 5–20.

Chernick, Howard, and Cordelia Reimers. 2004. "The Decline in Welfare Receipt in New York City: Push Versus Pull." *Eastern Economic Journal* 30(1, Winter): 3–29.

Chin, Margaret. 2005. "Moving On: Chinese Garment Workers After 9/11." In *Wounded City: The Social Impact of 9/11,* edited by Nancy Foner. New York: Russell Sage Foundation.

Dolfman, Michael L., and Solidelle F. Wasser. 2004. "9/11 and the New York City Economy: A Borough-by-Borough Analysis." *Monthly Labor Review* 127(6, June): 3–33.

Fiscal Policy Institute. 2001. "World Trade Center Job Impacts Take a Heavy Toll on Low-Wage Workers." (November 5). Available online at: http://www.fiscalpolicy.org.

———. 2002a. "The Employment Impact of the September 11 World Trade Center Attacks: Updated Estimates Based on the Benchmarked Employment Data." March 8. Available online at: http://www.fiscalpolicy.org.

———. 2002b. "Immigrant Workers Displaced by the September 11 World Trade Center Attacks." June 5. Available online at: http://www.fiscalpolicy.org.

Hotchkiss, Julie L., and Olga Pavlova. 2004. "The Impact of 9/11 on Hours of Work in the U.S." Working paper 2004–16a. Atlanta: Federal Reserve Bank of Atlanta (September).

CHAPTER 9

Child Care Arrangements in New York City After 9/11: A Return to Hearth and Home?

Sanders Korenman

In dangerous times, parents want their kids near them.
—Sue Shellenbarger,
"Are Your Children Safe Near Your Office?"
Wall Street Journal, September 27, 2001

But is September 11 a period that puts a full stop to one era and opens up a new, more community-minded chapter in our history? Or is it merely a comma, a brief pause during which we looked up for a moment and then returned to our solitary pursuits? In short, how thoroughly and enduringly have American values and civic habits been transformed by the terrorist attacks of last fall?
—Robert Putnam,
"Bowling Together,"
American Prospect, February 23, 2002

THE QUESTION raised by Robert Putnam has lingered since September 11, 2001: did the terrorist attacks enduringly realign American values and priorities? In this chapter, I consider the question of whether the terrorist attacks resulted in a renewed commitment to family life or a heightened concern for children's mental and physical health by examining whether home-based care of children increased after the attacks. After September 11, 2001, did parents more often care for their children at home or alter their child care arrangements so that they would be cared for by "close substitutes" for parents such as a nanny, babysitter, or relative? I also examine the question of whether children who were affected by the attacks physically or emotionally were more likely than other children in the wake of the attacks to be cared for by a parent, nanny, babysitter, or relative.

CONCERNS RAISED BY 9/11 FOR WORKING PARENTS

A Heightened Commitment to Family

After September 11, 2001, the expectation that the terrorist attacks would transform values was so widespread that it hardly seems necessary to cite examples. But now, more than three years after the attacks, we may need a few reminders.

In an article titled "Examine Your Priorities in the Wake of Attacks," the *Wall Street Journal*'s "work-life" reporter, Sue Shellenbarger (2001a), provided a prime example of the expectation that the terrorist attacks would fundamentally change values:

> Across the nation, at nearly every level of the work force, a subtle but far-reaching shift in priorities is under way. Values that were pre-eminent for many people—career, status, money, personal fulfillment—now are taking a back seat to more fundamental human needs: family, friends, community, connectedness with others. The change will color workers' decision-making for months, if not years.

The article focused particularly on the reactions of working mothers:

> Far more important to her now, Chicago businesswoman Linda Foster says, is "taking every day and making the most of it, with our kids and my husband and our friends. When something like this happens, you realize it's your family that matters most." . . . Last week, her old preoccupations—selling a previous home at a good price, getting her car repaired correctly—fell away. She says, "Maybe I don't need all this stuff. Maybe I need to concentrate on enriching my life with my family."

Despite finding expressions of increased family orientation among working women, however, the article ultimately suggested that employers would provide greater flexibility to employees with family concerns, and it downplayed the possibility of "a retreat to hearth and home."

Executives looking for historical parallels to guide a long-term response ... have failed to find them. The retreat to home and hearth after World War II comes up most often; that's what spawned the 1950s. Donna Klein of Marriott International predicts the terrorist attack, once again, "is going to shine the spotlight on family as the core component of society." But this time, she says, "there's a larger role for employers, because families generally are weaker, more scattered and more deeply involved in the workplace than they were 50 years ago. After World War II, there was a hearth and home to return to. Now, that has been irrevocably changed," she says. "The role of corporate America is going to be, 'What can we do to re-create some sense of safe place?' Does that include more flexibility, and more recognition of families as the key segment of society?" I think it does.

Interestingly, though, by the turn of the year 2002 the same reporter predicted that the renewed family orientation would endure (Shellenbarger 2002).

The coming year will bring deepening work-life conflict for millions, as workers' post-Sept. 11 reordering of priorities clashes with a recession-induced speed-up at work. The far-reaching shift in values predicted last September in this column, stressing family, friends and community over career, status and money, will continue to play out. "Sept. 11 has caused a remarkable number of people across the country to call a time-out for themselves, and ask two questions: What's really important to me? And, why am I here?" says Gil Gordon, a Monmouth Junction, N.J., consultant and author of *Turn It Off*, a book on drawing boundaries on work.

Effects on Children

Concerns about short-term dangers on the day of the attack and longer-term threats to the physical and emotional health of children were paramount in many New York parents' personal accounts of September 11, 2001. A New York Department of Health and Centers for Disease Control (CDC) survey of residents of lower Manhattan (south of Reade Street) revealed that 96 percent of Battery Park City residents had evacuated their apartments. When these respondents were asked about their concerns and needs, "topics of most interest were related to air quality and its safety and effect on children and adults; cleaning; rights as tenants; mental health; children's adjustment and financial assistance" (New York City Public Health Partnership 2002, 2).

Whether or not parents pulled their children home, there is no doubt that concern about the effect of the attacks on children changed parental behavior. Many families left or planned to leave the city permanently, expressly out of concern for the health and safety of children. For example, in an article entitled "Fear of Terrorism," the artist David Basseine wrote (Brustein 2003):

> About a month after 9/11, I decided that, after having lived in New York for 12 years, I wanted to move. . . . I was attached [to a Park Slope neighborhood] too, but more than that I was frightened by the risk to our children.
> With two kids, I just did not want to be in New York. We were in the middle of the anthrax scare, and I was opening my mail with gloves and a mask on. I was nervous about taking my kids on the subway. I didn't want to put them at risk.

Moreover, some evidence indicates that concerns for the well-being of children were not unfounded. Surveys and studies have linked health and emotional problems among children (and adults) to the attack on the World Trade Center (WTC). For example, respondents to the 2002 wave of the New York Social Indicators Survey (NYSIS) reported that their children suffered new health and emotional problems, that they and their children were more fearful, that they were reluctant to leave home, and that children feared that a parent might leave home and not return (Garfinkel et al. 2003). I review this evidence later in the chapter.

Children living well beyond lower Manhattan were also affected by the attack. A report commissioned by the New York City Public Schools (Applied Research Consulting 2002) found, six months after the WTC attack, a "broad range of mental health problems" among New York City schoolchildren in grades four through twelve. They reported an elevated prevalence of symptoms consistent with post-traumatic stress syndrome (PTSD) (10.5 percent), major depression (10.3 percent), anxiety (10.3 percent), agoraphobia (15 percent), and separation anxiety (12.3 percent). The report found a higher prevalence of symptoms of PTSD among younger children, children with a family member exposed to the attack, girls, those exposed to prior trauma, those personally exposed to the attack, and Hispanics.

Similarly, according to Deborah Phillips, Shantay Prince, and Laura Schiebelhut in an article published May 17, 2002 (*The Hoya*), 85 percent of fourth-through sixth-graders in two Washington, D.C., public schools reported that "their basic sense of security and safety [was] shaken by the attacks."

Evidence for physical risks to children is scarcer. A study in the *Journal of the American Medical Association* reported an increased risk of being small for gestational age among infants born to 187 pregnant women who were in the World Trade Center (12 women) or within ten blocks of it (175 women), on September 11, 2001 (Berkowitz et al. 2003). However, there were no significant differences (relative to a control group of private patients who delivered at

Mount Sinai Hospital over the same period) in mean gestational age, preterm birth, birthweight, or low birthweight. There was no correlation between the mother's reports of PTSD and infant health outcomes.

A second study of infant health compared women who gave birth at one of three downtown hospitals in lower Manhattan according to their reported exposure to the WTC site in the two weeks following September 11, 2001. No significant differences between the exposed group and the comparison group were found in a variety of indicators of infant health, including birthweight, length, and Apgar score. Although the difference in mean gestation (274.3 days versus 275.9 days, or 1.6 days) is statistically significant, the difference is tiny and unlikely to be consequential unless it is highly concentrated at the shortest gestations.

Child Care

There is also some evidence of increasing reluctance among New York parents to put their children in day care. A first bit of evidence appeared in an October 31, 2001, *Business Week* article (Pamela Mendels, "What's Next for On-Site Child Care?") that concluded: "With the exception of a few centers in New York and Washington, it's business as usual at employer-sponsored day-care facilities." For the most part, operators of on-site centers reported no changes in use as a result of the attack on the World Trade Center. Although the CEO of Bright Horizons Family Solutions, which runs 384 child care centers, reported that enrollment was up slightly, the CEO also reported that "a number of parents thinking of enrolling their children cancelled appointments to tour the centers after the September 11 massacres." Another CEO of a company that provides corporate backup center care saw a "noticeable drop" in attendance at several centers serving midtown and downtown New York, "including one about four blocks from the World Trade Center." Parents gave two main reasons for keeping kids out of the Manhattan centers: "a general sense of unease about the city's safety" and "wariness about taking children on public transportation systems."

Perhaps the most persistent evidence that the attacks raised new concerns for parents is the prominence given the subject in a series of articles by *Wall Street Journal* reporter Sue Shellenbarger, some of which I have already cited. The articles suggest that, at a minimum, the attack on the World Trade Center and the Pentagon heightened preexisting work-family tensions. Now "working families" could add terrorism fears, threats to the safety of children, and new child health and emotional problems to the list of prior concerns such as ear infections and the developmental quality of care.

In a striking example provided by Shellenbarger's September 27, 2001, article "Are Your Children Safe Near Your Office?" it was reported that the terrorist attacks had heightened fears about the safety of worksite (on-site) child care. The article in part attempted to reassure parents by documenting the truly heroic actions taken on the day of the attacks by the care providers at centers located in 5 World Trade and the Pentagon. Yet this article and others inevitably reminded readers that the attack on the federal building in Oklahoma City on April 19, 1995, had resulted in the death of nineteen children in an on-site center. The article concluded with the following thought: "Perhaps parents' biggest job is banishing fear—putting on a calm face, as these teachers did—so children can stay calm." But some parents may have concluded that their biggest job was to try to provide a safer location for their children.

In fact, this possibility is suggested by Shellenbarger's article "One Couple's Struggle with Work-Life Balance" (2001b), which chronicles the tribulations throughout 2001 of a working couple, Jason and Keely Krantz, who, before September, had decided that Keely would leave her job to care for their newborn at home. Here is the entry in that chronicle about the fall of 2001:

Autumn: Though the nation is reeling from terrorism and a slumping economy, the Krantzes have emerged stronger. . . . Edocs makes yet another offer to lure Keely back, a part-time, work-at-home deal she once would have coveted. She turns it down. Though she feels pangs of envy at her friends' career milestones, she's savoring the private joys of motherhood—seeing Aidan's face light up after brief separations, seeing her calm reaction to strangers. "I really know now that I wouldn't trade this for that," she says. Though unnerving, the terrorist assault has affirmed the value she places on family. So far, the Krantzes have been able to create a haven of their own at home. "We've survived a lot of different blows," Keely says, "and come out still strong."

Working parents, especially those in cities considered likely targets of future attacks, had to cope with leaving their kids each day and the fears that separation raises for children. A common fear among children after the attacks has been that a parent will go away and never return. In the minds of many children in hard-hit areas, "it's a real possibility that you go to work and don't come back," says Deborah Dugan, mother of two and executive vice president of Disney Publishing Worldwide in New York (Shellenbarger 2001c).

A survey conducted in Alameda County, California, four to six months after the attacks provided insight into the effect of the attack on early childhood teachers, administrators, and providers, as well as children in child care. Despite their distance from the attack, 20 percent of child care providers in the Alameda County survey reported that young (under age six) children in their care "expressed fears of becoming the victim of an act of terrorism, and 23% indicated that children had expressed more general fears of being harmed or

separated," and a third of providers surveyed had "persistent worries" that
something would happen to the children that they were caring for (Phillips et
al. 2002, 1).

These reports and information led us to investigate whether:

1. There is evidence that parents changed child care arrangements so that
   children could be closer to parents, relatives, or "home" (in the sense that
   either a parent was more likely to provide care for the child or the child
   was more likely to be cared for by a nanny or relative).
2. Those children who were adversely affected by the WTC attack are now
   more likely than other children to have a parent, relative, or nanny provide
   care.[1]

A few difficulties must be noted in drawing inferences about the effect of
9/11 from changes in behaviors between 1999 and 2002. Other changes over
this period may also have affected child care choices. The most important of
these are the economic downturn, welfare reform and the corresponding
expansion of child care subsidies, and expanded availability of after-school
programs.[2] I take a number of steps in my statistical analyses to control for
the influence of these factors; for example, I estimate models for subsamples
that are less likely to be affected by one or more of these changes.

Before turning to the data used for the analyses, I briefly summarize the
information available from vital statistics and census reports. First, there is
little evidence to date that fertility rates or infant mortality rates in New York
City were affected by the terrorist attack. The citywide infant mortality rate
was lower in 2002 than in 2001. There was no apparent break in the trend in
the weekly number of births thirty-six to forty weeks after September 11, 2001
(New York City Department of Health and Mental Hygiene 2003, 4, table 1;
53, figure WTC2). The number of births for 2002 was about 1 percent lower
than the number for 2001, and the birth rate fell by 0.1 per 1,000 population
to 15.4. However, this decline continues a downward trend in the rate from
its most recent peak of 19.1 in 1990. Finally, the U.S. census estimates that
New York City's population continued to grow after 2001, although the rate
of growth has slowed. Great uncertainty surrounds the census estimates,
which have been questioned (see, for example, Beveridge 2004).[3]

DATA

The data used for this analysis are taken from the 1999 and 2002 waves of
the Columbia University New York Social Indicators Survey (Social Indicators
Survey Center 2002, 2003; see also Garfinkel et al. 2003). The 2002 survey

instrument includes special WTC modules that contain a number of items regarding psychological and health effects of the attack. Interviews for the 2002 wave were conducted approximately six months after September 11, 2001; the 1999 wave interviews took place in late 1999 and early 2000.

The NYSIS sample is composed of two subsamples: a random sample and a supplemental sample that provides the large sample sizes needed for analysis of small populations or those with relatively low response rates. When weighted with sampling weights, the data represent the population of New York City. I examined the random subsample separately only to check whether the number of children under age thirteen and the number under age six differed significantly between 1999 and 2002. They did not. I do not discuss this issue further and proceed with an analysis of the (weighted) combined sample.

Families with children under age thirteen were asked a battery of questions regarding their child care arrangements in the past year. There were just over 600 such families in each wave of the survey, for a combined sample size of 1,230. Respondents can and do report use of multiple care arrangements. In some analyses, I examined whether the family used any of several different types of care. I also constructed a variable with five exclusive categories of child care arrangements as follows:

1. Parent presumed available for care (one or more parent not employed for pay outside the home); if not:
2. Out-of-home care (private day care or preschool, public preschool, or public after-school program); if not:
3. Nanny and/or babysitter care; if not:
4. Care by a relative (other than parents) or a friend; if not:
5. Other care, not specified (but all resident parents are employed).

This variable was defined to track as closely as possible increased or decreased parental care between 1999 and 2002. Because respondents may report multiple care arrangements, however, this measure is not as sensitive to switching children from out-of-home settings to care by a nanny, babysitter, or relative other than a parent. However, if this kind of change were made more often as a result of heightened fear of terrorism, I would expect to find more reports of multiple arrangements in 2002 than in 1999 among those who reported some use of out-of-home care. I found no noticeable increase between 1999 and 2002 in the use of nanny or family care among those who reported using out-of-home care. Still, the potential low sensitivity of this measure to switches from out-of-home care (other than switches to parent care) is a limitation.

RESULTS

Changes Over Time

Table 9.1 displays child care arrangements in 1999 and 2002 for the entire sample of families with a child age twelve or younger and subsamples of those with at least one child under age six and with no child under age six. Table 9.1 is our first check on whether child care arrangements appeared to change between 1999 and 2002.

The first panel of the table shows that, for all families with children under age thirteen, the share with one or more parent not employed increased by about two percentage points between 1999 and 2002. This increase could reflect either the recession (Parrott and Cooke, this volume) or an increased tendency of parents to leave (or not enter or reenter) employment in order to care for a child at home. However, on balance, this does not appear to the result of children being pulled from out-of-home care, since the proportion in out-of-home care also increased by about two percentage points, from 24 to 26 percent.

The proportion of families with a parent at home increased by more than five percentage points (or about 10 percent) among those with a child under age six, but fell slightly among those with no child under six (first row of the table). This pattern is suggestive of an increased tendency to care for young children at home. However, out-of-home care also increased (by more than four percentage points) among those with a preschooler, which is inconsistent with such an interpretation. There was also a relatively large decline in the proportion of young children cared for by a relative or friend.

The remaining panels of the table present results for three subsamples: families in which all resident parents are employed (either an employed single parent or married parents who are both employed); married couples; and single mothers. Use of out-of-home care increased substantially for working families with young children (from 44 percent to over 60 percent), while care by relatives and other (unspecified) arrangements fell. For those with no child under six (but with a child under thirteen), the proportion using out-of-home care fell nearly four percentage points.

Among married couples, the fraction with a parent at home increased by nearly six percentage points regardless of children's ages. Use of out-of-home care increased by about four percentage points among families with young children, but decreased by more than two percentage points among those with older children only.

The last panel shows tabulations for single mothers with no spouse or partner present.[4] Among single mothers with young children, the proportion using out-of-home care increased by more than twelve percentage points, even though, surprisingly, the proportion not employed increased by more than

TABLE 9.1   CHILD CARE ARRANGEMENTS IN NEW YORK CITY, 1999 AND 2002 (SAMPLE-WEIGHTED PROPORTIONS OF HIERARCHICAL VARIABLE)

Child Care Arrangement	All		Any Child Under Six		No Child Under Six	
	1999	2002	1999	2002	1999	2002
Entire sample						
One or more parent						
not employed	50.6	52.8	54.2	59.6	45.8	45.2
Out-of-home care	24.3	26.2	20.1	24.5	29.8	28.1
Nanny or sitter	5.4	4.3	6.2	5.3	4.4	3.1
Family or friends	13.6	11.0	13.0	8.1	14.4	14.3
Other	6.1	5.7	6.5	2.5	5.7	9.2
All parents employed						
One or more parent						
not employed	0.0	0.0	0.0	0.0	0.0	0.0
Out-of-home care	49.2	55.5	43.9	60.6	55.0	51.3
Nanny or sitter	10.9	9.1	13.5	13.2	8.0	5.7
Family or friends	27.5	23.3	28.4	19.9	26.5	26.2
Other	12.4	12.1	14.2	6.3	10.5	16.8
Married couples						
One or more parent						
not employed	54.2	60.1	60.0	65.8	47.1	52.7
Out-of-home care	21.7	22.7	17.1	21.0	27.4	24.9
Nanny or sitter	4.6	3.3	5.5	5.0	3.6	1.2
Family or friends	14.3	9.6	14.0	5.4	14.8	14.9
Other	5.1	4.4	3.4	2.8	7.2	6.3
Single mothers						
Parent not employed	41.2	34.7	37.9	41.5	45.2	28.5
Out-of-home care	26.8	39.1	25.4	37.7	28.5	40.5
Nanny or sitter	5.0	6.5	4.5	4.8	5.6	8.1
Family or friends	14.4	14.9	13.4	12.8	15.5	16.8
Other	12.6	4.8	18.8	3.2	5.3	6.2

Source: New York Social Indicators Survey (author's estimates).
Note: Sample is families with children age twelve and under. The "entire sample" includes unmarried cohabiting couples and single-father families that are not shown separately. "Care" is based on the following classification:

1. One or more parent not employed; if not:
2. Out-of-home care (public or private day care, preschool, before- and after-school programs); if not:
3. Nanny or babysitter, possibly with relative care; if not:
4. Family or friend care; if not:
5. All other care.

three percentage points. Relative care and other unspecified care declined. Among those with children over age six only, the proportion not employed fell markedly, from 45 percent to nearly 28 percent, or by more than one-third. Apparently, this is the group most affected by welfare reform (see, for example, Moffitt 2003). All forms of nonparental care increased for this group, especially out-of-home care (the use of which increased by twelve percentage points, or by nearly half).

Table 9.2 shows the proportion of families reporting any use of a child care arrangement. We also break out three subcategories of out-of-home care: private day care or preschool; public after-school programs; and public preschool (such as Head Start). Use of multiple types of care accounts for differences between the numbers reported in table 9.1 and table 9.2. For example, although 41 percent of families used out-of-home care in 1999, in 17 percent of families there was a parent who was not employed and used out-of-home care (table 9.2). Thus, in table 9.1 the corresponding figure for out-of-home care for the entire sample in 1999 is 24 percent (41 percent minus 17 percent). In general, however, when figures in table 9.2 indicate that any use of a type of care increased or decreased substantially, the corresponding category figure in table 9.1 shows a qualitatively similar change.

A few other figures in table 9.2 are worth noting. First, the majority of every group relied on family or friends for child care to some extent (for example, 57 percent for the entire sample in 2002), though very few relied on family and friends exclusively (for example, 11 percent for the entire sample in 2002; see table 9.1). Thus, in defining a five-category exclusive care arrangement variable, we in essence assume that care by family and friends is a secondary care arrangement when the family also uses out-of-home care or care by a nanny.

Second, table 9.2 clearly documents the expanded use of public after-school and preschool programs in this period. Use of after-school programs increased by eight percentage points, and the use of public preschool increased by six and a half percentage points. Interestingly, the increase in use of these programs was concentrated among married couples: the proportion of married couples with no children under age six who used after-school programs increased from 32 to 54 percent, whereas the use of such programs among single mothers with no child under six declined slightly. Similarly, the use of public preschool among married couples with a child under age six increased from 17 to 24 percent, but fell from 34 to 32 percent among single mothers with preschoolers.[5]

The focus of the analysis so far has been on how child care arrangements changed between 1999 and 2002. As noted, child care arrangements and propensities to be employed or to care for children at home could vary over time for reasons other than the terrorist attacks, such as the economic recession (Parrott and Cooke, this volume; Reimers, this volume). Moreover, child care

TABLE 9.2   ANY USE OF CHILD CARE ARRANGEMENTS IN PAST YEAR, 1999 AND 2002 (SAMPLE-WEIGHTED PROPORTIONS)

Child Care Arrangement	All		Any Child Under Six		No Child Under Six	
	1999	2002	1999	2002	1999	2002
Entire Sample						
One or more parent not employed	50.6	52.8	54.2	59.6	45.8	45.2
Out-of-home care	41.2	53.6	37.5	52.8	46.1	54.4
Private day care, preschool	16.8	20.7	18.1	27.2	15.2	13.4
Public after-school	34.3	42.4	26.6	32.6	40.0	48.6
Public preschool	20.4	26.9	22.2	27.0	n.a.	n.a.
Nanny or sitter	17.2	19.1	19.9	24.0	13.7	13.7
Family or friends	57.1	56.9	60.7	62.9	52.4	50.1
Other	6.1	5.7	6.5	2.5	5.7	9.2
All parents employed						
One or more parent not employed	0.0	0.0	0.0	0.0	0.0	0.0
Out-of-home care	49.2	55.5	43.9	60.6	55.0	51.7
Private day care, preschool	25.0	27.3	26.9	37.8	22.9	18.6
Public after-school	37.0	41.5	22.4	39.7	44.8	42.3
Public preschool	25.0	27.9	26.7	27.8	n.a.	n.a.
Nanny or sitter	24.7	23.1	28.9	31.3	20.2	16.3
Family or friends	70.9	69.3	73.8	77.2	67.7	62.8
Other	12.4	12.1	14.2	6.3	10.5	16.8
Married couples						
One or more parent not employed	54.2	60.1	60.0	65.8	47.1	52.7
Mother not employed	48.9	49.8	54.6	57.2	41.7	40.5
Out-of-home care	37.1	53.6	36.7	48.8	37.5	59.8
Private day care, preschool	14.5	19.0	16.1	24.8	12.4	11.5
Public after-school	29.3	42.4	25.7	25.3	32.2	54.3
Public preschool	16.1	23.6	17.0	23.8	n.a.	n.a.
Nanny or sitter	18.0	17.1	22.7	22.5	12.2	10.1
Family or friends	57.9	55.6	62.8	60.0	51.7	49.9
Other	5.1	4.4	3.4	2.8	7.2	6.3
Single mothers						
Parent not employed	41.2	34.7	37.9	41.5	45.2	28.5
Out-of-home care	49.2	60.4	41.1	65.2	58.7	55.9
Private day care, preschool	20.8	26.5	22.3	38.5	19.0	15.5
Public after-school	41.7	52.9	24.9	59.2	52.1	49.3
Public preschool	28.3	32.4	33.9	32.1	n.a.	n.a.
Nanny or sitter	13.6	21.5	14.7	26.2	12.2	17.2
Family or friends	57.8	60.4	58.4	62.4	57.1	59.5
Other	12.6	4.8	18.8	3.2	5.3	6.1

Source: New York Social Indicators Survey (author's estimates).
Note: Sample is families with children age twelve and under. The "entire sample" includes unmarried cohabitating couples and single-father families that are not shown separately. n.a. = no applicable.

arrangements differ according to the number and ages of children, the socio-economic resources of the family, and a variety of demographic characteristics. Clearly, it is important to control for these characteristics in examining changes in child care arrangements between 1999 and 2002.

Tables 9.3 and 9.4 show how child care arrangements varied according to sociodemographic characteristics of parents or families in our NYSIS samples for 1999 and 2002, respectively. For example, the first panel of table 9.3 shows that in 1999, 31 percent of mothers in families with a parent who was not employed lacked a high school degree (compared to 22 percent of all families and 10 percent of those with a child in out-of-home care). Compared to the entire sample, respondents in families in which a parent was not employed were more likely to be Hispanic, less likely to be black, and more likely, on average, to be headed by a married couple. These same basic patterns hold in 2002. However, a far lower proportion of families with an unemployed parent were headed by a single parent in 2002 (14 percent) than in 1999 (21 percent), a finding that most likely reflects the effects of welfare reform on the employ-ment of single mothers (and the effect of the recession on married couples).

In both years about 40 percent of mothers in families that employed a nanny were college graduates. Nanny care was also more common for pre-schoolers. College-educated mothers were disproportionately represented as well among those who used relative and friend care. Less-educated women and immigrants were more likely not to report a specific type of care. Finally, the proportion of those who reported no specific care type who had a child under age six fell markedly between 1999 and 2002, though this category makes up only 5 to 6 percent of the sample. College-educated mothers are disproportion-ately represented among users of out-of-home care, though the proportion of less-educated among this group doubled from 10 to 20 percent between 1999 and 2002.

Regression Estimates for Changes Over Time

Table 9.5 summarizes multinomial logit regression estimates of the changes between 1999 and 2002 in categorical child care arrangements. The figures in the table are the "year effects" (2002/1999) on the odds of being in the specified category relative to the base category (one or more parent not employed), controlling for the characteristics indicated (for example, demographic con-trols or demographic controls plus borough dummies).

Results are shown for the entire sample and various subsamples. For exam-ple, the out-of-home care (first) column shows how the odds of using out-of-home care (versus parent care) changed between 1999 and 2002. The figure 1.02 indicates an insignificant increase of 2 percent in the odds of out-of-home relative to parent care. Adding demographic and borough controls (models 2

TABLE 9.3   SAMPLE STATISTICS BY CHILD CARE ARRANGEMENT, 1999
(SAMPLE-WEIGHTED PROPORTIONS, UNLESS INDICATED)

Characteristics of Adult Respondent or Mother	One or More Parent Not Employed[a]	Out-of-Home Care[a]	Nanny or Sitter[a]	Family or Friends[a]	No Care Specified[a]	All
Mother's education						
Less than high school graduate	0.31	0.10	0.14	0.07	0.31	0.22
High school graduate	0.38	0.33	0.32	0.39	0.25	0.35
Some college	0.15	0.28	0.13	0.23	0.25	0.20
College graduate or higher	0.16	0.29	0.41	0.31	0.19	0.23
Respondent race, Hispanic						
Hispanic	0.42	0.28	0.25	0.37	0.34	0.36
Non-Hispanic black	0.19	0.38	0.35	0.22	0.20	0.25
Non-Hispanic White	0.23	0.22	0.23	0.26	0.15	0.23
Other and unknown	0.16	0.12	0.17	0.15	0.31	0.16
Mother's age (years)	34.8	35.5	34.7	34.8	39.0	35.2
Respondent immigrant	0.60	0.42	0.63	0.54	0.77	0.56
Number and ages of children under age thirteen						
One child under age six, none age six to twelve	0.19	0.22	0.28	0.28	0.23	0.22
Two or more children under age six, none age six to twelve	0.06	0.05	0.23	0.02	0.00	0.06
One or more under six and one or more age six to twelve	0.35	0.19	0.13	0.23	0.37	0.28
One child age six to twelve only	0.28	0.40	0.26	0.28	0.29	0.31
Two or more children age six to twelve, none under six	0.12	0.14	0.10	0.19	0.11	0.13
Living arrangement						
Respondent lives with spouse	0.63	0.52	0.50	0.62	0.48	0.59
Respondent lives with partner	0.16	0.12	0.23	0.07	0.02	0.13
Respondent single parent (no spouse or partner present)	0.21	0.36	0.27	0.31	0.50	0.28
Borough of New York City						
Bronx	0.23	0.20	0.19	0.12	0.12	0.20
Queens	0.28	0.38	0.26	0.32	0.47	0.32
Brooklyn	0.32	0.22	0.39	0.36	0.23	0.30
Staten Island	0.04	0.10	0.07	0.07	0.07	0.06
Manhattan	0.13	0.11	0.09	0.13	0.11	0.12
Sample size (unweighted)	266	186	39	93	32	616
Weighted proportion	0.51	0.24	0.05	0.14	0.06	1.00

Source: New York Social Indicators Survey (author's estimates).
[a]Category of hierarchical child care variable; see notes to table 9.1 for definition.

TABLE 9.4   SAMPLE STATISTICS BY CHILD CARE ARRANGEMENT, 2002
(SAMPLE-WEIGHTED PROPORTIONS, UNLESS INDICATED)

Characteristics of Adult Respondent or Mother	One or More Parent Not Employed[a]	Out-of-Home Care[a]	Nanny or Sitter[a]	Family or Friends[a]	No Care Specified[a]	All
Mother's education						
Less than high school graduate	0.35	0.20	0.18	0.13	0.43	0.28
High school graduate	0.35	0.27	0.22	0.29	0.21	0.31
Some college	0.13	0.26	0.19	0.24	0.11	0.18
College graduate or higher	0.17	0.27	0.41	0.34	0.25	0.23
Respondent race, Hispanic						
Hispanic	0.35	0.27	0.38	0.31	0.30	0.33
Non-Hispanic black	0.15	0.42	0.25	0.28	0.24	0.25
Non-Hispanic white	0.26	0.22	0.23	0.22	0.33	0.24
Other and unknown	0.24	0.09	0.14	0.19	0.13	0.18
Mother's age (years)	34.6	36.5	35.4	35.0	39.9	35.5
Respondent immigrant	0.62	0.52	0.65	0.43	0.69	0.58
Number and ages of children under age thirteen						
One child under age six, none age six to twelve	0.22	0.16	0.29	0.23	0.10	0.20
Two or more children under age six, none age six to twelve	0.13	0.05	0.15	0.04	0.06	0.09
One or more under six and one or more age six to twelve	0.25	0.28	0.22	0.10	0.08	0.23
One child age six to twelve only	0.23	0.35	0.19	0.39	0.54	0.30
Two or more children age six to twelve, none under six	0.17	0.16	0.15	0.23	0.22	0.18
Living arrangement						
Respondent lives with spouse	0.73	0.56	0.49	0.55	0.50	0.64
Respondent lives with partner	0.13	0.10	0.15	0.16	0.19	0.13
Respondent single parent (no spouse or partner present)	0.14	0.34	0.36	0.29	0.31	0.23
Borough of New York City						
Bronx	0.22	0.22	0.41	0.23	0.20	0.23
Queens	0.27	0.26	0.20	0.35	0.28	0.27
Brooklyn	0.31	0.36	0.15	0.28	0.43	0.32
Staten Island	0.07	0.04	0.03	0.07	0.07	0.06
Manhattan	0.13	0.12	0.21	0.07	0.02	0.12
Sample size (unweighted)	283	186	32	84	29	614
Weighted proportion	0.53	0.26	0.05	0.11	0.06	1.00

Source: New York Social Indicators Survey (author's estimates).
[a]Category of hierarchical child care variable, see notes to table 9.1 for definition.

TABLE 9.5   YEAR EFFECTS ON CHILD CARE CHOICES, 2002 VERSUS 1999
(RELATIVE ODDS FROM MULTINOMIAL LOGIT MODELS, BASE
CATEGORY = PARENT CARE PRESUMED)

Sample, Model	Out-of-Home Care	Nanny or Sitter	Family or Friends	Other	Sample Size
Entire sample					
1. No controls	1.02	0.76	0.77	0.91	1,230
2. Demographic controls	1.12	0.81	0.91	0.95	1,230
3. Demographic and borough controls	1.16	0.78	0.94	1.00	1,230
Various subsamples (demographic and borough controls)					
4. Child under age six	1.20	0.69	0.64	0.48	682
5. No child under age six	1.30	1.02	1.48	2.00*	548
6. Manhattan	0.83	0.28	0.87	0.10	148
7. College graduate (mother)	1.06	0.46	1.02	1.53	321
8. Married couple	1.13	0.47*	0.71	0.99	702
9. Married couple, child under age six	1.16	0.74	0.61	0.73	409
10. Married couple, no child under age six	1.09	0.48	1.27	0.78	293
11. Single parent	1.64*	1.53	1.15	1.68	380
12. Single parent, child under age six	0.94	0.73	0.60	0.13	178
13. Single parent, no child under age six	2.84**	3.36*	2.82*	9.40**	282

Source: New York Social Indicators Survey (author's estimates).
Notes: Data are weighted; sample weights are scaled to one for each year. Full sample is households with children age twelve and under. Demographic controls include mother's age and dummy variables for mother's education (4), race (3) and immigrant status of respondent, marital status (2), and dummy variables for number and ages of children (categories are one child under six, none six to twelve; two or more children under six, none six to twelve; at least one child under six and at least one six to twelve; one child six to twelve, none younger; and two or more children six to twelve, none younger).
**p ≤ .05; *.05 < p ≤ .10

and 3) raises the ratio to 1.16, suggesting increased use of out-of-home care, but the relative odds are not statistically different from 1.0. One explanation for finding no increase in parent care relative to out-of-home care might be that many parents wanted to care for a child at home but could not afford to do so. However, restricting the sample to those with a college degree (or higher) does not change the results: the odds ratio for out-of-home care relative to parent care is a bit smaller for this group than for the sample as a whole (1.06 rather than 1.16), but the difference is small, and neither indicates a statistically significant change. Restricting the sample to families with a preschooler raises this ratio, and the change in the relative odds is in the opposite direction to what would be expected if families were substituting parent care for out-of-home care as a result of the attack on the World Trade Center. Use of nanny and family care fell relative to home care for the entire sample and most subsamples, though again, these effects are not significant.

Where we do see significant changes are for single parents with no children under six. Use of most care modes increased relative to parent care at home (which, as we have seen, fell substantially); relative odds (2002/1999) approached or exceeded 3 for all types of care relative to parent care. Interestingly, for those with a child under six, there were no statistically significant changes in care arrangements, though use of nanny and family care fell relative to parent and out-of-home care.

Table 9.6 shows changes in reports of any use of care. For example, the row for model 3 shows that all categories of out-of-home care increased substantially and that parental and other types of care were stable. Use of out-of-home care increased substantially and significantly in all subsamples, though use of different types of out-of-home care varied differently for different groups. The largest (though not significant) increases in parent care were in Manhattan (model 7) and among families with a child under six (both married couples and single parents; models 9 and 12). These results suggest increased use of parental care for the most vulnerable (youngest) children; however, the higher increase in use of out-of-home care than parent care for families with preschoolers is inconsistent with this interpretation. Finally, results for the roughly one-quarter of families in which the mother had graduated from college are similar to results for the sample as a whole (compare model 7 to model 3, for example). Thus, it does not appear that those who (presumably) could most afford to increase their use of parent or nanny care did so more than the average family.[6]

Emotional and Health Effects and Child Care Arrangements

So far we have found little evidence that children were increasingly taken care of by a parent after the terrorist attack. This is not because children and parents were unaffected by the attack. As table 9.7 demonstrates, nearly one-fifth (18 percent) of parents reported that a reference child wanted to stay home as a result of the attack on the WTC; nearly half of respondents reported that they restricted their children's movements; and nearly half reported that

TABLE 9.6 YEAR EFFECTS ON ANY USE OF CHILD CARE MODE, 2002 VERSUS 1999 (COEFFICIENTS FROM LINEAR PROBABILITY MODELS, SAMPLE-WEIGHTED DATA)

Sample, Model	One or More Parent Not Employed	Out-of-Home Care	Private Day Care, Preschool	Public After-School	Public Preschool	Nanny or Sitter	Family or Friends	Sample Size
Entire sample								
1. No controls	0.023	0.124**	0.039	0.081**	0.065	0.019	−0.002	1,230
2. Demographic controls	−0.003	0.130**	0.055**	0.077***	0.065	0.024	0.020	1,230
3. Demographic and borough controls	−0.010	0.132**	0.056**	0.077***	0.067	0.024	0.022	1,230
Various subsamples (demographic and borough controls)								
4. With a child under age six	0.032	0.164**	0.099**	0.079	0.066	0.026	0.007	682
5. No child under age six	−0.067	0.096*	0.044	0.082*	n.a.	0.004	0.046	548
6. Manhattan only	0.077	0.244**	0.019	0.164	0.128	0.103	0.080	148
7. College graduate (mother)	0.004	0.126**	0.068	0.106*	−0.054	−0.040	−0.024	321
8. Married couples	0.020	0.175***	0.060**	0.101***	0.072	−0.006	0.007	702
9. Married couples, child under age six	0.048	0.141**	0.101**	−0.009	0.082*	−0.024	−0.009	409
10. Married couples, no child under age six	−0.017	0.231**	0.016	0.196**	n.a.	−0.001	0.051	293
11. Single parent	−0.077	0.045	0.059	0.059	0.010	0.048	0.001	380
12. Single parent, child under age six	0.062	0.169**	0.144***	0.322**	0.003	0.095	−0.023	178
13. Single parent, no child under age six	−0.187***	−0.063	−0.020	−0.067	n.a.	0.024	0.063	202

Source: New York Social Indicators Survey (author's estimates).

Notes: Data are weighted with sampling weights scaled to sum to one for each year.
Full sample is households with children age twelve and under. Demographic controls include mother's age and dummy variables for mother's education (3), race/Hispanicity (3) and immigrant status of respondent, marital status (2), and dummy variables for child age and number (categories are one child under six, none six to twelve; two or more children under six, none six to twelve; at least one child under six and at least one six to twelve; one child six to twelve, none younger; and two or more children six to twelve, none younger), where appropriate.
**p ≤ .05; *.05 < p ≤ .10; p-values based on robust standard errors.

TABLE 9.7   PROPORTION REPORTING EFFECTS OF THE WORLD TRADE CENTER
ATTACK, BY CATEGORICAL CHILD CARE ARRANGEMENT, 2002
(SAMPLE-WEIGHTED)

World Trade Center Effect[a]	All	One or More Parent Not Employed[b]	Out-of-Home Care[b]	Nanny or Sitter[b]	Family or Friends[b]	No Care Specified[b]
Adult effects						
Anyone in family lost job	0.16	0.18	0.11	0.11	0.14	0.26
Respondent wanted to stay home	0.47	0.49	0.45	0.45	0.47	0.29
Respondent cut child's freedom of movement	0.43	0.46	0.47	0.30	0.35	0.31
Child effects						
Child had new emotional or health problems	0.07	0.07	0.08	0.02	0.02	0.12
Child had problems sleeping	0.09	0.10	0.12	0.10	0.14	0.10
Child wanted to stay home	0.18	0.19	0.21	0.08	0.14	0.30
Child was worried respondent will go away and never return	0.29	0.29	0.36	0.12	0.27	0.29
Weighted sample count	614	324	161	26	68	35

Source: New York Social Indicators Survey (author's estimates).
[a]Except for "lost job," answered "yes" or "sometimes" to question about World Trade Center effect.
[b]Hierarchical child care category: see notes to table 9.1.

they (the parents) wanted to stay home more after the attack. And small proportions reported that their child had new health or emotional problems or
had trouble sleeping.

The reports of health and emotional problems resulting from the attack on
the World Trade Center suggest another way to examine whether the attack
affected child care choices in New York City. I examine whether those who
reported that they or their child experienced emotional or health difficulties
as a result of the attack on the WTC responded by caring for their child at
home or by removing the child from out-of-home care. Tabulations related to

this hypothesis are summarized in table 9.8. The figures in table 9.8 demonstrate that child care arrangements do not differ much according to reports of these WTC-related symptoms or difficulties. For example, in about 53 percent of families, a parent was not employed in the survey week in 2002. This proportion varied from 48.5 to 59 percent among families with various reported WTC-related difficulties.[7] Interestingly, reports that the child had new emotional or health problems or that the child feared that the parent would go away and not come back are associated with a somewhat higher likelihood of being in out-of-home care. This is the opposite of what would be expected if parents were more likely to provide care at home for a child adversely affected by the WTC attacks. In fact, it is more suggestive that out-of-home care is a (moderate) risk factor for these problems. Results presented in table 9.9 for proportions using any of the various care arrangements among those reporting each WTC-related difficulty are similar.

Table 9.10 shows the effects of reporting that someone in the family lost a job as a result of the WTC attack on the probability that the father and/or male partner or all parents were employed in the survey week in 2002. The upper panel pertains to all families and the lower panel to married-couple families. Clearly, a WTC-related job loss reduces the chance that the father or all resident parents were employed in 2002. These effects are statistically significant and large for males (whose odds of employment are reduced by half if the family reported a WTC-related job loss) and are not greatly affected by adding sociodemographic and borough controls. Differences in these effects vary somewhat across subsamples. The effects are largest for married men and single mothers with no children under age six.

SUMMARY AND DISCUSSION

We find little evidence that the attack on the WTC affected the child care arrangements of New York City families. First, parents did not appear more likely after the attacks than before to provide care at or close to home in response to increased fear of terrorism or to cope with problems their children developed as a result of the terrorist attack. Reliance on parent care, nanny care, or relative care did not appear to be greater after the attacks than before. Second, parents who reported that their children had new emotional or health problems or who expressed WTC-related fears also were not more likely to care for their children at home. Use of out-of-home care generally increased between 1999 and 2002 and was more rather than less prevalent among those who reported that their child had new health or emotional problems as a result of the attack on the WTC. These results were generally not affected by controlling for a child's age and a variety of sociodemographic characteristics of families.

Although the effects of welfare reform and the recession on child care

TABLE 9.8 CHILD CARE ARRANGEMENTS IN 2002 AMONG THOSE REPORTING EFFECTS OF WORLD TRADE CENTER ATTACK

World Trade Center Effect[a]	One or More Parent Not Employed[b]	Out-of-Home Care[b]	Nanny or Sitter[b]	Family or Friends[b]	No Care Specified[b]
All families	52.9%	25.8%	4.5%	11.2%	5.7%
Anyone in family lost job	59.5	18.5	3.0	9.8	9.2
Respondent wanted to stay home	55.9	25.7	3.9	10.9	3.6
Respondent cut child's freedom of movement	56.0	28.2	3.1	8.6	4.2
Child had new emotional and/or health problems	53.1	31.7	1.4	3.8	10.0
Child had problems sleeping	48.5	29.0	3.7	13.4	5.3
Child wanted to stay home	52.3	28.6	1.9	8.1	9.1
Child was worried respondent will go away and not return	50.9	31.8	1.7	10.0	5.5
Married couples	60.3	22.1	3.6	9.5	4.4
Anyone in family lost job	68.1	15.0	1.9	10.4	4.7
Respondent wanted to stay home	63.6	20.5	4.0	9.6	2.2
Respondent cut child's freedom of movement	63.3	26.4	1.2	5.7	3.5
Child had new emotional and/or health problems	60.0	29.0	0.0	1.8	9.3
Child had problems sleeping	58.7	21.8	0.0	14.9	4.6
Child wanted to stay home	60.9	25.2	0.0	6.9	7.1
Child was worried respondent will go away and not return	57.4	26.8	0.0	10.3	5.5
Single parents	34.7	39.1	6.5	14.9	4.8
Anyone in family lost job	42.7	39.5	0.0	13.3	4.5
Respondent wanted to stay home	37.6	38.1	8.3	12.7	12.7
Respondent cut child's freedom of movement	32.5	38.5	9.0	16.9	3.0
Child had new emotional and/or health problems	23.1	45.0	5.4	10.0	16.6
Child had problems sleeping	51.7	32.6	13.1	0.0	2.6
Child wanted to stay home	43.4	38.4	6.0	4.6	7.6
Child was worried respondent will go away and not return	33.7	41.7	6.8	11.2	6.5

Source: New York Social Indicators Survey (author's estimates).

[a] Except for "lost job," answered "yes" or "sometimes" to question about World Trade Center effect.

[b] Hierarchical child care category; see notes to table 9.1.

TABLE 9.9   PROPORTION REPORTING ANY USE OF CHILD CARE ARRANGEMENT
AMONG THOSE REPORTING AN EFFECT OF THE WORLD TRADE
CENTER ATTACK, 2002 (SAMPLE-WEIGHTED PROPORTIONS)

World Trade Center Effect[a]	One or More Parent Not Employed	Out-of-Home Care	Nanny or Sitter	Family or Friends
All	0.53	0.54	0.19	0.57
Adult effects				
Anyone in family lost job	0.60	0.56	0.11	0.57
Respondent wanted to stay home	0.56	0.50	0.20	0.56
Respondent cut child's freedom of movement	0.56	0.58	0.18	0.54
Child effects				
Child had new emotional and/or health problems	0.53	0.67	0.21	0.49
Child had problems sleeping	0.49	0.62	0.16	0.57
Child wanted to stay home	0.52	0.53	0.18	0.52
Child was worried respondent will go away and never return	0.51	0.56	0.20	0.52

Source: New York Social Indicators Survey (author's estimates).
[a]Except for "lost job," answered "yes" or "sometimes" to question about World Trade Center effect.

choices were quite apparent in these results and may have confounded my estimates of the effect of the terrorist attack, these results were also generally unaffected by restricting the sample to married couples (who were relatively unaffected by welfare reform) or families in which all parents were employed (who apparently escaped or recovered rapidly from recessionary job loss) or highly educated parents (who presumably could most easily afford to alter their child care arrangements). The result most consistent with 9/11 effects is the increase between 1999 and 2002 in the proportion of both married-couple and single-parent families in which a parent was not employed among those with a child under six years of age (table 9.6). We view this evidence as weak both because the estimated effect was not statistically significant and because the increase in the proportion with a parent at home was smaller than the increase in the proportion using out-of-home care. Nor should evidence of decreased parental employment for these groups be attributed entirely to the

TABLE 9.10   EFFECTS OF WORLD TRADE CENTER JOB LOSS ON
EMPLOYMENT OF MALE OR ALL CO-RESIDENT PARENTS IN
2002 (ODDS RATIOS FROM LOGISTIC REGRESSION,
SAMPLE-WEIGHTED DATA)

	All Resident Parents Employed[a]		Male Employed[b]	
Sample, Model	(Odds Ratio)	Sample Size	(Odds Ratio)	Sample Size
All families with children under thirteen				
1. No controls	0.72	602	0.47*	430
2. Demographic controls	0.88	602	0.53	430
3. Demographic and borough controls	0.91	602	0.54	430
Selected subsamples (demographic and borough controls)				
4. With a child under age six	0.60	330	0.43	249
5. With a child age six to thirteen, none younger	1.06	272	0.63	180
6. College graduate (mother)	0.93	164	0.24	136
7. Married couples	0.74	356	0.44*	356
8. Married couples, child under age six	0.55	209	0.35*	209
9. Married couples, child age six to thirteen, none younger	0.81	147	0.32	147
10. Single mother with children under age thirteen	0.53	156	n.a.	
11. Single mother, child under age six	1.07	72	n.a.	
12. Single mother, child age six to thirteen, none younger	0.43	83	n.a.	

Source: New York Social Indicators Survey (author's estimates).
[a]All employed = adult respondent and spouse or partner employed or employed single parent. Twelve married couples were dropped owing to missing employment status for the adult male.
[b]Employed male respondent or male spouse or partner of respondent.
**p ≤ 0.05; *.05 < p ≤ .10; n.a. = not applicable.

economic slowdown, since parents in families with no child under six were more likely to work (less likely to have a parent at home) in 2002 than in 1999, especially among single-parent families.

Although my failure to find evidence for a change in child care arrangements may be due to inadequate measures or confounding, it is worth considering the implications of these results, assuming they are correct. Does the absence of a change in child care arrangements mean that the terrorist attack did not result in a change of values and a reordering of priorities among New York parents? Perhaps values and priorities changed in the ways predicted and voiced but the link between values and behaviors is weak. There are many possibilities. Perhaps more parents would have preferred to care for their children at home but could not afford to do so. (However, we found no evidence of a shift to care at home among the more highly educated population.) Or perhaps those who acted on new priorities moved out of New York to the suburbs or lived there already—for example, in an attempt to provide a safer environment and find affordable housing with one income. We would not detect such changes in data drawn entirely from New York City. Another possibility is that the values change occurred but did not endure long enough to affect child care choices in 2002 (interviews were conducted between March and June 2002; see Garfinkel et al. 2003). For example, Putnam (2002) reports that the spike in religiosity and churchgoing after the attack on the WTC was short-lived. Reimers (this volume) concludes that the employment of disadvantaged women (but not men) was reduced by the attack on the World Trade Center in the last quarter of 2001 and that this effect did not endure through 2002. An interpretation of the evidence presented here that would be consistent with Reimers's findings is that there was a brief period of decreased employment of women, perhaps associated with an increased desire to be closer to their children, but that by mid-2002, when the NYSIS was fielded, this effect was no longer detectable. A final possibility is that behaviors did not change and families generally resumed their "normal" (previous) lives.

We anticipated that the group most likely to adjust their child care arrangements would be parents who wished to compensate for the emotional or health problems their children experienced as a result of the terrorist attack. Evidence that children in out-of-home care were more likely to have had these problems is inconsistent with this expectation. Instead, the evidence suggests the possibility that out-of-home care is a risk factor for elevated emotional problems linked to the terrorist attack and that parents had not, as of 2002, been able to offset fully these elevated risks.

I thank the Russell Sage Foundation for its generous support; Howard Chernick, Alan Krueger, and members of the working group on the economic effects of the 9/11 attack for their comments; Sandra Garcia, Irv Garfinkel, and Julian Tietler for their assistance with the NYSIS data; and Ana Champeny and Baruch Feldman for research assistance. I am responsible for all errors.

NOTES

1. We also investigated whether there was a decline in the number of children living in New York City and in Manhattan following September 11, 2001, and, using zip code information included in the NYSIS, whether the relationship between the distance to the WTC and child care arrangements changed between 1999 and 2001. We found no evidence of either.
2. Public funding for child care was increased in part because of 1996 welfare reform legislation, and public and private funding for after-school programs increased substantially between 1998 and 2002 (see Ansell 2004; After-School Corp. 2003).
3. Since births are well measured in vital records, if the population estimates were substantially upwardly biased, then the birth rate (which uses an estimated population as the denominator) should have fallen noticeably. It did not.
4. Unmarried cohabiting couples and single fathers are included in the full sample, but we do not show separate tabulations for them.
5. Further investigation of these trends is needed to determine to what degree they are the result of growing economic hardship among married couples, reduced categorical preferences for single parents, or expansion of eligibility for such programs into higher income brackets.
6. The "opportunity cost" in forgone earnings of caring for children at home is higher among the more highly educated.
7. Table 9.11 shows the intercorrelations of these effects; though the correlations are all positive, all are less than 0.4.

TABLE 9.11   CORRELATIONS OF WORLD TRADE CENTER EFFECTS

	Social Indicator Variable Name	wa1	wa5	wa6	wc1	wc2	wc4	wc5
Anyone in family lost job	wa1	1.00						
Respondent wanted to stay home	wa5	−0.13	1.00					
Respondent cut child's freedom of movement	wa6	−0.11	0.36	1.00				
Child had new emotional and/or health problems	wc1	0.05	−0.11	−0.19	1.00			
Child had problems sleeping	wc2	−0.02	0.17	0.20	−0.25	1.00		
Child wanted to stay home	wc4	−0.01	0.25	0.26	−0.26	0.31	1.00	
Child was worried respondent will go away and never come back	wc5	−0.15	0.24	0.30	−0.24	0.30	0.40	1.00

Source: New York Social Indicators Survey (author's estimates).

REFERENCES

After-School Corp. 2003. *The After-School Corporation Fifth-Year Report*. New York: The After School Corp. (November 1).

Ansell, Susan. 2004. "After-School Programs." *Education Week on the Web*. Available at: http://www.edweek.com.

Applied Research Consulting (ARC). 2002. *Effects of the World Trade Center Attack on New York City Public School Students: Initial Report to the New York City Board of Education*. New York: Columbia University Mailman School of Public Health and New York State Psychiatric Institute (May 6).

Berkowitz, Gertrud S., Mary S. Wolff, Teresa M. Janevic, Ian R. Holzman, Rachel Yehuda, and Philip J. Landrigan. 2003. "The World Trade Center Disaster and Intrauterine Growth Restriction." Letter. *Journal of the American Medical Association* 290(5): 595–96.

Beveridge, Andrew. 2004. "Estimating New York City's Population." *Gotham Gazette*, April 4. Available at: www.gothamgazette.com.

Brustein, Joshua. 2003. "Leaving New York." *Gotham Gazette*, September 9. Available at: www.gothamgazette.com.

Garfinkel, Irwin, Neeraj Kaushal, Julien Tietler, and Sandra Garcia. 2003. *Vulnerability and Resilience: New Yorkers Respond to 9/11*. New York: Columbia University School of Social Work, Social Indicators Survey Center (September).

Landrigan, Philip J., Paul J. Lioy, George Thurston, Gertrud Berkowitz, L. C. Chen, Steven N. Chillrud, Stephen H. Gavett, Panos G. Georgopoulos, Alison S. Geyh, Stephen Levin, Frederica Perera, Stephen M. Rappaport, Christopher Small, and the National Institute of Environmental Health Sciences (NIEHS) World Trade Center Working Group. 2004. "Health and Environmental Consequences of the World Trade Center Disaster." *Environmental Health Perspectives* 112(6, May): 731–39.

Meyers, Marcia K., and Shirley Gatenio. 2004. "Child Care in New York City." Unpublished paper. Seattle: University of Washington.

Moffitt, Robert. 2003. "The Temporary Assistance for Needy Families Program." In *Means-Tested Assistance Programs in the United States*, edited by Robert Moffitt. Chicago: National Bureau of Economic Research (NBER) and University of Chicago Press.

New York City Department of Health and Mental Hygiene. Bureau of Vital Statistics. 2003. *Summary of Vital Statistics 2002: The City of New York*. New York: New York City Department of Health and Mental Hygiene (December).

New York City Public Health Partnership. 2002. *Working Together to Create Healthy Communities* (no. 6, January). New York: New York City Public Health Partnership.

Phillips, Deborah, Nancy Crowell, Marcy Whitebook, and Joon Yong Jo. 2002. *Child Care Workers in the Aftermath of September 11th*. Berkeley: University of California, Center for the Study of Child Care Employment.

Putnam, Robert. 2002. "Bowling Together." *American Prospect* 13(3, February 11): 20–22.

Shellenbarger, Sue. 2001a. "Examine Your Priorities in the Wake of Attacks." *Wall Street Journal Online*. (September 21). Available at: http:www.careerjournal.com/columnists/workfamily/20010921-workfamily.html.

———. 2001b. "One Couple's Struggle with Work-Life Balance." *Wall Street Journal*

Online. (November 15). Available at: http:www.careerjournal.com/columnists/work family/20011115-workfamily.html.

————. 2001c. "Working Parents Face a New Kind of Pressure." *Wall Street Journal Online.* (October 25). Available at: http:www.careerjournal.com/columnists/workfamily/ 20011025-workfamily.html.

————. 2002. "Work-Life Changes for the Months Ahead." *Wall Street Journal Online.* (January 10). Available at: http:www.careerjournal.com/columnists/workfamily/2002 0110-workfamily.html.

Social Indicators Survey Center. 2002. *1999 New York City Social Indicators Survey: Documentation and Codebook.* Rev. ed. New York: Columbia University School of Social Work (March).

————. 2003. *2002 New York City Social Indicators Survey.* New York: Columbia University School of Social Work.

Vlahov, D., S. Galea, H. Resnick, J. Ahern, J. Boscarino, M. Bucuvalas, J. Gold, and D. Kilpatrick. 2002. "Increased Use of Cigarettes, Alcohol, and Marijuana Among Manhattan New York Residents After the September 11 Terrorist Attacks." *American Journal of Epidemiology* 155(11): 988–96.

PART III

The Fiscal Impact of 9/11

CHAPTER 10

The Fiscal Impact of 9/11 on New York City

Howard Chernick

THE SEPTEMBER 11 terrorist attack on New York's World Trade Center (WTC) was a terrible and severe shock for New York City along many dimensions: personal tragedy, social stress, political turmoil, economic dislocation, and fiscal and budgetary pressure. This chapter addresses the fiscal dimension of the 9/11 attack. I consider the magnitude of the additional costs incurred by the government of New York City, the effects on revenues, and the compensation received by the city, mainly from the federal government. In light of the tremendous budgetary pressure induced by the attack, the city has had to make difficult spending and revenue choices. In the last section of the chapter, the distributional impact of these choices is briefly assessed.

To assess the fiscal costs of the 9/11 attack I treat the public-sector costs of 9/11 as losses to New York City residents. As a result of the attack, many residents of New York City lost jobs and income. Almost all faced higher tax rates and reduced public services. Drawing on studies of the fiscal impacts that were done by various government agencies, I assess the overall dollar magnitude of these losses and the cost per resident. I then compare the losses to the compensation paid to New York City through the federal 9/11 assistance package to determine the net loss to New York City residents.

The impact of the attack on the city's budget includes the effect of the additional expenditures required, the increase in transfer payments, mainly for Medicaid, and the loss in city and state tax revenues. Not including the cleanup costs at the World Trade Center site, I estimate these costs to be at least $2.1 billion, or $260 per capita. This amount is between 0.5 and 1 percent

of personal income. Federal compensation for general budgetary relief will offset at most about one-third of these public-sector costs, leaving New York City
to make up a significant fiscal shortfall through tax increases and additional
borrowing. Perhaps somewhat surprisingly, the distributional impact of the
city's tax and spending responses to the 9/11 crisis has on balance been progressive—the net burden of tax increases and spending cuts has been borne
more by higher- than lower-income groups. The fiscal crisis arising from the
9/11 attack also had a severe impact on revenues to New York State. Except
for granting New York City permission to raise its tax rates and taking over a
small share of the city's debt obligations, the state has done little to compensate New York City for the fiscal costs of 9/11. I conclude that there is a strong
efficiency rationale for favoring dense areas such as New York City in the
distribution of federal assistance to combat terror.

The chapter begins with a general discussion of the fiscal and budgetary
situation in New York City following the 9/11 attack. I then summarize the
analytical approach of translating the public-sector costs back to individuals.
In the third section, I provide estimates of the various components of the
public-sector cost. The fourth section discusses the compensation received
from the federal government and estimates the net loss to New Yorkers
through the public sector. The last section considers briefly the distribution
by income group of the losses from 9/11. The conclusion considers the principles that should underlie federal assistance to prevent future terrorist attacks.

EXPENDITURE AND REVENUE TRENDS AFTER 9/11

After years of revenue surpluses, the combination of the national recession, the
bursting of the stock market bubble, and the 9/11 attack led to a severe deterioration in the fiscal condition of New York City. The budget gap for fiscal year
2002—from July 2001 to June 2002, covering the period of the 9/11 attack—
was largely dealt with by increased borrowing. With the approval of the state,
the city eventually issued an additional $2.1 billion in long-term debt under
the heading of New York City Transitional Finance Authority recovery bonds,
to be used largely to cover current expenditures. The annual cost of this additional borrowing is estimated at between $150 million and $180 million. In
fiscal year 2003 the city faced a deficit of $1.1 billion. The projected budget
gap for fiscal year 2004, as of January 2003, was $6.4 billion, about 14 percent
of total expenditures. The city responded to this fiscal pressure by increasing
borrowing, cutting expenditures, raising taxes, and substituting federal for local spending.

Expenditures

The adopted budget for fiscal year 2003 cut $1.5 billion from agency resources. Additional cuts during fiscal year 2003 brought the total expenditure reductions to $2.3 billion. The number of full-time equivalent employees was reduced from 315,000 to 300,000, or about 5 percent of the workforce. Personnel reductions have focused on the police department: the number of police is down from a maximum of 40,000 in 2001 to some 36,000 in 2004. There have also been substantial cuts in social service employment. Between August 2001 and August 2004, payroll data indicate a decrease of 38,000 in the number of government jobs in New York City, representing a 6.5 percent drop (New York City Office of Management and Budget 2004b). Since about 80 percent of government jobs in the city are local, these losses reflect primarily the actions of New York City government.

Fiscal Substitution

One way in which local governments deal with fiscal stress is to pressure higher-level governments to relax the local financial requirements for aided programs, thus allowing cities to substitute grants-in-aid for local funds. In the aftermath of 9/11, the city won approval by the federal government to spend a higher share of community development block grant (CDBG) funds for social services. This substitution freed up for alternative use some $19 million of city funds in fiscal year 2003. (New York City Independent Budget Office 2002a). The changes in the use of CDBG funds increased the city's reliance on federal funds for financing child welfare services even as the city reduced its own contributions for child care by 25 percent between 2001 and 2003 (New York City Independent Budget Office 2002b).

Tax Policy After 9/11

Figure 10.1 provides a summary picture of New York City's overall tax rate as a percentage of personal income and the tax response after 9/11.[1] The figure shows a steep decline in city tax burdens during the 1990s. By 2000 tax burdens had declined to a level not seen since the early 1960s. Since 2002 burdens have grown by almost a full percentage point. A part of the short-run change in tax burdens reflects changes in the denominator—personal income—with tax policy unchanged. A rough calculation based on the share of property tax in total city tax revenues shows that about two thirds of the increase in burdens stems from policy actions. This is because the base for the property tax is relatively insensitive to short-run changes in personal income. Nonetheless,

FIGURE 10.1   NEW YORK CITY TAX REVENUE AS THE SHARE OF PERSONAL
INCOME, 1970 TO 2005

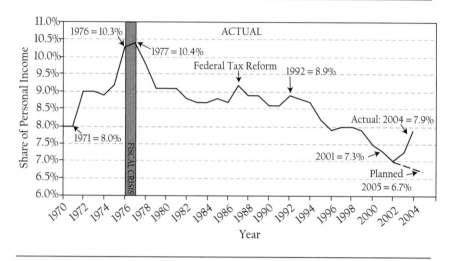

Source: City of New York (Office of Management and Budget 2001).

the magnitude of the increase, which exceeds substantially the increase associated with the previous economic downturn of the early 1990s, suggests the
crucial role played by tax increases in closing the large budget deficits caused
by the 9/11 attack and the recession.

Figure 10.2 shows New York City tax revenues for the major taxes and total
tax revenues from 1989 to 2004. Differences in the cyclical behavior of the property tax and personal income tax can be seen from the figure. As of January
2003, the projected budget gap for fiscal year 2004 was $6.4 billion, or about 14
percent of total expenditures. To address this deficit the city imposed a substantial array of tax increases. The tax increases are scheduled to sunset (automatically end) by 2005 or 2006. The nominal property tax rate was increased by 18.5
percent, raising revenues by $1.8 billion. The top bracket for the personal income
tax (PIT) was increased from 3.65 percent to 4.45 percent for taxable incomes
greater than $500,000. The city's sales tax rate was raised by 0.125 percentage
point from 2003 to 2005, bringing the combined state-city-transit authority sales
tax rate in New York City to 8.625 percent. Overall, personal income taxes were
increased by over $500 million per year between 2003 and 2005, while sales
taxes were increased by about $300 million in 2003 and 2004.

Reflecting the renewed strength in the New York City economy, particularly its real estate markets (Haughwout, this volume; Fuerst, this volume),

FIGURE 10.2   NEW YORK CITY REVENUES FROM PROPERTY, SALES, AND
                PERSONAL INCOME TAXES, 1989 TO 2004

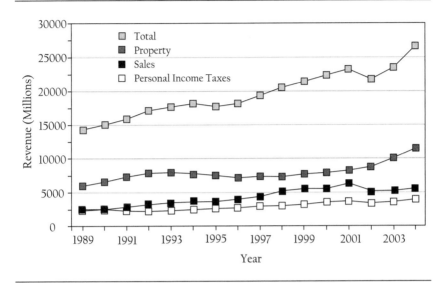

Source: New York State Comptroller (2003), New York State Division of Budget (2004), Comptroller, City of New York (2003), New York City Independent Budget Office (2004d).

tax revenues in 2004 ended up about 6 percent higher than projected at the start of the fiscal year. Projected revenues for 2005 are also above forecasts. A major source of this increase has been the strength of New York City's real estate–related taxes: the mortgage recording tax (MRT), the real property transfer tax (RPTT), and the commercial rent tax. These three taxes reached all-time highs in 2003, and yields for the first two, a function of the volume of transactions, have been extraordinarily robust in the past few years. Revenues from the real estate–related taxes equaled 14.3 percent of the real property tax revenues in 2003, 12.6 percent in 2004, and are projected at 11.7 percent of revenues in 2005. The mayor has taken advantage of the revenue performance to rebate a portion of the property tax increase, offering a $400 property tax rebate for owner-occupied residential property in both fiscal year 2005 and fiscal year 2006.

From 2001 to 2003, revenues from the personal income tax declined precipitously, by some 22.4 percent (New York City Independent Budget Office 2004a). The decline was reversed in 2004, with revenues expected to reach $5.4 billion. This represents a 20.9 percent increase over 2003. Almost 85 percent of this increase ($784 million) is due to the progressive rate increase that was imposed retroactively in 2003. PIT and corporate income tax revenues are heavily dependent on Wall Street firms' profits, which rebounded sharply in 2003. The overall behavior of New York City's tax base is broadly consistent with employment patterns in the city since 2001—notably, a very sharp decline, followed by a slow and uneven rate of recovery as of this writing.

The mayor argued that the 2003 and 2004 tax increases were necessary to stave off drastic service cuts and that the negative impact of these cuts on the well-being of New York City residents would have exceeded the adverse impact of the tax increases. If preserved services were valued less than forgone private income, the tax base would be expected to decline in response to the tax increase. Andrew Haughwout and his colleagues (2004) present evidence that past tax increases in New York City have had this effect. Although it is still too early for any comprehensive assessment, the growth in income and real estate values to date does not suggest an adverse effect from the rate increases. The market value of real estate increased by 17 percent between 2004 and 2005, and real estate–related taxes reached all-time highs in 2003 and 2004 (New York City Independent Budget Office 2004d).

A number of factors should limit the negative effects of the tax increase. If the increase is viewed as temporary—if the sunset provision is credible—this will tend to mute any long-run response. Second, as discussed earlier, New York City's tax burden prior to 9/11 was low in historic terms. In addition, both federal and state tax income tax burdens, particularly for high-income taxpayers, have fallen in recent years. This reduction in the cumulative tax burden on high-income New Yorkers should increase the ability of New York City to sustain rate increases on its high-income residents. Finally, tax rates have also risen in the counties surrounding New York in the post-9/11 period, reducing somewhat the competitive pressure the city would face if it were the only jurisdiction raising its taxes. However, there is a potential danger in that the net effect of the property tax changes has been to shift more of the burden onto nonresidential property, thus raising the costs of doing business in New York City.

The State Response

The loss to New York City residents would have been reduced if the state had chosen to function as a kind of public-sector insurer by reallocating fiscal resources from the rest of the state to New York City. Given the fiscal pressure on the state resulting from 9/11, an immediate increase in state assistance to New York City would have had to come either from a reallocation of the local assistance portion of the state budget or from an increase in state resources. Despite the grievous nature of the shock to New York City and the outpouring of sympathy and private charitable assistance for the victims of the 9/11 attack, the state budget was not significantly reallocated.

The major state contribution of direct assistance to New York City in the aftermath of 9/11 came through tax-enabling measures and permission to borrow to cover a portion of operating expenditures. The city was allowed to temporarily raise tax rates for the income tax and the general sales tax and to suspend the exemption for apparel priced under $110. Over the governor's veto, the state legislature also agreed to assume some $500 million of New York City's prior debt obligations. (That debt assumption is under court challenge.) The city was permitted to add some $2.1 billion in long-term debt, at an annual cost of $130 million to $150 million. The state also agreed to a temporary expansion in Medicaid coverage. In addition, the state, in conjunction with the federal government, relaxed some categorical restrictions on federal and state grants, thus giving the New York City increased budget flexibility and helping the city to substitute federal for local funds for social services.

The limited state response is in keeping with state fiscal policy toward New York City in the last ten years.[2] During this period the state has taken a number of steps that had an adverse impact on the city's fiscal base or its costs, including the elimination of the commuter tax in 1999, the distributional formula for the STAR (school tax relief) program, and intervention in collective bargaining for pension rights.[3] The last action has interacted with the extra overtime caused by the 9/11 attack to significantly increase overall pension costs for New York City. Though knotty issues of measurement are involved, under most assumptions New York City's net fiscal flow or balance of payments with the rest of the state has worsened in the past decade (Gardner 1999). The 9/11 disaster has done nothing to reverse that trend.

Changes in Public Assistance and Medicaid

Social welfare expenditures make up an important part of New York City's budget. As shown in table 10.1 and figure 10.3, the number of public assistance recipients fell dramatically between 1995 and 2003, from 1.16 million to 421,000. There was a slight rise from 2003 to 2004. In contrast, in the recessionary and slow growth period between 1989 and 1995, there was a 43 percent rise in the number of public assistance cases. The difference from the earlier period indicates that the responsiveness of the welfare caseload to New York City's business cycle has been substantially muted. Although the reasons have been widely debated, increased administrative hurdles to getting welfare, changes in family structure, changes in eligibility due to changes in the structure of jobs, and changes in fiscal incentives all play a role (New York City Independent Budget Office 2004b; Chernick and Reimers 2004). Whatever the reasons, the caseload data make clear that there was basically no increase in public assistance receipt in response to 9/11.

In contrast to public assistance, the number of food stamp recipients has increased by 20 percent between 2002 and 2004. However, because the food

TABLE 10.1   NUMBER OF NEW YORK CITY RECIPIENTS IN THE MAJOR
TRANSFER PROGRAMS (THOUSANDS), 1989 TO 2004

Year[a]	Public Assistance	Medicaid	Food Stamps
1989	813		
1995	1,161	1,843	1,458
1999	700	1,623	999
2001	519	1,578	836
2002	447	1,831	815
2003	421	2,204	854
2004	438	2,459	978

Source: New York City Department of Social Services (various years).
[a]The public assistance and food stamp numbers are the March numbers for the relevant year.
Medicaid numbers are for February.

stamps program is mainly federally funded, there is little direct fiscal impact
on New York City from the increase.

Equally as dramatic as the flatness in the public assistance rolls is the star-
tling increase in the number of Medicaid recipients. Since 2001, there has been

FIGURE 10.3   PUBLIC ASSISTANCE, FOOD STAMPS, AND MEDICAID
RECIPIENTS IN NEW YORK CITY, 1995 TO 2004

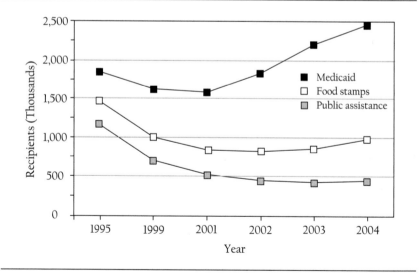

Source: New York City Department of Social Services (various years).

a 56 percent increase in the number of Medicaid and Family Health Plus recipients. As of April 2004, about 30 percent of the population of New York City
was enrolled in the Medicaid program. The fiscal costs of the program have
been growing at an average annual rate of 10.8 percent since 2001. The city's
total Medicaid liabilities will be nearly $4.5 billion in fiscal year 2004–2005.
Although the rate of increase in Medicaid spending is similar to the national
rate of increase over this period, it still represents an extraordinary fiscal burden. Medicaid expenditures will equal 9.6 percent of total city expenditures
in 2005, and 13.9 percent of city funds (New York State Comptroller 2002).

One of the sources of the sharp increase in Medicaid eligibility shown in
table 10.1 is directly related to the attack on the World Trade Center. The
9/11 attack brought down the city computer systems, including the Welfare
Management System (WMS). Because WMS holds the Medicaid eligibility
information for the city, the city was unable to provide regular determinations
of Medicaid eligibility. In response to the computer system shutdown, the city
and the state started offering four-month-long disaster relief Medicaid to low-
income families. The federal government allowed New York City to waive the
traditional eligibility requirements for Medicaid for four months.[4] A federal
waiver also allowed for the automatic recertification of coverage for those who
were already enrolled in Medicaid and were due for recertification during the
four-month period. Automatic recertification is important, since by one estimate at least 50 percent of Medicaid recipients in New York State lose their
eligibility as a consequence of the recertification process.[5]

It is difficult to separate out the longer-term effects on enrollment of the
special disaster relief program from other factors. Medicaid enrollment has
continued to grow since 2001, but the growth rate for 2003 was about half
that of 2002. Medicaid rolls grew by about 2.4 percent in 2001, 23.5 percent
in 2002, and 11.7 percent in 2003. The growth in 2002 was driven by the
implementation of Family Health Plus in New York City and the economic
downturn, as well as the DRM program. The 2003 growth rate slowed somewhat, but enrollment still grew rapidly. Cordelia Reimers (this volume) finds
that the increase in Medicaid participation was greater in New York City than
in five other large U.S. cities, bolstering the hypothesis that the 9/11 attack
was a major factor in the large increase in Medicaid enrollments.

THE COST OF THE 9/11 ATTACK

An Analytical Framework

Though my emphasis is on the public sector in New York City, I build up the
analysis from the conventional economic point of view that stresses the well-
being of individuals. The government's function is to provide the services de-

manded by its residents and to collect sufficient revenues to pay for those services. The economic well-being of residents depends on their after-tax income and the level of public services they receive. The loss suffered by New Yorkers owing to the 9/11 attack can therefore be divided into the loss in after-tax income and the loss in public services. To the extent that public-service levels are maintained, then to offset the loss in tax base, tax rates must rise, leading to a decrease in after-tax incomes.

After-tax income for a typical city resident i is equal to

$$y_i = (1 - \tau_I)I + \rho V + T - \tau_{prop}V \qquad (10.1)$$

where y is income after taxes, I is income before taxes, τ_I and τ_{prop} are local income and property tax rates, V is the value of property, ρ is the imputed rate of return on property, and T is income from transfers. Assuming that the level of public services does not change, then the cost to residents can be expressed completely in terms of the change in after-tax income. That change is equal to the decrease in before-tax income minus the increase in taxes, or

$$\Delta y_i = [\Delta I_i + \rho \Delta V_i + \Delta T_i] - [\Delta \tau_{prop}V_i + \tau_{prop}\Delta V_i + \Delta \tau_I I_i + \tau_I \Delta I_i] \qquad (10.2)$$

Equation 10.2 says that the loss in pre-tax income comes from a decline in earnings (ΔI) and the imputed annual value of destroyed property ($\rho \Delta V$), offset by an increase in transfers (ΔT). The second part of equation 10.2 shows that the change in taxes consists of two parts: the decrease in revenues at the pre-9/11 tax rates because the tax base has declined by ($\tau_{prop}\Delta V + \tau_I \Delta I$), and the offsetting increase in tax rates ($\Delta \tau_{prop}V + \Delta \tau_I I$) needed to maintain public services and pay for increased transfer payments. To simplify the notation, we now collapse the city's multiple taxes into a single rate τ and a single base B, the average tax base per resident. Ignoring intergovernmental grants, the city's tax rate is given by expenditures divided by the tax base B·N, that is, the average value multiplied by the number of residents N.[6]

$$\tau = [\text{Cost of Services} + \text{Transfers}]/(B \cdot N) \qquad (10.3)$$

The required change in the city tax rate is equal to

$$\Delta \tau = [\Delta s \text{ in Expenditures}]/B \cdot N - \tau(\Delta B/B) \qquad (10.4)$$

where the change in expenditures equals the change in the cost of services and the change in transfer payments. The total change in after-tax income is

$$\Delta y_i = (\Delta \text{Private Economy})_i + (\Delta \text{Public Economy})_I \qquad (10.5)$$

Applying the change in the tax rate in equation 10.4 to the individual resident's tax base B_i, the change in after-tax income from changes in the public economy is

$$(\Delta \text{Public Economy})_i = \Delta \tau \cdot B_i \qquad (10.6)$$

Equation 10.6 says that the change in after-tax income for resident i due to changes in the public sector is the required change in the tax rate, as shown in equation 10.3, multiplied by i's tax base. To reiterate, required tax changes result from an increase in required expenditures and a reduction in the tax base. Changes in transfers offset the decline in private income but require an increase in taxes to finance them.

To determine the total change in the economic well-being of New York City residents, we add up the changes from the private economy and the public economy for all individuals, with a weight ω_i applied to each individual.

$$\Delta W = \Sigma_i \, \omega_i \, \Delta y_i = \Sigma_i \omega_i [\Delta \text{Private Economy} + \Delta \text{Public Economy}] \qquad (10.7)$$

If we assign the same weight to each person ($\omega_i = 1$) and assume that the cost per unit of public services does not change, then the average welfare loss through the public sector from the 9/11 attack is the net change in transfers minus the change in expenditures plus the loss in tax revenues, or

$$\Delta W_{pub}/N = [\Delta \overline{T} - (1-m)\Delta \overline{T}] - \Delta EXP/N + \tau \Delta B \qquad (10.8)$$

where N is the resident population of New York City and m is the share of transfer payments paid by the state and federal governments. The first term in equation 10.8 is the change in the average transfer payment (Δ) minus the taxes needed to pay for those transfers. The term will be positive if a portion of the transfer cost is paid for by other governments. The second term is the expenditure increase required to keep services at their pre-9/11 level. This extra cost will have a negative effect on the well-being of residents. The third term is the reduction in tax revenue because of losses in the property base and the income or gross city product (GCP) base. These losses will also have a negative effect on well-being.

Two points should be noted about the expression in equation 10.8. First, the loss through the public sector is independent of the financing of the fiscal deficit from 9/11. The substantial increase in borrowing in fiscal year 2002 to maintain city services has the effect of spreading the costs of 9/11 over time and transferring costs to future residents and to landowners. However, the mix between tax increases and increased borrowing does not alter the magnitude of the costs.

Second, the aggregate loss to New York residents because of lower tax revenues ($\tau\Delta B$) is independent of the incidence of the tax losses and the incidence of the increase in tax rates to deal with the fiscal deficit. The formula for the public-sector losses measures the aggregate additional resources that are needed to maintain services for New York City residents, regardless of who pays for these. At least 20 percent of the increase in taxes imposed by New York City are likely to be borne by nonresidents through nonresident ownership of real estate and other taxable assets, purchases by nonresidents, and federal deductibility of local income and property taxes.[7]

To get the net per resident cost from the public economy, we subtract direct federal compensation per resident:

$$\text{Net Cost}/N = \Delta W_{pub}/N - \text{Compensation}_{Fed}/N \qquad (10.9)$$

Measuring the Losses from 9/11

In this section, we provide estimates for each of the components of the public-sector loss, as described in equations 10.7 and 10.8. Some of the components are not onetime costs incurred in fiscal year 2002 but flows of costs over several years. Therefore, I discount all costs beyond fiscal year 2002, using a social discount rate of 3.5 percent (Moore et al. 2004). To make the calculations easier to follow, I summarize all results from this section in table 10.2.

Changes in Transfer Payments and the Disaster Relief Medicaid Program   As discussed earlier, primarily as a consequence of the temporary relaxation of eligibility requirements under disaster relief Medicaid, the number of recipients grew by 25 percent, from 1.617 million to slightly more than 2 million in the period from September 2001 to May 2002.[8] The city originally estimated that about 35 percent (or 133,000 recipients) would then enter the traditional Medicaid program or Family Health Plus upon the expiration of the four-month period. The number of interviews for admission suggests that this estimate is fairly accurate, implying that state policy, abetted by federal waiver permission, allowed Medicaid eligibility to increase by about 271,000 people. It is estimated that the increase in Medicaid eligibility will cost the city an additional \$130 million in annual city-funded Medicaid expenditures (Comptroller, City of New York 2002). Since New York City pays 25 percent of the cost of traditional Medicaid expenditures, this implies a total increase of four times that amount, or \$520 million. Ignoring city residents' contribution to the state match, the average cost per resident from change in transfers is

$$\text{Change in Transfers} = \$520 \text{ million} - \$130 \text{ million} = \$390 \text{ million}$$
$$\div 8.1 \text{ million} = \$48 \text{ per capita.}$$

TABLE 10.2   THE FISCAL LOSS TO NEW YORK RESIDENTS FROM 9/11

Components of Public-Sector Loss	Total Cost	Cost per Resident
Net cost (gain) from increase in Medicaid transfers (2002)	$520 million (total increase in Medicaid spending – $130 million (city contribution) – $58.5 million (city share of state contribution) = $331 million	–$41
Increase in required expenditures (2002 to 2003)	$898.6 million	$111
Increase in required expenditures (2002 to 2006)	$1.09 billion	$135
Tax loss (2002 to 2003)	$2.472 billion	$330
Tax loss (2002 to 2010)	$3.95 billion	$488
New York City loss (2002 to 2003)	$3.04 billion	$400
New York City loss (2002 to 2010)	$4.71 billion	$582
Total loss per resident (2002 to 2003)	$400 New York City loss (2002 to 2003) + $59 New York City share of New York State tax loss	$459
Total loss per resident (2002 to 2010)	$582 + $59	$641
Federal budgetary compensation	$762 million (unrestricted) + $550 million (interest savings on refinancing)	$162
Net cost per resident (2002 to 2003)	–$41 transfer + $111 expenditures + $389 tax cost (New York City and New York State) – $162 federal compensation	$297 (0.8% of personal income)
Net cost per resident (2002 to 2010)		$479 (1.35% of personal income)

Source: Author's compilation.
Note: All multiyear estimates expressed as present discounted values in 2002.

The positive value for net transfers reflects the matching provisions for Medicaid: every local dollar for Medicaid is matched by roughly one state dollar and two dollars from the federal government. Thus, while city own-source revenues had to increase by $130 million a year to cover the city's share of the increase in Medicaid outlays, the total increase in medical spending was four times that amount, or $520 million. The extra Medicaid funds allowed New York City to provide medical services to those most affected by the 9/11 attack, at a fiscal cost to the government of New York City that was only one-quarter of the total resource cost. In standard budget accounting, Medicaid shows up as a significant fiscal cost, but when we take account of the fact that the extra spending goes directly to New York City residents, the transfer becomes a net gain to city residents. The estimate of $48 per resident reflects the fact that our method is to add up all of the public-sector costs (and benefits) from 9/11 and then average them over the number of residents. This average does not mean that all residents get a direct benefit from the Medicaid expansion, since the income standard for Medicaid makes only about one-third of New Yorkers eligible for Medicaid.

The $48 estimate overstates the average gain to city residents, because they must pay a share of the extra state matching expenditures required by the increase in Medicaid eligibility. Increased grants from New York State should not be counted entirely as a net gain to New York City residents. A lower bound on New York City's share of state revenues is given by the city's share of state personal income, which was about 45 percent in 2002. Hence, the per capita cost to New York City residents of the increased state funding for Medicaid in fiscal year 2002 can be approximated as (.45 multiplied by $130 million) divided by 8.1, or about $7 per capita. Subtracting this amount from the $48 figure,

$$\text{Average Net Gain from Increased Transfers}_{2002} = \$48 - \$7 = \$41.$$

Expenditure Increases   The main sources of increased expenditure for New York City from 9/11 have been increased overtime and security costs. The city also faces higher pension costs and exposure to higher claims costs. Costs for Medicaid also rose, but as discussed earlier, these higher costs were offset by higher in-kind transfers to newly eligible individuals.

The city has had to add additional security measures on an ongoing basis, assigning as many as 1,400 officers a day to security patrols. The Comptroller of the City of New York (2002) estimates that the city incurred $365 million in overtime costs related to the cleanup of the WTC site. Police overtime alone accounted for 70 percent of this total. WTC overtime in fiscal year 2003 was projected to equal about $14.4 million. The present discounted value of overtime is thus estimated to be $379 million. Numerous claims have also been filed against the city, totaling $8.2 billion as of August 2002. The Comptroller of the City of New York (2002) estimated that the city's liability for WTC claims is likely to be no higher than $350 million; that sum will be fully compensated by the federal government. In this section, we include the $350 million as a local cost. Federal compensation is considered in a subsequent section.

Extra pension expenses include $64.6 million for city employees who died in the attacks. There may also be future pension expenses from increased disability costs. Large amounts of overtime substantially raised the salaries of many police and firefighters. The inclusion of this extra pay in the pension calculation provided a strong incentive for many police and fire department members to retire after twenty years. In addition, the trauma of the attack itself has led to increased retirements. The comptroller's report estimates additional pension expenses of about $39 million per year from fiscal year 2003 through fiscal year 2006. The additional capital costs of replacing equipment and repairing or replacing buildings damaged or destroyed by the attack are estimated at $171 million from fiscal year 2002 to fiscal year 2006. The present discounted value of additional pension payments is $143.3 million. The present discounted value of the additional capital costs is $155.4 million.

To summarize, the present discounted value of the change in required expenditures is

$$\text{PDV } \Delta\text{Required Expenditures}_{2002-2003} = \$379 \text{ million} + \$350 \text{ million} + \$64.6 \text{ million} + \$37.8 \text{ million} + \$67.2 \text{ million} = \$898.6 \text{ million} = \$111 \text{ per capita; and}$$

$$\text{PDV } \Delta\text{Required Expenditures}_{2002-2006} = \$379 \text{ million} + \$350 \text{ million} + \$64.6 \text{ million} + \$143.3 \text{ million} + \$155.4 \text{ million} = \$1.09 \text{ billion} = \$135 \text{ per capita.}$$

Loss in Tax Revenues   Conceptually, the loss in tax revenues due to 9/11 is equal to

$$\Delta\text{Tax}_{9/11} = \tau\Delta\text{B(Attack)} = \Delta\text{Tax}_{\text{Actual}} - \Delta\text{Tax}_{\text{Recession}} + \Delta\text{Tax}_{\text{Policy}}$$

where τ is the average tax rate prior to 9/11, $\Delta\text{B(Attack)}$ is the decline in the tax base due to 9/11, $\Delta\text{Tax}_{\text{Recession}}$ is the decline in tax collections that would have occurred anyway owing to the economic slowdown, and $\Delta\text{Tax}_{\text{Policy}}$ is the increase in revenues due to an increase in tax rates on the 9/11-induced lower tax base. As discussed in the methodology section, offsetting changes in tax policy that reduce the actual revenue losses are counted as part of the 9/11 impact. As measured by gross city product, New York City's economic slow-down began in January 2001.[9] The actual change in tax revenues from 2001 to 2002 was a negative $1.5 billion, or 6.4 percent of revenues. Using several different estimation methods, the comptroller's office, in its report one year after the attack (Comptroller, City of New York 2002), estimated that the bulk of the reduction in taxes from 2001 to 2002 was due to the impact of 9/11. Its estimates range from $1.0 billion to $2.0 billion.[10] The comptroller's office estimates that the 9/11 impact in 2003 was $928 million, comprising a decrease of $184 million in property taxes and $744 million in nonproperty taxes. Because of the attack, market values in lower Manhattan fell by $3.6 billion from 2002 to 2003. The actual change in property taxes in 2003 reflects the decline in the property base, together with an 18.5 percent rate offset that began in the second half of fiscal year 2003. Nonproperty taxes fell by 11 percent in fiscal year 2002, while property taxes increased by 6.4 percent.

A more recent estimate of the loss in tax revenues, based on an updated forecast for August 2001 and actual tax revenues for 2002 and 2003, raises the overall magnitude of the losses but revises the timing so that they are somewhat lower in 2002 but higher in 2003 and beyond (New York City Office of Management and Budget 2004a). OMB estimates a greater continuing effect of 9/11 on revenues, because employment has been slower to recover than originally anticipated, and part of that slowness is attributed to 9/11.

OMB estimates that tax losses in 2002 were $926 million, about 4.3 percent of tax revenues, and $1.6 billion in 2003. The $1.6 billion figure equals 7.1 percent of 2003 revenues, after accounting for policy changes. Over the two-year period following the terrorist attack, the estimated loss equals 5.7 percent of revenues. In 2004 and 2005, the loss in business-sensitive taxes will be about $420 million, while property tax losses are estimated at about $125 million at least until 2010. Over the two years following the attack, the tax loss is

$$\text{PDV of Tax Loss}_{2002\text{-}2003} = \$2.472 \text{ billion} = \$330 \text{ per capita.}$$

The estimated total tax losses over the eight-year period from 2002 to 2010 equal

$$\text{PDV of Tax Loss}_{2002\text{-}2010} = \$926 \text{ million (2002)} + \$1.546 \text{ billion (2003)} + \$495$$
$$\text{million (2004)} + \$491 \text{ million (2005)} + \$492 \text{ million}$$
$$(2006\text{-}2010) = \$3.95 \text{ billion} = \$488 \text{ per capita.}$$

Total Losses Through the Public Sector   Assuming that the additional transfers and personnel expenditures are incurred for just one year after the attack, the total losses to the public sector over the two-year period following 9/11 would be approximately equal to

$$\text{PDV of Per Capita Loss}_{2002-2003} = \text{Net Transfers} + \text{Required Expenditure Increase}$$
$$+ \text{Tax Loss} = -\$41 + \$111 + \$330 = \$400 \text{ per capita.}$$

Computing estimated losses through fiscal year 2010,

$$\text{PDV of Per Capita Loss}_{2002-2010} = -\$41 + \$135 + \$488 = \$582 \text{ per capita.}$$

Compensation for the Attacks

New York State   For the purposes of assessing the public-sector costs to New York City residents, the State of New York should be treated as an overlapping governmental unit that is both financed by and helps to provide financing to the residents of New York City. Conceptually, the public-sector loss to city residents from the loss in state tax revenues due to the attack is equal to the proportion of the total state tax loss due to 9/11 that can be imputed back to the residents of New York City. This proportion is roughly equal to New York City's personal income as a fraction of total state personal income, which is about 45 percent.

The economy of New York City makes up a substantial portion of total economic activity in New York State, with well over 50 percent of gross state product (GSP) produced within the city.[11] In no other state is the largest city even close to New York City in terms of its relative importance in the state. Because the New York City economy is so large relative to the entire state, the fiscal shock to New York City was also a fiscal shock at the state level. The correlation is magnified by the fact that the city and the state share common tax bases for the sales tax and the personal and corporate income taxes. Figure 10.4 shows state and city tax revenues in the 1990s and 2000s. Although the two series track each other closely, the figure shows that the state suffered a larger revenue reduction than New York City in 2002 and 2003. The reduction was greater for the state because all the major revenue sources for the state are sensitive to economic conditions in the short run, while city revenues are somewhat more inelastic because at least 40 percent of its tax revenue comes from the more cyclically stable property tax and property related taxes.

A very rough estimate of the one-year loss in tax revenues to New York State can be given by taking an estimate of the decline in GCP of $17.5 billion (Comptroller, City of New York 2002) and multiplying that amount by the average New York State tax rate of 6 percent. This gives an estimate of $1.05 billion. Multiplying this number by the personal income share in New York

FIGURE 10.4   NEW YORK CITY AND NEW YORK STATE TAXES, 1989 TO 2004

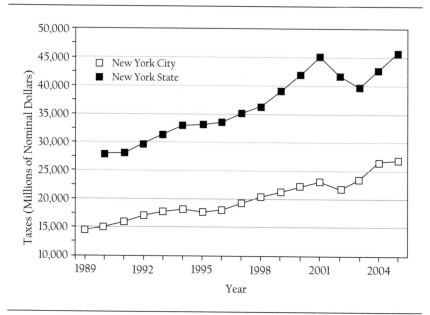

Source: Comptroller, City of New York (2003), New York City Independent Budget Office (2004d).

City yields a state tax loss of about $473 million, or $59 per capita. Adding this amount to the total city costs gives a total loss through the public sector equal to

$$\text{PDV of Public-Sector Loss}_{2002-2003} = \text{New York City Loss} + \text{New York State Loss}$$
$$= \$400 + \$59 = \$459 \text{ per resident.}$$

The present discounted value through 2010 equals

$$\text{PDV of Public-Sector Loss}_{2002-2010} = \$582 + \$59 = \$641 \text{ per capita.}$$

Federal Response to the 9/11 Attack

In the aftermath of 9/11, President Bush pledged $20 billion in aid to New York City to assist with recovery. The aid came in three allotments: September 11 emergency appropriations that totaled $11.235 billion and provided cash assistance to individuals, local governments, and small businesses; the Liberty

Zone Economic Package, enacted in the spring of 2002, which granted $5 billion in tax relief to businesses located in downtown Manhattan;[12] and a supplementary emergency appropriation package enacted in July 2002 that appropriated an additional $5.436 billion to New York City. This brought federal appropriations to a total of $20.4 billion.

The New York City Independent Budget Office (2004c) divides federal assistance into three categories. About 30 percent of the total funding, some $6.33 billion, went for emergency response needs. Federal funds were allocated for two specific purposes: rescue, recovery, and cleanup under the oversight of the Federal Emergency Management Agency (FEMA), and redeveloping the WTC site and revitalizing its vicinity through targeted cash assistance. The second phase focuses on economic recovery and includes $4.43 billion. The third phase, worth $9.71 billion, is for long-term rebuilding.

Typically the federal government does not provide general fiscal relief to governments that have been hit by natural disasters. However, in the case of the 9/11 attack, $1.7 billion, or about 8 percent of the total federal reimbursement, was provided to the city of New York. Of that amount, $762 million was from a transfer of the remainder of the original congressional appropriation and went for unrestricted budgetary relief. The other part of general relief was achieved by waiving federal rules on the onetime refinancing of municipal debt, thus allowing New York City to take advantage of lower interest rates for some of its general obligation debt. The cost to the federal government of this provision was $937 billion. The actual budget savings to New York City in 2003 was estimated at slightly more than $500 million. The difference is the wedge between the tax savings realized by lenders and the savings in interest costs to the borrower. Adding the budgetary saving from the refinancing to the direct budgetary relief, federal compensation for general fiscal costs was

$$\text{General Federal Budget Compensation} = \$762 \text{ million} + \$550 \text{ million}$$
$$= \$162 \text{ per capita.}$$

Net Cost to New York City Residents

Putting all of the estimates together, the cost to the residents of New York City residents through the public sector for the period 2002 through 2003 is equal to

$$\text{PDV of Net Cost}_{2002-2003} = \Delta\text{Net Transfers} + \Delta\text{Government Expenditures} + \Delta\text{Tax}$$
$$\text{Costs}_{\text{New York City} + \text{New York State}} - \text{Federal Compensation} =$$
$$-\$41 + \$111 + \$389 - \$162 = \$297.$$

Taking the estimates of losses through 2010, we compute

$$\text{PDV of Net Cost}_{2002-2010} = \$641 - \$162 = \$479.$$

Per capita personal income in New York City in 2002 was equal to $35,378. Hence, as a share of personal income, the present discounted value of the net cost to residents of New York City over the two-year period following the 9/11 attack was equal to roughly eight-tenths of 1 percent of personal income in 2002. Recurring public-sector losses from the destruction of property will raise this estimate somewhat, as will the future costs of servicing the additional debt issued by the city to cover costs in fiscal year 2002. The present discounted value of net costs per capita through 2010 equals 1.35 percent of personal income. Thus, depending on the time frame, the present discounted value of costs to New York City residents ranges from about 0.8 percent to 1.35 percent of personal income in the year of the attack. Ignoring the Medicaid transfer, federal general compensation to the government of New York City offset about one-third of the total public-sector cost. Federal tax deductibility will reduce the net burden of the tax increases by about 20 percent (Schlain 2004), that is, from $389 per capita to $311 per capita. If we take into account the federal deductibility of state and local income and property taxes, as well as the federal matching contribution for Medicaid, the net cost becomes

$$\text{PDV}_{2002-2003} \text{ (deductibility included)} = -\$41 + \$111 + \$389 - \$162 - \$78 = \$219$$
$$= 0.6 \text{ percent of personal income.}$$

With this accounting rule, federal compensation is equal to roughly 56 percent of the public-sector costs from 9/11.

DISTRIBUTIONAL IMPACTS

City Responses

In my analysis of the net public-sector costs of 9/11, I have simply taken the aggregate amounts from each category and divided by the resident population. This approach ignores the question of whether particular groups have been disproportionately affected. The net distributional impact of the fiscal responses to 9/11 represents the aggregate impact of the incidence of tax changes, spending adjustments, and additional borrowing. A complete analysis is very difficult and has not been attempted here. However, we may roughly summarize the incidence as follows:

1. *Tax increases*: The property tax increase was proportional for all income classes. Since the residential property tax in New York City is regressive, the proportional increase compounds the regressivity (Chernick 1987). In the 2005 budget, the city has provided rebates to owners of class 1 properties, which comprise one-, two-, and three-family homes, and owners of cooperatives and condominiums. The rebates will probably increase the regressivity of the residential portion of the property tax, because they shift the burden from owners to renters. However, the net effect is also to shift the burden from residential to commercial properties, a shift that is likely to be progressive in its incidence effects. The sales tax increase is regressive. The increase in the income tax is highly progressive. The net effect of all the tax changes is to leave the overall incidence pattern of New York City taxes similar to the pre-9/11 pattern.

2. *Incidence of expenditure changes*: One major change, the expansion of Medicaid and Family Health Plus coverage, is highly progressive. Selective small cuts—for example, in libraries and senior citizen centers and social services—have had their greatest impact on lower-income New Yorkers. The impact of cuts in the number of police are probably about equal across income classes. However, the fact that the incidence of crime has continued to fall, even as police staffing levels have dropped, suggests that prior to 9/11 New York City was "overpoliced" and that the cuts have had little marginal impact.

3. *Additional borrowing*: The additional long-term borrowing to help the city get through the 2002–2003 fiscal year will be borne by future generations of New Yorkers and by current landowners to the extent that future debt service costs are capitalized in land values.

As a rough summary, the net distributional impact of the fiscal changes in response to 9/11 has probably been slightly more progressive (more favorable to low-income households) than the prior net fiscal burden by income class.

SUMMARY AND CONCLUSIONS

The 9/11 terrorist attack plunged New York City into a deep fiscal crisis. Revenues fell dramatically and costs rose. The city dealt with the crisis by a mixture of expenditure cuts, tax increases, and increased borrowing. Before the attack, tax burdens in the city had declined to a level not seen since the early 1960s. Since 2002, tax burdens (taxes raised as a proportion of personal income) have grown by almost a full percentage point, though they remain low in historic terms. The recovery of tax revenues in fiscal years 2004 and 2005, particularly owing to the strength of the real estate markets, has enabled the city to avoid even harsher cuts.

Compensation from the federal government has been significant. I estimate that in present value terms the direct costs to the public sector from the 9/11 attack, not including cleanup costs at the WTC site, were equal to somewhere between 0.8 percent and 1.35 percent of 2002 personal income. Direct federal compensation will offset about one-third of these public-sector costs. If we include automatic federal matching funds for Medicaid and the federal tax deductibility, federal compensation rises to over half of the direct costs.

Overall, most of the $20.4 billion in federal compensation will go for replacement of private capital and public infrastructure in the immediate vicinity of the attack. Only a small proportion has taken the form of fiscal relief to the New York City government, and an even smaller proportion has gone to assist displaced workers. Edward Glaeser and Jesse Shapiro (2002) and Andrew Haughwout (this volume) question whether it is efficient for the federal government to provide the bulk of its compensation to New York City in the form of place-based subsidies to replace lost office buildings in lower Manhattan. Glaeser and Shapiro argue that it would have been both fairer and more efficient if more of the money had gone to compensate workers and residents hurt by the attack and to the city government to reduce the need for additional taxes. It is important to recall, however, that at least 23 percent of an unprecedented $2.7 billion in private charitable contributions from around the country went to New York City workers and residents (Dixon and Stern 2004).

Guidelines for the Allocation of Federal Antiterror Funds

Although federal direct compensation to New York City has been substantial, there is little doubt that subsequent federal antiterror appropriations have shortchanged the city. In adhering to the "something for everyone" criterion for these funds, the political process has favored rural over urban states and penalized large cities. Given the greater likelihood of attack in dense cities, and the greater losses that would result, it is inefficient to allocate federal monies on a per capita basis. Although it is perhaps not surprising that the politics of federal grants-in-aid for homeland security have quickly reverted to politics as usual, it is useful to review the reasons for a different type of allocation rule.

What is the appropriate federal response to the problem of preventing future terrorist attacks, and in particular, should big cities, especially New York, receive a greater share of antiterrorism assistance? Protection against terrorist attack should rightly be seen as a pure public good that is national in scope. The external costs from a terrorist attack at a given location and the external benefits from lowering the probability of future attacks are enormous. Indeed, the WTC attack has had widespread national consequences, both economically and politically.[13] Because local governments are not likely to take into full account the national impacts of terrorist acts, decentralized decisions by local governments are likely to lead to underinvestment in antiterror activities. Hence, federal funding to reduce the likelihood of future attacks is entirely appropriate.

The basic constitutional guarantee of security of person places the responsibility for protection against terrorism squarely at the federal level. However, given the U.S. tradition of decentralized government and its sheer size, there is a strong case on efficiency grounds for having the federal government deputize local governments as agents in protecting against terrorist attacks. The total amount of antiterrorism assistance to municipalities is a national decision that reflects the trade-offs between this use of funds and other means of protecting the country, as well as the overall assessment of the risk of terrorist attack. However, in allocating the appropriated funds across the country, an efficient allocation is one that equalizes the benefits of an additional dollar of federal antiterrorism aid across cities (or states). The benefit of a dollar of aid may be defined as the change in the probability of attack multiplied by the average expected loss. Although the chances of future terrorist attacks are, of course, unknown, in terms of the probability of attack and the expected loss, these benefits are directly proportional to urban density (Schwabish and Chang, this volume). Cities often plead that because their needs are special, they deserve greater federal assistance. In the case of antiterrorism assistance there is a very strong rationale for heeding these pleas and making the award of aid directly proportional to factors such as urban density.

I would like to thank Robert Inman for suggesting the analytical framework and other helpful comments. I also thank two anonymous reviewers and members of the New York City Recovery Project economic group, especially Andrew Haughwout, Cordelia Reimers, and James Parrott, for helpful comments on earlier drafts. I would also like to thank staff members of the New York City Independent Budget Office, for considerable help with data and interpretation, and Olesya Tkacheva, for research assistance.

NOTES

1. Personal income for New York City is estimated as a share of the estimate for the New York metropolitan area (U.S. Department of Commerce 2004).
2. For example, despite numerous adjustments and special provisions of the state

formulas for distributing school aid, the city's share of state aid to education has remained approximately constant over the last ten years. In 1999 New York City received 35.5 percent of state education aid, though it enrolls 38 percent of the state's students (Campaign for Fiscal Equity 2000).

3. These policies are discussed in detail in a number of reports; for a summary, see Bowles (2002). The distribution of state aid is discussed in Chernick and Reschovsky (2001). The elimination of the commuter tax is considered in Chernick and Tkacheva (2002).

4. Beneficiaries were allowed to enroll by attesting that all the information they provided on the simplified, one-page application was correct. Only applicant identity was verified. To qualify for disaster relief Medicaid (DRM), applicants had to meet the eligibility standards for Family Health Plus, the state's supplementary health insurance program for families who have low incomes but are ineligible for Medicaid. Income eligibility levels for Family Health Plus are 133 percent of the federal poverty level for parents and 100 percent of the federal poverty level for single adults and childless couples. All that was required of those who signed up for DRM was filling out a two-page form attesting that they would meet the requirements of Family Health Plus. Legal immigrants were also allowed to enroll in DRM, mostly because the program's launch coincided with the state's intention to open enrollment to this population anyway.

5. One study estimates that about 50 percent of Medicaid recipients who do not receive cash assistance are involuntarily disenrolled each year. For Medicaid beneficiaries also receiving cash assistance, the involuntary disenrollment figure is estimated at 85 percent. This study found that recertification is most likely to screen out lower-income families and that most of those screened out are in fact still eligible (Lipson et al. 2003).

6. For simplicity, I ignore intergovernmental grants in the conceptual framework, though they are taken into account in the next section.

7. Excluding the federal deductibility of local taxes, Helen Ladd and John Yinger (1991, ch. 6 app.) estimate that in the 1980s about 15 percent of New York City's taxes were exported to nonresidents. A recent estimate is that 21 percent of the 2003 to 2006 PIT surcharge is offset through federal deductibility (Schlain 2004).

8. I obtained most of the information on disaster relief Medicaid in communications with Rachelle Celebrezze of the New York City Independent Budget Office.

9. The Comptroller of the City of New York dates recessions based on quarterly changes in gross city product. Changes in GCP are in turn based on the number of jobs located in the city. Between the pre-recession peak of 3.754 million jobs and September 2001, the city lost 48,000 jobs.

10. The actual reduction was lower than $2 billion because of the growth in property taxes. Property tax revenues for 2002 were unaffected by 9/11 because they were determined by assessed values set in June 2001.

11. About 42 percent of the total number of state jobs are in New York City, and about 45 percent of state personal income is received by residents of New York City. Because a substantial portion of income generated in New York City is received by nonresidents (37 percent of earned income in 1996), the share of New York State output produced within the borders of New York City is well over 50 percent.

12. The Liberty Zone Economic Package also includes $1.2 billion in savings from allowing New York City and New York State to issue $8 billion in tax-exempt bonds to be used for private investment in offices, residential units, and utilities.

13. The 2005 *Economic Report of the President* estimates that the 9/11 attack caused the U.S. economy to lose 900,000 jobs in the three months following the attack (Council of Economic Advisers 2005).

REFERENCES

Bowles, Jonathan. 2002. "Sympathy, but No Support." New York: Center for an Urban Future (April 3). Available at: http://www.nycfuture.org/content/reports/report_view.cfm?repkey=64.

Campaign for Fiscal Equity. 2000. "Reforming New York's Flawed Finance System." *Evidence Policy Reports from the CFE Trial.* (November, Volume 2).

Chernick, Howard. 1987. "Taxes." In *Setting Municipal Priorities, 1988,* edited by Charles Brecher and Raymond Horton. New York: New York University Press.

Chernick, Howard, and Cordelia Reimers. 2004. "The Decline in Welfare Receipt in New York City: Push Versus Pull." *Eastern Economic Journal* 30(1): 3–30.

Chernick, Howard, and Andrew Reschovsky. 2001. "Lost in the Balance: How State Policies Affect the Fiscal Health of Cities." Discussion paper. Washington, D.C.: Brookings Institution, Center on Urban and Metropolitan Policy (March).

Chernick, Howard, with Olesya Tkacheva. 2002. "The Commuter Tax and the Fiscal Cost of Commuters in New York City." *State Tax Notes* 25(6, August 5): 451–56.

Comptroller, City of New York. 2002. *One Year Later: The Fiscal Impact of 9/11 on New York City* (September 4). Available at: http://www.comptroller.nyc.gov/bureaus/bud/reports/impact-9-11-year-later.pdf.

———. 2003. "Comprehensive Annual Financial Report of the Comptroller for the fiscal year ended June 30, 2003." Available at: http://www.comptroller.nyc.gov/bureaus/acc/CAFR_FYJun03/CAFR_FY_Ending_June03.pdf.

Council of Economic Advisers. 2005. *Economic Report of the President.* Washington: U.S. Government Printing Office (February). Available at: http://www.whitehouse.gov/cea/erpcover2005.pdf.

Dixon, Lloyd, and Rachel Stern. 2004. *Compensation for Losses from the 9/11 Attacks.* Santa Monica, Calif.: RAND Institute for Civil Justice. Available at: http://www.rand.org/pubs/monographs/2004/RAND_MG264.pdf.

Gardner, Kent. 1999. "The Fiscal Balance Among New York State regions." Rochester and Albany, N.Y.: Center for Governmental Research (January).

Glaeser, Edward, and Jesse M. Shapiro. 2002. "Cities and Warfare: The Impact of Terrorism on Urban Reform." *Journal of Urban Economics* 51(2): 205–24.

Haughwout, Andrew, Robert Inman, Steven Craig, and Tom Luce. 2004. "Local Revenue Hills: Evidence from Four U.S. Cities." *Review of Economics and Statistics* 86(May): 570–85.

Ladd, Helen, and John Yinger. 1991. *America's Ailing Cities: Fiscal Health and the Design of Urban Policy.* Baltimore: Johns Hopkins University Press.

Lipson, Karen, Eliot Fishman, Patricia Boozang, et al. 2003. "Rethinking Recertification:

Keeping Eligible Individuals Enrolled in New York's Public Health Insurance Programs." *Commonwealth Fund* (August). Available at: http://www.cmwf.org/usr_doc/lipson_recertification_656.pdf.

Moore, Mark, Anthony Boardman, Aidan Vining, David Weimer, and David Greenberg. 2004. "'Just Give Me a Number!' Practical Values for the Social Discount Rate." *Journal of Policy Analysis and Management* 23(4, Fall): 789–812.

New York City Department of Social Services. Human Resources Administration. Various years. *HRA Facts.* Available at: http://www.nyc.gov/html/hra/html/hrafacts.html.

New York City Independent Budget Office. 2002a. "Rising Homelessness Threatens Higher City Costs." *Inside the Budget* (September). Available at: http:www.ibo.nyc.ny.us.

———. 2002b. "City's Reliance on State and Federal Funds for Child Care Grows." Background paper. Available at: http://www.ibo.nyc.ny.us/.

———. 2004a. "Analysis of the Mayor's Preliminary Budget for 2005" (May 15). Available at: http:www.ibo.nyc.ny.us.

———. 2004b. "Despite Recession, Welfare Reform and Labor Market Changes Limit Growth in Public Assistance." Fiscal brief (August). Available at: http:www.ibo.nyc.ny.us.

———. 2004c. "Three Years After: Where Is the $20 Billion in Federal WTC Aid?" *Inside the Budget* (August 11). Available at: http://www.ibo.nyc.ny.us.

———. 2004d. "A Brighter Fiscal Picture, But Reasons for Caution." *Fiscal Outlook* (December). Available at: http://www.ibo.nyc.ny.us.

New York City Office of Management and Budget. 2001. *City of New York Executive Budget FY2001: Budget Summary.* New York: New York City OMB.

———. 2004a. "Impact of 9/11 on New York City Tax Revenue." Memo (September 15). New York: New York City OMB.

———. 2004b. *Monthly Report on Current Economic Conditions* (September 21). Available at: http://www.ci.nyc.ny.us/html/omb/pdf/ec09_04.pdf.

New York State Comptroller. Office of the State Deputy Comptroller. 2002. *Review of the Four-Year Financial Plan for the City of New York (Fiscal Years 2000 Through 2003).* Report 10–2000 (December). Available at: http://www.osc.state.ny.us/osdc/rpt1000/rpt1000.htm.

———. 2003. *Comprehensive Annual Financial Report for Fiscal Year Ended March 31, 2003.* Available at: http://www.osc.state.ny.us/finance/finreports/cafr03.pdf: expenditures.

New York State Division of the Budget. 2004. *Financial Plan Overview, Part I.* Available at: http://publications.budget.state.ny.us/fy0405app2/appd2_part1.pdf.

Schlain, Karen. 2004. "New York City and the Federal AMT: The Future Is Now." *State Tax Notes* (February 23).

United States Department of Commerce, Bureau of Economic Analysis. 2004. "The Sources and Methods for the Annual Estimates of County Personal Income, 1996–2002." Available at: http://www.bea.doc.gov./bea/regional/articles/lapi2002/overview.pdf.

INDEX

Boldface numbers refer to figures and tables.